CHILDREN'S RIGHTS IN INTERCOUNTRY ADOPTION

European Family Law Series

CHILDREN'S RIGHTS IN INTERCOUNTRY ADOPTION

A European Perspective

Claire Fenton-Glynn

intersentia
Cambridge – Antwerp – Portland

Intersentia Ltd
Sheraton House | Castle Park
Cambridge | CB3 0AX | United Kingdom
Tel.: +44 1223 370 170 | Email: mail@intersentia.co.uk

Distribution for the UK:
NBN International
Airport Business Centre, 10 Thornbury Road
Plymouth, PL6 7 PP
United Kingdom
Tel.: +44 1752 202 301 | Fax: +44 1752 202 331
Email: orders@nbninternational.com

Distribution for the USA and Canada:
International Specialized Book Services
920 NE 58th Ave. Suite 300
Portland, OR 97213
USA
Tel.: +1 800 944 6190 (toll free)
Email: info@isbs.com

Distribution for Austria:
Stämpfli Verlag AG
Wölflistrasse 1
Postfach 5662
3001 Bern
Switzerland
Tel.: +41 31 300 66 77
Email: verlag@staempfli.com

Distribution for other countries:
Intersentia Publishing nv
Groenstraat 31
2640 Mortsel
Belgium
Tel.: +32 3 680 15 50
Email: mail@intersentia.be

Children's Rights in Intercountry Adoption. A European Perspective
Claire Fenton-Glynn

ISBN 978-1-78068-228-0
D/2014/7849/64
NUR 822

GPRC Guaranteed Peer Reviewed Content

British Library Cataloguing in Publication Data. A catalogue record for this book is available from the British Library.

To Dan and Catriona Simmonds

ACKNOWLEDGEMENTS

This book has developed from my doctoral thesis, completed at the University of Cambridge in 2013. During this time, I have benefited enormously from the advice, encouragement, comments and criticisms of many friends and colleagues, both on this manuscript, and in reaction to talks and papers that have been based on it.

In particular, I would like to express my gratitude to my doctoral supervisor, Dr Andrew Bainham, for his willingness to share his time and extensive expertise, and to Dr Jens Scherpe, for his advice and unwavering support in all aspects of academic life over the last four years. I would also like to thank Professor Jonathan Herring for his insightful comments and constructive discussions in examining the thesis.

The research in this book could not have been undertaken without invaluable assistance from many colleagues who helped me to find foreign texts or provided translations: Humberto Cantu Rivera, Tom Coppen, Philippe de Bonneval, Marco Devesas-Campos, Elena Kazamia, Demetrio Maltese, Nora Markard, Sergii Masol, Natasa Mavronicola, and Rumiana Yotova. Thank you for so generously sharing your knowledge and skills.

Finally, thanks must go to Shaun Berg, who gave me my first chance, and helped me to become the lawyer, academic and person I am today.

CONTENTS

Acknowledgements vii
Table of Cases xiii

Chapter 1. Introduction 1

1.1. The Importance of Europe 6
1.2. Structure of the Book 7

Chapter 2. Combating Abuses: International and Regional Regulation 11

2.1. United Nations Convention on the Rights of the Child 12
2.2. Hague Convention on Protection of Children and Co-operation in Respect of Intercountry Adoption 16
2.3. Revised European Convention on the Adoption of Children 2008 18
2.4. Proposing Normative Guidelines 18

Chapter 3. Intercountry Adoption and the Domestic Child Welfare System: The Principle of Subsidiarity 21

3.1. Subsidiarity in Practice: Waiting Periods and Necessary Conditions . . . 22
3.2. Continuity of Culture, Language, Religion and Ethnicity 30
3.3. The Place of Domestic Alternatives 34
3.3.1. Institutional Care: Can It Ever be Appropriate? 35
3.3.2. Foster Care: Alternative or Smoke-Screen? 41
3.4. Impact of Intercountry Adoption on the Domestic Child Welfare System 43
3.4.1. Sending Countries 43
3.4.2. Receiving Countries 47
3.5. Conclusion 48

Chapter 4. Consenting Adults: Giving and Receiving Consent to Adoption . 51

4.1. Consent by the Birth Mother 53
4.1.1. How Soon Is Too Soon? The Timing of a Mother's Consent and its Revocation 54
4.1.2. Promoting Assistance during the Adoption Process 60
4.1.3. Conclusion 65

4.2. Consent by the Father 66
4.2.1. The Importance of Establishing Paternity. 66
4.2.2. Who Is Required to Give Consent to an Adoption Order?. 67
4.2.3. Establishing Paternity: Registration, Acknowledgement and Court Order 72
4.2.4. Identifying the Father: Investigation and Determination 75
4.3. Conclusion 80

Chapter 5. Buying Babies: The Inducement of Consent 81

5.1. International Instruments 81
5.2. Elements of Consent 83
5.2.1. "Free" Consent. 83
5.2.2. Is Consent Ever Free? 86
5.3. Payments and Compensation 89
5.4. Improper Financial Gain in Adoption. 95
5.4.1. "Approved Non-Accredited Bodies". 99
5.4.2. Independent and Private Adoption 100
5.5. Conclusion 103

Chapter 6. Compulsory Adoption: Adoption Without Consent. 105

6.1. Loss of Parental Rights and Parental Misconduct 106
6.2. Overriding a Refusal to Consent. 108
6.3. Abandonment, Lack of Contact and Disinterest 110
6.4. Legal Assistance to Parents 113
6.5. Conclusion 114

Chapter 7. Child Participation: Autonomy and Protection 117

7.1. International Instruments 118
7.2. Adoption in Europe. 121
7.3. Autonomous Decision-Making. 122
7.3.1. Strict Age Limits 122
7.3.2. Age Limits with Exceptions for Capable Children 126
7.3.3. Age Limits with Exceptions for Best Interests 127
7.3.4. No Age Limit or Laws on Consent 128
7.3.5. European Convention on Human Rights 130
7.4. Participation of Younger Children 133
7.5. Participation and the Protection of the Child's Welfare. 139
7.6. Conclusion 145

Chapter 8. Adoptive Parents: Eligibility, Preparation, and Support 147

8.1. Adoptive Parents and the Rights of Children: Complementary or Contradictory? 148
8.1.1. Intercountry Adoption: An Emerging Market 148
8.1.2. A Right to a Child? 151
8.2. Qualifications of Adoptive Parents 154
8.2.1. International Instruments 154
8.2.2. The Age of Adopters: How Old Is Too Old? 155
8.2.3. Marital Status: Single Adoption 163
8.2.4. Marital Status: Unmarried Couples 166
8.2.5. Adoption by Same-Sex Couples: Changing Social Perceptions? . 169
8.2.6. Conclusion 172
8.3. Facilitating the Adoption: Counselling, Contact, Monitoring and Support 172
8.3.1. Counselling of Prospective Adoptive Parents 173
8.3.2. Establishing a Pre-Adoption Relationship 177
8.3.3. Post-Adoption Services 179
8.4. Conclusion 183

Chapter 9. Who Am I? The Child's Right to Identity 185

9.1. International Instruments 185
9.1.1. United Nations Convention on the Rights of the Child 185
9.1.2. Hague Convention on Intercountry Adoption 188
9.1.3. Revised European Convention on the Adoption of Children ... 189
9.2. The Right to Access Information? 190
9.2.1. Why Is Access to Information Important for a Child? 190
9.2.2. The Child's Access to Information in Europe 191
9.3. Secrecy and Birth Parents 197
9.3.1. Must Information Be Recorded? 197
9.3.2. Balancing the Rights of Biological Parents and Children 207
9.4. Conclusion 210

Chapter 10. Conclusion 211

List of Legislation 217
Literature 223
Index 247

TABLE OF CASES

EUROPEAN COMMISSION ON HUMAN RIGHTS

B, R and J v Federal Republic of Germany (Appl. No. 9639/82) Decision of 15 March 1984. 70
Berrehab v the Netherlands (Appl. No. 10730/84) Decision of 21 June 1988 . . . 69
ED v Ireland (Appl. No. 25054/94) Decision of 18 October 1995. 33
MB v United Kingdom (Appl. No. 22920/93) Decision of 6 April 1994. 69
VS v Germany (Appl. No. 4261/02) Admissibility Decision of 22 May 2007. 59
X v Belgium and the Netherlands (Appl. No. 6482/74) Decision of 10 July 1975. . . . . 152, 165, 166
X v the Netherlands (Appl. No. 8896/80) Decision of 10 March 1981 162
X v United Kingdom (Appl. No. 7626/76) Decision of 11 July 1977 69

EUROPEAN COURT OF HUMAN RIGHTS

Airey v Ireland (Appl. No. 6289/73) Judgment of 9 October 1979; [1979] ECHR 3 114
Anayo v Germany (Appl. No. 20578/07) Judgment of 21 December 2010; [2010] ECHR 393 69
EB v France (Appl. No. 43546/02) Judgment of 22 January 2008; [2008] ECHR 55. . . . . 162, 171
Evans v United Kingdom (Appl. No. 6339/05) Judgment of 10 April 2008; [2007] ECHR 264. 151
Fretté v France (Appl. No. 36515/97) Judgment of 26 February 2002; [2002] ECHR 156. . . . . 162, 171
Gas and Dubois v France (Appl. No. 25951/07) Judgment of 15 March 2012 168
Gaskin v United Kingdom (Appl. No. 10454/83) Judgment of 7 July 1989; [1989] ECHR 13 208
Godelli v Italy (Appl. No. 33783/09) 25 September 2012 209
Hokkanen v Finland (Appl. No. 19823/92) Judgment of 23 September 1994; [1994] ECHR 32. 132

Johansen v Norway (Appl. No. 17383/90) Judgment of 7 August 1996; [1996] ECHR 31 .... 105, 110
Kearns v France (Appl. No. 35991/04) Judgment of 10 January 2008; [2008] ECHR 1 .... 59, 64
Keegan v Ireland (Appl. No. 16969/90) Judgment of 26 May 1994; [1994] ECHR 18 .... 22, 69
Kutzner v Germany (Appl. No. 46544/99) Judgment of 26 February 2002, [2002] ECHR 160 87
Marckx v Belgium (Appl. No. 6833/74) Judgment of 13 June 1979; [1979] ECHR 2 .... 53, 69
McMichael v United Kingdom (Appl. No, 16424/90) Judgment of 24 February 1995; [1995] ECHR 8 71
Neulinger and Shuruk v Switzerland (Appl. No. 41615/07) Judgement of 6 July 2010; [2010] ECHR 1053 111
Nielsen v Denmark (Appl. No. 10929/84) Judgment of 28 November 1988; [1988] ECHR 23 130–131
Odièvre v France (Appl. No. 42326/98) Judgment of 13 February 2003; [2003] ECHR 86 .... 69, 194, 198, 199, 202, 203, 207–209
Olsson v Sweden (No 2) (Appl. No. 13441/87) Judgment of 27 November 1992; [1992] ECHR 75 .... 27, 143
P, C and S v the United Kingdom (Appl. No. 56547/00) Judgment of 16 July 2002; [2002] ECHR 604 .... 110, 114
Pini and Others v Romania (Appl. No. 78028/01) Judgment of 22 June 2004; [2005] ECHR 275 22
R and H v United Kingdom (Appl. No. 35348/06) Judgment of 31 May 2011; [2011] ECHR 844 .... 64, 110
Raw and Others v France (Appl. No. 10131/11) Judgment of 7 March 2013; [2013] ECHR 199 144
Rozanski v Poland (Appl. No. 55339/00) Judgment of 18 May 2006; [2006] ECHR 545 .... 70, 73
Sahin v Germany (Appl. No. 19301/92) Judgment of 10 April 2001; [2001] ECHR 266 .... 125, 128, 136, 137
Saviny v Ukraine (Appl. No. 39948/06) Judgment of 18 December 2008 87
Schneider v Germany (Appl. No. 17080/07) Judgment of 15 September 2011; [2011] ECHR 2416 .... 69, 70
T v United Kingdom (Appl. No. 24724/94) Judgment of 16 December 1999; [1999] ECHR 170 131
Todorova v Italy (Appl. No 33932/06) Judgment of 13 January 2009; [2009] ECHR 69 57
W v United Kingdom (Appl. No. 9749/82) Judgment of 8 July 1987; [1987] ECHR 17 64
Wagner and JMWL v Luxembourg (Appl. No. 76240/01) Judgment of 28 June 2007 164–166

Wallova and Walla v Czech Republic (Appl. No. 23848/04) Judgment of 26 October 2006 88
X and Others v Austria (Appl. No. 19010/07) Judgment of 19 February 2013; [2013] ECHR 148 . . . . . 168, 170
X v Croatia (Appl. No. 11223/04) Judgment of 17 July 2008; [2008] ECHR 641 64
X, Y and Z v United Kingdom (Appl. No. 21830/93) Judgment of 22 April 1997; [1997] ECHR 20 143
Zaunegger v Germany (Appl. No. 22028/04) Judgment of 3 December 2009; [2009] ECHR 1982 71

FRANCE

Enfance et Familles v F et A, Court of Appeal of Riom, 16 December 1997 (1998) JCP II 10147 200
TGI La Roche-sur-Yon (29 July 1993) BICC 1 March 1994, No 302 143

NETHERLANDS

Valkenhorst II (HR 15 April 1994) *NJ* 1994 194

NEW ZEALAND

C v S and W (2006) High Court Napier, CIV-2005-441-776 140

SPAIN

Recurso de Casacion num. 2854/1994, Sentencia del TS de 21 septiembre 1999 200

UNITED KINGDOM

A Local Authority v GC [2009] 1 FLR 299 57
Birmingham City Council v S [2006] EWHC 3065 (Fam); [2007] 1 FLR 1223 66
Flintshire County Council v K [2001] 2 FLR 476 81
M (A Minor) [1997] EWCA Civ 2766 41

Mabon v Mabon [2005] EWCA Civ 634; [2005] 2 FLR 1011 .... 135, 143, 144
R (G) v Nottingham City Council [2008] EWHC 152 (Admin); [2008] 1 FLR 1660 54
R (Thomson) v Minister of State for Children [2005] EWHC 1378 (Admin)... 151
Re C (A Child) v XYZ County Council [2007] EWCA Civ 1206; [2008] 1 FLR 1294 .... 66, 79
Re C (Adoption: Legality) [1999] 1 FLR 370 .... 93, 100, 149
Re C (Foreign Adoption: Natural Mother's Consent: Service) [2006] 1 FLR 318 86
Re D (Paternity) [2006] EWHC 3545 (Fam); [2007] 2 FLR 26 74
Re E (A Minor) (Wardship: Medical Treatment) [1993] 1 FLR 386........ 129
Re G (Foreign Adoption: Consent) [1995] 2 FLR 534........ 86
Re H (Minors) (Local Authority: Parental Rights) (No 3) [1991] Fam 151 68
Re H (Paternity: Blood Test) [1996] 2 FLR 65........ 186
Re J (Abduction: Children's Objections) [2011] EWCA Civ 1448; [2012] 1 FLR 457 118
Re K (Adoption & Wardship) [1997] 2 FLR 230........ 55
Re L (An Infant) (1962) 106 SJ 611, CA 109
Re M (Adoption or Residence) [1998] 1 FLR 570 .... 108, 109
Re P (Adoption: Unmarried Couple) [2008] UKHL 38........ 168
Re R (A Minor) (Contact) [1993] 2 FLR 762 192
Re W [1971] AC 682........ 108
S v S [1992] 2 FLR 31 129
S v S; W v Official Solicitor [1972] AC 24 75
Watson v Nikolaisen [1955] 2 QB 286........ 200
X and Y (Foreign Surrogacy) [2008] EWHC 3030 (Fam); [2009] 1 FLR 733........ 55, 94, 97
X County Council v C [2007] EWHC 1771 (Fam)........ 78

UNITED STATES

GP, 842 So 2d 1062 (Florida) 78
In re Baby Girl Clausen (1993) 442 Mich. 648; 502 NW 2d 649........ 55
US v Focus on Children US District Court of Utah, Sealed Indictment (2007) <www.brandeis.edu/investigate/adoption/docs/FOCindictment.pdf> [1 February 2013] (Utah)........ 61, 85, 91
US v Lauryn Galindo No CR 03–0187 Z (Washington District Court) 85, 91

CHAPTER 1
INTRODUCTION

Intercountry adoption began as a humanitarian practice, first used to assist children orphaned by World War II and subsequently those in the aftermath of the conflicts in Korea and Vietnam. However, in the years since, it has evolved into a multi-million dollar business, marred by widespread accusations of human rights abuses, and concern over the law's ability to prevent them.

European[1] jurisdictions play a central role in intercountry adoption, both as countries of origin for children being placed, and as receiving countries. In 2010, 50 per cent of all children involved in intercountry adoption worldwide were sent to countries within Europe,[2] while three European states – France, Spain and Italy – have been in the top five receiving states in the world for the past 15 years.[3] In addition, of the approximately 30,000 children involved in intercountry adoption per year worldwide,[4] around one third come from European jurisdictions.[5]

---

1 For this book, I refer to Europe in the wider sense, including all 47 member states of the Council of Europe: Albania, Andorra, Armenia, Austria, Azerbaijan, Belgium, Bosnia and Herzegovina, Bulgaria, Croatia, Cyprus, the Czech Republic, Denmark, Estonia, Finland, Former Yugoslav Republic of Macedonia (FYR Macedonia), France, Georgia, Germany, Greece, Hungary, Iceland, Ireland, Italy, Latvia, Liechtenstein, Lithuania, Luxembourg, Malta, Moldova, Monaco, Montenegro, the Netherlands, Norway, Poland, Portugal, Romania, Russia, San Marino, Serbia, Slovakia, Slovenia, Spain, Sweden, Switzerland, Turkey, Ukraine, and the United Kingdom.

2 Peter Selman, "The Global Decline of Intercountry Adoption: What Lies Ahead?" (2012) 11(3) *Social Policy and Society* 381, 383.

3 European Union, *International Adoption in the European Union* (2009, European Parliament) 43 <www.childoneurope.org/issues/adoption/Report%20EP%20international%20adoption_EN.pdf> [7 February 2013].

4 Peter Selman, "Global Trends in Intercountry Adoption: 2001–2010" (2012) 44 *Adoption Advocate* 1, 2.

5 In 2009, the European Union estimated that this figure was one-half of all adoptions worldwide, but this must be adjusted down in the light of the fall in Russian adoptions (see UNICEF, *TransMONEE Database* (2012) <www.transmonee.org/> [22 May 2013]; European Union, *International Adoption in the European Union* (2009) 9). Given the difficulties in acquiring information concerning intercountry adoption, it is not always possible to access exact and current figures. Selman suggests that the number of European children being placed in intercountry adoption has dropped by a third since 2004, although he is not clear which European countries are included in this estimate (Peter Selman, "The Global Decline of Intercountry Adoption: What Lies Ahead?" (2012) 11(3) *Social Policy and Society* 381, 390). In addition, key sending states are often in a state of flux, as a rise in adoptions can denote problems in regulation – as was seen in Romania – and be followed by a moratorium on

Europe is also very interdependent when it comes to intercountry adoption, with the majority of children from European states of origin being sent to receiving countries within Europe. While practice in receiving countries is more varied, as can be seen below, adoptions within the region still make up a significant proportion of the overall figures.

Percentage of children sent to other European jurisdictions[6]

Sending States	Percentage to Europe
Albania	67%
Armenia	28%
Azerbaijan	7%
Bosnia and Herzegovina	92%
Bulgaria	69%
Croatia	100%
Czech Republic	94%
Estonia	28%
FYR Macedonia	80%
Georgia	6%
Hungary	88%
Latvia	86%
Lithuania	72%
Moldova	29%
Montenegro	Not available
Poland	74%
Portugal	56%
Romania	78%
Russia	36%
Serbia	100%
Slovakia	99%
Turkey	87%
Ukraine	60%

intercountry placements. As such, the number of children placed in intercountry adoption, and the states from which they come, can vary dramatically from year to year.

6 European Union, ibid., 9. Figures represent intercountry adoptions in the year 2004. Note that Portugal identified itself as both a sending and receiving country, and is therefore listed in both tables.

Percentage of children received from other European jurisdictions[7]

Receiving States	Percentage from Europe
Andorra	Not available
Austria	Not available
Belgium	12%
Cyprus	100%
Denmark	10%
Finland	16%
France	21%
Germany	48%
Greece	Not available
Iceland	0%
Ireland	65%
Italy	64%
Liechtenstein	50%
Luxembourg	0%
Malta	24%
Monaco	Not available
Netherlands	2%
Norway	4%
Portugal	Not available
San Marino	Not available
Slovenia	Not available
Spain	38%
Sweden	16%
Switzerland	28%
United Kingdom	5%

In this context, the question that this book aims to answer is very simple: how can we best protect the rights of children involved in intercountry adoption in Europe?

The book will neither encourage greater use of intercountry adoption as a placement for children, nor advocate for it to be curtailed. Instead, it recognises that intercountry adoption can provide a valuable placement option for certain children, provided that it is appropriately regulated. The question remains how this regulation can be achieved whilst ensuring that unnecessary bureaucracy does not *de facto* limit adoptions that should take place.

7 European Union, ibid., 9. Figures represent intercountry adoptions in the year 2004. Note that Portugal identified itself as both a sending and receiving country, and is therefore listed in both tables.

The international community has attempted to regulate the intercountry adoption system through the 1993 Hague Convention on Protection of Children and Co-operation in Respect of Intercountry Adoption (Hague Convention). While this Convention, which has 93 contracting states, has provided important procedural safeguards and effectively coordinated responsibilities between sending and receiving states, it defers extensively to domestic authorities in deciding how best to protect substantive rights.

As such, it still remains necessary to undertake a more detailed investigation of the human rights principles that must complement these procedural requirements. Using the United Nations Convention on the Rights of the Child (UNCRC) as the foundation for analysis, this book provides an examination of the application of children's rights in the field of intercountry adoption. In doing so, it will use European jurisdictions as examples of both good and bad practice in order to illustrate the issues that arise in the practical implementation of these principles, and make normative suggestions as to how intercountry adoption can be effected in a manner that protects the rights of children in Europe.

In advancing normative propositions for the regulation of intercountry adoption, this book will not be suggesting that uniform laws should be adopted across all 47 European states. Especially in the field of family law, there will be different historical, social and financial considerations that will come into play when deciding how best to implement human rights obligations, as has long been recognised by the European Court of Human Rights.[8] Instead, the book will explore the human rights principles that should be followed in conceiving an intercountry adoption system that provides comprehensive protection for the rights of children, within which there is scope for different approaches as to how best to comply with these obligations.

The focus of this book is specifically on the rights of children in intercountry adoption placements with unknown prospective parents; relative and step-parent adoptions fall outside the scope of inquiry. Although the rights of birth parents and adoptive parents, as well as public policy considerations, will also be evaluated, in proposing a framework for intercountry adoption the rights and welfare of the child himself or herself will be the guiding principle. This approach is mandated by the UNCRC, which under article 21 requires that states that recognise or permit adoption – either domestic or intercountry – ensure that the best interests of the child shall be the paramount consideration. The Hague Convention is also predicated on ensuring that intercountry adoption takes place "in the best interests of the child and with respect for his or her fundamental rights as recognised in international law".[9] It requires that before any child is deemed eligible for adoption, matched with prospective adoptive

8 See discussions of the margin of appreciation under article 8.

9 Article 1(a).

parents, or transferred to a receiving state, the authorities must determine that this would be in the child's best interests.[10]

In this context, children's rights and children's interests should be seen as complementary. This book will not rehearse the debate concerning protection and autonomy, or whether they are truly antithetical,[11] but instead work within the guidance provided by the international instruments. The rights of the child as set out by the UNCRC will be used to provide a framework of rules for intercountry adoption, taking into account the role of the welfare principle in article 3 of that Convention. This principle, which states that the best interests of the child shall be a primary consideration in any action concerning children, acts as an overarching interpretative tool in determining the content of the state's obligations under the Convention, as well as a mediating principle used to resolve conflicts between competing rights.[12] It is not intended to be a stand-alone principle that overrules the enumerated rights in the UNCRC, but as a mechanism for deciding the most appropriate implementation of these rights.[13]

This focus on the rights of the child does not mean, however, that the rights of birth and adoptive parents can be wholly dismissed. The respective rights of the parties in the adoption triad should not be viewed as inevitably in conflict, but as interrelated and potentially complementary, and it is therefore important that these are analysed and taken into consideration within the child rights framework.

It should also be remembered that although rights language, and the law in general, can be a very potent tool in protecting children, it cannot work alone. Protection under the law can only be fully effective if accompanied by education,

---

10 See articles 4, 16, 21 and 24.

11 Although this topic will be considered briefly in Chapter Seven. See, for example, John Eekelaar, "The Interests of the Child and the Child's Wishes: The Role of Dynamic Self-Determinism" (1994) 8 *International Journal of Law, Policy and the Family* 48; Jane Fortin, "Children's Rights: Are the Courts Now Taking Them More Seriously?" (2004) 15 *King's College Law Journal* 253; Michael Freeman, "Taking Children's Rights More Seriously" (1992) 6 *International Journal of Law, Policy and the Family* 52; Martin Guggenheim, "Ratify the UN Convention on the Rights of the Child, But Don't Expect Any Miracles" (2006) 20 *Emory International Law Review* 43; Martha Minow, "Whatever Happened to Children's Rights?" (1995) 80 *Minnesota Law Review* 267; Robert Mnookin, "Child-Custody Adjudication: Judicial Functions in the Face of Indeterminacy" (1975) 39 *Law and Contemporary Problems* 226; Laura Purdy, "Why Children Shouldn't Have Equal Rights" (1994) 2 *International Journal of Children's Rights* 223; Hillary Rodham, "Children Under the Law" (1973) 43 *Harvard Educational Review* 487; Michael S Wald, "Children's Rights: A Framework for Analysis" (1979) 12 *University of California, Davis, Law Review* 255.

12 See Philip Alston, "The Best Interests Principle: Towards a Reconciliation of Culture and Human Rights" (1994) 8(1) *International Journal of Law, Policy and the Family* 1; Jean Zermatten, "The Best Interests of the Child Principle: Literal Analysis and Function" (2010) 18 *International Journal of Children's Rights* 483.

13 Thorbjørn Jagland (Council of Europe Commissioner for Human Rights), *Adoption and Children: A Human Rights Perspective* (28 April 2011) <https://wcd.coe.int/wcd/ViewDoc.jsp?id=1780157> [30 May 2011].

professional training and research. Law provides the structure under which good practice can be implemented, but law enacted alone without appropriate foundations laid to support it will achieve little. It is not the intention of this book to go into great detail concerning areas of good practice that can be developed to implement the law in an effective manner – this is outside the scope of the study. Instead, it will focus on the promotion of strong laws to provide a framework for good practice, and provide protection for children through judicial and legislative mechanisms.

1.1. THE IMPORTANCE OF EUROPE

Europe provides a unique opportunity to examine the practice of intercountry adoption. Crucially, it contains both states that act as countries of origin for children entering into intercountry adoption – for example Albania, Armenia, Bulgaria, Estonia, Latvia, Lithuania, Georgia, Poland, Russia and Ukraine – and states that act as receiving countries, where children are placed with adoptive parents – for example Denmark, France, Germany, Italy, the Netherlands, Norway, Spain, Sweden, Switzerland, and the United Kingdom.[14] This divide between sending and receiving states provides a rare opportunity to examine both sides of the practice within a region, and the mechanisms that can be put in place at each end of the process to ensure that the rights of the child are adequately protected.

Furthermore, the European human rights system provides an unrivalled opportunity to regulate intercountry adoption on a regional level. The European Convention for the Protection of Human Rights and Fundamental Freedoms – more commonly known as the European Convention on Human Rights (ECHR) – and its enforcement mechanism, the European Court of Human Rights (ECtHR), create a unique legal space in which human rights can be protected in a manner unprecedented in international and regional law. In addition to the analysis presented on the 47 European states, the book will examine the jurisprudence of the Court as it applies to intercountry adoption. This is of particular importance as it can create region-wide norms that must be followed, but equally, it can undermine international human rights principles where its own judgments are not similarly enlightened or progressive.

It is important to bear in mind that this is not a work of comparative law – it does not study in depth the laws of any one country, nor examine the practical implementation of these laws. Instead, it takes the form of a description of foreign legal data; how different countries approach the regulation of intercountry adoption. At the same time, this book does not purport to provide an exhaustive overview of the legislation and practice across European states.

14 It should be noted that these states are quite precisely divided between eastern and western Europe.

The purpose of using the practice of European jurisdictions is not to provide an encyclopaedic list of legislation, but to use the example of certain states to indicate good and bad practice, and highlight interesting areas of divergence for comparison. Due to considerations of language and accessibility of sources, some jurisdictions are more prevalent in this analysis, while for others, only minimal information is available. The book is not evaluating the practice of states to provide an overview of the practice of intercountry adoption in Europe, but to better understand the different ways in which the rights of children can be implemented or violated through using practical examples of state practice.

1.2. STRUCTURE OF THE BOOK

Intercountry adoption is usually evaluated as an end product rather than there being an examination of the individual decisions that lead to a child being placed. This book will analyse every aspect of the decision-making process, from who has the right to be named a parent, to the child's own decision-making capacity, to the assistance an adoptive parent is given post-placement. Too often intercountry adoption is considered as a distinct practice, separated from normal child protection procedures and domestic laws. This book will firmly place intercountry adoption back in the domestic sphere, albeit guided by international and regional human rights obligations. For this reason, some chapters of the book will appear to apply equally to domestic adoption; this is as it should be. Although there may be additional considerations in the practice of intercountry adoption, at heart it should be considered as akin to any other alternative care placement, subject to the same scrutiny, the same protections.

Following this introductory chapter, Chapter Two will examine the framework of instruments that will be used as the foundation for analysis throughout the book. This includes not only the UNCRC and Hague Convention outlined above, but also the Revised European Convention on the Adoption of Children of 2008. It will discuss the fundamental principles of these conventions as they relate to intercountry adoption, and their applicability to domestic European law.

Chapter Three begins the substantive analysis of human rights obligations in intercountry adoption by considering the application of the principle of subsidiarity. This principle, which requires that all domestic alternatives be considered and deemed inappropriate before intercountry adoption is authorised, is one of the cornerstones of the international regulation of adoption. This chapter will illuminate the role of the principle of proportionality under the ECHR in ensuring the appropriate use of domestic alternatives by European states, while examining the importance of facilitating family reunification. Further, it will analyse the use of "waiting periods" before a child can be placed in intercountry adoption, and the arguments that have been formulated against these. In particular, the debate concerning the use of institutional care for children, and whether this can ever be an appropriate alternative to an out-of-country placement, will be considered. Finally, the chapter will examine the impact of intercountry adoption on the domestic child welfare systems of both sending and receiving states, and the ways in which excessive use of intercountry adoption may affect these.

Chapter Four commences the analysis of perhaps the most controversial aspect of intercountry adoption: consent. This chapter examines the voluntary placement of children, beginning with an often-overlooked question: who must give their consent to the adoption? When considering the place of the mother, this is relatively straightforward, and the chapter moves on to consider the assistance the mother must be given before making a decision concerning adoption, and how soon after the child's birth that decision can be made. On the other hand, the role of the biological father is much more complex. Identifying the father is important for protecting the rights of the child, as it provides the additional possibility of domestic placement, either through the father himself, or his extended family. This chapter will look at the practices across Europe for the establishment of paternity through presumption, recognition and court order. Further, it will consider mechanisms for investigating paternity, and how the rights of the child in this respect can be balanced with the rights of the mother, and of the father himself.

Chapter Five will examine the improper inducement of consent, which lies at the heart of many of the intercountry adoption scandals over the past 25 years. The prevention of the sale of, or traffic in, children was one of the driving forces behind the drafting of the Hague Convention, as well as the Optional Protocol to the UNCRC on the Sale of Children, Child Prostitution and Child Pornography. This chapter will analyse the restrictions and procedures that have been put in place by these instruments, and the areas in which they fall short. In particular, it will look at the practice of improper gain and independent adoptions, and the role they play in undermining the international regime.

Many children involved in intercountry adoption are not placed with parental consent, but are adopted when this has been overridden or dispensed with. Chapter Six will investigate the circumstances in which this can occur, and the balance that states must achieve between protecting the child's right to maintain his or her family ties, and ensuring a safe and stable environment for the child's development. This is particularly important in the context of what is termed child "abandonment", which is a common way that children are placed in an intercountry adoption, often unnecessarily, and will be examined in this chapter.

The final issue concerning consent involves not the parents, but the child himself or herself. This is an aspect of adoption law that has received little attention, especially in intercountry adoption where the common perception is that children are adopted as young babies. Contrary to that belief, Chapter Seven will show that older children are also being placed in intercountry adoption, and highlight the importance of ensuring that they are able to participate in the decision-making process either directly or indirectly. It will look not only to the age at which the child should be able to make an autonomous decision on whether or not he or she wants to be adopted, but also how those not yet mature enough to do so should also have their views considered. Further, the means by which children can have their interests independently represented will be evaluated, and the implications of this for children of all ages.

Chapter Eight shifts the focus from consent to the decision-making processes concerning adoptive parents. It will look at three key issues: eligibility, preparation and support; but first, it will determine whether there is a right to adopt, and how prospective adoptive parents have shaped the intercountry adoption marketplace. In relation to the eligibility of prospective adoptive parents, this chapter will analyse the age of adopters, and whether there should be a minimum or maximum age or age difference between the adopters and child. It will also look at adoption by single persons and unmarried couples, as well as the controversial issue of adoption by homosexuals, and the evolution of practice throughout Europe. The final part of the chapter will examine the mechanisms put in place to assist prospective adoptive parents, including pre-adoption counselling and post-adoption services, and determine whether they are of benefit in promoting a stable and healthy relationship with adopted children.

The final substantive chapter concerns an adopted child's ability to access information on his or her biological origins. The chapter will discuss not only the *negative* obligation on the state not to prevent a child from accessing his or her original birth records, but also the *positive* obligation to ensure that such records exist in the first place. In doing so, it will consider the practice of anonymous birth and the use of "baby-boxes" to anonymously relinquish children, and how these interfere with the rights of the child. More than any other, this chapter will focus on the balance between the rights of the child, the birth parents, and the adoptive parents, as well as the pressure placed by public policy considerations.

Finally, Chapter Ten will present my conclusions as to how best we can protect the rights of children involved in intercountry adoption in Europe, highlighting the areas where good practice has already been established, and those in which there are still substantial improvements needing to be made. It will conclude that for an effective system that protects the rights and welfare of the child, intercountry adoption must not be seen as a stand-alone practice, but must be integrated into the domestic child welfare system with similar scrutiny, safeguards and protection.

CHAPTER 2
COMBATING ABUSES: INTERNATIONAL AND REGIONAL REGULATION

International adoption worldwide is governed primarily by two international instruments: the United Nations Convention on the Rights of the Child, which has been ratified by all European states; and the Hague Convention on Intercountry Adoption, which has been ratified by all but three.[1] In addition to these international instruments, the Revised European Convention on the Adoption of Children of 2008 (ECA 2008) provides a regional mechanism for regulating the practice. Although this Convention has fewer signatories than the international instruments, its regional nature and the specificity of its provisions make it an important element of the legal regime. These instruments will provide the core for the analysis of state practice in this book, and for developing normative guidelines for the protection of children's rights in intercountry adoption.

Although the European Convention on Human Rights will play a central role in this book, its provisions will not be used as a basis for analysing state practice. Instead, the decisions of the ECtHR themselves will be examined for compliance with the rights of the child as contained in the instruments above, focusing in particular on whether they promote children's rights in this area, or rather undermine the international human rights principles.

The reason for treating the ECHR differently from these other international and regional instruments is two-fold. First, and most importantly, the Convention is not a children's rights instrument. As Eekelaar and Dingwall argue, the structure of the ECHR suggests that "the minds of the drafters were not directed at the child within the family, but on the relationship between the adult members and the outside world."[2] Children and minors are only mentioned twice in the main body of the Convention: under article 5(1)(d) (the right to liberty and security) an exception to the right is permitted where a minor is

1 See below.

2 John Eekelaar and Robert Dingwall, *Human Rights: Report on the Replies of Governments to the Enquiry under Article 57 of the European Convention on Human Rights* (1987, Council of Europe) 17.

detained for the purpose of educational supervision or for bringing him or her before a legal authority; and under article 6(1) (the right to a fair trial) which allows for the exclusion of the press or public from a trial where the interests of a juvenile require. Both these articles thus provide exceptions to general rights for adults in order to provide additional protection for children in the area of juvenile justice, rather than providing children with rights that they can enforce against the state. The adult-centred approach to the Convention can also be seen in its approach to the issue of education; ostensibly a child's right, under article 2 of Protocol 1 this is formulated in such a way that its primary function has been to protect the right of parents to direct their child's education in conformity with their own beliefs.[3] Further, the jurisprudence of the Court is developed through addressing the specific complaints of individuals. As it is very rare for a child to bring a case on his or her own without being joined to a parent's petition – the case law largely reflects the interests and concerns of adults.

The second reason for treating the ECHR as an object of analysis, rather than a tool for developing normative guidance for the practice of intercountry adoption, is the nature of the Convention's enforcement mechanism, the European Court of Human Rights. The object of this book is to take the basic children's rights principles in international and regional law and give content to them when applied to situations involving intercountry adoption. In addition to not containing children's rights principles as outlined above, the ECHR's more general provisions are already applied to practical situations and given content by the Court. As such, it is more appropriate to analyse the Court's decisions for compliance with the framework provided by other child-centred and adoption-focused instruments.

2.1. UNITED NATIONS CONVENTION ON THE RIGHTS OF THE CHILD

The most important of these instruments is the 1989 United Nations Convention on the Rights of the Child, the principal international convention concerning children's rights, and the most widely ratified human rights instrument in the world. Every European state is party to the Convention and, as such, bound by its provisions under international law.[4]

The Convention contains both civil and political, as well as social, economic and cultural, rights, and is underpinned by four key principles: the principle of

3 This article reads: "No person shall be denied the right to education. In the exercise of any functions which it assumes in relation to education and to teaching, the State shall respect the right of parents to ensure such education and teaching in conformity with their own religious and philosophical convictions."

4 Only Somalia, South Sudan and the United States are not parties to the Convention (although both Somalia and the United States are signatories).

non-discrimination; the best interests of the child; the right to life, survival and development; and respect for the views of the child. These are the fundamental obligations of states to children within their jurisdiction, used to guide the implementation of other rights under the Convention.[5]

The UNCRC has two provisions that deal directly with adoption. The first, article 20, considers the place of domestic alternative care, and provides that a child who is deprived of his or her family environment shall be entitled to special protection and assistance from the state. The Convention also sets out guidelines for the provision of alternative care, stating that:

> "Such care could include, *inter alia*, foster placement, kafalah of Islamic law, adoption or if necessary placement in suitable institutions for the care of children. When considering solutions, due regard shall be paid to the desirability of continuity in a child's upbringing and to the child's ethnic, religious, cultural and linguistic background."[6]

This article is deliberately wide in scope, considering a variety of different placement options for children who have been deprived of their family environment. This reflects the different cultural and religious traditions among contracting states, as well as the different financial resources. Of key importance in this article is the explicit consideration of institutional care and its implications for the subsidiarity principle in article 21, as well as the preference for continuity in the child's upbringing where possible, both of which will be discussed in detail in Chapter Three.

The second article of the UNCRC of central importance to the regulation of adoption is article 21. This article considers both domestic and intercountry adoption, and was one of the most controversial articles in the drafting process. Such was the contentious nature of this article that the drafting group had nearly twice the number of participants as the next largest group.[7] In 1982, the Working Group on the Draft Convention on the Rights of the Child, an auxiliary body of the UN Commission for Human Rights, adopted the following text:

> "1. The States Parties to the present Convention shall undertake measures, where appropriate, to facilitate the process of adoption of the child. Adoption of the child shall be authorized only by competent authorities who determine, in accordance with applicable law and procedures, and on the basis of all pertinent and reliable information, that the adoption is permissible in view of the child's status concerning

5 See Rachel Hodgkin and Peter Newell, *Implementation Handbook for the Convention on the Rights of the Child* (3rd ed, 2007, UNICEF) 35.

6 Article 20(3) UNCRC.

7 David Johnson, "Cultural and Regional Pluralism in the Drafting of the UN Convention on the Rights of the Child", in Michael Freeman and Philip Veerman (eds), *The Ideologies of Children's Rights* (1992, Kluwer Law) 104.

> parents, relatives and guardians and that, if required, the appropriate persons concerned have given their informed consent to the adoption on the basis of such counselling as may be necessary.
> 2. The States Parties to the present Convention shall take all appropriate measures to secure the best interests of the child who is the subject of intercountry adoption. States Parties shall ensure that placements are made by authorized agencies or appropriate persons under the adequate supervision of competent authorities, providing the same safeguards that are applied in exclusively domestic adoptions. The competent authorities shall make every possible effort to ensure the legal validity of the adoption in the countries involved. States Parties shall endeavour, where appropriate, to promote these objectives by entering into bilateral or multilateral agreements."[8]

This import of this draft is significantly different to the final article that was adopted in the Convention in 1989. Despite the fact that the majority of the requirements in the text are substantially the same, albeit organised in a different fashion, the main difference lies in the first sentence of subparagraph one, which states that signatories shall undertake measures "to facilitate the process of adoption". This obligation, which encourages the practice of adoption, is in stark contrast to the eventual text that places intercountry adoption as a practice of last resort.

This shift of focus was a result of the different states that were involved in the drafting process. The working text was drafted predominantly by the Western delegations, while the final text had to balance the proposal with the interests of two other groups with opposing approaches to intercountry adoption. On the one hand, some delegations wished to strengthen controls over intercountry adoption, rather than encourage it, while others were philosophically opposed to the practice in the first place, and did not want it mentioned in the Convention at all.[9] As a result, the final text was a compromise between these positions, with an acknowledgement of intercountry adoption still remaining, but with the removal of the reference to the facilitation of adoption, as well as stricter rules concerning the conditions under which adoption could occur.[10]

These additional restraints on intercountry adoption notwithstanding, there is still a substantially affirmative focus to the eventual formulation. The final text of article 21 of the 1989 United Nations Convention on the Rights of the Child reads:

8 Office of the United Nations High Commissioner for Human Rights, *Legislative History of the Convention on the Rights of the Child* (2007) HR/PUB/07/1.

9 David Johnson, "Cultural and Regional Pluralism in the Drafting of the UN Convention on the Rights of the Child", in Michael Freeman and Philip Veerman (eds), *The Ideologies of Children's Rights* (1992, Kluwer Law), 105.

10 Ibid.

> "States Parties that recognize and/or permit the system of adoption shall ensure that the best interests of the child shall be the paramount consideration and they shall:
> (a) Ensure that the adoption of a child is authorized only by competent authorities who determine, in accordance with applicable law and procedures and on the basis of all pertinent and reliable information, that the adoption is permissible in view of the child's status concerning parents, relatives and legal guardians and that, if required, the persons concerned have given their informed consent to the adoption on the basis of such counselling as may be necessary;
> (b) Recognize that inter-country adoption may be considered as an alternative means of child's care, if the child cannot be placed in a foster or an adoptive family or cannot in any suitable manner be cared for in the child's country of origin;
> (c) Ensure that the child concerned by inter-country adoption enjoys safeguards and standards equivalent to those existing in the case of national adoption;
> (d) Take all appropriate measures to ensure that, in inter-country adoption, the placement does not result in improper financial gain for those involved in it;
> (e) Promote, where appropriate, the objectives of the present article by concluding bilateral or multilateral arrangements or agreements, and endeavour, within this framework, to ensure that the placement of the child in another country is carried out by competent authorities or organs."

The most important aspect of article 21, however, is the imperative that the best interests of the child be the paramount consideration in adoption. While the majority of rights in the UNCRC are subject to the requirement that the welfare of the child be a primary consideration – as provided for in article 3 – this wording makes clear that in matters of adoption, no other rights or interests, including those of birth parents, prospective adopters, or economic or political considerations, should be considered equal to those of the child.[11]

The purpose of this elevation of children's rights in the context of adoption is to ensure that, in the common parlance, a family is found for a child, not a child for a family. The practice of adoption is as old as recorded history, yet its origins predominantly lie in the promotion of the social, political and economic interests of the adopter.[12] The adoption of young children for the purposes of social care is relatively recent, and article 21 reaffirms this role, placing adoption as a solely child-focused practice, which cannot be effected for any reasons other than for the child's welfare.[13]

---

11 United Nations Commission on Human Rights, *Report of the Working Group on a Draft Convention on the Rights of the Child* (2 March 1989, United Nations) E/CN.4/1989/48, [359]–[364].

12 See, for example, adoption under Roman law to create ties between wealthy families, and to create male heirs.

13 See Rachel Hodgkin and Peter Newell *Implementation Handbook for the Convention on the Rights of the Child* (3rd ed, 2007, UNICEF) 295.

2.2. HAGUE CONVENTION ON PROTECTION OF CHILDREN AND CO-OPERATION IN RESPECT OF INTERCOUNTRY ADOPTION

The Hague Convention is the principal international instrument focused solely on the adoption of children. It is not a human rights convention as the UNCRC is, but a treaty under private international law whose main focus is to put in place procedural safeguards to help ensure an efficient system of intercountry adoption by allocating responsibilities between states of origin (or sending states) and receiving states. However, this does not mean that the instrument is devoid of normative assumptions, as will be discussed below.

The Hague Convention is the product of the Hague Conference on Private International Law (Hague Conference), which has 74 members who are usually involved in the drafting of any conventions of the Conference.[14] However, given the subject matter of the Convention on Intercountry Adoption, it was considered that non-member states should be allowed to participate in the drafting, as well as become parties to the subsequent instrument.[15] It was acknowledged that to be able to effectively deal with the issue of intercountry adoption, the participation of as many states as possible was essential, and in particular, the inclusion of states of origin was indispensable.[16] Because the focus of the Hague Convention is the co-operation between states involved in both sides of intercountry adoption, and ensuring that there are procedural safeguards which these authorities follow, it was felt that a multilateral convention was required which did not simply codify private international law rules, but created a wide-reaching mechanism for the co-operation of states.[17]

This wide participation was particularly important given the failure of the previous attempt by the Hague Conference to regulate the practice of adoption. In 1965, the member states of the Conference drafted the Hague Convention on Jurisdiction, Applicable Law and Recognition of Decrees Relating to Adoption. This Convention only needed three ratifications to enter into force, which it achieved 13 years later in 1978, but it was never ratified by more than those three states.[18] The Hague Convention on Intercountry Adoption of 1993 has been

---

14 There are 73 individual member states to the Conference, as well as the European Union, which is a member as a regional economic integration organisation. States that are members of the European Union are also members of the Conference in their own right.

15 Gonzalo Parra-Aranguren, *Explanatory Report on the Convention on Protection of Children and Co-operation in Respect of Intercountry Adoption* (1993) [8], <www.hcch.net/index_en.php?act=publications.details&pid=918> [7 February 2013].

16 Ibid., [5].

17 Ibid., [8].

18 Switzerland, Austria and the United Kingdom. This Convention is no longer in force, as it has been denounced by the states that had previously ratified it.

substantially more successful, having been ratified by 93 states, including 44 of the 47 European states. Unfortunately, among those states that have not ratified it are two of the most prolific sending states in Europe, Russia and Ukraine, in addition to Bosnia and Herzegovina. Russia has, however, signed the Convention, but as of May 2014 has not ratified it.

The avowed object of the Convention is to establish a system of co-operation amongst states to ensure that the best interests of the child and his or her fundamental rights under international law are respected. This is achieved by introducing procedural safeguards to allocate responsibility for decision-making amongst Contracting States, rather than regulating the basis upon which that decision is made.

The procedural requirements placed on intercountry adoption under the Hague Convention are in principle quite simple. The central feature of the Convention is the establishment of Central Authorities by each state,[19] which are responsible for ensuring compliance with the Hague Convention, and act as the focal points for intercountry adoption within that jurisdiction.[20] Depending on whether the country in question is a sending or receiving state, the Central Authority will play a different role. In a state of origin, the Central Authority must determine whether a child is suitable for adoption,[21] including ensuring that the necessary consents have been obtained,[22] the child's opinion has been sought if necessary,[23] and that domestic placements have been considered.[24] On the other hand, it is the responsibility of the Central Authority in the receiving state to ensure that the prospective parents are eligible and suitable to adopt,[25] that they have received appropriate counselling,[26] and that the child will be authorised to reside in that state.[27]

The Convention works on the concept of mutual recognition: an adoption recognised in one contracting state is also recognised in all others. Such recognition can only be refused if the adoption is manifestly contrary to its public policy, taking into account the best interests of the child.[28]

19 A state can choose to establish only one Central Authority, or several with one acting as the main focal point (an example of the latter being Spain, where there is a central authority for each internal jurisdiction).

20 Central Authorities can delegate some of their functions to accredited bodies, as will be discussed in Chapter Five, but remain responsible for the overall functioning of the system.

21 Article 4(a) Hague Convention.

22 Article 4(c).

23 Article 4(d).

24 Article 4(b).

25 Article 5(a).

26 Article 5(b).

27 Article 5(c).

28 Article 24.

2.3. REVISED EUROPEAN CONVENTION ON THE ADOPTION OF CHILDREN 2008

One of the principal reasons for which Europe was chosen as the area of study for this book was the strength of the regional human rights laws and enforcement mechanisms. The Council of Europe covers 47 member states and has drafted over 200 treaties and protocols, as well as thousands of recommendations and resolutions by the Parliamentary Assembly.

Of particular importance is the 2008 Revised European Convention on the Adoption of Children. This treaty, which entered into force in September 2011, has been signed by Armenia, Belgium, FYR Macedonia, Hungary, Iceland, Montenegro, Portugal, Serbia, and the United Kingdom, and further ratified by Denmark, Finland, the Netherlands, Norway, Romania, Spain and Ukraine.

This instrument is especially important as it is more expansive than the general principles contained in the UNCRC, and contains detailed substantive requirements covering such issues as consent to adoption, qualifications of adoptive parents, and access to information on the child's origins. It is a revision of the original European Convention on Adoption drafted in 1967,[29] with the impetus for reform lying in the need to update its provisions to take into account the changing nature of family law and adoption over the last 40 years. In particular, it was regarded as important to reconsider the standards in light of the Hague Convention, and the decisions of the European Court of Human Rights.[30]

While this Convention is not uniformly binding, and still leaves some elements of discretion, it can be a useful tool in guiding the evaluation of domestic legislation, and interpreting the provisions of the UNCRC. It is the only human rights instrument that provides a detailed analysis of the rights of parents and children in adoption, and although it is rather cautious in its approach to some issues and does not always provide the highest standard of protection for children's rights, it provides a practical starting point for analysis.

2.4. PROPOSING NORMATIVE GUIDELINES

These three conventions will combine to form the basis of the examination of the practice of intercountry adoption in this book. As stated above, the UNCRC will

---

29 This Convention has been ratified by Austria, the Czech Republic, Denmark, FYR Macedonia, Germany, Greece, Ireland, Italy, Latvia, Liechtenstein, Malta, Norway, Poland, Portugal, Romania, Sweden, Switzerland, and the United Kingdom (although it has since been denounced by Norway and Sweden, and partially denounced by the United Kingdom). It has also been signed by France, Iceland and Luxembourg.

30 Council of Europe, *Explanatory Report to the European Convention on the Adoption of Children (Revised)* (2008) [7] <http://conventions.coe.int/Treaty/en/Reports/Html/202.htm> [18 January 2013].

form the foundation of the analysis of children's rights, but the way in which its articles are interpreted and applied in the specific context of intercountry adoption will be informed by these other instruments. Importantly, although they each have different approaches, scope and import, they share the common guiding principle of the best interests of the child, which will also guide this book.[31]

This does not mean, however, that the provisions of these instruments will be endorsed unthinkingly or go unchallenged when they are out of date or insufficiently precise, or where they have failed to deal appropriately with an issue. Academic writing and research, the work of non-governmental agencies and interpretation by international organisations will all play a part in defining the scope of children's rights, and how they should be interpreted.

The fact that not all 47 states across Europe are party to each of the conventions being considered does not detract from their relevance in developing a framework for the protection of children in intercountry adoption. Whether they have been ratified by the state in question or not, these instruments remain an important indicator of the current international approach, and a reference point for further inquiry. In addition, they prompt consideration of the major problems that may arise in relation to intercountry adoption, and present mechanisms to address these. Together, these instruments provide a background against which intercountry adoption is played out in Europe, and a basis for analysis of the rights of children involved in this practice, which will be developed throughout this book.

---

31 Article 3 UNCRC; article 1 Hague Convention; preamble, article 4 ECA 2008.

CHAPTER 3

INTERCOUNTRY ADOPTION AND THE DOMESTIC CHILD WELFARE SYSTEM: THE PRINCIPLE OF SUBSIDIARITY

Before considering the substantive aspects of adoption – who must consent to an adoptive placement, how adoptive parents are chosen, what information a child can have access to – we must first look to the place of intercountry adoption in the scheme of child care alternatives, and when it can be considered to be in the best interests of a child to be adopted outside his or her country of origin.

Article 21 of the UNCRC regulates the place of intercountry adoption within the domestic sphere, requiring that it only be considered "if the child cannot be placed in a foster or an adoptive family, or cannot in any suitable manner be cared for in the child's country of origin". This requirement to consider domestic placements before an intercountry adoption is known as the principle of subsidiarity, and is also contained in article 4(b) of the Hague Convention, which permits an intercountry placement only where the sending state authorities "have determined, after possibilities for placement of the child within the State of origin have been given due consideration, that an intercountry adoption is in the child's best interests". Although this formulation is somewhat weaker than that contained in the Convention on the Rights of the Child, referring only to "due consideration" of domestic options, rather than the much clearer imperative in the UNCRC, it arguably has the same import. The Explanatory Report on the Hague Convention confirms that article 4(b) represents an express acceptance of, and obligation to comply with, the subsidiarity principle, and that states must ensure that no domestic or internal measures are available before considering intercountry adoption.[1]

The principle of subsidiarity is one of the cornerstones of the international regulation of intercountry adoption although, as will be seen below, it is not without its critics. The importance of this principle lies in the integration of intercountry adoption into the national child protection system: intercountry adoption cannot be seen as a stand-alone practice, but must be part of a holistic approach to child

---

1 Gonzalo Parra-Aranguren, *Explanatory Report on the Convention on Protection of Children and Co-operation in Respect of Intercountry Adoption* (1993) [120]–[122] <www.hcch.net/index_en.php?act=publications.details&pid=918> [7 February 2013].

welfare that recognises that intercountry adoption is simply the last in a line of alternative care options. As such, the principle requires that these domestic alternatives are carefully considered, and that intercountry adoption is not used prematurely in a way that would endanger the child's right to stay with his or her family where possible, and to maintain his or her cultural, linguistic, religious and ethnic identity where appropriate. Further, it is intended to ensure that intercountry adoption is not promoted to the detriment of the domestic welfare system, and is seen as an extension of this system, rather than an alternative to it.

In Europe, perhaps the most influential instrument in ensuring that the principle of subsidiarity is respected is the European Convention on Human Rights, through the application of the principle of proportionality under article 8. Article 8(1) provides that everyone has the right to respect for private and family life; however, this can be interfered with under article 8(2) if it is in accordance with the law and necessary in a democratic society. In order for a measure to be "necessary" in a democratic society, it must comply with the principle of proportionality, that is, the interference with the private or family life must be no more than is necessary, and the Court will examine whether there could have been less intrusive measures taken which would have minimised the disruption of family life for the children and parents involved, while still protecting the welfare of the child.[2]

Thus the issue of proportionality dominates the evaluation of child protection measures under the ECHR. In essence, it obliges the state to ensure that any action taken to protect the child is no more than is necessary in that particular situation. Where family assistance would enable the family to stay together, the state must not separate them; where temporary care would suffice, long-term solutions cannot be implemented; and, most importantly for these purposes, where suitable domestic placements are available, intercountry adoption should not be considered.[3] In this way, it adds content to the principle of subsidiarity by creating in effect a hierarchy of care options that requires that intercountry adoption be used as a practice of last resort, and only after all domestic options, and especially family reunification, have been considered and found unavailable or inappropriate.[4]

3.1. SUBSIDIARITY IN PRACTICE: WAITING PERIODS AND NECESSARY CONDITIONS

The relationship between domestic placement and intercountry adoption in Europe, and how this is regulated, varies remarkably between different

---

2 See, for example, *Keegan v Ireland* [1994] ECHR 18.

3 See, for example, *Pini and Others v Romania* [2005] ECHR 275.

4 See Andrew Bainham, "The Politics of Child Protection in Romania" (2009) 17 *International Journal of Children's Rights* 527, 537.

jurisdictions. For example, such is the emphasis on domestic care in Austria, Denmark, Iceland, Italy, the Netherlands, Norway and Spain, that foreign parents are not permitted to adopt children in these states, unless they are already legal residents.[5] Even greater restrictions are in place in Sweden, where adopters must be permanent residents or citizens, while in Switzerland, the prospective adopters must show habitual residence, and that they have fully integrated into Swiss life, culture and social norms.[6] On the other hand, England requires prospective adopters to have been living in part of the British Islands for a year,[7] Cyprus two years,[8] and Monaco ten years.[9]

It should be noted, however, that all these countries are traditionally receiving countries for intercountry adoption, rather than sending countries. In sending countries, the legislation is more nuanced, and a better perspective on different implementations of the subsidiarity principle can be obtained.

In Azerbaijan,[10] Estonia,[11] Hungary,[12] Latvia[13] and Slovenia,[14] the principle is adopted in its simplest form, with the legislation merely stipulating that a child may only be placed for intercountry adoption where it is not be possible for him or her to be cared for within the country. Similarly, Croatia only allows intercountry adoption if there is a "particular interest", interpreted restrictively to mean children for whom care cannot be found domestically,[15] while Bosnia and Herzegovina only permits foreigners to adopt if there is "overwhelming justification".[16] Montenegro enforces the principle of subsidiarity in a yet more emphatic manner, as the law prohibits intercountry adoption, but permits an exception if no adopter can be found domestically.[17]

While legislation in this manner is important for the normative weight it carries, without further measures to ensure that it is effectively regulated, it is

---

5 United States: Department of State, *Country Information*, <http://adoption.state.gov/country_information.php> [21 December 2012].

6 Ibid.

7 Section 49(2) Adoption and Children Act 2002.

8 Section 3(1) Adoption Law 1995.

9 Article 245 Civil Code.

10 Article 117.5 Family Code.

11 Section 165(6) Family Law Act 2009.

12 Yves Brulard and Letitia Dumont, *Comparative Study Relating to Procedures for Adoption Among the Member States of the European Union, Practical Difficulties Encountered in this Field by European Citizens within the Context of the European Pillar of Justice and Civil Matters and Means of Solving these Problems and of Protecting Children's Rights* (2007, European Union) 208.

13 Section 169 Civil Law.

14 Article 140 Marriage and Family Relations Act 1976.

15 Article 127 Family Act. In most instances, these will be older children, or those suffering from disabilities (Petar Sarcevic et al, *Family Law in Croatia* (2011, Kluwer Law) 149).

16 Interpreted to mean that no family can be found for the child domestically, and that intercountry adoption would be in the child's best interests (United States: Department of State, above n 5).

17 Article 125 Family Law.

little more than a statement of intent. In particular, it leaves no guidance as to the length of time that the authorities must spend searching for a domestic placement, raising the possibility that children could be kept in substandard care for inappropriate amounts of time waiting for a domestic placement, or alternatively, that insufficient attempts are made to find a family within the state of origin and the child is prematurely sent abroad.

To combat such difficulties, many states have placed statutory time limits on the search for a domestic placement, ranging from three months in Armenia[18] and Poland,[19] to six months in Albania,[20] Bulgaria,[21] the Czech Republic,[22] Lithuania,[23] Moldova[24] and Slovakia,[25] eight months in Georgia[26] and Russia,[27] and one year in Serbia[28] and Ukraine.[29] These limits are helpful, not only because they give the state time to evaluate family reunification options, and search for domestic solutions that maintain the child's ethnic, linguistic and cultural identity, but also because it can help stop abusive practices in intercountry adoptions. Where a child has to be placed on a domestic adoption list first, there are no incentives for an intermediary to improperly induce consent from birth parents, as will be discussed in Chapter Five.

Given the vast differences between the lengths of time mandated by different states, however, how do we evaluate the appropriate time period

18 Article 112(4) Family Code.

19 Hague Conference, *Country Profile: Poland* (2010) <www.hcch.net/index_en.php?act=publications.details&pid=5093&dtid=42> [14 January 2012]. This includes two months searching within the local area, and one month searching within the region. If at this stage a domestic placement is still not found, the child's data is sent to a central database for placement in intercountry adoption.

20 Article 257 Family Code. However, exceptions can be made to the six month waiting period in the best interests of the child, if the delay may be harmful to the child's health (article 23(2), Law No 9695 of 19 March 2007).

21 Article 89(2) Family Law.

22 Hague Conference, *Country Profile: Czech Republic* (2010) <www.hcch.net/index_en.php?act=publications.details&pid=5116&dtid=42> [14 January 2012]. This includes three months in which the regional authorities search for a placement within the region, followed by three months in which the Ministry of Labour and Social Affairs tries to find a placement anywhere within the entire country.

23 Article 3.224 Civil Code.

24 Article 116(3) Family Code.

25 Brulard and Dumont, above n 12, 436.

26 Hague Conference, *Country Profile: Georgia* (2010) <www.hcch.net/index_en.php?act=publications.details&pid=5118&dtid=42> [14 January 2012].

27 Article 124(4) Family Law 1995. Although this article only requires six months on the federal database before an intercountry adoption is considered, the child must have spent one month on the local database, and one month on the regional database before they are placed on the federal register, making the waiting period eight months (see United States: Department of State, above n 5).

28 Article 106 Family Act.

29 Ukraine, *State Party Report to the UN Committee on the Rights of the Child* (3 March 2010) CRC/C/UKR/3-4, [89].

within which family reunification and domestic placement should be pursued? The answer is that this will depend on the particular situation in the jurisdiction in question, and the circumstances of the individual child. On the one hand, three months is an extremely short period of time to attempt to find a suitable family for a child domestically, or to determine whether family reunification is possible. On the other, in a country where there are almost no domestic placements available, a waiting period of 12 months may be excessively damaging, given the evidence that age is an important factor in predicting the likelihood of a successful adoptive placement.[30] Research on child development shows that the longer children are left in inadequate care, the greater the chance that their long-term well-being will be compromised.[31] A study by Van den Dries et al found that children who were adopted before 12 months of age were as securely attached to their adoptive parents as non-adopted children, but that children adopted after this time showed more evidence of attachment disorders.[32] Children start to develop secure attachments between the ages of six months and two years, and during this time need sensitive care-giving and consistent responsiveness. As such, a delay in finding an adoptive placement can be particularly detrimental for those children who are left in institutional care during this period. This was seen in a study undertaken in relation to children adopted from Romanian orphanages. Chisholm found that children who had spent at least eight months in a Romanian orphanage had significantly greater insecure attachment patterns, as compared to Canadian-born non-institutionalised children, and children who had been adopted from Romania before the age of four months.[33]

In 2001, a more specific study was undertaken in the United Kingdom in relation to children adopted from Romanian orphanages, which identified specific domains of dysfunction in these children, as compared to children adopted from within the United Kingdom. It found that there was no difference in the rate of emotional problems, peer difficulties and conduct problems between the two groups, and no association within the sample of Romanian adoptees with the age at the time of entry into the United Kingdom. In contrast, attachment problems, inattention/overactivity, quasi-autistic problems and cognitive impairment were much more common in the Romanian adoptees, and there was significant association with the age at entry,

---

30 Elizabeth Bartholet, "International Adoption: Thoughts on the Human Rights Issues" (2007) 13 *Buffalo Human Rights Law Review* 151, 180.

31 Rebecca Brown and Harriet Ward, *Decision-making within a child's timeframe* (2013, Childhood Wellbeing Research Centre) 88.

32 L Van den Dries, F Juffer, MH Van IJzendoorn, MJ Bakermans-Kranenburg, "Fostering security? A meta-analysis of attachment in adopted children" (2009) 31 *Children and Youth Services Review* 410.

33 Kim Chisholm, "A Three Year Follow-up of Attachment and Indiscriminate Friendliness in children Adopted from Romanian Orphanages" (1998) 69(4) *Child Development* 1092.

and the rate of problems. The study found that the proportion of adoptees with normal functioning among those who left Romania before the age of six months was 70 per cent, and that the chances of normal social functioning were substantially less the older the child was at the time of leaving the institution.[34]

The delay in finding a permanent placement for a child is one of the biggest controversies surrounding the subsidiarity principle, especially where the domestic child welfare system is underdeveloped. Sara Dillon has argued that although family reunification and community-based solutions are desirable, they are simply not practical in some countries where there are neither the resources nor the willing families to provide them. Without adequate monitoring of whether these solutions are actually capable of providing solutions for children, she suggests that they are dangerous distractions that promise much, but achieve little.[35] Where the child is being cared for – or rather, not cared for – in an unsuitable institution in the meantime, this can have dramatic effect on the subsequent growth and development of the child, as the studies above have shown. Such deprivation will be a violation of the child's rights under article 6(2) of the UNCRC, which guarantees to the maximum extent possible the survival and development of the child, and article 27, which recognises the right to a standard of living adequate for the child's physical, mental, spiritual, moral and social development.

At a domestic level, this problem also emerges when balancing family reunification and domestic adoption, and the need to combat "drift" in foster care. One of the strategies conceived to combat this has been parallel planning, which simultaneously makes attempts towards family reunification whilst establishing a care plan based on alternative care if this should fail. This mechanism could be equally used to ensure that while a domestic placement is being searched for, a foreign family is also being screened and prepared in case this does not eventuate.

The result is that it is not so much the time limit that is important, but what the authorities are working to achieve during this time. For example, in Albania, during the six-month waiting period, all opportunities for national adoption must have been exhausted,[36] and in Bulgaria, at least three candidate adopters must have been nominated for the child, with none of them filing an application.[37] Other countries, however, simply rely on the existence of the child's name on a register, and fail to place additional duties on authorities to diligently search for a domestic placement, or for family reunification to be

34 Michael L Rutter et al, "Specificity and Heterogeneity in Children's Responses to Profound Institutional Privation" (2001) 179 *British Journal of Psychiatry* 97.

35 Sara Dillon, "The Missing Link: A Social Orphan Protocol to the United Nations Convention on the Rights of the Child" (2007) 1 *Human Rights and Globalization Law Review* 39, 58–59.

36 Article 257 Family Code.

37 Article 113 Family Code.

effectively explored.[38] Without such requirements, either in law or in practice, there is little point in enforcing an arbitrary delay in placement.

In addition to searching for adequate domestic care, this time should also be used to facilitate family reunification where possible. States have an obligation to enable a child to grow up with his or her family where possible, and as such, must take appropriate measure to reintegrate the child into their family environment. Unfortunately, this is not always a priority of states. A particularly problematic example of this in Europe is Bulgaria, where family reunification services are limited to trying to locate the child's parents, and do not extend to mechanisms that would facilitate the child's reintegration in the family, such as financial and social support.[39] In particular, there is little work done to help parents to maintain contact with children in care, and visits are limited by procedural requirements and narrow time constraints.[40] In visiting institutional care facilities in Bulgaria, Andy Bilson noted that rather than being provided with support to reconnect with the child, visiting parents were made to sit in a corridor with their child, with a member of staff watching over them.[41] As he points out, parents and families require positive encouragement and support to visit their children and re-establish relationships, not hindrances.[42]

The issue of family reunification was taken up by the European Court of Human Rights in the case of *Olsson v Sweden (No 2)*,[43] where the Court made clear that the right to contact must be real and effective, not just on paper. In this case, the authorities had removed the applicants' children and placed them in separate homes significant distances away from their parents, meaning that the parents were not able to visit them easily. The Court found that this violated the right to respect family life under article 8 as it did not allow for the ultimate aim of family reunification to be achieved.[44]

---

38 The Hague Special Commission noted the suggestion that in some countries, there was an absence of a real search for domestic solutions (Hague Conference, *Report and Conclusions of the Special Commission on the Practical Operation of the Hague Convention of 29 May 1993 on Protection of Children and Co-operation in Respect of Intercountry Adoption 28 November–1 December 2000* (2001) [28] <www.hcch.net/upload/scrpt33e2000.pdf> [7 February 2013]).

39 Andy Bilson, *The Development of Gate-Keeping Functions in Central and Eastern Europe and the CIS: Lessons from Bulgaria, Kazakhstan and Ukraine* (2010) 10 <www.unicef.org/ceecis/overview_Report_20_August_preface.doc> [7 June 2012].

40 For example, parents often have to obtain a medical certificate before visiting (ibid.).

41 Ibid.

42 Ibid.

43 *Olsson v Sweden (No 2)* [1992] ECHR 75.

44 In the English context, see section 22C(8) of the Children Act 1989, under which the local authority must ensure that a looked after child's placement is such that it allows, *inter alia*, the child to live near his or her home, it does not disrupt his or her education or training, and if the child has a sibling also in care, they are able to live together.

In this way, attempts at family reunification must be based on viable community solutions, and not be purely administrative. Further to this, the duty to search for an appropriate in-country placement should also extend to an obligation on the state to develop domestic alternatives to institutional care, including encouraging kinship care, fostering and domestic adoption. Many countries do not have a tradition of these practices, and as such, create a dangerous dichotomy between institutional care and intercountry adoption.[45] Several countries have tried to address this issue, particularly in former communist states where institutional care was the norm.[46] In 2005 in Ukraine, for example, the government created a new State Department of Adoption and Protection of the Rights of a Child, and since this time the number of domestic adoptions has increased, while intercountry adoptions have fallen.[47] It also created a system of funded foster care, which has led to an increase in the number of children in foster homes by almost 500 per cent.[48] Correspondingly, the number of children in institutions fell by 18.4 per cent between 2004 and 2008, with the number of children below the age of three falling by 30.1 per cent.[49] Similarly, the Czech Republic has established the "Right to Childhood" initiative, which aims to create a network of professional foster parents,[50] and Slovakia has developed a system of professional family care that has increased the number of families seven fold.[51]

Romania's child protection system has also seen a shift from residential care to family-based solutions. From 1998 to 2011, the number of children in residential care fell by over 40%, while the number of children in family care more than doubled, as can be seen by the table below.

---

45 For example, foster care was only introduced into Romania in 1998 (Michael Hancock (Rapporteur, Council of Europe Parliamentary Assembly), *The Rights of Children in Institutions: follow-up to Recommendation 1601 (2003) of the Parliamentary Assembly* (8 February 2005) <http://assembly.coe.int/ASP/Doc/XrefViewHTML.asp?FileID=10786&Language=en> [7 February 2013]).

46 UNICEF, *Guidance Note on Intercountry Adoption in the CEE/CIS/Baltics Region* (2003, UNICEF) <www.unicef.org/ceecis/Guidance_note_Intercountry_adoption.pdf> [1 September 2011].

47 Bilson, above n 39, 15.

48 Ibid., 16.

49 Ibid., 13.

50 University of Nottingham, *Child Abandonment in the Czech Republic* (2012) <www.nottingham.ac.uk/iwho/research/projects/childabandonment/czechrepublic.aspx> [22 October 2012].

51 University of Nottingham, *Preventing Child Abandonment in Slovakia* (2012) <www.nottingham.ac.uk/iwho/documents/childabandonment/slovakia/preventing-child-abandonment.pdf> [25 October 2012].

Number of children in the child protection system in Romania: 1998–2011[52]

Year	Number of children in residential care	Number of children in family care (extended family, foster care)
1998	38,597	17,044
1999	33,356	23,731
2000	57,181	30,572
2001	49,965	37,553
2002	43,234	43,092
2003	37,660	46,568
2004	32,679	50,239
2005	28,786	47,723
2006	26,105	47,871
2007	25,114	48,172
2008	34,437	47,159
2009	23,696	45,550
2010	23,183	43,817
2011	22,742	43,518

However, although these countries have shown some success, there is still a long way to go to reduce the placement of children in inappropriate institutional care in Europe. In this regard, the 2000 Hague Convention Special Commission suggested that the principle of subsidiarity in the Hague Convention and the UNCRC not only imposes a positive obligation on the sending state to develop domestic family support and child care services, but that there is also a corresponding duty on receiving states to support this development.[53]

One of the ways this has been traditionally achieved is through the payment of compulsory "contributions" by adoptive parents to the domestic child welfare system, either directly to the institution from which the child is taken, or to the state itself.[54] However, the problem with promoting development in this manner can be seen in the situation that developed in Romania following the 1997 adoption reforms. At this time, the government introduced a "points system" to

52 Romanian Office for Adoption, <www.adoptiiromania.ro/statistics.html>, as presented by Ingi Iusmen, "The EU and International Adoption from Romania" (2013) 27(1) *International Journal of Law, Policy and the Family* 1, 14.

53 Hague Conference, *Report and Conclusions of the Special Commission on the Practical Operation of the Hague Convention of 29 May 1993 on Protection of Children and Co-operation in Respect of Intercountry Adoption 28 November–1 December 2000* (2001) [24] <www.hcch.net/upload/scrpt33e2000.pdf> [7 February 2013].

54 For example, in Albania, there is a compulsory contribution to the Albanian Adoption Committee of $1,000 (Decision of the Council of Ministers No 544 (21 March 1994); Hague Conference, *Country Profile: Albania* (2010) <www.hcch.net/index_en.php?act=publications.details&pid=5081&dtid=42> [14 January 2012]).

allocate the number of children that each agency could place in intercountry adoption. The more the agency contributed to the development of domestic welfare system, the more children it could place in intercountry adoption. As Dickens points out, this system built a cycle that linked the viability of domestic services to placing children in foreign families, thus encouraging intercountry adoption and bringing it into the mainstream of child welfare options.[55] It also meant that the state itself had a vested interest in continuing intercountry adoption, compromising the integrity of the system. Furthermore, although this scheme did bring some much needed money into the country, *Romania Libera* reported that in 1999 only US$4 million of an estimated US$30 million that was obtained from intercountry adoption was actually spent on child protection services.[56]

It is thus important that any assistance provided to states to develop the domestic child welfare system does not develop into the main source of funding, or create a reliance on continued intercountry placements. The practice of "voluntary" contributions, and the possibility they raise for the improper inducement of consent will be further discussed in Chapter Five.

3.2. CONTINUITY OF CULTURE, LANGUAGE, RELIGION AND ETHNICITY

In addition to ensuring the best possible chances for family reunification, the principle of subsidiarity also allows the child to maintain his or her cultural, linguistic, religious and ethnic identity wherever possible. This corresponds with article 20(3) of the UNCRC, which requires that "[w]hen considering solutions, due regard shall be paid to the desirability of continuity in a child's upbringing" in line with these four considerations. The Hague Convention also recognises the importance of these factors, requiring that where a Central Authority is satisfied that a child is adoptable, it shall give due consideration to the child's upbringing and to his or her ethnic, religious and cultural background in determining whether a placement with the particular prospective adoptive parents is in the best interests of the child.[57]

As these instruments suggest, ethnicity, culture, language and religion should not be overriding issues that would prevent the finding of a family placement where this is appropriate. However, it should be considered as an aim of the system, to guide the search for the most appropriate family.

There are several states that, in addition to the general principle of subsidiarity, have incorporated the requirement for continuity with the child's ethnicity,

---

55 Jonathan Dickens, "The Paradox of Inter-country Adoption: Analysing Romania's experience as a sending country" (2002) 11 *International Journal of Social Welfare* 76, 78.

56 Ibid., 78–9.

57 Article 16(1) Hague Convention.

culture, language or religion into their legislation. For example, in Estonia, there is a requirement that if possible, the need for maintaining the national, religious, cultural and linguistic origins of the child shall be taken into account in making an adoption decision,[58] and in Georgia, the authorities must take into consideration religious and ethnic conformity.[59] Further in Armenia,[60] Lithuania[61] and Russia,[62] any decision on alternative care must take into account the ethnic origin of the child, affiliation to a certain religion and culture, his or her native tongue, and the possibility of ensuring continuity in the child's upbringing and education.

However, such considerations have been heavily criticised, not only in terms of intercountry adoption, but also in domestic practice. Critics have argued that the focus on maintaining the child's cultural and ethnic identity through the preference for domestic placement runs counter to the best interests of children, as it unnecessarily delays placement for little or no benefit. In particular, Bartholet suggests that for children needing intercountry adoption, there is no real cultural or ethnic identity to give up. She argues that these children will otherwise live in inadequate institutions or on the streets, and thus not in a situation where they can appreciate their ethnic and cultural heritage,[63] and that these children will in fact face discrimination based on their ethnic status if they remain.[64]

None of these arguments is persuasive in displacing the principle of subsidiarity. It is incorrect to assert that because a child is living on the streets or in an institution, he or she does not have an ethnic, religious, linguistic or cultural identity that should be maintained if possible. No child, no matter what the living situation, is completely divorced from his or her surroundings. Each child has his or her own attachments, experiences, and community that should not be distained or dismissed. Moreover, the threat of discrimination in the country of origin should not be seen as a driving factor towards intercountry adoption, or even a justification for it.

It is interesting to note that on a domestic level, England has recently introduced legislation that removes the requirement on adoption agencies to give due consideration to the child's religious persuasion, racial origin and cultural and linguistic background.[65] The government contends that these aspects of the

---

58 Section 147(1) Family Law Act 2009.

59 Hague Conference, *Country Profile: Georgia* (2010) <www.hcch.net/index_en.php?act=publications.details&pid=5118&dtid=42> [14 January 2012].

60 Article 111 Family Code.

61 Article 3.224(5) Civil Code.

62 Article 123(1).

63 Elizabeth Bartholet, "What's wrong with adoption law?" (1996) 4 *International Journal of Children's Rights* 263, 269; "International Adoption: Propriety, Prospects and Pragmatics" (1995) 13 *Journal of the American Academy of Matrimonial Law* 181, 202.

64 Elizabeth Bartholet, "International Adoption: Propriety, Prospects and Pragmatics" (1995) 13 *Journal of the American Academy of Matrimonial Law* 181, 202.

65 Children and Families Act 2014.

child's background will continue to be considered under the requirement that the agency give due consideration to "the child's needs, background and any other relevant characteristics", but that the shift of emphasis away from an explicit consideration of ethnicity will help to ensure that the disproportionate number of children in care of African descent and from other ethnic minorities are not faced with long waiting periods for an adoption by a family of the same ethnic origin.[66] This was a concern expressed by the UN Committee on the Rights of the Child in its 2008 Concluding Observations on the United Kingdom.[67] However, it is important to note that the Committee explicitly recommended that when facilitating the adoption of these children, cultural background should be taken into due account.[68]

The overrepresentation of children from ethnic minorities in the care system is a problem that also occurs in other areas of Europe. For example, in Romania and Bulgaria, Roma children make up 60–80 per cent of children in institutions,[69] while in Slovakia, in a study of ten maternal units, eight felt that there was an overrepresentation of ethnic minorities among the children who had been abandoned, with six reporting that Roma infants were frequently abandoned.[70] This problem is exacerbated by the fact that there is a shortage of prospective adoptive parents from ethnic minorities on a domestic level in many jurisdictions.[71]

However, it is not just children from minorities whose ethnicity, culture, language and religion should be considered. In the context of intercountry adoption, any child being placed in a foreign placement will potentially lose one, if not all, of these connections. In a study on behalf of the British Association for Adoption and Fostering, women who had been adopted by British parents from Hong Kong in the 1960s were asked their feelings on their Chinese looks and heritage. 75 per cent of participants reported times when they wished they looked less Chinese when growing up, although only 19 per cent reported still experiencing this feeling.[72] 54 per cent also recalled feeling uncomfortable when people commented on their looking different from their adoptive family, while 43

66 United Kingdom: Department for Education, *Consideration of the Children and Families Bill Provisions in Light of the European Convention on Human Rights and the United Nations Convention on the Rights of the Child* (2013) [13]–[17], <http://media.education.gov.uk/assets/files/pdf/e/140213%20echr%20and%20uncr%20note%20for%20publication%20final%20lao.pdf> [2 May 2013].

67 (20 October 2008) CRC/C/GBR/CO/4, [46].

68 Ibid., [47].

69 Velina Todorova, "Family Law in Bulgaria: Legal Norms and Social Norms" (2000) 13 *International Journal of Law, Policy and the Family* 148, 166.

70 University of Nottingham, *Data Collected from Maternity Units in Slovakia* (2012) <www.nottingham.ac.uk/iwho/documents/childabandonment/slovakia/data-collected-from-maternity-units.pdf> [14 January 2013].

71 See, for example, Gwen Rule, *Recruiting Black and Minority Ethnic Adopters/Foster Carers* (2006, British Association for Adoption and Fostering).

72 Alan Rushton et al, "Assessing Community Connectedness and Self-Regard in a Mid-Life Follow-up of British Chinese Adoptions" (2012) 36 *Adoption and Fostering* 62.

per cent reported feeling uncomfortable at times in certain situations in the UK because of reactions to their Chinese appearance.[73] Further studies have shown that appearance discomfort and discrimination is linked to higher levels of problem behaviours and adjustment difficulties.[74] In addition, research indicates that trans-racially adopted children score lower on racial identity measures than children who are adopted by parents of the same race. This is particularly problematic as confusion of ethnic identity and perceived discrimination has been associated with behavioural problems and psychological distress.[75]

The obvious solution to these problems is to encourage more families to adopt domestically, both from majority and minority groups;[76] however it could take a considerable length of time for such alternatives to coalesce. In the meantime, it may be in the best interests of the children involved to grow up in a family environment, even if it is not within their own ethnic, racial, linguistic or cultural group.

This is the approach that has been taken by the European Commission on Human Rights the only time it has been faced with the issue of the maintenance of cultural identity. The case of *ED v Ireland*[77] was brought by the father of a child placed for adoption. He and the child's mother were both members of the travelling community, and although he admitted that he could not currently provide care for the child, he argued that adoption would mean the loss of the child's access to his traveller heritage and his "true" identity. Instead, he argued for the child to be placed in long-term fostering, while being educated concerning his heritage, and upon adulthood he could choose which life he wished to lead.

The Commission held that it was within the state's margin of appreciation to decide that the child's need for a permanent family was greater than the need to maintain his cultural heritage, and that it would not interfere with the balancing process undertaken by the domestic authorities. While this decision is hardly surprising given the nature of the Commission as an international supervisory

73 Ibid., 68.

74 W Feigelman, "Adjustments of transracially and inracially adopted young adults" (2000) 17 *Child and Adolescent Social Work Journal* 165; Femmie Juffer, "Children's Awareness of Adoption and Their Problem Behaviour in Families with 7-Year-Old Internationally Adopted Children" (2006) 9 *Adoption Quarterly* 1.

75 Marianne Cerderblad et al, "Mental Health in International Adoptees as Teenagers and Young Adults: An epidemiological study" (1999) 40 *Journal of Child Psychology and Psychiatry and Allied Disciplines* 1239. See also Susan Smith et al, *Finding Families for African American Children: The role of race and law in adoption from foster care* (2008, Evan B Donaldson Institute) 6.

76 There is an additional concern that even where there are families from such minorities willing to adopt, they are unable to do so because the requirements for adoptive parents are skewed in favour of white, middle-class families. This subject cannot be explored in this book, but should be kept in mind when considering the choice between prospective adoptive parents domestically and from abroad, and comparing their suitability, to ensure that the richer or more traditional families are not automatically given preference.

77 (Appl. No. 25054/94) Decision of 18 October 1995.

body, it reaffirms the need for balance and the weighing of options in the best interests of the child, and that neither ethnicity nor permanency should be given definitive weight.

Culture, religion, language and ethnicity should not be completely ignored in choosing an adoptive family, but nor should they be the only consideration, blocking a placement where it is the most appropriate option. As with any decision concerning adoption, the individual child's best interests should be the guiding principle, and this must balance the need for a permanent placement in a stable and loving family and the interest in being placed in an environment that will enable him or her to develop in a positive manner. In enabling this, the choice of appropriate adoptive parents is imperative: even where parents do not come from the same background, they must be willing and able to encourage the child to appreciate his or her heritage. As with special needs children, parents should be selected who have the ability to address the particular needs of the child, and steps must be taken to ensure that the child continues to develop a positive racial, cultural and ethnic identity. While affirming a child's heritage through books and appropriate toys is important, steps must be taken not only for the child to *know* about his or her background, but *appreciate* it, and not see it is something inferior.

The maintenance of culture, language, religion and ethnicity must thus be considered in the same way as family reunification: as a goal to be achieved where possible, but one that cannot be pursued indefinitely to the detriment of the child's chances of achieving a permanent family. It is a justification for the principle of subsidiarity to be respected, but not for it to be dogmatically pursued.

3.3. THE PLACE OF DOMESTIC ALTERNATIVES

As discussed above, the principle of subsidiarity in international law requires that intercountry adoption only be contemplated when there is no suitable care for the child in the country of origin. But the question remains: what is "suitable" care? The principal debate in this area has surrounded the use of institutional care for children in many eastern European countries, and whether this can ever be appropriate, but the question also extends to other forms of domestic care such as foster care and kafalah.

According to UNICEF, there are three principles that should guide decisions regarding alternative care for children:

"1. Family based solutions are generally preferable to institutional placements;
2. Permanent solutions are generally preferable to temporary ones; and
3. Domestic solutions are generally preferable to those involving another country."[78]

---

[78] Dan O'Donnell, *Child Protection: A Handbook for Parliamentarians* (2004, UNICEF) 115 <www.unicef.org/ceecis/Guide_Enfants_OK.pdf> [7 February 2011].

However, often the best that can practically be achieved in this respect is one or two out of three, and the difficulty lies in determining which to follow. The following sections will discuss domestic alternatives to intercountry adoption, and the place they should hold on the spectrum of care options available to authorities.

3.3.1. INSTITUTIONAL CARE: CAN IT EVER BE APPROPRIATE?

One of the main arguments in favour of intercountry adoption is the assertion that children would otherwise be left in institutional care in their countries of origin. However, while all agree that institutionalisation is not suitable for children in the long term, it is not as clear cut whether intercountry adoption should automatically be preferred to this type of care, or whether it can at times be appropriate for certain children, for a short period of time.

When listing possible alternative care placements, article 20 of the Convention on the Rights of the Child states that such care could include "foster placement, kafalah of Islamic law, adoption or if necessary placement in suitable institutions for the care of children." Given the clear preference in the UNCRC for a family environment as expressed in the preamble,[79] however, and the predication of the use of institutional care with "if necessary", it appears that it is not a mechanism which is favoured under this instrument, nor is it a favoured practice generally.

The Hague Convention is even less enthusiastic about the use of institutional placements for children, with its preamble stating that the Convention recognises "that intercountry adoption may offer the advantage of a permanent family to a child for whom a *suitable family* cannot be found in his or her State of origin".[80] The use of "suitable family" rather than "suitable care" appears to rule out the use of institutions, and highlights the importance that the Convention places on family care for a child. The Explanatory Report to the Convention is even more explicit, stating "the placement of a child in a family, including in intercountry adoption, is the best option among all forms of alternative care, in particular to be preferred over institutionalization."[81]

The term "institution" has extremely negative connotations, particularly in light of the horror of Romanian institutions revealed after the fall of Ceauşescu.

79 The UNCRC preamble provides: "Recognizing that the child, for the full and harmonious development of his or her personality, should grow up in a family environment, in an atmosphere of happiness, love and understanding".

80 My emphasis.

81 Gonzalo Parra-Aranguren, *Explanatory Report on the Convention on Protection of Children and Co-operation in Respect of Intercountry Adoption* (1993) [46] <www.hcch.net/index_en.php?act=publications.details&pid=918> [7 February 2013].

However, these were examples of worst practice, and should not be used as an illustration of all institutional care. Group care is not unusual in Europe, and the highest rate of institutionalised children under three is in fact in the French community in Belgium.[82] In different countries this form of care performs different functions, and to label all non-family environments as "institutional settings" is to narrow the scope of care too greatly. For example, institutional care in the form of residential units is used extensively in France in order to determine the child's individual needs. This can allow childcare professionals to assess the children, and determine the most suitable care and carers for them, without putting them through numerous foster families and causing additional disruption. Warman and Roberts observe that in France, residential placement may be chosen in preference to a family placement to ensure that the child is ultimately placed with the correct family. They suggest that while an appropriate family is being found, the child would be placed in an institution to prevent them bonding with a temporary family, as children need stable attachments that are not repeatedly broken.[83]

In addition, residential homes are used in the French and Danish systems for therapeutic interventions, where a child has emotional and behavioural difficulties. These allow professionals to work with the child, while simultaneously searching for appropriate family care.[84] In England, residential units can be used for parenting appraisal: families are placed in these units for assessment to provide reports for social services departments, as well as for legal proceedings. They can also act as an educational tool, and provide instruction on parental and caring responsibilities as a preventative measure before taking children into state care.

As such, institutional care is still a prevalent practice in some western European states for children with specific needs, and for specific purposes. However, in many eastern European countries it has traditionally been used as a general alternative to foster placement for children separated from their families. For example, out of a total of 33,076 children in care in the Czech Republic in 2010, 22,414 were in residential care, while only 9,662 were placed under guardianship or in a foster family. Several other states, including Armenia, Azerbaijan, Bulgaria, Bosnia and Herzegovina, Croatia, Georgia, Lithuania, Montenegro and Ukraine also had lower numbers of children in state care living with families than in institutions.[85] In addition, in Russia, one of the largest countries of origin for children placed in intercountry adoption, 305,701 children were listed in institutions in 2010 with a further 430,604 placed under guardianship or with foster families.[86]

---

82 United Nations Committee on the Rights of the Child, *Concluding Observations: Belgium* (18 June 2010) CRC/C/BEL/CO/3–4, [46].

83 Andrea Warman and Ceridwen Roberts, *Adoption and Looked after Children – an International Comparison* (Working Paper 2003/1, Department of Social Policy and Social Work, University of Oxford) 48.

84 Ibid., 44.

85 UNICEF, *TransMONEE Database* (2012) <www.transmonee.org/> [22 May 2013].

86 Ibid.

The physical and psychological effects of poor quality institutional care on children, and in particular on young children, are well documented. This is acknowledged in General Comment 7 from the Committee on the Rights of the Child on "Implementing Child Rights in Early Childhood", which recognises that "low-quality institutional care is unlikely to promote healthy physical and psychological development and can have serious negative consequences for long-term social adjustment, especially for children under three but also for children under five years old."[87]

Indeed Kevin Browne, in his study on children in institutions in Europe, suggested that even in high-quality institutions, the length of stay should be no longer than three months for children younger than three years of age, as this period of time already constitutes a significant proportion of the child's life. He cites research that suggests that more than six months in such facilities results in developmental delay.[88] This was similarly emphasised by a Canadian study of institutionalised children in Romania that found that children who had spent eight months or more in an orphanage were delayed in social, motor and language development.[89]

For this reason, in recent years there have been widespread initiatives to prevent the use of inappropriate institutional care for young children. In Romania, no child under the age of two may now be placed in an institution,[90] while in Slovakia, from January 2012 every child under six has been required to be placed in a family.[91] Similarly, the Czech Republic has launched the "Right to Childhood" initiative, which aims to ensure that by 2014–2016, no child under three will be placed in an institution.[92] Romania has also closed down the worst institutions that caused such contention in the early 1990s, and established facilities that provide family-type care, with "maternal assistants" within a family setting. These institutions replicate as closely as possible a family environment, with preferably no more than 12 people in a setting, a domestic environment, and opportunities for children to be involved in the normal routines of life, including cleaning, cooking, playing and education.[93]

---

87 (20 September 2006) CRC/C/GC/7/Rev.1, [36].

88 Kevin Browne and Catherine Hamilton-Giachritsis, *Mapping the Number and Characteristics of Children under Three in Institutions Across Europe at Risk of Harm* (2005, University of Birmingham) 26.

89 Elinor Ames, *The Development of Romanian Orphanage Children Adopted to Canada* (1997, Simon Fraser University).

90 Except where he or she has a severe disability that requires this (article 60(1) Law No 272/2004).

91 University of Nottingham, *Child Abandonment in Slovakia* (2012) <www.nottingham.ac.uk/iwho/research/projects/childabandonment/slovakia.aspx> [25 October 2012].

92 <www.mpsv.cz/files/clanky/13456/strategy.pdf> [2 May 2014].

93 Romania: Ministry of Labour, Social Solidarity and Family, *"Children First" Human Rights in Child Protection: A Manual of Good Practice* (2005, European Union). This practice is also prevalent in France, especially for children for whom it is felt a placement with family would not be suitable, for example teenagers or children with special needs (Warman and Roberts, above n 83, 22).

Despite these initiatives, there still remain an alarmingly high number of children in poor quality institutional care throughout these countries and others in the area, and a lack of focus on domestic family-based solutions. This means that in many countries, a dichotomy is being unnecessarily created between intercountry adoption and poor quality institutional care, with many calling for an increase in intercountry adoption to "save" children from these institutions.

However, it is necessary to consider the reasons that these children have been placed in care. A large number of children in Europe have been placed in alternative care because of disabilities, either mental or physical. A recent study undertaken by UNICEF has highlighted the number of children with disabilities in residential (institutional) care.

Number of children with disabilities in residential care: 2011[94]

	Number of children in residential care (to the nearest 100)	Number of children with disabilities in residential care
Armenia	5,000	2,484
Azerbaijan	9,200	2,459
Bosnia and Herzegovina	2,300	1,570
Bulgaria	6,900	2,402
Czech Republic	22,900	11,218
FYR Macedonia	700	378
Hungary	6,900	1,741
Latvia	2,000	466
Lithuania	7,100	3,698
Romania	23,300	8,747
Russian Federation	293,300	138,114
Serbia	3,100	1,485
Slovakia	6,400	917
Slovenia	1,200	1,180

In addition, in certain jurisdictions, alternative care has been traditionally used by parents as a temporary care option, where children can be placed for a short period of time. This practice was common in Romania and Bulgaria, and emphasises the need for effective support mechanisms for families, rather than the quick placement of children for intercountry adoption. As such, very few children in so-called "orphanages" across Europe are orphans in the true sense of the word, and have predominantly been placed in care because of an inability to care for the child, for social or economic reasons.

94 UNICEF, *TransMONEE Database* (2013) <www.transmonee.org/> [14 May 2014].

There have been many well-documented cases where a child who has been adopted from a foreign "orphanage" has been subsequently found not to have been abandoned or orphaned as originally thought, but simply placed in state care while the family was seeking to rectify temporary financial or social problems.[95] For this reason, assistance to the family is vitally important to ensure that children are being cared for by the state only where their birth family is inadequate, not because the family is unable to care for them for reasons of material poverty. This is highlighted by the Guidelines for the Alternative Care of Children, a resolution of the United Nations Human Rights Council formally welcomed by the UN General Assembly. Article 14 of these Guidelines reads:

> "Financial or material poverty, or conditions directly and uniquely imputable to such poverty, should never be the only justification for the removal of a child from parental care, for receiving a child into alternative care, or for preventing his/her reintegration, but should be seen as a signal for the need to provide appropriate support to the family."[96]

The Convention on the Rights of the Child makes clear the necessity of family assistance, both in the preamble,[97] and in the substantive provisions. Article 18(2) of the Convention obliges states to "render appropriate assistance to parents and legal guardians in the performance of their child-rearing responsibilities", while article 19(2) requires the provision of "[e]ffective procedures for the establishment of social programmes to provide necessary support for the child and for those who have the care of the child". This is also highlighted in the preamble of the Hague Convention, which requires "that each State should take, as a matter of priority, appropriate measures to enable the child to remain in the care of his or her family of origin".

---

95 Examples of this can be seen in the adoption by Angelina Jolie of a Somalian child who she believed to be an orphan, and in Madonna's adoption of a Malawian boy whose father later came to retrieve him from the care home only to find he had been adopted (see Benyam D Mezmur, "From Angelina (to Madonna) to Zoe's Ark: What are the 'A-Z' Lessons for Intercountry Adoptions in Africa?" (2009) 23 *International Journal of Law, Policy and the Family* 145, 147; Angella Johnson, *Madonna's Adopted Baby's Father Tells How He Was Powerless to Stop Her* (15 October 2006, Daily Mail) <www.dailymail.co.uk/news/article-410451/Madonnas-adopted-babys-father-tells-powerless-stop-her.html> [7 April 2011]; Raphael Tenthani, *Malawi Welcomes Madonna Adoption* (13 June 2009, BBC News) <http://news.bbc.co.uk/2/hi/entertainment/8098719.stm> [7 April 2011]).

96 United Nations Human Rights Council, *Draft Resolution to the General Assembly: Guidelines for the Alternative Care of Children* (15 June 2009) A/HRC/11/L.13. Formally welcomed by consensus in the General Assembly on 20 November 2009.

97 Stating that: "Convinced that the family, as the fundamental group of society and the natural environment for the growth and well-being of all its members and particularly children, should be afforded the necessary protection and assistance so that it can fully assume its responsibilities within the community".

The effect that material poverty can have on the placement of children was seen in Romania, where from 1991 to 2000, in the climate of economic hardship following the fall of Ceauşescu, the number of children who were separated from their families for purely economic reasons doubled,[98] and between 1990 and 1997, the rate of institutionalisation of children under three years old increased by more than 60 per cent.[99] Financial assistance in this situation would not only have prevented the separation of some of these children from their families, but would have also reduced the burden on child care institutions, which were insufficient in quality and quantity to cope with the children needing care.[100] In such circumstances, not only would fewer children have been subsequently placed in intercountry adoption when these institutions were found to be patently inappropriate, but this would also have represented a *financial saving* for states given the high cost of institutional care. The University of Nottingham estimates that in Bulgaria, while it costs no more than €1,200 per year to support a child to stay in his or her family, €3,367 is needed to care for a child in an institution.[101] Similarly, in 2005 Everychild suggested that in Russia, Ukraine, Romania and Moldova, foster care was three times more expensive than providing social services to vulnerable families.[102]

What can be seen from this discussion is that institutional care, although in its worst form inadequate and undesirable, can be carefully designed and tailored to meet the specific needs of certain groups of children, as has been the case in France, Denmark and England, as well as recent reforms in Romania. However, this is often not the case in eastern European jurisdictions, where the preference for institutional over family-based care is creating a reliance on intercountry placements to provide adequate care for children without families. This can only be addressed with a fundamental shift in the way child welfare services are provided in the jurisdictions in question, which is slowly beginning to materialise, and an additional emphasis on family assistance to prevent the need for alternative care in the first place.

---

98 Velina Todorova, "Children's Rights in Bulgaria after the End of Communism" (2009) 17(4) *International Journal of Children's Rights* 623, 626.

99 Dickens, above n 55, 77.

100 The Committee on the Rights of the Child has expressed concern over the placement of children in care for reasons of poverty in several jurisdictions, including, for example, Azerbaijan (*Concluding Observations* (12 March 2012) CRC/C/AZE/CO/3–4, [52]), and the Czech Republic (Concluding *Observations* (4 August 2011) CRC/C/CZE/CO/3–4, 2011, [45]).

101 University of Nottingham, *Causes and Consequences of Child Abandonment: Bulgaria* (2012) <www.nottingham.ac.uk/iwho/documents/childabandonment/bulgaria/causes-and-consequences-of-child-abandonment.pdf> [3 June 2012].

102 Richard Carter, *Family Matters: A Study of Institutional Childcare in Central and Eastern European and the Former Soviet Union* (2005, Everychild) <http://p-ced.com/reference/Family_Matters_summary.pdf> [7 February 2013].

3.3.2. FOSTER CARE: ALTERNATIVE OR SMOKE-SCREEN?

A second question that must be addressed is whether foster care should be considered as an appropriate domestic alternative to intercountry adoption. Sara Dillon is highly critical of foster placement, stating that "national foster care will give the appearance of having dealt with a certain subset of social orphans, while denying them the best possible permanency options."[103] She argues that the solution should instead be an out-of-country placement that would provide more permanency.

This line of reasoning resolutely ignores the primary purpose of foster care, which is to provide protection and support for the child while simultaneously facilitating family reunification. A foster care placement can serve as a short-term solution that allows the family time to deal with whatever issues led to the separation in the first place, whether these be financial, social or psychological.

A secondary use of foster placement can be seen in long-term foster care as an alternative to adoption. While countries such as the US and England view adoption as the preferred choice for the permanent care of young babies and children, where they cannot stay with their families, this is not necessarily the case in all jurisdictions, For example, in France, the welfare of the child is viewed as being best served by maintaining blood and kinship ties, and as such fostering does not have the same pejorative connotations.[104] Permanency should not be assumed to lie solely with establishing a legal tie with a new family, but should reflect the need for continuity and stability in the child's care.

The advantages of long-term foster care were set out by Ward LJ in the English case of *M (A Minor),* in which he held that "[l]ong-term fostering does enable the child to have the best of both worlds by feeling she belongs to both families though she must reside with and will anyway usually choose to live with only one – the one who gives her the daily love and care."[105] However, he also acknowledged that adoption could also be beneficial for some children, stating that "[t]he significant advantage of adoption is that it can promote much needed security and stability, the younger the age of placement, the fuller the advantage."[106]

Those who advocate strongly for adoption as the most appropriate solution for providing stability and security often focus on the needs of children who are taken into care at a very young age, who may rightly benefit from a new family.

---

103 Sara Dillon, "The Missing Link: A Social Orphan Protocol to the United Nations Convention on the Rights of the Child" (2007) 1 *Human Rights and Globalization Law Review* 39, 74.

104 Andrew Cooper, "International Perspectives on Child Protection" in Malcolm Hill, Anne Stafford and Pam Green Lister (eds), *International Perspectives on Child Protection* (2002) 135 <www.scotland.gov.uk/Resource/Doc/1181/0009926.pdf> [9 March 2011].

105 [1997] EWCA Civ 2766.

106 Note that this decision was handed down before the implementation of the Human Rights Act 1998, and therefore no analysis of article 8 rights was undertaken.

However, it is important to remember that children entering care are often significantly older when separated from their families, and therefore their needs will potentially differ. For an older child, "permanency" may mean remaining within his or her culture as discussed above, and maintaining the ties already formed with family, friends and society, while having the security of a long-term placement. Children do not operate in a vacuum – they are part of a society with interlinking ties to their siblings, extended family, friends, neighbourhood, community, school, and faith – and thus when they are removed from their environment, they face potential disruption of *all* aspects of their life and identity.

The table below shows that the number of children under two years of age left without parental care in the Czech Republic, Estonia, Hungary, Lithuania and Serbia is only a small proportion of the whole. While children under two make up a larger percentage in Armenia, they are still in the minority.

Age of children left without parental care: 2011[107]

	Total number of children left without parental care in 2011	Children left without parental care in 2011 aged 0–2 years
Armenia	241	101
Czech Republic	6,019	669
Estonia	2,573	324
Hungary	5,457	1,099
Lithuania	2,305	992
Serbia	2,571	180

Although this is only a small cross-section of countries, as wider data is unavailable, it supports the proposition that, in these countries at least, while some children may be suited to a clean and complete break with their family of birth, the large majority will have ongoing emotional connections both to that family and to their society, language, environment and culture which would make adoption, and especially an intercountry adoption, undesirable.

The ultimate aim of all child protection authorities must be to promote the welfare of the child through establishing stability and minimising disruption in his or her life. Assumptions as to the best mechanism to achieve this vary significantly across jurisdictions; while some attach more weight to the legal irrevocability and life-long implications of adoption in achieving stability, others focus on the maintenance of kinship and identity. It would be imprudent to suggest that any of these approaches is more beneficial to the welfare and rights of the child in all circumstances. The differing approaches highlight the diverse needs of children who are taken into care, depending on their

[107] UNICEF, *TransMONEE Database* (2013) <www.transmonee.org/> [14 May 2014].

individual situation. For this reason, it is important to take a flexible approach to child protection, in which all options are considered carefully and thoroughly, but none is presupposed to be the best solution for all children. While stability and permanency through adoption may be extremely important for some children, especially those who are very young when placed in care, others might benefit more from the maintenance of their identity and already established links with their birth family. As such, the imperative for intercountry adoption will be different for each child, and especially older children may experience greater harm being placed in a foreign permanent family than, for example, being cared for in a domestic long-term fostering arrangement, or even in an institutional setting. For this reason, it is important to consider all domestic care options before intercountry adoption, adapting to the needs of the child.

3.4. IMPACT OF INTERCOUNTRY ADOPTION ON THE DOMESTIC CHILD WELFARE SYSTEM

The final issue that must be considered in the context of the principle of subsidiarity relates not to the individual child, but to the domestic welfare system as a whole, and the role that intercountry adoption can play in distorting it to the detriment of all children involved. The effects of intercountry adoption can be seen in both sending and receiving states: while in sending states, intercountry adoption can divert resources away from the domestic welfare system, and suppress domestic adoption, in receiving states the practice can result in hard-to-place children not being placed in family care.

3.4.1. SENDING COUNTRIES

Perhaps the most dramatic impact of intercountry adoption on the domestic system was seen in the 1990s in Romania, which was the scene of what has been one of the most controversial chapters in the history of intercountry adoption. Before 1989, intercountry adoption was virtually unknown in Romania, but after the fall of Ceauşescu and the opening of the country to the world, the distressing situation of children in institutional care that came to light led to many foreigners applying to adopt Romanian children.

In addition to the problems that arose in relation to the adoptions themselves – including inducement of consent, which will be discussed in detail in Chapter Five – the influx of intercountry adoptions had a negative effect on domestic adoption. The drop in national adoptions in comparison with intercountry adoptions can be seen in the table below.

National and intercountry adoption cases in Romania: 1992–2000[108]

	1992	1993	1994	1995	1996	1997	1998	1999	2000
National adoption	3,200	2,792	2,389	1,538	662	197	840	1,710	1,291
Intercountry adoption	891	2,038	1,789	1,057	1,658	851	2,017	2,575	3,035

The reasons for this were examined by Ambrose and Coburn: they suggest that the domestic adoption process was seen as "excessively cumbersome", and since such adoptions were processed for free, there was no incentive for them to be utilised in place of the more lucrative intercountry adoptions.[109] They found that Romanian adopters were rarely able to adopt infants, who were reserved for foreign adopters, and in the first ten months of 2000, the average age of domestic adoption was three years old, while intercountry adoption was ten months.[110]

Perhaps the most troubling effect of intercountry adoption on the domestic welfare system is that due to the large profits it generates, it has the potential to bring children into the welfare system who would not otherwise be there. The Independent Group for International Adoption Analysis in Romania reported that intercountry adoption stimulated the abandonment of children in Romania who would otherwise have remained with their families,[111] while UNICEF suggests that in eastern Europe an increase in the number of adoptions is often accompanied by a rise in institutional placements, and where national legislation requires that only children in institutions may be placed in intercountry adoption, this has simply led to a rise in "relinquishments" to institutions.[112]

Similar allegations were levelled against the Vietnamese system by the US Department of State in 2008, when it reported that monetary donations to orphanages in exchange for the supply of adoptable children were distorting adoption patterns. It noted that:

108 Dirk Westhof, *Flow Model Institutionalised Children in Romania and the Determining Variables* (2005) <www.crin.org/docs/resources/treaties/crc.40/GDD_2005_Flowstudy_children_in_residential_care_Romania.pdf> [15 May 2012].

109 Michael W Ambrose and Anna Mary Coburn, *Report on Intercountry Adoption in Romania* (2001) 7 <http://pdf.usaid.gov/pdf_docs/PNACW989.pdf> [30 January 2012].

110 Ibid.

111 Independent Group for International Adoption Analysis, *Re-organising the International Adoption and Child Protection System* (2002) <www.afaener.org/Rapport_FINAL_ang.doc> [30 January 2012].

112 UNICEF, *Guidance Note on Intercountry Adoption in the CEE/CIS/Baltics Region* (2003, UNICEF) <www.unicef.org/ceecis/Guidance_note_Intercountry_adoption.pdf> [1 September 2011].

> "Under US Immigration law, children can be adopted if they are orphans due to the whereabouts of their birth parents being unknown (desertion) or if one or both birth parents have permanently relinquished custody of their child to the orphanage (termed 'abandonment' by US Immigration law but commonly referred to as relinquishment). Prior to the suspension of adoption in 2002, 80% of cases were relinquishments, and 20% were abandonments. Since the Memorandum of Agreement (MOA) [Bilateral Agreement] went into effect in 2005, those figures have flipped with over 85% of the cases involving desertions. Orphanages not involved in ICA, however, have reported to the Embassy that they have not seen any increase in the number of deserted children, and the vast majority of children in these facilities are children in care. Post [the Embassy] has received multiple, credible reports from orphanage officials that facilitators are deliberately staging fraudulent desertions to conceal the identity of the birth parents."[113]

This problem was also experienced in Cambodia; despite the moratorium on intercountry adoption in 2001, a survey by the US Agency for International Development found that by 2005, there was no build-up of children in orphanages, with the numbers remaining roughly the same, indicating that the children who were placed in intercountry adoption from Cambodia before the moratorium were a distinct group of children, separate from true orphans or those who genuinely needed alternative care.[114] As such, intercountry adoption can cause a vicious cycle, where children need to be placed in intercountry adoption because they are in institutions, but are in institutions because of the practice of intercountry adoption.

Further, as Jonathan Dickens suggests, intercountry adoption can also undermine the availability of quality social workers and professionals within the domestic sector. As intercountry adoption often draws in large fees, it can afford to pay better salaries and offer better working conditions than can the local welfare authorities.[115]

One of the problems in this regard is the practice of "donations" that are given by adoptive parents to orphanages or institutions, which encourage these organisations to promote intercountry adoption over domestic. The Albanian Central Authority reports that prospective adoptive parents often provide child care institutions from which they adopt with various types of aid such as medication, clothing, food and toys,[116] while it is also legal to

113 United States: Department of State, *Summary of Irregularities in Adoptions in Vietnam* (25 April 2008) <http://vietnam.usembassy.gov/irreg_adoptions042508.html> [10 January 2012].

114 David M Smolin, "Child Laundering: How the Intercountry Adoption System Legitimizes and Incentivizes the Practices of Buying, Trafficking, Kidnaping, and Stealing Children" (2006) 52 *Wayne Law Review* 113, 145.

115 Dickens, above n 55, 81.

116 Hague Conference, *Country Profile: Albania* (2010) <www.hcch.net/index_en.php?act=publications.details&pid=5081&dtid=42> [14 January 2012].

accept donations in Armenia,[117] Georgia[118] and Latvia.[119] In the Czech Republic, Lithuania and Poland, donations are also permitted, but only after the adoption process has been completed.[120] While it is important that donations are not permitted before approval for adoption is given, the requirement that they only be undertaken after the adoption does not prevent their having an influence on the process. Where an institution knows it can expect some sort of donation or payment, even if it is to come later, it can encourage it to place more children in intercountry adoption than would otherwise be the case. Worryingly, private institutions in Poland are permitted to *require* such payment – although public institutions may not do so – making it not so much a voluntary donation, but a fee collected directly by the institution itself.[121]

Payments encourage competition between prospective adoptive parents, between accredited bodies and agencies, and between receiving states. Although the Hague Convention prohibits contact between the prospective adoptive parents and the institution before the child has been deemed eligible to adopt,[122] it is permitted before the matching is completed, allowing for preference to be given to those who pay (or offer) the most, rather than those who are most appropriate to care for the child. Where certain bodies or agencies are known to suggest the parents they work with give a higher "donation" than others,[123] they may be preferred over others, and likewise receiving states.[124] For this reason, countries such as Estonia, Portugal, Romania and Slovakia prohibit any kind of donation or sponsorship to the institution or organisation that the child is staying with,[125] although whether or not this is always obeyed is questionable.

---

117 Hague Conference, *Country Profile: Armenia* (2010) <www.hcch.net/index_en.php?act=publications.details&pid=5115&dtid=42> [14 January 2012].

118 Donations are only permitted with the approval of the government authorities (Hague Conference, *Country Profile: Georgia* (2010) <www.hcch.net/index_en.php?act=publications.details&pid=5118&dtid=42> [14 January 2012]).

119 These must be documented, however (Hague Conference,, *Country Profile: Latvia* (2010) <www.hcch.net/index_en.php?act=publications.details&pid=5087&dtid=42> [14 January 2012]).

120 Hague Conference, *Country Profile: Czech Republic* (2010) <www.hcch.net/index_en.php?act=publications.details&pid=5116&dtid=42> [14 January 2012]; Hague Conference, *Country Profile: Lithuania* (2010) <www.hcch.net/index_en.php?act=publications.details&pid=5209&dtid=42> [14 January 2012]; Hague Conference, *Country Profile: Poland* (2010) <www.hcch.net/index_en.php?act=publications.details&pid=5093&dtid=42> [14 January 2012].

121 Hague Conference, *Country Profile: Poland* (2010) <www.hcch.net/index_en.php?act=publications.details&pid=5093&dtid=42> [14 January 2012].

122 Article 29.

123 In many instances, the amount and type of donation will be guided by the agency, rather than be at the sole initiative of the adoptive parents.

124 See B Mathieu, *L'argent, premier écueil et dernier tabou de l'adoption* (1 October 2008, L'Expansion) <www.lexpansion.lexpress.fr> [14 January 2013]; Hague Conference, *A Discussion Paper on the Financial Aspects of Intercountry Adoption* (2012) <www.hcch.net/index_en.php?act=events.details&year=2012&varevent=284> [14 January 2013].

125 Hague Conference, *Country Profile: Estonia* (2010) <www.hcch.net/index_en.php?act=publications.details&pid=5242&dtid=42> [14 January 2012]; Hague Conference, *Country Profile:*

3.4.2. RECEIVING COUNTRIES

It is not only sending countries that are affected by an influx of intercountry adoption. Where healthy, young children are available relatively easily from other countries, the domestic system of child protection in receiving countries can be suppressed, and fewer options become available for those children who need particular assistance within their own country. This is particularly the case for older children or children with special needs, who may be prevented from being placed domestically with a family because of a prevalence of more "desirable" adoptees coming into the country, which in turn could lead to increased institutionalisation for these children. In addition, public and professional attention is diverted from hard-to-place domestic children when there is the possibility of adopting babies from overseas.

This phenomenon can be seen in many countries in western Europe where domestic adoption is relatively low but intercountry adoptions are high. In France, around 800 children are adopted domestically every year,[126] whereas in 2008 3,271 children were adopted from abroad by French families.[127] Similarly, Sweden has reported averaging 15 to 20 domestic adoptions per year, with 912 intercountry adoptions in 2009,[128] and the Netherlands recorded 40 domestic adoptions[129] and 682 intercountry placements in 2009.[130]

In these countries, the low domestic adoption rates reflect the importance of kinship, and the belief that family ties should not be broken except under the most exceptional circumstances. As such, foster care is a much more common practice, with families previously having been willing to take children into their homes without the need for legal confirmation of the arrangement through adoption. However, many families who would have otherwise fostered children domestically may now be opting instead to parent younger, healthier children from other countries, leaving domestic so-called "unadoptable" children without family care.

Similar effects are seen in the United States, which is the largest receiving state in the world, but yet has hundreds of thousands of children waiting for

---

Portugal (2010) <www.hcch.net/index_en.php?act=publications.details&pid=5094&dtid=42> [14 January 2012]; Romania: article 70 Law No 273/2004; Hague Conference, *Country Profile: Slovakia* (2010) <www.hcch.net/index_en.php?act=publications.details&pid=5095&dtid=42> [14 January 2012].

126 Hague Conference, *Country Profile: France* (2010) <www.hcch.net/index_en.php?act=publications.details&pid=5086&dtid=42> [14 January 2012].

127 France: Ministère des Affaires Étrangeres et Européennes, *Intercountry Adoption in France* (2010) <www.diplomatie.gouv.fr/fr/IMG/pdf/Adoption_FinaleAng_BD.pdf> [9 March 2011].

128 Sweden: Intercountry Adoptions Authority, *Annual Adoption Statistics* (2010) <www.hcch.net/upload/wop/adop2010pd05_se.pdf> [9 March 2011].

129 Statistics Netherlands, *Adoption* (2013) <www.cbs.nl/en-GB/menu/themas/veiligheid-recht/cijfers/extra/mappingworld-2-adoptie.htm> [9 March 2011].

130 Netherlands: Ministerie van Justitie, *Adoptie: trends en analyse* (15 March 2010) <www.hcch.net/upload/wop/adop2010pd05_nl.pdf> [9 March 2011].

adoption domestically. These "waiting" children are comprised nearly entirely of older, minority or special needs children,[131] many of whom are in turn placed in intercountry adoption. The USA in fact sends more children for intercountry adoption than such European sending states as Albania, Armenia, Azerbaijan, the Czech Republic, Estonia, Georgia, Hungary, Latvia, Lithuania, Portugal and Slovakia.[132]

As such, not only may individual children in both sending and receiving countries be damaged by the precipitous use of intercountry adoption, but also the interests of all children in need of alternative care may be jeopardised. It is important that these more wide-reaching effects be carefully considered before intercountry adoption is advocated as a child-saving solution for children in care. Intercountry adoption is not, and never can be, a panacea; it is only an option for a small minority of children in state care, even in the most prolific sending countries. For example, in 2009, the Czech Republic reported approximately 9,662 children in the care of foster parents or guardians, but only 549 adoptions, either domestic or intercountry. In Russia, these figures were 430,604 in family care, and 11,157 adoptions; in the Ukraine, 68,508 and 3,496.[133] For this reason, we cannot simply look for the quickest way to get some children out of a terrible situation, leaving others in greater danger, but must reconstruct domestic care systems to ensure that they provide adequate standards of care for all who require it. Where intercountry adoption is jeopardising that system, leading to more children abandoned than there otherwise would be, or leading to longer stays in care for certain categories of children, its regulation should be carefully reconsidered.

3.5. CONCLUSION

To truly achieve its aims, the principle of subsidiarity requires much more than a preference for domestic solutions over intercountry adoption. It requires that all possible steps be taken to ensure that the child is provided with the greatest opportunity to stay with his or her family and to maintain a cultural, linguistic

---

131 Nearly 60 per cent of these children were non-white, over 60 per cent were six years of age or older, and 30–40 per cent were estimated to have physical health problems (Kimberly D Krawiec, "Altruism and Intermediation in the Market for Babies" (2009) 66 *Washington and Lee Law Review* 203, 230–231).

132 Peter Selman, "Global Trends in Intercountry Adoption: 2001–2010" (2012) 44 *Adoption Advocate* 1, 14; Peter Selman, *The Impact of Intercountry Adoption on the Well-Being of Children in Europe* (2007) <www.ciimu.org/webs/wellchi/conference_3/selman.pdf> [21 February 2013]; Australian Intercountry Adoption Network, *International Adoption Statistics* (2010) <www.aican.org/statistics.php?region=0&type=birth> [26 February 2013]; Hague Conference, *Statistics* (2010) <www.hcch.net/index_en.php?act=conventions.publications&dtid=32&cid=69> [14 January 2013].

133 UNICEF, *TransMONEE Database* (2012) <www.transmonee.org/> [22 May 2013].

and ethnic identity, and to build a domestic welfare system that can facilitate this. The biggest obstacle to achieving these aims is the widespread use of institutional care among states of origin for intercountry adoption, due to a lack of assistance to families and underdeveloped family care alternatives such as fostering and domestic adoption.

In order for the principle to be effective, states must develop domestic mechanisms that support families, to ensure that separation is not due to financial and material poverty, and to keep children out of state care wherever possible. Where state care is necessary, the primary aim of the authorities should be achieving reunification of the family while providing short-term care that is appropriate and allows the child to develop in a healthy manner. It is only after these attempts fail that long-term solutions can be considered, first on a domestic level, and then internationally. These solutions can take a number of different forms, depending on the needs of the child, and should not be considered as a one-size-fits-all approach. The best interests of the child lie in achieving permanency and a healthy environment in which to develop, which can mean different things for each individual child, depending on his or her age, needs and background. In deciding this, attention must be paid to the views of the child (where these are expressed), and what he or she wishes for in a placement, in order to preserve his or her autonomy, and provide the best possible opportunity for success.

CHAPTER 4

CONSENTING ADULTS: GIVING AND RECEIVING CONSENT TO ADOPTION

When family reunification and other alternative care mechanisms are not appropriate or have been exhausted, the focus must shift to ensuring that the adoption process is completed in a manner that safeguards the rights of the child. The following chapters will consider the issue of parental consent to adoption – who must give it, how it can be obtained, and when it can be dispensed with.

While obtaining parental consent may initially be seen as relating primarily to parental rights, this is an area of the law where stronger safeguards for parents can lead to greater protection for the child involved. Ensuring appropriate consent pursues two primary goals: first, preventing the unnecessary separation of families; and second, ensuring that placements are not disrupted.[1] Where consent has been obtained in a legitimate manner, the child is not deprived of the right to stay with his or her family wherever possible, whereas an effective mechanism for dispensing with consent where appropriate ensures that the child is protected and placed in a new family where this is necessary. On the other hand, it is also in the interests of the child to be secure in his or her new family placement, and for this not to be challenged at a later date where consent has been improperly obtained or dispensed with, making it vital that appropriate procedures are followed from the beginning.

The UNCRC does not concern itself greatly with the issue of consent to adoption. Although article 21(a) refers to the need for "the persons concerned [to] have given their informed consent to the adoption on the basis of such counselling as may be necessary", it fails to go into further detail as to who the "persons concerned" may be, when consent may be given, what form it must take, or the process by which such consent may be overridden.

The Hague Convention goes into somewhat more detail regarding the conditions for consent, although it still leaves many areas unexplored. Chapter II of the Convention establishes certain requirements that must be met before an intercountry adoption can take place, allocating responsibility for meeting these

1 See Elizabeth J Samuels, "Time to Decide? The Laws Governing Mothers' Consents to the Adoption of their Newborn Infants" (2005) 72 *Tennessee Law Review* 509.

requirements between states of origin and receiving states. Article 4 sets out the responsibilities of the former, the majority of which are dedicated to ensuring that the appropriate consents have been obtained.

As such, an intercountry adoption can only take place within the scope of the Hague Convention if the authorities:

> "(c) have ensured that
> (1) the persons, institutions and authorities whose consent is necessary for adoption, have been counselled as may be necessary and duly informed of the effects of their consent, in particular whether or not an adoption will result in the termination of the legal relationship between the child and his or her family of origin,
> (2) such persons, institutions and authorities have given their consent freely, in the required legal form, and expressed or evidenced in writing,
> (3) the consents have not been induced by payment or compensation of any kind and have not been withdrawn, and
> (4) the consent of the mother, where required, has been given only after the birth of the child."

As such, like the UNCRC, the Hague Convention leaves the identity of those whose consent is needed to the discretion of domestic authorities. However, the additional restrictions on payment and compensation are of particular importance, and will be discussed in detail in Chapter Five. In addition, the restriction on the consent of the mother after birth is an important shift in adoption practice, which is also echoed in the more recent Revised European Convention on the Adoption of Children of 2008.

Although, as discussed in Chapter Two, the ECA 2008 does not as yet have widespread ratification across Europe, its detailed consideration of the human rights principles involved in adoption makes it of considerable importance. Article 5 of the Revised Convention sets out the consents necessary before an adoption can occur, including specific details concerning the identity of those who must consent and how consent may be dispensed with. It reads:

> "1. Subject to paragraphs 2 to 5 of this article, an adoption shall not be granted unless at least the following consents to the adoption have been given and not withdrawn:
> (a) the consent of the mother and the father; or if there is neither father nor mother to consent, the consent of any person or body who is entitled to consent in their place;
> (b) the consent of the child considered by law as having sufficient understanding; a child shall be considered as having sufficient understanding on attaining an age which shall be prescribed by law and shall not be more than 14 years;
> (c) the consent of the spouse or registered partner of the adopter.
> 2. The persons whose consent is required for adoption must have been counselled as may be necessary and duly informed of the effects of their consent, in particular

> whether or not an adoption will result in the termination of the legal relationship between the child and his or her family of origin. The consent must have been given freely, in the required legal form, and expressed or evidenced in writing.
> 3. The competent authority shall not dispense with the consent or overrule the refusal to consent of any person or body mentioned in paragraph 1 save on exceptional grounds determined by law. However, the consent of a child who suffers from a disability preventing the expression of a valid consent may be dispensed with.
> 4. If the father or mother is not a holder of parental responsibility in respect of the child, or at least of the right to consent to an adoption, the law may provide that it shall not be necessary to obtain his or her consent.
> 5. A mother's consent to the adoption of her child shall be valid when it is given at such time after the birth of the child, not being less than six weeks, as may be prescribed by law, or, if no such time has been prescribed, at such time as, in the opinion of the competent authority, will have enabled her to recover sufficiently from the effects of giving birth to the child."

While this Convention adds substantially more content to the principles in the UNCRC and Hague Convention, it is by no means comprehensive, and continues to leave a large scope for discretion. However, it does raise the important issues of adoption without consent, which will be discussed in Chapter Six, as well as the place of the mother or father without parental responsibility, which will be considered in relation to unmarried fathers in section 4.2.

In the sections below, the procedure for obtaining consent from the birth mother and father will be considered separately, as they raise very different issues and human rights considerations. While for the mother, the most important considerations will be the support she is given in making the decision, the father must pass the initial hurdle of being recognised as a parent before being granted any say in the adoption process.

4.1. CONSENT BY THE BIRTH MOTHER

In most European jurisdictions, the relationship between the mother and the child is confirmed simply through the act of giving birth, if she so wishes,[2] although exceptions to this arise in relation to surrogacy and assisted reproduction.[3] This book will not discuss these exceptions, and will instead use

---

2 This is also the case under the ECHR; see *Marckx v Belgium* [1979] ECHR 2. In some jurisdictions, a birth mother may choose not to establish this legal relationship, as will be discussed in relation to anonymous birth in Chapter Nine.

3 See, for example, Andrew Bainham, "What is the Point of Birth Registration?" (2008) 20(4) *Child and Family Law Quarterly* 459; MJ Vonk, "Tensions Between Legal, Biological and Social Conceptions of Parenthood in Dutch Family Law" (2007) 11(1) *Electronic Journal of Comparative Law*; Janet L Dolgin, "Just a Gene: Judicial Assumptions About Parenthood" (1992–1993) 40 *UCLA Law Review* 637.

the term "birth mother" to refer to the woman who gave birth to the child, no matter what the precise biological relationship. For the purposes of adoption, the more important issue lies in the way in which the mother, once she has given birth, can consent to the placement of her child, and the assistance she is given when coming to this decision.

4.1.1. HOW SOON IS TOO SOON? THE TIMING OF A MOTHER'S CONSENT AND ITS REVOCATION

The timing of consent given by a mother for the placement of her child for adoption is crucial to ensuring that her rights, and those of the child, are not violated. Women need to be protected from making life-changing decisions in the immediate aftermath of birth, and the practice of allowing birth mothers to give their consent at this time exploits their weakness when they are most vulnerable. A mother needs to recover from the effects of the birth and the hormones involved with pregnancy, and time should be given for her to reflect on her decision in a less stressful and emotionally charged situation.

This will be of benefit to both the mother and the child, as it means that they will not be separated prematurely or before the mother has time to reflect.[4] Reports from several European countries suggest that pressure is routinely brought to bear on mothers in hospitals to abandon their children, especially if they belong to an ethnic minority, putting them in a vulnerable position. For example, a study by Andy Bilson in eastern Europe found that in Ukraine and Bulgaria, medical staff often advise parents that it would be in the child's best interests to be placed in an institution or adopted,[5] and Bilson and Markova report that upon entry into hospital, an administrator asked all Roma mothers if they wanted to keep their babies, and routinely filled out the adoption forms on their behalf.[6] These findings are supported by a 2005 UNICEF report on Romania, which found that when mothers were asked who had encouraged them in their decision to abandon their children, 80 per cent indicated medical staff, while 12 per cent indicated social workers.[7] Thus,

---

4 Any removal of the child must also comply with law, and not be taken without judicial sanction: *R (G) v Nottingham City Council* [2008] EWHC 152 (Admin); [2008] 1 FLR 1660 is a particularly pertinent example of the dangers that may arise.

5 Andy Bilson, *The Development of Gate-Keeping functions in Central and Eastern Europe and the CIS: Lessons from Bulgaria, Kazakhstan and Ukraine* (2010) 17 <www.unicef.org/ceecis/overview_Report_20_August_preface.doc> [7 June 2012].

6 Andy Bilson and Galina Markova, "But You Should See Their Families: Preventing Child Abandonment and Promoting Social Inclusion in Countries in Transition" (2007) 12(3) *Social Work and Social Sciences Review* 29, 37.

7 Ecaterina Stativa et al, *The Situation of Child Abandonment in Romania* (2005, UNICEF) 98 <www.ceecis.org/child_protection/PDF/child%20abandonment%20in%20Romania.pdf> [7 January 2013].

placing a minimum waiting period before the mother gives the child up for adoption will not only give her additional time to consider her options, but also assist in ensuring that her decision is not overly influenced by pressure from medical professionals.

In addition, if the child is placed for adoption and the mother later changes her mind, this can have a disastrous effect on the stability of the child and can cause substantial legal wrangling. This was seen in the US *Baby Jessica Case*,[8] where a mother signed a release relinquishing her parental rights before the 72-hour waiting period had expired. The child was immediately placed with another family, and when the mother sought to revoke her release, two years of litigation ensued.[9]

In this respect, an intercountry adoption can exacerbate the difficulties involved in a premature placement: once a child has been taken to the receiving state with a new family, there is little scope to investigate the circumstances in which the adoption order has been made. In many cases, it is seen as a *fait accompli*, and even where irregularities have occurred, the courts have chosen to confirm the order rather than create further disturbance in the child's life. This was acknowledged in the English case of *X and Y (Foreign Surrogacy)*, when the High Court found that

> "it is almost impossible to imagine a set of circumstances in which by the time the case comes to court, the welfare of any child (particularly a foreign child) would not be gravely compromised (at the very least) by a refusal to make an order."[10]

Despite these vulnerabilities, the UNCRC does not address the issue, and the Hague Convention contains minimal guidance, requiring that the consent of the mother can be given only after the birth of the child, but leaving it to the discretion of states as to how soon after the birth consent can be given.[11] On the other hand, the more recent ECA 2008 requires that a mother's consent cannot

---

8 *In re Baby Girl Clausen* (1993) 442 Mich. 648; 502 NW 2d 649.

9 Although this case was ultimately decided on the rights of the father in the case, who the mother had failed to name, it exemplifies the problems that arise when appropriate time is not given to the mother after birth.

10 [2008] EWHC 3030 (Fam); [2009] 1 FLR 733, [24]. An exception to this was seen in the case of *Re K (Adoption & Wardship)* [1997] 2 FLR 230, which involved a Bosnian child who had been brought to England for medical treatment, and whose foster parents subsequently tried to adopt her. Although all adoption from Bosnia had been stopped, and the child had a grandfather and aunt in Bosnia who wanted to care for the child, adoption was granted by the court. This was overturned on appeal, with the court finding that the adoption procedure had been fatally flawed. This case highlights that although in cases of surrogacy or adoption where the parents are unknown, the welfare of a foreign child already brought into England and cared for by prospective adopters will normally require an adoption order, where a child has family ready and willing to care for him or her, this will not be the case.

11 Article 4(c)(4) Hague Convention.

be given until six weeks after birth.[12] The explicit reasoning behind the inclusion of this requirement was to "avoid premature adoptions to which mothers give their consent as a result of pressure exerted before the birth of the child or before their physical health and psychological balance have been restored after the child's birth."[13]

The legislation in Europe varies vastly from country to country with regards to the timing of consent, ranging from before birth (Slovakia),[14] to immediately after birth (Slovenia),[15] 30 days (Spain[16] and Bulgaria),[17] six weeks (Cyprus,[18] the Czech Republic,[19] England,[20] Latvia,[21] Malta,[22] Portugal,[23] Serbia,[24] Switzerland[25] and Turkey),[26] eight weeks (Estonia[27] and Germany),[28] 60 days (Romania),[29] two months (Belgium,[30] Norway[31] and Ukraine),[32] to three months (Denmark,[33] Greece,[34] Iceland,[35] Lithuania[36] and Montenegro).[37] Only in Finland and Sweden is there any reference to the emotional and physical state of the mother, with consent only permitted after she has sufficiently recovered from

12 Article 5(5) ECA 2008.

13 Council of Europe, *Explanatory Report to the European Convention on the Adoption of Children (Revised)* (2008) [37] <http://conventions.coe.int/Treaty/en/Reports/Html/202.htm> [18 January 2013].

14 Yves Brulard and Letitia Dumont, *Comparative Study Relating to Procedures for Adoption Among the Member States of the European Union, Practical Difficulties Encountered in this Field by European Citizens within the Context of the European Pillar of Justice and Civil Matters and Means of Solving these Problems and of Protecting Children's Rights* (2007, European Union) 444.

15 There is no law regarding the time after birth that the mother can consent to adoption, therefore it is possible for her to give consent from the moment the child is born (ibid., 449).

16 Article 177 Civil Code.

17 Article 89(2) Family Law.

18 Section 6(3)(a) Adoption Act 1995.

19 Section 68a Act No 94/1963 Sb on Family.

20 Section 52(3) Adoption and Children Act 2002.

21 Section 169 Civil Law.

22 Article 118(2) Civil Code.

23 Article 1982(3) Civil Code.

24 Article 98(3) Family Act.

25 Article 265(b)(1) Civil Code.

26 Article 310 Civil Code.

27 Section 152(2) Family Law Act 2009. The parent's consent can be given before this, but it will not enter into force until eight weeks after birth.

28 Section 1747(2) Civil Code. However, the father may consent to the adoption of the child before birth if the parents are not married to each other (section 1747 Civil Code).

29 Article 16(1) Law No 273/2004.

30 Article 348–5 Civil Code.

31 Section 7 Act of 28 February 1986, No 8 relating to Adoption.

32 Article 217(3) Family Code.

33 Except in exceptional circumstances (article 8(2) Adoption (Consolidation) Act).

34 Article 1551 Civil Code.

35 Article 8 Adoption Act No 130/1999.

36 Article 3.209(3) Civil Code.

37 Article 124 Family Law.

the child's delivery (and in Finland, in any case no earlier than eight weeks after birth).[38]

The case of England is a particularly interesting example, as although the consent given by a mother to an adoption is ineffective if it is given less than six weeks after the child's birth, a distinction is made between consent to *placement for adoption*, and consent to *adoption* itself.[39] This distinction puts birth parents in a vulnerable position, as consent to placement carries with it numerous legal consequences in relation to the adoption, including restrictions on parents' ability to require the return of their child.[40] Furthermore, once prospective adopters have applied for an adoption order the parents cannot withdraw their consent to placement and can only oppose the adoption application with the leave of the court.[41] In this way, parents are put at a distinct disadvantage if consent to placement is already given during a time when it has been deemed iniquitous to allow them to give consent to adoption, thus allowing a loophole in their protection and also that of the child.[42]

In the one case that it has dealt with of this kind, the European Court of Human Rights endorsed the six-week waiting period in the ECA 2008, and stressed the necessity of ensuring that a mother has time to reflect on her decision, especially when that decision is made shortly after birth.

In *Todorova v Italy*,[43] a mother gave birth to twins, but on the day of their birth requested that she not be legally recognised as their mother, and that her name not be revealed. Four days after this, the mother requested time to reflect before deciding whether or not to recognise her children, and asked that they be placed in a temporary family or placement until she could make a decision. Despite this, less than a month after the children's birth, the courts declared them adoptable, without hearing the mother. The ECtHR found that there had been a violation of the mother's rights under article 8; although the Court recognised that the interests of the children required that their future be decided as soon as possible, it found that such speed was not necessary in this case, and the complete disregard for the rights of the mother was a violation of her right to respect for family life. In particular the Court held that

> "in disputes of this nature, where the consequences are of extreme importance as they affect the family relationship, the State had a positive obligation to ensure that the consent given by the applicant to the abandonment of her children was informed, and had been surrounded by adequate safeguards."[44]

---

38 Finland: section 15 Adoption Act 22/2012; Sweden: section 4:5a Children and Parents Code (1949:381).

39 Section 52(3) Adoption and Children Act 2002.

40 Sections 30 et seq, Adoption and Children Act 2002.

41 Section 47(3) Adoption and Children Act 2002.

42 See *A Local Authority v GC* [2009] 1 FLR 299.

43 [2009] ECHR 69.

44 Ibid., [82].

While the dangers of allowing consent too soon after birth have been made clear, there are also dangers on the other end of the spectrum, where the child is left in limbo for an extended period of time. While both the mother and child have an interest in ensuring that consent is not given too early, the child also has an interest in ensuring that he or she is placed in a stable and secure environment as soon as possible. Excessive delays in obtaining consent for adoption can prejudice the development of the child, especially where he or she is placed in institutional care in the meantime.[45] Thus, a careful balance must be struck between ensuring that the mother has time to recover after birth and that the child can stay with his or her family wherever possible on the one hand, and that the child can be placed in a new family and allowed to develop from the earliest possible opportunity on the other.

A similar balance between the child's competing interests must also be struck when considering rules concerning the revocation of consent validly given. On the one hand, states must legislate to ensure that the child is not separated from his or her parents if they are willing to care for him or her, but on the other hand, they must prevent the disruption of the placement of the child with an alternative family if this is not in the best interests of the child.

Practice across Europe in this area varies widely, with consent becoming immediately binding in Germany[46] and Portugal,[47] while in other states, consent can be revoked within a certain time period, ranging from 30 days (Andorra,[48] Serbia[49] and Romania),[50] to six weeks (Turkey[51] and Switzerland),[52] two months (France),[53] three months (Luxembourg[54] and Albania)[55] or even six months (Monaco).[56] In France and Luxembourg consent can still be revoked after this time, but whether or not the child will be returned to the parents will depend on an evaluation of the child's best interests.[57]

45 See Chapter Three.
46 Section 1750(2) Civil Code.
47 Article 1983 Civil Code.
48 Article 12 Qualified Law on Adoption of 21 March 1996.
49 Article 98(4) Family Act.
50 Article 16(2) Law No 273/2004.
51 Article 310 Civil Code.
52 Article 265b Civil Code.
53 Article 348–3 Civil Code.
54 Article 351–3 Civil Code.
55 Or until the court has made the adoption order. If the prospective parents refuse to return the child once consent is withdrawn, the parents may petition the court for the return of the child, if this is in the child's best interests (article 248 Family Code).
56 Article 254 Civil Code.
57 France: After two months, the parents can withdraw their consent if the child has not been placed for adoption, but this can be refused by a judge in the interests of the child (article 348–3 Civil Code); Luxembourg: The birth parents can still ask for the child's return after three months if he or she has not been placed for adoption. In this case if the authorities refuse to return the child, a tribunal will decide whether it is in the interests of the child to allow the revocation (article 351–3 Civil Code).

Other countries link the revocation of consent to events in the adoption proceedings, for example, before the commencement of the adoption case (Poland),[58] before the child is placed with prospective adopters (Azerbaijan[59] and the Czech Republic)[60] or before the court order for adoption (Armenia,[61] Belgium,[62] Estonia,[63] Finland,[64] Greece,[65] Ireland,[66] Lithuania,[67] Moldova,[68] Russia[69] and Ukraine).[70] Denmark, on the other hand, allows the revocation of consent before the final adoption order, unless the consent has been withdrawn unreasonably with regard to the welfare of the child.[71]

The European Court of Human Rights has touched on this matter briefly, in the case of *Kearns v France*,[72] which will be discussed in more detail below concerning counselling for birth parents. In this case, a mother who had placed her child for adoption argued that the time period of two months for withdrawing her consent was insufficient, and thus interfered with her right to respect for family life under article 8 of the ECHR. In reaching its decision, the Court emphasised that the state must balance the interests of the biological mother with those of the child, with the child's interests being paramount. It found that it was in the interests of the psychological and legal stability of the child to seek a new family as quickly as possible, and France had not overstepped its margin of appreciation by restricting revocation to two months.

This decision is hardly surprising, as just a year previously, in the case of *VS v Germany*, the Court had found that the German law prohibiting any revocation of consent was in compliance with article 8.[73] In this case, a 16-year-old girl had given her consent to the adoption of her ten-month-old child, but later wished to revoke this, claiming she had been put under pressure to give her consent and deeply regretted her actions. The Court ruled that although consent was irrevocable in Germany, it was possible to annul the consent in certain

58 Article 119(1) Family Code.
59 Article 122.2 Family Code.
60 Section 68(a) Act No 94/1963 Sb on Family.
61 Article 118(2) Family Code.
62 Article 348-8 Civil Code, and at the latest six months after the filing of the adoption petition.
63 Section 155(3) Family Law Act 2009.
64 Section 17 Adoption Act 22/2012.
65 Article 1554 Civil Code.
66 Section 14(6) Adoption Act 1952.
67 Article 3.212 Civil Code: "The court shall not approve of the revocation of the consent to adoption if a year has elapsed since the limitation of the parental authority, which has not been lifted, or if the court ascertains that the parents try to revoke their consent to adoption only for material gain."
68 Article 125 Family Code.
69 Article 129 Family Law 1995.
70 Article 217(6) Family Code.
71 Article 9(1) Adoption (Consolidation) Act.
72 *Kearns v France* [2008] ECHR 1.
73 (Appl. No. 4261/02) Admissibility Decision of 22 May 2007.

circumstances, and the German courts had held extensive hearings into whether the girl's consent had been valid.

In both of these cases, the Court considered the variance of practices in European states concerning the revocation of consent. It emphasised that states hold a wide margin of appreciation, and as long as the various interests at stake have been balanced, it will be reluctant to interfere. Since the Court accepted the revocation laws of Germany, which are the strictest in Europe (along with Portugal), it seems unlikely that other more lenient laws will be contrary to article 8.

With respect, this is an area in which the Court has placed too great a weight on the decisions of the domestic authorities and highlights its deficiencies when dealing with issues of children's rights. When considering the binding nature of consent, flexible rules must apply that can adapt to the individual circumstances of the case, which in particular the German system is unable to do. Although it is important that the child feels secure in his or her prospective adoptive placement, and that prospective adoptive parents feel likewise, this must be weighed against the right of the child to grow up with his or her family of birth wherever possible. A prohibition on revocation of consent altogether, or placing a specific time limit on this, is insufficiently tailored to the interests of children, as it applies irrespective of whether an alternative family has been found for the child, or whether he or she faces a prolonged stay in unsatisfactory care. A more nuanced approach is needed, founded on the stage of adoption proceedings coupled with a decision based on the welfare of the child. No country has adopted such laws as yet, although Denmark is the closest where it allows consent to be withdrawn as long as this is not unreasonable with regard to the welfare of the child. As no international or regional convention has considered this yet, and the approach of the ECtHR has been overly deferent, this is an area where the rights of both parents and children are compromised.

4.1.2. PROMOTING ASSISTANCE DURING THE ADOPTION PROCESS

The second area in which birth mothers – and for that matter, fathers – are potentially subject to a particular disability is in the area of counselling and assistance during the adoption process. This is especially important in assisting an understanding of the nature of the adoption, and whether or not it will result in a complete termination of the relationship between the child and the birth parents, as well as ensuring that there are no misunderstandings concerning the process of adoption.

This is an area in which the international conventions are more specific in their requirements, although still leaving considerable leeway for domestic authorities. While article 21(a) of the UNCRC provides a wide requirement that "the persons concerned have given their informed consent to the adoption on the basis of such counselling as may be necessary", article 4(c)(1) of the Hague Convention goes one step further in requiring that those whose consent is necessary

> "have been counselled as may be necessary and duly informed of the effects of their consent, in particular whether or not an adoption will result in the termination of the legal relationships between the child and his or her family of origin."

The ECA 2008 echoes this requirement almost exactly.

The requirement of informed consent, especially in the context of the legal consequences of adoption, is particularly important in the area of intercountry adoption as differing practices exist throughout the world as to the legal effects of adoption for the relationship between the child and his or her birth family.

This was highlighted in the indictment in the case of *US v Focus on Children*, filed in the Utah District Court in 2007. Focus on Children was an intercountry adoption agency that arranged adoptions of Samoan children for American citizens. According to the indictment, the families of these children were falsely told that they were signing their children up to an educational program, where the children would be schooled in America and return at the age of 18. Such an arrangement would be consistent with the local concept of adoption and fostering, and the adoption documents were drawn up in English, which the majority of the families did not read.[74] Similar practices have been recorded in Vietnam[75] and the Marshall Islands,[76] and are reported to be widespread in many sending countries.[77]

It is not only accurate information that is needed, but also assistance in fully understanding the adoption process, and in coming to terms with the decision. Many mothers who are giving birth are young, illiterate and suffering considerable hardship.[78] It is important in such cases that these vulnerabilities are not taken advantage of, and that a mother's lack of competence or understanding is not exploited. UNICEF reported in Romania in 2005 that

---

74 *US v Focus on Children*, US District Court of Utah, Sealed Indictment (2007) <www.brandeis.edu/investigate/adoption/docs/FOCindictment.pdf> [1 February 2013].

75 United States: Department of State, *Summary of Irregularities in Adoptions in Vietnam* (25 April 2008) <http://vietnam.usembassy.gov/irreg_adoptions042508.html> [10 January 2012].

76 Jini L Roby and Stephanie Matsumura, "If I Give You My Child, Aren't We Family?: A study of birthmothers participating in Marshall-Islands-US adoptions" (2002) 5(4) *Adoption Quarterly* 7.

77 It is important to note in this respect that several sending countries in Europe allow simple adoption, which maintains the legal tie between the birth parents and their children (e.g. Bulgaria, Luxembourg, Poland, Portugal and Slovakia) meaning that the potential for confusion arises.

78 FJ Pilotti, "Intercountry Adoption – Trends, Issues and Policy Implications for the 1990s", in *Childhood* (1993, Instituto Interamericano del Nino) 165–177.

29 per cent of mothers who abandoned their children were under the age of 20, with another 28 per cent between the ages of 20 and 24.[79] Further, 63 per cent were single mothers, and 94.2 per cent were unemployed.[80] A similar picture emerges in Lithuania, where 73 per cent of mothers who abandoned their children were unemployed, with 40 per cent not having acquired secondary education.[81] Further, 67 per cent of children in Bulgarian institutions came from single parent families.[82] In a survey by the University of Nottingham of 89 maternity units across nine European countries,[83] 75 per cent cited poverty and financial hardship as a possible cause of child abandonment,[84] with 72 per cent stating problems with housing and homelessness.[85]

These figures demonstrate the vulnerable position of many birth mothers, which, added to the hardships and emotions of childbirth, may place them in a position where they feel unable to keep their children. Although a mother should at no time be discouraged from giving up her child if that is what she feels is best for both herself and the child, it is important that she be given the opportunity to think through her decision carefully, and with all relevant information.

To this end, some European states have included specific requirements for counselling for both mothers and fathers in their legislation and practice. Finland is a particularly good example of this, with the 2012 Adoption Act requiring that before consent is given, a consultation be arranged with the parents to explain the purpose, conditions and legal consequences of adoption. Parents must also be informed of the financial assistance and social services available to them if they wish to keep their child.[86] Belgian law makes similar

---

79 Stativa et al, above n 7, 31–32.

80 Ibid., 32.

81 Lithuania: Institute for Social Research, *Every Child Counts* (2005) 44 <www.sociologija.eu/media/file/every%20child%20counts.pdf> [6 June 2012]. This is compared to 89 per cent of the population (aged between 20 and 64) who had achieved at least upper secondary education in 2007 (Eurostat, *Total population having completed at least upper secondary education* (2012) <http://epp.eurostat.ec.europa.eu/tgm/table.do?tab=table&init=1&language=en&pcode=tps00065&plugin=1> [23 November 2012]). A similar picture is seen in Latin America, where a study found that the majority of birthmothers whose children were placed in intercountry adoption were aged between 14 and 18, were functionally illiterate, and either unemployed or worked in the informal sector (street vendors, beggars, prostitutes) (Pilotti, above n 78).

82 Kevin Browne, Shihning Chou and Kate Whitfield, *Child Abandonment and its Prevention in Europe* (2012, University of Nottingham) 8 <http://resourcecentre.savethechildren.se/content/library/documents/child-abandonment-and-its-prevention-europe> [7 February 2013].

83 Bulgaria, the Czech Republic, France, Hungary, Lithuania, Poland, Romania, Slovakia, and the United Kingdom.

84 Including 100 per cent of hospitals in Romania and the Czech Republic (Browne, Chou and Whitfield, above n 82, 11).

85 Including 100 per cent in hospitals in Slovakia and the Czech Republic (ibid.).

86 Sections 14, 21, 24 Adoption Act 22/2012.

provision, requiring the mother and father to be informed of the consequences of adoption by both social services and the tribunal before whom they given their consent. Such information must relate to their rights and assistance and advantages offered to families, as well as possible ways to resolve social, financial, psychological or other problems that may be posed by their situation.[87]

In other states, counselling is not required, but the court or authority taking the parents' consent must explain the consequences of adoption and its legal effects.[88] This is the case in England, where a CAFCASS officer (Children and Family Court Advisory and Support Service) must witness the consent of a parent or guardian to adoption.[89] In the organisation's guidance document, the officer is required to ensure that the consent given is unconditional, and given with a full understanding of the nature and effect of the order. Furthermore, the officer is advised to be vigilant about factors that might invalidate consent, such as incapacity due to mental ill health or learning disability.[90] By placing this obligation on government officials, the English parliament has established an additional check to ensure that the rights of children and their parents are protected.[91]

The impact that counselling can have may be seen in statistics reported from Germany, where in one study between 50 and 75 per cent of women who sought anonymity on birth changed their minds once counselling was provided.[92] Further, as can be seen in the table below, figures from Ukraine suggest that counselling can greatly affect the number of children abandoned in maternity units.

---

87 Article 348.4 Belgian Civil Code. In Latvia, the parents are required to sign a declaration stating: "I am informed regarding the possibility to receive social assistance and social services provided for families with children." (Hague Conference, *Country Profile: Latvia* (2010) <www.hcch.net/index_en.php?act=publications.details&pid=5087&dtid=42> [14 January 2012]).

88 Cyprus: section 7 Adoption Act 1995; Estonia: section 152(6) Family Law Act 2009; Ireland: section 39 Adoption Act 1952, section 3 Adoption Act 1976; Lithuania: article 3.212(4) Civil Code; Malta: article 119(1) Civil Code; Poland: Hague Conference, *Country Profile: Poland* (2010) <www.hcch.net/index_en.php?act=publications.details&pid=5093&dtid=42> [14 January 2012]; Portugal: article 1982(1) Civil Code; Slovakia: section 183(2) Civil Code.

89 Family Procedure Rules 2010, rule 16.32.

90 United Kingdom: CAFCASS, *Guidance for Witnessing Consent to the Making of an Adoption Order (in Partner and other Non-Agency Adoptions)* (2007) [6.4] <www.cafcass.gov.uk/pdf/CONSENT%20TO%20THE%20MAKING%20OF%20AN%20ADOPTION%20ORDER%20FPR%200411v2.pdf> [6 January 2012].

91 Of course, government regulation of consent does not necessarily ensure protection of rights, and has been one of the major problems in intercountry adoption in countries such as Cambodia, Guatemala and India. See, for example, David M Smolin, "Child Laundering: How the Intercountry Adoption System Legitimizes and Incentivizes the Practices of Buying, Trafficking, Kidnapping, and Stealing Children" (2006) 52 *Wayne Law Review* 113.

92 Deutscher Ethikrat, *Anonymous Relinquishment of Infants: Tackling the Problem* (2009, German Ethics Council) 28, <www.ethikrat.org/files/der_opinion_anonymous-relinquishment-of-infants.pdf> [15 June 2012].

Effect of counselling on child abandonment in Ukraine: 2004–2010[93]

	Number of children abandoned at maternity units	Number of children not abandoned after mothers received counselling
2004	1,549	102
2005	1,249	274
2006	998	431
2007	1,027	492
2008	909	522
2009	865	423
2010	719	524

The European Court of Human Rights has made clear on numerous occasions the procedural requirements inherent in the right to respect for family and private life under article 8. In particular, it has found that a parent has the right to be involved in the decision-making process to a degree sufficient to provide them with appropriate protection of their interests.[94] The exact requirements of article 8 will depend on the particular circumstances of the case, and the seriousness of the decision in question, but the authorities must ensure that in any case concerning adoption, parents who have established "family life" have the opportunity to be adequately informed of the process and involved in the procedure.[95]

The content of this procedural requirement was explored in the case of *Kearns v France*.[96] This case involved an Irish woman who fell pregnant through an extra-marital relationship. In February 2002 she travelled to France with her mother and a French lawyer, and requested an anonymous birth under French law. The day after the child's birth, in the presence of a nurse acting as an interpreter, she signed the record placing the child in state care. In May, the child was placed for adoption with a new family; however, in July, the mother returned to the hospital seeking the return of her child. When this was refused, as the two-month time period within which she could revoke her consent had passed, she made an application to the ECtHR alleging a violation of her right to respect for family life under article 8. She argued that the French authorities had a positive obligation to make all necessary arrangements to ensure that she understood the precise implications of her actions, including a clear and accurate translation of the technical legal provisions concerning her.[97]

93 Browne, Chou and Whitfield, above n 82, 7.

94 See, for example, *W v United Kingdom* [1987] ECHR 17; *R and H v United Kingdom* [2011] ECHR 844.

95 *X v Croatia* [2008] ECHR 641.

96 *Kearns v France* [2008] ECHR 1.

97 Ibid., [52].

The Court rejected her argument on the grounds that as an Irish national she had specifically chosen to give birth in France to take advantage of the anonymous birth laws in that jurisdiction. Furthermore, it held that the presence of a doctor and nurse with knowledge of English was sufficient, and article 8 cannot be construed as requiring the authorities to ensure the presence of qualified interpreters.

While the application failed on the facts, this case opens the door to the possibility of requiring states to ensure that birth parents sufficiently understand the consequences of placing a child for adoption. The fact that the applicant had chosen to travel to France for the birth was extremely detrimental to her case, but it is arguable that a mother who was already living in the country concerned and did not understand the procedure due to language or the complicated nature of the law in this area would be in a strong position to claim a violation of article 8. This case made clear that sufficient information and advice in a language that the parent can understand is still vital, even if these conditions were satisfied in the particular circumstances.

Although the international instruments are clear that the *effects* of consent must be clearly explained, there is a need for greater use of counselling for birth parents considering placing their child for adoption. While in theory, counselling "as may be necessary" is an appropriate requirement, the spirit of this safeguard has unfortunately not been taken up by many states who leave birth parents without psychological assistance when making this momentous decision.

4.1.3. CONCLUSION

In order to protect the rights of the child, it is important that he or she is not placed in adoption where it was possible to stay within his or her family; thus the rules concerning voluntary consent to adoption must be carefully tailored to provide birth mothers with time and assistance to make a careful and considered decision. On the other hand, the right of the child to be placed in a secure and stable environment as soon as possible, which will not be later disrupted, must also be considered, and a flexible approach should be taken that can assess the needs of the child in the individual circumstances.

This is an area which has been slow to develop in Europe; although procedural safeguards have been enforced through the ECtHR concerning participation in the decision-making process when a child has been removed from a family against the parents' wishes, there is relatively little consideration of voluntary placement of children and the protection of the mother in this respect.

If there is little consideration of the place of the mother, however, the place of the birth father in adoption proceedings is even more tenuous, often being overlooked or given only minor consideration. The next section will look at the role of fathers: how they can be recognised, and why it is important to do so.

4.2. CONSENT BY THE FATHER

4.2.1. THE IMPORTANCE OF ESTABLISHING PATERNITY

The importance of determining, and legally recognising, paternity for a child can be seen in three principal respects.[98]

First, article 7 of the UNCRC provides the right of every child to know and be cared for by his or her parents as far as possible. Although these rights may be seen as joint and severable, one will often flow from the other, and any restriction on the circumstances in which the father is identified and recognised can seriously impede the realisation of the child's right to be cared for by him. Although the father may not always be easily identifiable, where he is, there should be no distinction between the parents based on gender, with both taking equal responsibility for caring for the child, rather than the emphasis being placed solely on the mother as primary carer.

Second, and most importantly in the context of intercountry adoption, where the mother is unable to look after the child, the father or his extended family may be able to step in and provide an alternative home. Kinship care can be an important alternative care mechanism for children who are separated from their immediate families, and denying the biological father recognition effectively halves the potential placement options for the child. This was recognised in the English case of *Birmingham City Council v S*, where the Court held that:

> "Adoption is a last resort for any child. It is only be [sic] considered when neither of the parents nor the wider family and friends can reasonably be considered as potential carers for the child. To deprive a significant member of the wider family of the information that the child exists who might otherwise be adopted, is a fundamental step that can only be justified on cogent and compelling grounds."[99]

Finally, even if the father is not going to provide care for the child, it is important in terms of the child's right to know his or her origins. As will be discussed in

---

98 The acknowledgement of paternity is also important to the interests of both the father (who has a right to know and care for his child) and the state (whose welfare obligations can be lowered by passing responsibility onto fathers to support their children) however consideration of these issues does not fall within the ambit of this book.

99 [2006] EWHC 3065 (Fam); [2007] 1 FLR 1223, [73]. Cf *Re C (A Child) v XYZ County Council* [2007] EWCA Civ 1206; [2008] 1 FLR 1294, where Lady Justice Arden held that the Adoption and Children Act 2002 does not require, as a matter of policy, preference to be given to the child's natural family ([43]).

Chapter Nine, knowledge of origins can be important in forming a child's identity, and protects his or her rights to privacy and autonomy.

In this way, the place of the father in a child's life is intimately connected with the realisation of his or her rights in relation to adoption. Where acknowledgement of the father is denied, the child's rights to identity, to know and be cared for by his or her parents, and to be placed in intercountry adoption only as a last resort are jeopardised. This section will thus explore the circumstances in which the father can be involved in adoption proceedings, and where his consent is needed before a child can be placed in another family.

4.2.2. WHO IS REQUIRED TO GIVE CONSENT TO AN ADOPTION ORDER?

The primary distinction in laws regarding consent to adoption lies between the married, and unmarried, father. While in every European jurisdiction the married father has the same rights as the mother in consenting or objecting to an adoption order,[100] the unmarried father is placed in a somewhat more tenuous position.

The most restrictive jurisdiction concerning unmarried fathers is that of Malta, where only the mother of a child born out of wedlock need consent to the adoption, whether or not the father has recognised the child, contributed to his or her maintenance, or even cared for him or her.[101] Although in such circumstances the court must *hear* the father, his wishes or views do not have to be adhered to.[102]

Such an approach is inherently discriminatory, and relies on outdated assumptions concerning the attitudes, and aptitudes, of unmarried fathers. It assumes that mothers will be the primary carers for children, and that fathers play little or no role in their lives, and nor do they deserve to. Fortunately, the majority of jurisdictions do not adopt such a restrictive approach, although, as will be seen, the position of mothers is generally elevated over that of the unmarried father.

A significant number of countries require consent only from those parents who have acquired parental responsibility or who have custody of the child,[103]

100 The exception to this is in countries that recognise anonymous birth, in which case the mother, married or not, can give birth to a child secretly and place him or her for adoption. These jurisdictions, and the implications for fathers, will be discussed in Chapter Nine.

101 Article 115(3)(b) Civil Code.

102 Article 115(4)(b) Civil Code.

103 This must be differentiated from the discussion below as to parents who "have not lost parental responsibility". To have lost parental responsibility means that there has been neglect or abuse of the child, whereas acquiring it in the first place depends on political decisions in the country as to who deserves to be a parent.

including in Austria,[104] Denmark,[105] England,[106] Iceland,[107] Ireland,[108] Norway[109] and Sweden.[110] In each of these jurisdictions, an unmarried mother has sole parental responsibility or custody, although in all but Austria (where parental responsibility may only be granted upon joint application)[111] the father can apply to the courts to acquire this should he wish to do so.[112]

Several other countries base their adoption consent laws on the level of involvement with the child. In the Netherlands, adoption can only be ordered if neither parent raises an objection, but this can be ignored if the parent in question has not, or hardly ever, lived with the child as a family,[113] while in Switzerland, consent is not required from a parent who has not cared for the child to any meaningful degree.[114] Similarly in Latvia, although the consent of both the mother and father is needed, if custody is only vested in one of them, the consent of the other can be dispensed with if it is refused without good cause.[115] These laws require the unmarried father to be engaged with the

104 Article 181 Civil Code.

105 Article 7(2) Adoption (Consolidation) Act.

106 Section 52 Adoption and Children Act 2002.

107 Article 7 Adoption Act No 130/1999 (custody).

108 Only the guardian or the person who has control over the child (section 14 Adoption Act 1952).

109 Section 7 Act of 28 February 1986, No 8 relating to Adoption (custody).

110 Section 4:5a Children and Parents Code (1949:381) (custody).

111 Articles 166, 167 Civil Code.

112 Denmark: if parents are not married, the mother acquires sole custody unless the parents have shared a joint address within the ten months preceding the birth of the child. This can be altered by a joint agreement, or a court order (articles 7, 14 Act on Parental Responsibility); England: the father can acquire parental responsibility through birth registration, a formal agreement with the birth mother, or through a parental responsibility order under section 4(1)(c) of the Children Act 1989. When determining whether to grant a parental responsibility order, the courts will treat the child's best interests as paramount, and will consider the degree of commitment shown to the child, the degree of attachment between the child and the father, and the reasons for which the father is applying for parental responsibility (*Re H (Minors) (Local Authority: Parental Rights) (No 3)* [1991] Fam 151); Iceland: unmarried mothers have sole custody, but the father can make an application to the court (chapter II, Act in Respect of Children No 76/2003); Ireland: where the father and mother of an infant are not married, the father must make an application to the court to be appointed a guardian of the child (section 6A Guardianship of Children Act 1964); Norway: although the unmarried mother will have sole parental responsibility, the father can initiate judicial proceedings under the Children Act for custody, which will be decided according to the best interests of the child. However, the parent without parental responsibility will still be entitled to be heard at the adoption proceedings (sections 35(1), 48, 56 Act of 8 April 1981, No 7 relating to Children and Parents); Sweden: while the unmarried mother will have sole custody from the child's birth, parents can agree to joint custody by means of registration, or the father can initiate court proceedings. The parent without custody must still be heard in the adoption proceedings (sections 6:3(1), 6:4(2) and 6:6 Children and Parents Code (1949:381)).

113 Article 1:228 Civil Code.

114 Section 265a(1) Civil Code.

115 Section 169 Civil Law.

child's life, although this can be substantially difficult where the mother does not agree. Cyprus, on the other hand, also requires consent from any person who is liable by virtue of any order or agreement to contribute to the maintenance of the child, meaning that financial as well as social ties are considered.[116]

This approach, based on the care and commitment to the child, is substantially similar to that taken by the ECtHR in this area. For a father to have substantive or procedural rights in relation to the adoption of his biological child, he must first establish that he has family or private life with the child under article 8. Although the Court has long held that family life automatically exists between a mother and her child from the moment of birth in all but the most exceptional cases,[117] the same is not true for the father. Where a child is born within wedlock, family life has been found to exist automatically between the father and the child;[118] however, when the child is born to unmarried parents, the father will have to prove that he has established some kind of relationship with the child – a mere biological relationship is insufficient.[119] This can be extremely difficult, especially in cases concerning adoption where the mother gives the child up immediately after birth, or does not allow the father to have contact, and he is thus denied the opportunity of forming any connection with his child.[120]

This issue was addressed in the recent case of *Anayo v Germany*,[121] when the Court established a new form of protection under article 8 for *desired* family life (under the guise of private life). This case involved a man who had a relationship with a married woman for two years before she fell pregnant with twins. However, before the birth she returned to her husband, who was thus legally registered as the father of the children, and they refused the biological father contact. The Court held that the applicant, having never cohabited with his

116 Section 4(4)(a) Adoption Act 1995.

117 See *Marckx v Belgium* [1979] ECHR 2; *Odièvre v France* [2003] ECHR 86; *X v United Kingdom* (Appl. No. 7626/76) Decision of 11 July 1977.

118 *Berrehab v the Netherlands* (Appl. No. 10730/84) Decision of 21 June 1988.

119 *Schneider v Germany* [2011] ECHR 2416, [80].

120 An exception is made for fathers who have had a committed relationship with the child's mother, and if the couple had planned the pregnancy or were in a long-term relationship, family life can be found to exist between the child and father notwithstanding the fact that they have never met. This was the case in *Keegan v Ireland*, where the Court held that where there was a "marriage like" relationship between the mother and father that was sufficient to constitute family life between them, any child that was born out of this relationship *ipso jure* also formed part of this family unit (even if the relationship broke down before the child's birth) ([1994] ECHR 18). Cf. *MB v United Kingdom*, where the child was born as a result of an unplanned pregnancy during an extra-marital affair that had lasted six or seven months. In this case, the Commission found that there was no family life under article 8, even though the fact that the father had never seen the child was because the mother had obstructed his access ((Appl. No. 22920/93) Decision of 6 April 1994).

121 [2010] ECHR 393.

children or the mother, nor even met the children, did not have a relationship of sufficient consistency to qualify as having existing family life with them. Nevertheless, the Court noted that this was not the applicant's fault, as it was the result of the refusal of the mother to let him see the children. In a very cautious decision, the Court did not exclude that the applicant's intended relationship with his children fell within the definition of "family life" under article 8, and confirmed that, at the least, his "private life" was interfered with by a refusal of the German courts to allow him contact with his biological children.

While this case concerned contact, and not consent to adoption, it opens the door to greater recognition for unmarried fathers where they have been denied the opportunity to establish a relationship, and thus family life, with their child.[122] Nevertheless, the mother is still placed in a much stronger position, with the father needing to prove that he has taken steps to show commitment to the child (even if these are obstructed), while the mother automatically obtains rights from the moment of birth.

This refusal to recognise the equal importance of mothers and fathers in a child's life relies on, and perpetuates, outdated stereotypes. The difference in treatment between married and unmarried fathers reinforces the traditional conservative notion of what society considers a family *should* be, namely two parents joined in marriage, and punishes fathers who do not conform to this. As Bainham argues, there is a "tendency to equate the absence of cohabitation with the absence of responsibility" on the part of a father.[123] This was clearly seen in the 1984 European Commission on Human Rights case of *B, R and J v Federal Republic of Germany*, where an unmarried couple bringing up their child together applied for joint care and custody of the child. This was refused as under German law only the mother of a child born out of wedlock could have custody, with the authorities arguing that since the unmarried father may not be willing to assume any family obligations, it was in the child's best interests to exclude the father from acquiring equal legal status. The Commission agreed with this, and found that any discrimination against an unmarried man in

---

122 This case also involved complex issues concerning the relationship between biological and legal fatherhood. Because the children already had a legal father, it was not a matter of providing the child with two parents, but of the benefits of a relationship with a biological parent. It has since been applied to putative fathers who wish to establish paternity, although this was limited to establishing paternity for the purposes of contact with the child, not to overturn the legal presumption of parenthood within a marriage (see *Schneider v Germany* [2011] ECHR 2416).

123 Andrew Bainham, "When is a Parent Not a Parent? Reflections on the Unmarried Father and his Child in English Law" (1989) 3 *International Journal of Law, Policy and the Family* 208, 234. This can also be seen in the dissenting opinion in the ECtHR case of *Rozanski v Poland* where the judges noted that "[t]here is always a risk that paternity claims might be raised in a frivolous or vexatious way and be used to harass mother and child" ([2006] ECHR 545, [2]).

relation to his child arose from the couple's decision not to marry, and was therefore justifiable.[124]

Although this case was decided almost 30 years ago, presumptions about the different role of mothers and fathers, and the importance of the marriage tie, continue to pervade the Court's judgments. In the 1996 case of *McMichael v United Kingdom*, the Court found that the government's aim to provide a mechanism for identifying "meritorious" fathers to whom to accord parental rights was legitimate, as it protected the interests of the child and the mother, and that the conditions placed on unmarried fathers for obtaining parental rights were proportionate.[125] In particular, the Court approved of the Commission's finding that "it is axiomatic that the nature of the relationships of natural fathers with their children will inevitably vary, from ignorance and indifference at one end of the spectrum to a close stable relationship indistinguishable from the conventional matrimonial-based family unit at the other."[126] This approach was reaffirmed once more in the 2009 case of *Zaunegger v Germany*.[127]

Despite the conservative approach of the Court to article 8, relying on commitment to the child or mother in determining a father's substantive or procedural rights, most European jurisdictions simply require the consent of "both parents" to the adoption, regardless of their relationship with the child and even if they do not exercise parental authority, as long as they have not been *deprived* of this for abuse or neglect. This is the case in, for example, Albania,[128] Andorra,[129] Armenia,[130] Azerbaijan,[131] Belgium,[132] Bulgaria,[133] Croatia,[134] the Czech Republic,[135] Estonia,[136] France,[137] Greece,[138] Lithuania,[139] Luxembourg,[140]

124 (Appl. No. 9639/82) Decision of 15 March 1984.

125 [1995] ECHR 8, [98].

126 Ibid.

127 [2009] ECHR 1982. In this case, the court found that although domestic authorities could differentiate between unmarried mothers and fathers, the father must be given some opportunity of establishing a relationship with the child, and that care and custody could not be denied without an assessment of the child's best interests.

128 Article 246 Family Code.

129 Article 10 Qualified Law on Adoption of 21 March 1996 (as long as filiation has been established).

130 Article 118 Family Code.

131 Article 122 Family Code.

132 Article 348–3 Civil Code (as long as filiation has been established).

133 Article 89(1)(2) Family Code.

134 Petar Sarcevic et al, *Family Law in Croatia* (2011, Kluwer Law) 146.

135 Section 67(2) Act No 94/1963 Sb on Family.

136 Section 152(1) Family Law Act 2009.

137 Article 348 Civil Code (as long as filiation has been established).

138 Article 1550 Civil Code.

139 Article 3.212(1) Civil Code.

140 Article 351 Civil Code (as long as filiation has been established).

Moldova,[141] Monaco,[142] Poland,[143] Portugal,[144] Russia,[145] Serbia,[146] Slovenia,[147] Spain[148] and Ukraine.[149]

Importantly, Romania requires the consent of both parents *even if they have been deprived of parental responsibility or parental rights*.[150] However, this can be dispensed with if it is being abusively withheld and adoption is in the best interests of the child.[151] This is an important statement of principle, enacted after the adoption abuses that were widespread during the 1990s in that country. As a result, "abandonment" can no longer be used as a quick way to place a child in adoption, as the parents will still need to be located and consent to this. Although the mechanism for dispensing with consent is quite straightforward, this law nonetheless places a valuable check on improper placement in adoption.

4.2.3. ESTABLISHING PATERNITY: REGISTRATION, ACKNOWLEDGEMENT AND COURT ORDER

It can thus be seen that in the majority of European jurisdictions, the unmarried father will in principle be involved in the adoption decision, even if this is subject to some restrictions. However, the ability of the father to be involved is predicated on his recognition as a legal parent, and as such, it is important to review how legal paternity is established throughout Europe.[152]

In many jurisdictions, the joint registration of parents of a child born out of wedlock, or recognition by the father with the consent of the mother, is permitted, or even encouraged.[153] This promotes a spirit of joint responsibility

---

141 Article 124 Family Code.

142 Article 250 Civil Code (as long as filiation has been established).

143 Article 119(1) Family Code.

144 Article 1981 Civil Code. Under this law, even if parents are minors or do not have parental authority, they must still consent, as long as the child is not under a protective order by the court.

145 Article 129 Family Law 1995.

146 Article 99 Family Act.

147 Article 141 Marriage and Family Relations Act 1976.

148 Article 177(2)(ii) Civil Code.

149 Article 217 Family Code. In Georgia, a similar mechanism provides that an adoption of a child born outside wedlock requires the consent of the mother, but the order may not be made if the father has filed a petition for establishment of paternity (article 1252 Civil Code).

150 Articles 11, 12 Law No 273/2004.

151 Articles 12(2), 13 Law No 273/2004.

152 This book will only cover the establishment of legal paternity where no other father has been identified. It will not consider how the presumption of paternity can be overturned by a biological father of a child born to a mother married to a different man, nor will it consider how paternity can be disputed by a man who claims not to be the father, but who has been so named.

153 See, for example, Armenia: article 35(3) Family Code; Austria: articles 163c(1) and 163d(1) Civil Code; Azerbaijan: article 44.3 Family Code; Belgium: articles 319 and 319*bis* Civil Code; Croatia: Petar Sarcevic et al, *Family Law in Croatia* (2011, Kluwer Law) 134; Denmark:

for the child (even if the mother is still given the defining role), and is intended to foster cooperation. However, even where the mother does not consent, and registration cannot be achieved by agreement, in the majority of states, a father is able to establish paternity through a court order.[154] While in some states, such as the Czech Republic and the Netherlands, a court can overrule the mother's refusal to consent to recognition by the father based on psycho-social reasoning,[155] by far the more common mechanism is the establishment of paternity based solely on biological reality, available in, for example, Armenia,[156] Croatia,[157] the Czech Republic,[158] Estonia,[159] Finland,[160] France,[161] Georgia,[162] Greece,[163] Iceland,[164] Ireland,[165] Latvia,[166] Lithuania,[167]

section 2(1) Children Act; Estonia: sections 84 and 89(1) Family Law Act 2009, Finland: sections 15 and 16a Paternity Act 1975; Georgia: article 1190(1) Civil Code; Germany: sections 1592 and 1595 Civil Code; Iceland: article 4 Act in Respect of Children No 76/2003; Ireland: sections 7 and 7A Births and Deaths Registration Act 1880; Italy: articles 250–254 Civil Code; Latvia: section 155 Civil Law; Lithuania: articles 3.141–3.145 Civil Code; Luxembourg: article 335 Civil Code; Malta: article 86 Civil Code; Moldova: article 47(5) Family Code; Monaco: article 235 Civil Code; Montenegro: article 105 Family Law; Norway: section 4 Act of 8 April 1981, No 7 relating to Children and Parents – this is not required if parents are cohabiting; Romania: article 56 Family Code; Russia: article 48(3) Family Law 1995; Serbia: articles 47(4) and 50 Family Act; Slovakia: Slovakia, *State Party Report to the UN Committee on the Rights of the Child* (21 September 2006) CRC/C/SVK/2, [184]; Slovenia: articles 87, 90 Marriage and Family Relations Act 1976; Spain: articles 120, 124 Civil Code; Sweden: sections 1:3 and 1:4 Children and Parents Code (1949:381); Ukraine: article 126(1) Family Code. In France (article 332 Civil Code) and Switzerland (article 260b Civil Code), paternity based on acknowledgement by the father can only be challenged on the basis that the applicant is not, in fact, the father.

154 This approach was tacitly accepted by the ECtHR in the case of *Rozanski v Poland*. This case concerned a putative father who wished to register his paternity, but could not do so as the mother did not consent, and the possibility of commencing judicial proceedings was at the discretion of the authorities. The Court found that this circumstance placed the Polish legislation in violation of article 8. The system has since been changed ([2006] ECHR 545).

155 In the Czech Republic, the mother's refusal to consent can be overridden if she cannot consider the importance of her conduct, or if gaining her consent is obstructed by an impediment that can hardly be overcome (section 52(3) Act No 94/1963 Sb on Family). Further, in the Netherlands, the court can replace mother's consent provided that the recognition will not harm the mother's interests in an undisturbed relationship with her child (article 1:204 Civil Code).

156 Article 36 Family Code.

157 Petar Sarcevic et al, *Family Law in Croatia* (2011, Kluwer Law) 125.

158 Section 54 Act No 94/1963 Sb on Family.

159 Section 94 Family Law Act 2009.

160 Section 22(2) Paternity Act 1975.

161 Article 327 Civil Code. However, this can only be instigated by the mother or the child.

162 Article 1190(2) Civil Code.

163 Article 1475 Civil Code.

164 Articles 10, 15, 17 Act in Respect of Children No 76/2003.

165 Sections 35(1) and 38 Status of Children Act 1987.

166 Section 157 Civil Law.

167 Article 3.146(8) Civil Code.

Luxembourg,[168] Malta,[169] Moldova,[170] Monaco,[171] Montenegro,[172] Norway,[173] Poland,[174] Russia,[175] Serbia,[176] Slovakia,[177] Slovenia,[178] Spain,[179] Sweden[180] and Ukraine.[181]

On the other hand, in Azerbaijan, the father has no mechanism to establish paternity if the mother objects, no matter whether he can prove his biological relationship or not, thus placing the power solely in the hands of the mother.[182] If she does not wish for a father to be recognised and registered, he will not be. Restrictions are also placed on fathers in Belgium, Germany and England, where the court will decide whether or not to order DNA tests or recognise the father based on the welfare of the child. In Belgium, if the child is over 12 months, the court may refuse recognition where it is manifestly contrary to the interests of the child,[183] while in England the courts have found that although it is possible to compel a child to undergo scientific testing to establish paternity, this can only be done if it is in the child's best interests.[184]

It must be noted that in England, the order for biological tests to establish paternity is not dismissed, but instead suspended. A practical example of this was seen in the English case of *Re D (Paternity)* in which a child was vehemently opposed to participating in scientific testing, and wanted nothing to do with the putative father. The Court held that although it was in the child's best interests to know the truth about his paternity, and to know sooner rather than later, it was not in his best interests to force him to undergo tests that he was resolutely

168 Article 340 Civil Code. Proceedings must be instituted within two years of the child's birth.

169 Article 86 Civil Code.

170 Article 48 Family Code.

171 Article 232 Civil Code.

172 Article 99 Family Law.

173 Section 6 Act of 8 April 1981, No 7 relating to Children and Parents.

174 Article 85(1) Family Code. However, it should be noted that the biological father cannot claim paternity unless no other father is currently registered. If there is a father registered by presumption or acknowledgement, this cannot be challenged (Stanislawa Kalus and Magdalena Habdas, *Family Law in Poland* (2011, Kluwer Law) 109).

175 Article 49 Family Law 1995.

176 Article 57 Family Act.

177 Slovakia, *State Party Report to the UN Committee on the Rights of the Child* (21 September 2006) CRC/C/SVK/2, [184].

178 Article 90(2) Marriage and Family Relations Act 1976. The father must bring an action within one year of finding out that the mother does not consent to acknowledgement, and within five years of the child's birth.

179 Article 124 Civil Code.

180 Section 1:5 Children and Parents Code (1949:381).

181 Article 128(1) Family Code.

182 Unless the mother is dead, unable to be found or deprived of legal capacity (Article 44 Family Code).

183 Article 322 Civil Code.

184 See *Re D (Paternity)* [2006] EWHC 3545 (Fam); [2007] 2 FLR 26. This line of jurisprudence applies only to situations where the father is known and seeking recognition of paternity – it does not apply where the father is not known and permission is sought to identify him, which is discussed below.

against. As such, it stayed the order to undergo testing without limit of time, but with liberty to restore, and in the meantime instructed the guardian to explain to the child that the truth was easier to live with than to be in doubt, and that the issue could not be put off indefinitely.[185]

This approach is the most consistent with the UNCRC, ensuring that the child has the right to know and be cared for by *both* his or her parents, but allowing a degree of autonomy to the child to decide how, and when, he or she wishes to know these parents. Importantly, though, this autonomy is not absolute, and the authorities ensure that the child is given guidance to help him or her understand all the information, and why knowledge of both parents is important.

It is thus clear that throughout Europe there is a consensus (with Azerbaijan being the only exception) that the father should have some mechanism for establishing his paternity outside wedlock, either through consent or through a court order. However, this is only the case where he *knows* of the existence of the child. If he is not aware of the birth, either through ignorance or concealment, the possibility of obtaining a paternity order is purely theoretical. As such, it is important to examine the mechanisms in place in certain European states to ensure that the father is identified.

4.2.4. IDENTIFYING THE FATHER: INVESTIGATION AND DETERMINATION

In Croatia, Montenegro and Slovenia, this is achieved by placing an obligation on the registrar to contact the mother of a child born outside of wedlock, and ask her to give a statement concerning the identity of the father.[186] In England, new laws have recently been enacted under which where birth registration is undertaken by the mother herself, she is required to give information at that time concerning the identity of the father, except where she does not know his identity or whereabouts, or where she has reason to fear for her safety or that of the child if the father is contacted.[187]

---

185 Ibid. Note that this was a case involving a child who already had an established relationship with another man whom he considered to be his father, and was in fact being cared for by that man's mother, and his resistance to biological testing should be understood in this context. Another important factor in this case was that the child was not influenced by the biological mother one way or another, so could be truly seen to be making his own decision. See also *S v S; W v Official Solicitor* [1972] AC 24.

186 Croatia: Petar Sarcevic et al, *Family Law in Croatia* (2011, Kluwer Law), 135; Montenegro: article 100 Family Law; Slovenia: article 91 Marriage and Family Relations Act 1976.

187 This requirement was introduced by the Welfare Reform Act 2009. As of May 2014, the relevant part of this Act was yet to enter into force (note also that exceptions also apply to a child who has no father as he or she was conceived via certain types of IVF, where the father

These requirements are somewhat weak and allow the mother to avoid identifying the father by simply claiming ignorance. However, a more comprehensive investigation of the situation is undertaken by the authorities in Austria and Finland. In Austria, the authorities must ensure that paternity is established, except if the child's welfare would be adversely affected by such a determination,[188] while in Finland, there is an investigation of paternity by the Child Welfare Authorities.[189] However, such an investigation can be terminated by the mother if she objects to it (Finland),[190] or if she exercises her right not to disclose the name of the father (Austria).[191] Leaving the power as to whether or not the father is identified in the hands of the mother severely curtails the rights of the child and once again relies on an outdated stereotype concerning the role of men and women in caring for children. Moreover, it reinforces the myth that unmarried fathers are, *a priori*, less worthy or capable of caring for their children, and that mothers should be free to decide whether to involve them or not.

A more strict approach is taken in several Nordic jurisdictions. For example, in Iceland, there is a legal obligation on the mother to declare the paternity of her child born out of wedlock.[192] Where a child's paternity has not been stated within six months, the National Registry notifies a magistrate, who issues a letter to the mother insisting that she make arrangements for the declaration of paternity. She is informed of her duties in this regard and of the right of the child, as well as of the right of a man who believes himself to be the father of a child to instigate legal proceedings.[193]

In Denmark, on the other hand, the regional state administration has an obligation to institute filiation proceedings in cases where paternity has not been established.[194] The mother is summoned to a meeting, in which she has a duty to disclose information concerning with whom she has had sexual relations.[195] However, a violation of this duty is not punishable – although the authorities can bring a case before a court if it appears she is withholding information, if she claims not to be able to identify the father the case will simply be dismissed.[196]

has died, or where the father lacks capacity within the meaning of the Mental Capacity Act 2005).

188 Article 163a(1) Civil Code.

189 Section 8 Paternity Act 1975.

190 Section 8(2) Paternity Act 1975.

191 Article 163a(1) Civil Code.

192 Article 1 Act in Respect of Children No 76/2003.

193 Article 7 Act in Respect of Children No 76/2003. A similar situation occurs in Portugal, where the Civil Registry Office must refer the matter to the courts to investigate the identity of the father if he is not named on the birth registration (article 1864 Civil Code). The Court will then interview the mother to see who she thinks the father is (article 1865 Civil Code).

194 Article 7(1) Children Act.

195 Article 8(1) Children Act.

196 Hans Viggo Godsk Pedersen and Ingrid Lund-Andersen, *Family Law in Denmark* (2011, Kluwer Law) 85.

In Norway and Sweden, the investigation goes one step further, with legislation placing an obligation on the authorities to establish the identity of the father, with or without the help of the mother.[197] For example, in Sweden, if a father is not registered by the mother at birth, the governmental Social Welfare Committee is obliged to investigate paternity by making enquiries of the mother, as well as other persons who may be able to shed light on the situation.[198] The Committee will explain to the mother the legal, social and psychological importance of establishing paternity for her child, and also has various coercive measures at its disposal, including the fact that she will not receive child support if she refuses to cooperate without a valid reason.[199] The Committee can also seek a court order for DNA tests if there are a number of candidates for paternity.

This investigation is only stopped if it proves impossible to find the necessary information, if the continuation of the investigation would be detrimental to the child or expose the mother to stresses that cause danger to her mental health, or if the mother has already consented to the child's adoption. With regard to the latter, the Committee has an obligation to investigate the paternity of a child who has been placed for adoption; however, this may also be discontinued if the mother refuses to cooperate.[200] This exception undermines some of the principal reasons for which the father's identity is important, and highlights the fact that the investigation is concerned less with the child's rights, and more with removing the burden of supporting the mother from the welfare state. Nevertheless, even with undesirable limitations and exceptions, these jurisdictions establish identification of the father as the legal norm, which can contribute to creating a societal norm.[201]

---

197 Norway: section 5 Act of 8 April 1981, No 7 relating to Children and Parents; Sweden: section 5:2 Children and Parents Code (1949:381).

198 Section 2:4 Children and Parents Code (1949:381).

199 Section 4(1) Welfare Act (1996:1030).

200 Kees Jan Sarloos, *Dissertation: European Private International Law on Legal Parentage?* (2010, Maastricht University) 49.

201 Another mechanism is in place in the United States, where 30 states have introduced putative father registries. These allow a man to register his sexual relationship with a woman, in order to be informed of any subsequent court proceedings concerning the child. In some states, such as Florida, Virginia and Utah, any man who engages in a sexual relationship with a woman is deemed to be on constructive notice that a pregnancy, and subsequent adoption proceedings, may occur. As such, he has a duty to protect his own interests and must register with the putative fathers registry, otherwise there is no obligation on the state to seek him out for notification of any proceedings (Florida Statute section 63.088; Virginia Code section 6.3–2–1250 (E); Utah Code 2 78–30–4.13(1)(a)). In Illinois, on the other hand, if a putative father does not register within 30 days of birth, not only is he not entitled to notification of proceedings, but he is barred from asserting any interest in the child. In this way, failure to register constitutes a waiver of all rights, but also an abandonment of the child. A lack of knowledge of the pregnancy or birth is not deemed to be an acceptable reason for a lack of registration (750 Illinois Compiled Statutes 50/12.1). See also Laura Oren, "Unmarried Fathers and Adoption: 'Perfecting' or 'Abandoning' an Opportunity Interest" (2007) 36 *Capital University Law Review* 253, 270.

There have been many objections to such investigations, however, with concerns that they constitute an invasion of the right of the mother to privacy. The English law is a pertinent example of this, where although courts have been willing to make orders directing the mother to disclose identifying information about the father, and have authorised local authorities to seek to persuade mothers as to the benefits of doing so, where the mother continues to be recalcitrant, they have been unwilling to take further steps to force her cooperate.

This approach was epitomised by Mr Justice Munby in *X County Council v C*, where he held that:

> "The whole process [of seeking to force the mother to cooperate] smacks too much of the Inquisition to be tolerable. And it is not to be justified merely because we believe, however strongly, that what we are doing is being done in the best interests of a child ... We can reason with someone in the mother's position. We can seek to persuade. But we should not seek to force or to coerce."[202]

He was "deeply uncomfortable" with the proposition that women should be cross-examined for information on the father, and even more so that they should be open to imprisonment for criminal contempt of court for lying about the extent of their knowledge.[203]

There is no doubt that imprisonment of reluctant mothers would be counterproductive, as this would be contrary to the interests of the child. Coercion of mothers through other means such as cutting off welfare payments or child support is also unattractive, as it once again punishes the child, and may jeopardise his or her wellbeing. The solution must be to create circumstances in which mothers and fathers are treated equally, and the identification of the father is the social norm, which is what England has tried to achieve with its new laws concerning joint registration at birth, with the mother having to provide an explanation if she does not record a father.

It is also important to consider that there will be cases where the mother is genuinely ignorant of the identity of the father. This possibility was countered in Florida by the introduction of a law that required the mother to advertise in the media to establish his identity. The controversial laws obliged a mother of a child put up for adoption who did not name the father (whether through ignorance or unwillingness) to place a notice in a newspaper containing her name, a description of the possible father and of the mother including age, race, hair colour, height, weight, and the likely date and place of conception. Unsurprisingly, this law was later invalidated on the grounds that it was an unconstitutional intrusion on the privacy rights of mothers, including the right to avoid disclosure of personal matters.[204]

202 [2007] EWHC 1771 (Fam), [40]–[41].

203 Ibid., [38]–[39].

204 *GP*, 842 So 2d 1062. See also Jeffrey Parness, "Adoption Notices to Genetic Fathers: No to Scarlet Letters, Yes to Good-Faith Cooperation" (2005) 36(1) *Cumberland Law Review* 63.

A more nuanced approach has been adopted in Sweden, as was seen above, where the authorities invite the mother to name people that it *could* be, and investigate these possibilities. This system walks the thin line between the mother's right to privacy, and the right of child to be cared for by his or her parents and to know his or her origins; this is further strengthened by the mechanism under which the investigation can be halted if it would be detrimental to the child or expose the mother to stresses that cause danger to her mental health.

In addition to concerns regarding the mother's privacy and wellbeing, it is also important to consider that extensive investigations may result in a delay in placement for adoption. This has been one of the key concerns of intercountry adoption advocates, who argue that children are being placed in institutions and foster care for unconscionable periods of time while investigating placement options that may never eventuate.

The issue of delay was considered by the English Court of Appeal in *Re C (A Child) v XYZ County Council* where it was held that where the child was to be placed for adoption, there was no obligation to make *any inquiries* into the identity of the birth father unless these would genuinely further the prospect of finding a long-term carer for the child without delay.[205]

In this case, the mother had hidden the pregnancy from her family, friends and colleagues and immediately after the birth informed the local authority that she wished for the child to be adopted. The local authority applied to the courts for guidance as to the steps to be taken concerning identification of the father, and whether they should explore the possibility of placement with extended family. The Court considered that any further investigations into the father would delay the adoption process to the detriment of the child, and although the benefit to the child of knowing the identity of his or her father was acknowledged, it was not considered as important as providing the child with a permanent home as quickly as possible.

While in principle, when placing knowledge of identity against long-term care and development of the child, a quick placement will be preferable, this is a false dichotomy that fails to take into consideration the other benefits that identifying the father may bring, and overemphasises the possible delays this may incur. Where an intercountry adoption is being considered, identifying the child's father not only allows the child to have knowledge of his or her identity, it also raises the possibility that the child could be cared for within the country of origin, either by the father or by the extended family. Although some, such as Bartholet, argue that this results in an unnecessary delay with little hope of success, this relies once again on the assumption of unmeritorious and unwilling fathers, presupposing that unmarried fathers will not want to care for their children.[206]

---

205 [2007] EWCA Civ 1206; [2008] 1 FLR 1294, [3], Arden LJ.

206 See, for example, Elizabeth Bartholet, "International Adoption: Thoughts on the Human Rights Issues" (2007) 13 *Buffalo Human Rights Law Review* 151, 193.

Nor do delays have to be extensive. An investigation into the identity of a father, and his willingness to care for the child, does not have to, and indeed should not, take an inordinate amount of time. However, it is his right, and the right of the child, for this to be undertaken. Intercountry adoption should be a mechanism used to provide families for children who cannot be cared for by their own; to disregard the search for half the child's biological family would mean that instead of saving orphans, intercountry adoption would be creating them.[207]

4.3. CONCLUSION

The areas of law discussed in this chapter are much-overlooked features of the adoption framework, left to the discretion of domestic authorities with minimal guidance from the international instruments. It is in these areas, however, that a significant difference can be made in ensuring that children who are placed in intercountry adoption are only those for whom it is truly necessary.

The procedures set out in this chapter all revolve around ensuring that the child has the greatest chance of staying with his or her family of birth, through identifying all members of that family, and making sure that the decision to place the child for adoption is fully informed, and not made under pressure or emotional stress.

However, an even greater danger to the rights of children and birth parents in this respect lies in the ability of intercountry adoption to generate substantial profits, leading to many individuals and agencies seeking to exploit birth parents by improperly inducing their consent through payments, compensation, or misrepresentation. It is this dilemma that must now be considered.

---

207 See EJ Graff, *The Seamier Side of International Adoption* (10 May 2009, New York Times) <http://roomfordebate.blogs.nytimes.com/2009/05/10/celebrity-adoptions-and-the-real-world/> [19 April 2011].

CHAPTER 5

BUYING BABIES: THE INDUCEMENT OF CONSENT

One of the most serious problems that arises in relation to intercountry adoption, and the one that is most publicised by the media, is that of the improper inducement of consent from birth parents. Wherever intercountry adoption has occurred, there have been allegations of the buying of children, of birth parents being deceived, and of improper practices on the part of those facilitating the adoption process.

Although these problems are not confined to intercountry adoption, they generally do not arise in relation to domestic transactions, in large part because of the financial incentives that are associated with the intercountry adoption system.[1] This section will look at the requirements for valid consent under the international instruments, and the practical problems that have arisen in this regard. In doing so, it will use examples from various countries involved in intercountry adoption, including non-European countries.[2] However, the purpose of this chapter is not to enumerate all the scandals that have arisen concerning intercountry adoption in the last 25 years, nor to claim that all systems suffer from the same defects. It will bring attention to these incidents only to better understand the practices that the law must consider when regulating this area in Europe.

5.1. INTERNATIONAL INSTRUMENTS

The improper inducement of consent in relation to adoption is not explicitly considered under the UNCRC, with article 21 only covering improper gain by intermediaries, which will be discussed in more detail below. However, article 35 requires that member states take "national, bilateral and multilateral

1 This distinction has become less clear-cut in cases of surrogacy, and particularly private agency adoptions in the United States where competition exists for children (see, for example, *Flintshire County Council v K* [2001] 2 FLR 476).

2 Although the context of this book is regulation in Europe, examples of difficulties that have arisen in other countries can serve to illuminate areas that may also be problematic if rules are not appropriately drafted and enforced in Europe.

measures to prevent the abduction of, sale of, or traffic in children for any purpose or in any form", which has been taken up in the Optional Protocol to the UNCRC on the Sale of Children, Child Prostitution and Child Pornography. The Optional Protocol has 163 parties, including all European states save the Czech Republic, Ireland and Russia, who have signed but not ratified the Protocol.

This Protocol, which specifically refers to the Hague Convention on Intercountry Adoption, defines the sale of children as "any act or transaction whereby a child is transferred by any person or group of persons to another for remuneration or any other consideration",[3] and includes illegal adoption. Article 3(1)(ii) of the Optional Protocol requires that states ensure the punishment of those who improperly induce consent for adoption, while article 3(5) obliges states to take all appropriate legal and administrative measures to ensure that all those involved in adoption comply with the applicable international instruments.

More precise, however, are the provisions of the Hague Convention in this area. The impetus for the drafting of this Convention derived from the "very serious problems" that were being posed by intercountry adoption throughout the world, both for the rights of children, and for birth families.[4] Article 1 of the Convention, which contains its aims and objectives, states that in addition to establishing safeguards to ensure that adoptions take place in the best interests of the child and with respect for his or her fundamental rights, the purpose of the Convention is to ensure co-operation between states to prevent the abduction, sale of, or traffic in children.[5]

As was made clear in the Explanatory Report, however, the Convention does not prevent these practices directly, but rather works to counter them indirectly.[6] It does not regulate the criminal aspects of illicit activities in the field of intercountry adoption, but simply establishes civil and administrative procedures that make such activities more difficult.[7]

One of these procedures is the regulation of the giving and receiving of consent to intercountry adoption. The inducement of consent can be broken into two separate but related concepts, both of which are outlined in article 4 of the Convention. The first, in article 4(c)(2), requires that parents have given their consent freely; the second, under article 4(c)(3), requires that any consent given has not been induced by payment or compensation of any kind.

---

3 Article 2 Optional Protocol to the Convention on the Rights of the Child on the Sale of Children, Child Prostitution and Child Pornography (2000) 2171 UNTS 227.

4 Gonzalo Parra-Aranguren, *Explanatory Report on the Convention on Protection of Children and Co-operation in Respect of Intercountry Adoption* (1993) [2] <www.hcch.net/index_en.php?act=publications.details&pid=918> [7 February 2013].

5 Article 1(b) Hague Convention.

6 Parra-Aranguren, above n 4, [52].

7 Ibid., [53]–[54].

These two requirements for valid consent, although complementary, have widely different implications. While infringements of the former have been considered by all commentators as a violation of the rights of the child and the birth family, opinion is more varied with respect to the latter. Furthermore, whereas violations of the principle of free consent are generally more clear-cut, the line between payments inducing consent and free-standing donations is harder to define. These debates, and their implications for children and families involved in intercountry adoption, are set out below.

5.2. ELEMENTS OF CONSENT

5.2.1. "FREE" CONSENT

As outlined above, article 4(c)(2) of the Hague Convention requires that the parents have given their consent freely, which the Explanatory Report suggests is intended to prohibit consent that has been influenced by fraudulent claims or deliberate misrepresentations, as well as that induced by coercion by family, government, adoption facilitators or other third parties.[8] Unfortunately, allegations of malpractice in this area are widespread, and arise in a number of different countries. Pressure amounting to duress and undue influence has been reported, and birth mothers are alleged to have been coerced by their families, communities, or adoption facilitators to give up their children, and threatened or punished if they do not do so.[9] While some of these actions could be dealt with under the criminal law, it is extremely difficult to detect and enforce in situations of intra-familial coercion.[10]

8 Ibid., [141].

9 See United Nations International Commission Against Impunity in Guatemala (CICIG), *Report on Players Involved in the Illegal Adoption Process in Guatemala since the Entry Into Force of the Adoption Law (Decree 77-2007)* (2010) 5 <http://cicig.org/uploads/documents/informes/INFOR-TEMA_DOC05_20101201_EN.pdf> [7 February 2013]; David M Smolin, "The Two Faces of Intercountry Adoption: The Significance of the Indian Adoption Scandals" (2005) 35 *Seton Hall Law Review* 403; EJ Graff, *Anatomy of an Adoption Crisis* (12 September 2010, Foreign Policy) <www.foreignpolicy.com/articles/2010/09/07/anatomy_of_an_adoption_crisis?page=0,0> [4 February 2012].

10 In addition, the collusion of medical officials in inducing consent for adoptions is not uncommon. As was discussed in Chapter Four, studies in Ukraine, Bulgaria and Romania indicate that medical staff, hospital administrators and social workers have encouraged mothers to place children for adoption (Andy Bilson, *The Development of Gate-Keeping functions in Central and Eastern Europe and the CIS: Lessons from Bulgaria, Kazakhstan and Ukraine* (2010) 17 <www.unicef.org/ceecis/overview_Report_20_August_preface.doc> [7 June 2012]; Andy Bilson and Galina Markova, "But You Should See Their Families: Preventing Child Abandonment and Promoting Social Inclusion in Countries in Transition" (2007) 12(3) *Social Work and Social Sciences Review* 29, 37; Ecaterina Stativa et al, *The Situation of Child Abandonment in Romania* (2005, UNICEF) 98 <www.ceecis.org/child_protection/PDF/child%20abandonment%20in%20Romania.pd> [7 January 2013]. There have

To combat illegal inducement of consent, states have introduced requirements as to whom consent must be given. In Albania,[11] Andorra[12] and Cyprus,[13] consent must be given before a court, ensuring that there is judicial oversight of the system. However, other jurisdictions are much less strict in their requirements, with Denmark,[14] Georgia[15] and Hungary[16] allowing consent to be given before the social service authorities or other government official, and Azerbaijan[17] and Bulgaria[18] requiring only that the consent be notarised. In Armenia[19] and the Czech Republic[20] the oversight is even less rigorous, and consent may be taken by an official in the institution in which the child is staying before the adoption.

Regrettably, the involvement of judicial officials does not ensure the legality of the process. Judges were widely alleged to be colluding in enabling illegal adoptions from Guatemala,[21] and the cooperation of the police in other forms of human trafficking across the globe has been widely reported.[22] As the OSCE reports, "there is a very strong correlation between trafficking and corruption",[23] and the integrity of state officials cannot automatically be assumed. This has been one of the major arguments put forward in favour of allowing private and independent adoptions, as will be discussed below. However, despite these difficulties, the involvement of government and judicial officials in ensuring that

---

also been arrests of public officials in prominent sending countries such as Cambodia, Guatemala and Vietnam).

11 Article 247 Family Code.

12 Article 12 Qualified Law on Adoption of 21 March 1996.

13 Section 6 Adoption Act 1995.

14 Article 8(1) Adoption (Consolidation) Act.

15 Hague Conference, *Country Profile: Georgia* (2010) <www.hcch.net/index_en.php?act=publications.details&pid=5118&dtid=42> [14 January 2012].

16 Hague Conference, *Responses to Questionnaire of April 2010 on the abduction, sale of, or traffic in children and some aspects of the practical operation of the 1993 Hague Intercountry Adoption Convention: Hungary* (2010) <www.hcch.net/index_en.php?act=publications.details&pid=5451&dtid=33> [14 January 2012].

17 Article 122 Family Code.

18 Article 89(6) Family Code.

19 Article 118 Family Code.

20 Hague Conference, *Responses to Questionnaire of April 2010 on the abduction, sale of, or traffic in children and some aspects of the practical operation of the 1993 Hague Intercountry Adoption Convention: Czech Republic* (2010) <www.hcch.net/index_en.php?act=publications.details&pid=5451&dtid=33> [14 January 2012].

21 United Nations International Commission Against Impunity in Guatemala (CICIG), above n. 9.

22 For example, in 2007, the Albanian Ministry of the Interior referred to the Public Prosecution Office 157 criminal cases for corruption or trafficking against 219 police officers (Children's Human Rights Centre of Albania et al, *Albania Alternative Report to the Optional Protocol of the Convention on the Rights of the Child on the Sale of Children, Child Prostitution, and Child Pornography* (2012) 18, <www2.ohchr.org/english/bodies/crc/docs/ngos/Albania_AlbanianCoalitionAgainstChildTraffickingSexualExploitationofChildren_CRC61OPSC%20Report.pdf> [10 January 2013]).

23 L Mann and I Dolea, *OSCE Trial Observation Manual for the Republic of Moldova* (2006, OSCE/ODIHR) 79.

consent has been given freely and not been improperly induced continues to be the optimal situation, being substantially better than no oversight at all.

The involvement of state officials in confirming consent can also be beneficial in safeguarding another element of free consent – ensuring that the birth parents fully comprehend what it is they are consenting to. In different jurisdictions, domestic practices vary relating to the consequences of an adoption or a child being taken into care, and at times these have been exploited to give rise to illegal intercountry adoptions through fraud and misrepresentation.[24] This is particularly the case where "simple" adoption is used in the domestic system, under which the bond with the birth family is maintained and only a limited legal relationship is established with the adoptive family.[25]

This was highlighted in the indictment in the case of *US v Focus on Children* regarding children adopted from Samoa, as discussed in Chapter Four. A similar situation occurred in Cambodia with the well-publicised case of Lauryn Galindo, who worked with Cambodian "recruiters" who enticed poor families to place their children for adoption by telling them of the better life that they would have in the United States and promising an ongoing relationship with them, notwithstanding that this would not occur.[26]

Unfortunately, these are not uncommon stories, and similar allegations have arisen in relation to other countries also.[27] It is for this reason that the Hague Convention requires that all persons whose consent is necessary "have been

24 In addition to giving incorrect information, there have been reports of adoption facilitators tricking or drugging birth mothers into putting their thumbprint (as a signature) on blank pieces of legal paper, which are subsequently filled in to read as consent to adoption of the baby (see United Nations Committee on Human Rights, *Report of the Special Rapporteur on the Sale of Children, Child Prostitution and Child Pornography, Addendum: Report on the Mission to Guatemala* (27 January 2000, United Nations) E/CN.4/2000/73/Add/2, [35]).

25 International Social Service, *Fact Sheet No. 29: 'Simple Adoption' versus 'Full Adoption': The Effects of Adoption* (2007, ISS/IRC) <www.iss-ssi.org/2009/assets/files/thematic-facts-sheet/eng/29.Adoption%20simple-full.%20eng.pdf> [1 March 2011]. In the Explanatory Report to the Hague Convention, it was emphasised that the majority of countries have several different types and systems of adoptions, even within their country, all having different legal consequences. See Parra-Aranguren, above n 4, [134]. Within Europe, there are several countries that allow both simple and full adoption, including, inter alia, Belgium, Bulgaria, France, Italy, Luxembourg, Montenegro, Poland, Portugal and Slovakia.

26 Similar practices have been recorded in Vietnam, and are reported to be widespread in many sending countries (see United States Embassy: Hanoi, *Summary of Irregularities in Adoptions in Vietnam* (25 April 2008) <http://vietnam.usembassy.gov/irreg_adoptions042508.html> [22 October 2011]).

27 See for example: in Vietnam, United States Embassy: Hanoi, ibid.; in Nepal, Thomas Bell, *Nepal comes to terms with foreign adoption tragedy* (28 September 2011, BBC News) <www.bbc.co.uk/news/world-south-asia-15066220> [16 February 2012]; in Sierre Leone, EJ Graff, *The Makeni Children* (9 August 2011, Slate) <www.slate.com/articles/double_x/doublex/features/2011/the_makeni_children/that_was_the_last_time_we_ever_saw_these_children.html> [16 February 2012]; in Haiti, Karen Smith Rotabi, *Inter-country Adoption: Steep Declines in International Adoptions by US Parents Reflect Mixed Record* (18 November 2011, RH Reality Check) <www.rhrealitycheck.org/article/2011/11/18/intercountry-adoption-steep-declines-in-the-us> [21 November 2011].

counselled as may be necessary and duly informed of the effects of their consent, in particular whether or not an adoption will result in the termination of the legal relationship between the child and his or her family of origin".[28]

An example of good practice can be seen in the English approach in this area, where the courts have been careful to ensure that the consent of the birth parent has been obtained for the full termination of parental rights, and that this does not happen without their knowledge by operation of law. This was seen most pertinently in the case of *Re G (Foreign Adoption: Consent)*,[29] which involved a child born in Paraguay whose mother gave her consent to a simple adoption (full adoption not being available in Paraguay to a child who had living parents), and agreed to the fact that the child would be taken to the UK with English adoptive parents. However, when the adoptive parents applied to the English courts for an adoption order in that jurisdiction[30] the Court held that the birth mother must be given notice of the proceedings, as she had not given her consent to an order that would have the effect of a full adoption.[31] This approach is in line with article 27 of the Hague Convention, which prohibits the conversion of a simple adoption into a full adoption without the appropriate consent of the birth parents.[32] Unfortunately, however, such scrutiny cannot always be seen in either sending or receiving countries, leaving both children and parents in a vulnerable position.

5.2.2. IS CONSENT EVER FREE?

Even where such direct coercion, duress, fraud or misrepresentation is not present, questions must be raised as to the circumstances under which consent

28 Article 4(c)(1) Hague Convention.

29 [1995] 2 FLR 534.

30 This had to occur as the Paraguayan adoption was not recognised in England. Some of these difficulties are ameliorated by the ratification of the Hague Convention, which in article 23 provides for the recognition by operation of law of adoptions which have taken place in other Hague Convention parties, meaning that there does not have to be adoption proceedings in both the state of origin and the receiving state. Such recognition can only be refused if the adoption is manifestly contrary to its public policy, taking into account the best interests of the child (article 24 Hague Convention).

31 The need for additional consent in this case can be contrasted with the case of *Re C (Foreign Adoption: Natural Mother's Consent: Service)* [2006] 1 FLR 318, which concerned a child born in Papua New Guinea and adopted by an English couple working there at the time. As in *Re G*, the mother knew that the child would be taken to England, but in this case had given consent to an irrevocable adoption that would terminate all ties between herself and her daughter. As such, the Court held that when deciding an application for adoption under English law, her consent was valid for both the Papua New Guinean adoption, and also the English proceedings.

32 Although this article is a valuable protection of parental and children's rights, it does not address the problem that arises where parents have been misled into thinking they had given consent to a simple adoption that retained the relationship with their child, while actually signing away all parental rights and connection.

can truly be described as "freely" given. As David Smolin points out, the requirement of individual and free choice, under which the mother is an autonomous agent, does not fit the reality of the lives of most relinquishing mothers, and in many situations, mothers will feel that giving up their child is their only option in the face of financial hardship, lack of assistance, and societal pressures.[33] Such was the concern in England regarding this issue that the wording of the Adoption Act 1976, which referred to giving consent "freely", was changed to "unconditional" consent in the Adoption and Children Act 2002, to reflect the understanding that the decision to place a child for adoption is a very difficult one and the term "free" may not appropriately convey this.[34]

As was discussed in Chapter Four, birth mothers often come from vulnerable groups within society. In Romania and other parts of eastern Europe, Roma children have been disproportionately represented in adoptions,[35] while the majority of mothers who abandon their children are young, single and unemployed.[36] They often do not have the support and assistance needed to raise a child, either from their families, the wider community, or the state.[37]

Further, the financial inequality between birth and adoptive parents has been one of the key criticisms of intercountry adoption.[38] It has been argued by Smolin that since most birth parents are living on very low incomes, a relatively small amount of money would be sufficient to keep the family together, let alone the vast sums paid by adoptive parents to agencies to secure an intercountry adoption. This is an ethical dilemma, and arguably one that cannot be resolved through judicial mechanisms but must be addressed on political and social levels. As Bartholet points out, "long-term solutions lie in

---

33 David M Smolin, "The Two Faces of Intercountry Adoption: The Significance of the Indian Adoption Scandals" (2005) 35 *Seton Hall Law Review* 403, 489.

34 United Kingdom: Secretary of State for Health, *Adoption: A New Approach* (2000, HM Stationary Office) [8.27]–[8.28]. See also John Condon, "Psychological Disability in Women Who Relinquish a Baby for Adoption" (1986) 144 *Medical Journal of Australia* 117, 117.

35 Jolie Chai, *Forced Removal of Romani Children from the Care of their Families* (2005, European Roma Rights Centre) <www.errc.org/article/forced-removal-of-romani-children-from-the-care-of-their-families/2290> [3 February 2012]. See also, for example, Niki Kitsantonis and Matthew Brunwasser, *Baby Trafficking is thriving in Greece* (18 December 2006, New York Times) <www.nytimes.com/2006/12/18/world/europe/18iht-babies.3939121.html> [3 February 2012].

36 Ecaterina Stativa et al, *The Situation of Child Abandonment in Romania* (2005, UNICEF) 31–32 <www.ceecis.org/child_protection/PDF/child%20abandonment%20in%20Romania.pd> [7 January 2013].

37 There is a growing line of jurisprudence under the ECtHR requiring states to consider providing educational and psychological assistance to parents before children are taken into state care (see, for example *Kutzner v Germany* [2002] ECHR 160, *Saviny v Ukraine* [2008] ECHR 1741). However, the Court has yet to consider whether assistance should be provided before a child is placed voluntarily in adoption or alternative care.

38 See, for example, David M Smolin, "Intercountry Adoption as Child Trafficking" (2004) 39(2) *Valparaiso University Law Review* 281, 303–304; Elizabeth Bartholet, "International Adoption: Current Status and Future Prospects" (1993) 3(1) *The Future of Children* 89, 90.

reallocating social and economic resources, both among countries and within countries",[39] and this is not something that can be achieved in a short space of time.[40]

Smolin has suggested that it be mandatory that a family be offered assistance to stay together before any decision to give up the child is made, to ensure that the child is not being relinquished simply due to poverty.[41] This is in line with article 14 of the UN Guidelines for the Alternative Care of Children, which requires that financial or material poverty never be the justification for receiving a child into alternative care, but instead should be a signal to provide the family with appropriate support.[42] However, while these principles are laudable, economic reality prevents this from being universally achievable. The majority of sending states do not have the financial means to provide such assistance, and as a socio-economic right, the obligation to provide such support is limited by the availability of state resources.[43]

One solution to this could be to create a fund from payments made in valid intercountry adoptions, and offer this as support to each family. However, this would create a *de facto* welfare system in the country supported by intercountry adoptions, and may even operate to drive the push for more adoptions.[44] As the 2000 Special Commission on the Practical Operation of the Hague Convention pointed out, the support given to domestic services should not be such that it

39 Elizabeth Bartholet, "What's Wrong with Adoption Law?" (1996) 4 *International Journal of Children's Rights* 263, 269.

40 It should also be recognised that financial inequality is present in the majority of adoptions, whether voluntary or as a result of child protection measures, whether domestic or international (see, for example, Kristen Shook, "Does the Loss of Welfare Income Increase the Risk of Involvement with the Child Welfare System?" (1999) 21(9–10) *Children and Youth Services Review* 781, 782; Dorothy E Roberts, *Shattered Bonds: The Color of Child Welfare* (2002, Basic Civitas Books) 27; Duncan Lindsay, *The Welfare of Children* (1994, Oxford University Press) 153; Kristen Shook Slack, "Understanding the Risks of Child Neglect: An Exploration of Poverty and Parenting Characteristics" (2004) 24(9) *Child Maltreatment* 395; ED Jones and R McCurdy, "The Links Between Types of Maltreatment and Demographic Characteristics of Children" (1992) 16(2) *Child Abuse and Neglect* 201). It would be impractical, and extremely damaging, to eliminate all alternative child care mechanisms as a result of this, but it is nonetheless important to try to minimise the impact that such inequality has on the decision-making processes of birth parents and continue to strive through political, economic and social means to ensure greater equality in the future. See Smolin, above n 38, 310–11.

41 Ibid.

42 United Nations Human Rights Council, *Draft Resolution to the General Assembly: Guidelines for the Alternative Care of Children* (15 June 2009) A/HRC/11/L.13. Formally welcomed by consensus in the General Assembly on 20 November 2009. The ECtHR in *Wallova and Walla v Czech Republic* also indicated that where the separation of a family is due purely to a lack of material resources – in this case, a lack of suitable housing – the national authorities must address this by means other than separation (note that this case involved involuntary placement of children into state care, rather than voluntary placement) ((Appl. No. 23848/04) Judgment of 26 October 2006).

43 See, for example, article 4 UNCRC.

44 See discussion of the points system in Romania in Chapter Three.

would create a dependency on this income, and thus on intercountry adoption continuing and flourishing.[45]

As such, as Bartholet rightly suggests, this is not a problem that can be solved overnight, nor is it one to which a legal solution is readily available. Nevertheless, it must be a factor that is considered in the design and implementation of intercountry adoption legislation to ensure that not only individual placements, but the system as a whole, provides protection to families and children that is as comprehensive as possible given the available resources.

5.3. PAYMENTS AND COMPENSATION

In addition to the requirement that consent be given by the birth parents freely, article 4 of the Hague Convention requires that parents' consents "have not been induced by payment or compensation of any kind".[46] Furthermore, the Optional Protocol to the UNCRC includes within the definition of "sale of children", "improperly inducing consent, as an intermediary, for the adoption of a child in violation of applicable international legal instruments on adoption."[47]

One of the ways in which the Hague Convention tries to prevent payments and improper inducement is through the prohibition on contact between the prospective adoptive parents and the biological parents, or any other person who has the care of the child, until after certain conditions have been met. These include the child having been declared adoptable, an intercountry adoption being deemed to be in his or her best interests, and the appropriate consents having been obtained from the biological parents.[48] However, while this prohibition is important in preventing direct payments from prospective adoptive parents, it does not prevent indirect payments. Nor does it prevent the biological parents giving consent, knowing that later it is common practice for adoptive parents to give them some form of compensation. The Hague Convention permits "gifts" to the birth family and other bodies involved in the adoption process after the adoption has taken place, as long as there is transparency in the transaction, as was discussed in Chapter Three.[49]

---

45 Hague Conference, *Report and Conclusions of the Special Commission on the Practical Operation of the Hague Convention of 29 May 1993 on Protection of Children and Co-operation in Respect of Intercountry Adoption 28 November–1 December 2000* (2001) [47] <www.hcch.net/upload/scrpt33e2000.pdf> [7 February 2013].

46 Article 4(c)(3) Hague Convention.

47 Article 3(1)(a)(ii) Optional Protocol on the Sale of Children, Child Prostitution and Child Pornography.

48 Article 29 Hague Convention.

49 Hague Conference, *The Implementation and Operation of the 1993 Hague Intercountry Adoption Convention: Guide to Good Practice: Guide No 1* (2008) 65 <www.hcch.net/upload/adoguide_e.pdf> [7 February 2013].

Unfortunately, despite the prohibition in the international instruments, examples of baby buying, and inducement of consent by payment or compensation, abound in intercountry adoption. In Romania, adoption facilitators were reported to negotiate with mothers to abandon their children,[50] while in Cambodia they have been accused of offering money or food to birth families in return for their consent to adoption.[51] Prior to the shutdown of intercountry adoption in Guatemala, the UN Special Rapporteur on the Sale of Children, Child Prostitution and Child Pornography (UN Special Rapporteur) reported that the *majority* of cases of intercountry adoption in that country involved criminal offences including the buying and selling of children.[52]

In 1993, Elizabeth Bartholet argued that there was no evidence that such practices occurred, and that even if they did, they were isolated events and not widespread practice.[53] Bartholet suggested that there was an ample supply of children in institutions who were genuinely in need of homes, so there was no need for payments to be made for the surrender of children.[54] Unfortunately, such assertions have since been disproved. In the last 20 years there have been reports of widespread baby buying in numerous countries including Cambodia,[55] Ethiopia,[56] Guatemala,[57] Haiti,[58] India,[59] Romania,[60] Sri Lanka,[61]

---

50 Independent Group for International Adoption Analysis, *Re-organising the International Adoption and Child Protection System* (2002) <www.afaener.org/Rapport_FINAL_ang.doc> [30 January 2012].

51 Karen Smith Rotabi, *Inter-country Adoption: Steep Declines in International Adoptions by US Parents Reflect Mixed Record* (18 November 2011, RH Reality Check) <www.rhrealitycheck.org/article/2011/11/18/intercountry-adoption-steep-declines-in-the-us> [21 November 2011].

52 United Nations Committee on Human Rights, *Report of the Special Rapporteur on the Sale of Children, Child Prostitution and Child Pornography, Addendum: Report on the Mission to Guatemala* (27 January 2000, United Nations) E/CN.4/2000/73/Add/2, 13.

53 Elizabeth Bartholet, "International Adoption: Current Status and Future Prospects" (1993) 3(1) *The Future of Children* 89, 96.

54 Ibid.

55 United States: Department of Homeland Security, *Backgrounder: Operation Broken Hearts* (19 November 2004) <www.ethicanet.org/galindo_backgr.pdf> [5 February 2012].

56 Kathryn Joyce, *How Ethiopia's Adoption Industry Dupes Families and Bullies Activists* (21 December 2011, The Atlantic) <www.theatlantic.com/international/archive/2011/12/how-ethiopias-adoption-industry-dupes-families-and-bullies-activists/250296/?single_page=true> [8 February 2013].

57 United Nations Committee on Human Rights, above n 52.

58 SOS Children's Villages: Canada, *Haitian Children Sold for only $1.20* (21 February 2011) <www.soschildrensvillages.ca/News/News/child-charity-news/Pages/Haitian-Children-Trafficked-611.aspx> [16 February 2012].

59 David M Smolin, "Child Laundering: How the Intercountry Adoption System Legitimizes and Incentivizes the Practice of Buying, Trafficking, Kidnaping, and Stealing Children" (2006) 52 *Wayne Law Review* 113.

60 Independent Group for International Adoption Analysis, *Re-organising the International Adoption and Child Protection System* (2002) <www.afaener.org/Rapport_FINAL_ang.doc> [30 January 2012].

61 Janaka Perera, *Call for Re-Opening 'Prem Nivasa' Case* (23 January 2012, Asian Tribune) <www.asiantribune.com/news/2012/01/22/call-re-opening-'prem-nivasa'-case> [16 February 2012].

Vietnam,[62] and even China.[63] These practices have been reported not only in the media, but have been the subject of UN reports and judicial investigations in the United States and in countries of origin.[64] These are not unsubstantiated allegations, but verified accounts.

Bartholet is correct, however, that there are many children throughout the world that are genuinely without families and who could potentially benefit from intercountry adoption. However, this does not necessarily lead to the conclusion that there is therefore no need for facilitators to induce families to give their children up for adoption.

First, there is a problem with the type of children who are usually in institutional care in need of adoption. One of the principal reasons why prospective adoptive parents wish to undertake an intercountry adoption is the desire to adopt a young, healthy infant, which can take up to ten years in some sending countries – for example, the United States – but less than a year in intercountry adoptions.[65] However, contrary to popular belief, there is not a large number of such children available for adoption from institutional care, with available research indicating that most are older, suffering from disabilities, or otherwise thought to be "undesirable".[66] Second, the majority of children in institutional care still have some remaining family, who may have placed the child due to an inability to care for them on a temporary basis.[67]

Unfortunately, as Margaret Turano so aptly put it, "[b]abies, like any commodity, are subject to the law of supply and demand",[68] and when there are not enough children available for adoption in institutional care who fit the desirable characteristics that adoptive parents are searching for, facilitators often act to ensure that there is a ready supply. This was seen particularly in Guatemala, with the UN Special Rapporteur reporting that "recruiters use middlemen to seek out pregnant women who ... might be willing to give up their children or to sell them",[69] with estimates of the amounts given to birth mothers

62 Schuster Institute for Investigative Journalism, *Adoption: Vietnam* (22 February 2011) <www.brandeis.edu/investigate/adoption/vietnam.html> [5 February 2012].

63 See Schuster Institute for Investigative Journalism, *News Reports of Adoption Irregularities in China* (22 February 2011) <www.brandeis.edu/investigate/adoption/ChinaNews.html> [5 February 2012].

64 See, for example, United Nations Committee on Human Rights, above n 52; *US v Lauryn Galindo* No CR 03-0187 Z (Washington District Court); *US v Focus on Children* US District Court of Utah, Sealed Indictment (2007) <www.brandeis.edu/investigate/adoption/docs/FOCindictment.pdf> [1 February 2013].

65 See Jonathan G Stein, "A Call to End Baby Selling: Why the Hague Convention on Intercountry Adoption Should be Modified to Include the Consent Provisions of the Uniform Adoption Act" (2002) 24 *Thomas Jefferson Law Review* 39, 64.

66 See Chapter Three.

67 See UNICEF, *TransMONEE Database* (2012) <www.transmonee.org/> [22 May 2013].

68 Margaret V Turano, "Black Market Adoptions" (1976) 22(1) *Catholic Lawyer* 48, 48.

69 United Nations Committee on Human Rights, above n 52, [36].

ranging from Q6000 to Q7000 (around US$750 to US$900).[70] Such practices ensure that there is a supply of adoptable infants who are young and healthy[71] and whose parental ties have already been terminated (legally or otherwise).

Member states of the Hague Convention have adopted different approaches to payments and compensation made to birth parents, and when this should act as an impediment to adoption. In Ukraine, the prohibition is rather weak, amounting only to a restriction on enforcing agreements made to make payments to birth parents. In Bulgaria, on the other hand, there is no prohibition on payments to birth parents, as long as these have not *induced* their consent, a fact that the birth parents must confirm to a notary.[72] This is a very difficult provision to enforce, relying on the subjective intent of the birth parents, and on their own confirmation before government officials, where they are unlikely to self-incriminate.

On the other end of this spectrum is the approach of the United States to illegal adoption under the Optional Protocol to the Convention on the Rights of the Child. Upon ratifying this instrument, the US Government stated that the Senate's consent to the Protocol was subject to the understanding "that the term 'Improperly inducing consent' ... means knowingly and wilfully inducing consent by offering and giving compensation for the relinquishment of parental rights."[73] This reservation puts the onus back on the intentions of the adoptive parents or adoption facilitator, rather than on the consequences of the payments or compensation or the intent of the birth parents. As such, it is dangerously narrow, as it does not allow for the substantial effect that any offer of payment may have in countries of origin, no matter how well intentioned that offer may be.

It can be extremely difficult to determine when consent has been induced, or where payment has been ancillary to the decision to relinquish a child. In the United States, when dealing with domestic adoption, the law differentiates between payments that create any obligation on the parent to relinquish the child, and those that do not. Generally under US domestic law, significant expenses are permitted, including living expenses and medical expenses, but

70 ILPEC Guatemala, *Adoption and the Rights of the Child in Guatemala* (2000) [46] <www.iss-ssi.org/Resource_Centre/Tronc_DI/ilpec-unicef_english_report_2000.pdf> [5 September 2011].

71 In some countries, for example Vietnam, there have been reports of children being returned to the families from which they were bought if they were later found not to be healthy (United States: Department of Homeland Security, *Backgrounder: Operation Broken Hearts* (19 November 2004) <www.ethicanet.org/galindo_backgr.pdf> [5 February 2012]).

72 Article 89(6) Family Code. An additional safeguard is provided in the requirement that the Minister of Justice give consent for all intercountry adoptions, which will be refused where substantial offences have been committed in the course of the adoption procedure. It is not clear what may constitute "substantial offences" and what offences may be committed without affecting the consent of the Minister (Article 117 Family Code).

73 United States, Reservation to the Optional Protocol to the Convention on the Rights of the Child on the Sale of Children, Child Prostitution and Child Pornography.

cannot be made conditional on subsequent consent to adoption.[74] Indeed, this is one of the reasons why some prospective adoptive parents choose to turn to intercountry adoption, as under the domestic system, they may pay thousands of dollars only to have the birth mother change her mind.

However, as Smolin points out, domestic practice often confuses the intercountry adoption situation, as there is an impression that since it is legal to offer thousands of dollars to birth parents domestically in some countries, payment of what may seem in comparison small sums to birth parents in intercountry adoption is also legitimate.[75] This disregards the fact that while the average income in Europe's largest sending country, Russia, is US$13,911, in receiving countries such as France this figure is US$27,789 in the Netherlands US$25,740, and in Norway US$30,465.[76] What may seem to be reasonable compensation in these receiving countries may in sending countries be sufficient to induce consent to adoption for financial reasons.

For this reason, many European states prohibit any payment or compensation whatsoever to change hands during the adoption process. For example, in Denmark, an adoption order may not be issued if any of the parties required to give consent are to give or receive any kind of payment whatsoever, including compensation for loss of income.[77] Similar legislation exists in England,[78] Estonia,[79] Finland[80] and Iceland.[81]

Cypriot courts will also refuse to make an adoption order unless it has confirmed that there has been no payment or reward made, or agreed to be made, in relation to the consent. However, an exception is made for payments that are sanctioned by the presiding court itself.[82] While there is no problem in theory with courts deciding on what payments are acceptable, it is important this does not inadvertently circumvent the prohibition against payments, as was seen in the English case of *Re C (Adoption: Legality)*.[83] In this case, the adoptive mother had been turned down by domestic adoption agencies on numerous occasions as an unsuitable adoptive parent. After employing an independent agent to prepare a parenting report, she engaged a lawyer in Guatemala who

---

74 See Smolin, above n 38, 303.

75 Ibid., 311.

76 OECD, *Better Life Index* (2012) <www.oecdbetterlifeindex.org/> [8 February 2013].

77 Article 15 Adoption (Consolidation) Act.

78 Sections 95–96 Adoption and Children Act 2002.

79 Section 147(2) Family Law Act 2009.

80 Section 5 Adoption Act 22/2012.

81 Article 14 Adoption Act No 130/1999.

82 Article 7(1)(c) Adoption Act 1995. This is also seen in Malta where article 119(c) Civil Code requires that before making the adoption order, the court will ensure that the applicant has not received or agreed to receive, and that no person has made or given or agreed to make or give to the applicant, any payment or other reward in consideration of the adoption except such as the court may sanction.

83 [1999] 1 FLR 370.

facilitated an adoption for her in that country,[84] and in doing so, made payments that were beyond what could be justified as "reasonable expenses".[85]

As the adoption was not undertaken under the Hague Convention, on the child's arrival in England the adoptive mother applied for an English adoption order. Despite the illegal payments, and serious concerns on the part of social workers, the guardian and the court about the ability of the adoptive mother to provide for the needs of the child, the court granted the adoption order as the least damaging alternative. In doing so, the court waived the procedural breaches that had occurred, as any other decision would be contrary to the welfare of the child. He could not be taken away from the adoptive mother under domestic child welfare legislation,[86] and would in all likelihood continue to remain in the UK and be brought up by the applicant. All that would be different would be his legal status, and denying him this would be contrary to his welfare.[87]

The court noted that "[e]xcept for the very unusual case where there is a claim for a return of the child to the natural family, in all the reported cases the welfare considerations seem to have led the court to authorise or waive whatever breaches have occurred in the particular case".[88] In this way, adoptive parents know that even if they commit offences, including illegal payments or even not being approved as fit to adopt, they will in all likelihood be retrospectively authorised, thus giving little incentive to follow the law. Worryingly, the judge in this case reported that, at the time, there were 300 overseas adoptions conducted every year in England in accordance with the proper procedures, and between 75 and 100 that were not.[89]

Even where parents are trying to act within the law, retrospective approval of payments can create significant uncertainty, leaving it unclear to actors as to the legality of their actions. For this reason, it is important that if the court is to monitor payments, it does so in advance of the child's placement with prospective parents taking place, and establishes clear and easily available guidelines as to how it will conduct any evaluation.

---

84 This aspect of the case will be discussed below.

85 [1999] 1 FLR 370, 381.

86 Section 31 of the *Children Act* requires that the child be suffering, or is likely to suffer, significant harm before a care order is made concerning him or her.

87 [1999] 1 FLR 370, 376.

88 Ibid., 382. This problem was raised in relation to international surrogacy arrangements in the English case of *Re X and Y (Foreign Surrogacy)*. In this case, an English couple contracted with a Ukrainian woman to be their surrogate mother, paying her a monthly stipend, as well as €25,000 upon a live birth. Notwithstanding that these payments significantly exceeded the amount permitted under English law for surrogacy arrangements ("expenses reasonably incurred"), the courts retrospectively approved them. However, in giving this approval, Hedley J admitted that he was uncomfortable with the process, noting that by the time a case of this kind comes to court, the child's welfare would often be gravely compromised if the court refused to make an order ([2008] EWHC 3030 (Fam); [2009] 1 FLR 733, [24]).

89 Although this figure is now 15 years old, it serves as an interesting example of the dangers that arise when a permissive attitude is taken towards such conduct ([1999] 1 FLR 370, 376).

Clarity is of particular importance where criminal sanctions are imposed on those who make improper payments, for example in Albania, Spain, Sweden and Switzerland.[90] Unfortunately, however, criminal sanctions are not present in every state for those involved in illegal payments to facilitate adoption, a fact that the UN Committee on the Rights of the Child has consistently expressed its concerns over.[91] More worryingly, however, is the fact that in several European states the conduct of the birth parents is also criminalised. For example, in Romania, any parent of a child who requests or receives money or other material profits given in return for the adoption of a child faces a punishment of two to seven years imprisonment.[92]

While it is by no means desirable that birth parents should request or receive payment in return for placing their child for adoption, to penalise their conduct rather than, or as well as, that of the agency or adoptive parents who are making the payments is to punish the weaker party, who is often already the victim of exploitation and disadvantage. Further, it discourages birth parents from coming forward to report where their consent has been improperly obtained. A more effective response lies in criminalising the conduct of the buyers who are exploiting the weakness and vulnerability of birth parents, often on a systemic basis, rather than the birth parents for whom it will likely be a one-off occurrence.

5.4. IMPROPER FINANCIAL GAIN IN ADOPTION

The inducement of consent of birth parents flows from the existence of a demand for children for adoption, and the large sums of money that can potentially be made in facilitating an intercountry placement. For this reason, it is important not only to regulate payments to the birth family, but also to regulate the financial aspects of the intercountry adoption system as a whole so that it

---

90 Albania: article 124(a) Criminal Code; Spain: article 221(1) Criminal Code; Sweden: section 7:2 Penal Code (1962:700); Switzerland: article 23, Federal Law relative to the Hague Convention on adoption and of protection of children in cases of intercountry adoption.

91 See for example, the concluding observations on the Optional Protocol concerning Albania ((5 October 2012) CRC/C/OPSC/ALB/CO/1); Azerbaijan ((12 March 2012) CRC/C/OPSC/AZE/CO/1); Belgium ((11 June 2010) CRC/C/OPSC/BEL/CO/1); Bosnia and Herzegovina ((1 October 2010) CRC/C/OPSC/BIH/CO/1); FYR Macedonia ((30 November 2012) CRC/C/OPSC/MKD/CO/1); Greece ((20 July 2012) CRC/C/OPSC/GRC/CO/1); Montenegro ((1 October 2010) CRC/C/OPSC/MNE/CO/1); Serbia ((11 June 2010) CRC/C/OPSC/SRB/CO/1).

92 Article 70(1) Law No 273/2004. This same punishment is also given to an individual who intermediates or facilitates the adoption for the purpose of gaining material profits (article 70(2)). Similarly, in Spain, anyone who, for compensation, delivers a child for adoption shall be punished (article 221(1) Criminal Code).

remains a child protection mechanism, rather than a money-making enterprise involving the sale of, or traffic in, children.[93]

This concern was addressed in article 21(d) of the UNCRC, which requires that states take all appropriate measures to ensure that placements in intercountry adoption do not "result in improper financial gain for those involved in it". This was a controversial provision in the drafting stages, as some states wished for *any* financial gain to be prohibited in the intercountry adoption system. In particular, during the working group on the drafting of this article, the representative of Venezuela argued that in suggesting that it was legitimate to make "proper" financial gain from intercountry adoption, the door was opened for trafficking in children.[94] She suggested that "it was not possible to combat a market for children which obviously existed in the world and at the same time to institutionalize that market by permitting persons dealing with intercountry adoption to make 'financial gain'."[95]

Nevertheless, the provision was adopted by consensus, and its import later incorporated into the Hague Convention, article 32 of which reads:

> "1. No one shall derive improper financial or other gain from an activity related to an intercountry adoption.
> 2. Only costs and expenses, including reasonable professional fees of persons involved in the adoption, may be charged or paid.
> 3. The directors, administrators and employees of bodies involved in an adoption shall not receive remuneration which is unreasonably high in relation to services rendered."

This is reinforced by article 8 of the Convention, under which Central Authorities are obliged to take all appropriate measures to prevent improper financial or other gain, and deter all practices contrary to the objects of the Convention. While this instrument does not iterate how this is to be achieved, or impose penalties for a breach of these provisions, it is clear that prevention of improper practices in this field can only be accomplished through regulation and monitoring of the bodies involved in intercountry adoption.

One way that this has been achieved has been through the implementation of strict limitations on the actors who can be involved in this practice. While the Hague Convention requires a Central Authority – or several – to be established in each contracting state to ensure the implementation of the Convention, it also allows this Authority to delegate its functions to accredited bodies, subject to certain conditions. These include that the accredited body shall only pursue non-profit objectives, that it be directed and staffed by persons who are qualified by

---

93 Cf Elisabeth M Landes and Richard A Posner, "The Economics of the Baby Shortage" (1978) 7 *Journal of Legal Studies* 323.

94 United Nations Commission on Human Rights, *Report of the Working Group on a Draft Convention on the Rights of the Child* (2 March 1989, United Nations) E/CN.4/1989/48, [356].

95 Ibid., [729].

their ethical standards and by their training or experience to work in intercountry adoption, and that it be subject to supervision as to its composition, operation and financial situation.[96]

The number of accredited bodies varies from state to state. In many countries, such as Albania, Armenia, the Czech Republic, Georgia, Lithuania, Montenegro, Portugal, Slovakia and Slovenia, no accredited bodies are permitted to operate and all adoptions must go through the Central Authority itself, placing (in principle) a tight control on adoption. On the other hand, Italy has 65 bodies accredited under its Central Authority, and Spain 43, while Germany has 14, Greece eight, and the Netherlands six.

In many receiving countries that do permit accredited bodies, to ensure that only costs and expenses, including reasonable professional fees, are charged,[97] the Central Authority provides strict oversight of the fees requested of adoptive parents. Such a mechanism was actually proposed by the United States during the drafting process of the Convention, in response to fears concerning the loose definition of "reasonable" fees, and the latitude it may give accredited bodies.[98] While this was rejected in favour of more flexible language in the final instrument, several European countries have adopted this approach. For example, in Andorra, the criteria for setting the fees to be paid in adoption are included in a contract signed between the government and the individual accredited body, although the actual fee itself is not fixed.[99] Similarly, the costs of adoption in Finland are controlled by legislation, although the fee is set by the accredited body itself,[100] while Italy sets a maximum limit on fees that can be charged by accredited bodies both in Italy itself (€3,600) and in the sending country (€10,000).[101] On the other hand, states such as Norway and Sweden do not control the fees that accredited bodies can charge in advance, but instead examine the accounts of these bodies annually to ensure that no improper financial gain is being made.[102]

An additional check is put on accredited bodies in some countries by requiring them to state in advance the fees that will be charged to prospective adopters, and how they will be spent. In Denmark, the accredited body has to inform the Central

96 Chapter III, Hague Convention.

97 For a discussion of "reasonable" fees in relation to payments made to surrogate parents, see *X and Y (Foreign Surrogacy)* [2008] EWHC 3030 (Fam); [2009] 1 FLR 733.

98 Parra-Aranguren, above n 4, [531].

99 Hague Conference, *Country Profile: Andorra* (2010) <www.hcch.net/index_en.php?act=publications.details&pid=5082&dtid=42> [14 January 2012].

100 Hague Conference, *Country Profile: Finland* (2010) <www.hcch.net/index_en.php?act=publications.details&pid=5243&dtid=42> [14 January 2012].

101 Hague Conference, *Country Profile: Italy* (2012) <www.hcch.net/index_en.php?act=publications.details&pid=5153&dtid=42> [14 January 2012].

102 Hague Conference, *Questionnaire on Accredited Bodies in the Framework of the Hague Convention of 29 May 1993 on Protection of Children and Co-operation in Respect of Intercountry Adoption: Norway* (2009) <www.hcch.net/upload/wop/adop2010_no.pdf> [21 February 2013]; Hague Conference, *Country Profile: Sweden* (2010) <www.hcch.net/index_en.php?act=publications.details&pid=5097&dtid=42> [14 January 2012].

Authority of the fees it intends to charge, and if it wishes to increase that fee at any stage, it must inform the Authority in advance.[103] Similarly, in Italy, when an accredited body is applying for authorisation to undertake intercountry adoption facilitation, it must inform the Central Authority of the fees that it intends to charge, and if these are exceeded, disciplinary proceedings will be triggered.[104]

Although a fee schedule known in advance is of crucial importance for prospective adoptive parents and Central Authority oversight, of equal importance is a detailed breakdown of where the money will be spent. In particular, despite some sending countries – for example, the Czech Republic, Estonia, Georgia, Latvia, Poland and Portugal – requiring that all intercountry adoption services be free of charge, save for minor translation and notary expenses,[105] some states have reported that accredited bodies in receiving states have charged prospective adoptive parents for work that has been carried out for free.[106] For this reason, in Norway, in addition to all fees being published on the websites of the accredited bodies, the accredited body must also inform the Central Authority of the fees paid locally by them to government agencies and child caring institutions in the country of origin.[107]

However, as the Hague Guide to Good Practice points out, it is not simply the payment of official fees that is problematic, but also the unofficial and unaccounted for fees that are required to "expedite" paperwork, or help "facilitate" the adoption, without which Central Authorities and adoption agencies find that their applications are indefinitely delayed.[108] In this way, blame for profit-making activities should not be placed solely on accredited agencies, but, as the Hague Conference itself acknowledges, on "lawyers, notaries, public servants, even judges and university professors, [who] have either requested or accepted excessive amounts of money or lavish gifts from prospective adoptive parents".[109] Such transgressions can only be prevented by strict accountability, transparency and, most importantly, solidarity among states parties to the Convention. Where all parties refuse to pay such "donations", the practice will quickly be stamped out; however, as long as some

---

103 Hague Conference, *Country Profile: Denmark* (2010) <www.hcch.net/index_en.php?act=publications.details&pid=5128&dtid=42> [14 January 2012].

104 Hague Conference, *Country Profile: Italy* (2012) <www.hcch.net/index_en.php?act=publications.details&pid=5153&dtid=42> [14 January 2012].

105 Hague Conference on Private International Law, *Country Profiles* (2010) <www.hcch.net/index_en.php?act=conventions.publications&dtid=42&cid=69> [14 January 2012].

106 Hague Conference, *The Implementation and Operation of the 1993 Hague Intercountry Adoption Convention: Guide to Good Practice: Guide No 2* (2012) [352] <www.hcch.net/upload/adoguide2en.pdf> [22 February 2013].

107 Hague Conference, *Country Profile: Norway* (2010)<www.hcch.net/index_en.php?act=publications.details&pid=5090&dtid=42> [14 January 2012].

108 Hague Conference, *The Implementation and Operation of the 1993 Hague Intercountry Adoption Convention: Guide to Good Practice: Guide No 1* (2008) [235]–[236] <www.hcch.net/upload/adoguide_e.pdf> [7 February 2013].

109 Parra-Aranguren, above n 4, [527].

parties continue to participate in this practice, the system will be distorted and preference given to parents, agencies and states that are willing to pay.

5.4.1. "APPROVED NON-ACCREDITED BODIES"

The delegation of the powers and responsibilities of the Central Authorities to accredited bodies was a "very sensitive issue" in the drafting process of the Hague Convention.[110] Some participants resisted its inclusion, arguing that from experience "most of the abuses in intercountry adoptions arise because of the intervention of such 'intermediaries' in the various stages of the adoption proceedings."[111] Even more controversial, however, was the inclusion in the Convention of "approved non-accredited bodies".

Article 22(2) of the Convention allows a state to declare that certain functions of the Central Authority may be carried out by other bodies or persons that meet the requirements of integrity, professional competence, experience and accountability, and are qualified by their ethical standards and by their training or experience to work in the field of intercountry adoption (so-called "approved non-accredited bodies"). The functions that are permitted to be carried out by approved non-accredited bodies are restricted to those of preparing the reports on the prospective adoptive parents and on the child, matching parents with a child, and organising for the transfer of the child from the state of origin to the receiving state. Unlike "accredited bodies", however, approved non-accredited bodies are permitted to operate for a profit. The state must declare any such bodies that are authorised to operate to the Hague Bureau, and supervise their activities.

Article 22 represents a concession on the part of the drafters of the Convention to the most prolific actor in the intercountry adoption system, the United States.[112] As the Hague Conference itself admits, it is a compromise "between those who wanted the greatest safeguards possible developed in the Convention, and those who wished to preserve some freedom for individuals to operate."[113]

Although approved non-accredited bodies are subject to the same limitations on improper financial gains as are accredited bodies, allowing any profit to operate as a motivation for an intercountry adoption raises questions of objectivity and impartiality, and, as Watkins argues, is contrary to the Convention's objective of preventing the sale of, or traffic in, children.[114] It allows

110 Ibid., [242].

111 Ibid.

112 See Dawn Watkins, "Intercountry Adoption and the Hague Convention: Article 22 and Limitations upon Safeguarding" (2012) 24(4) *Child and Family Law Quarterly* 389, 404–405.

113 Hague Conference, *The Implementation and Operation of the 1993 Hague Intercountry Adoption Convention: Guide to Good Practice: Guide No 2* (2012) [619] <www.hcch.net/upload/adoguide2en.pdf> [22 February 2013].

114 Watkins, above n 112, 400.

scope for market forces and financial considerations to influence decision-making, in contradiction to the requirement under article 21 of the UNCRC that the best interests of the child always be the paramount consideration in decisions concerning adoption. An example of this can be seen in the ability of a Central Authority to delegate responsibility for compiling the report on the child who is the subject of the adoption, including deciding whether the adoptive placement is in his or her best interests under article 16(d).[115] Where an adoption agency has a vested financial interest in placing the child for adoption, its objectivity in coming to a decision as to whether this is in the child's best interests must be questioned. There should be no other priority or concern for an organisation when making decisions on a child's future than how best to promote the welfare of the child.

Another potential concern arising from profit-making agencies was seen in the English case of *Re C (Adoption: Legality)*, discussed above. In this case, the mother had been turned down for approval to adopt in two different English counties, and by a special needs adoption agency, for reasons including her ill health and her limited understanding of adoption issues. The applicant subsequently commissioned a parenting home study report from an independent agent, in contravention of English law, which prohibits anyone but an adoption agency from making arrangements for the adoption of a child. According to the judge in the case, this report was striking in its superficiality, and did not cover obvious and vital issues, including the ability of the applicant to understand the issues raised by adoption, or the emotional cultural needs of a child adopted from one culture to another.[116] In addition, it failed to mention the fact that the applicant had been deemed unfit to adopt a child domestically on three separate occasions. This report was used to complete an adoption in Guatemala, and as discussed above, the English courts retrospectively approved the illegal conduct, and allowed the adoption order.

The Court noted that many prospective adoptive parents who were rejected as adopters of English children were seeking children in other countries using independent reports and acknowledged that by allowing the application, it was effectively recognising a two-tier adoption system, under which children adopted domestically are granted substantially more protection than those coming from other jurisdictions.

5.4.2. INDEPENDENT AND PRIVATE ADOPTION

While adoptions involving accredited bodies and approved non-accredited bodies, regardless of their flaws, fall within the scope of the Hague Convention,

115 Although the final responsibility for the report remains with the Central Authority (article 22(5) Hague Convention).

116 [1999] 1 FLR 370, 375.

there are two other types of intercountry adoptions that do not comply with this instrument: independent adoptions and private adoptions.

Independent adoptions are those in which prospective adopters are approved as eligible to adopt in their home state by the appropriate authorities, and then travel to the state of origin to find a child to adopt directly without the assistance from the Central Authority or an accredited body in that state.[117] Thus the "independence" referred to is in the matching stage – it is the prospective adoptive parents themselves who make the match (or an adoption agency acting on their behalf). Private adoptions, on the other hand, are defined as those that are organised directly between the birth parents and adoptive parents, without the involvement of the state authorities in either jurisdiction before the approval of the match.

Although the majority of European states prohibit any form of independent or private adoption, independent intercountry adoptions continue to be permitted in the Czech Republic, Denmark,[118] Finland, Greece, Slovakia and Switzerland, and private adoptions in the Czech Republic, Finland, Greece, Slovakia.[119] Further, Austria, Cyprus, France and Germany, while prohibiting independent and private adoptions in countries that have ratified the Hague Convention, permit both forms of adoption in all other countries.[120]

While these adoptions are not strictly contrary to the Hague Convention – they simply fall outside its framework – they are contrary to the spirit of the instrument, and allow substantially more scope for abusive practices. They are

117 Hague Conference, *The Implementation and Operation of the 1993 Hague Intercountry Adoption Convention: Guide to Good Practice: Guide No 1* (2008) 16 <www.hcch.net/upload/adoguide_e.pdf> [7 February 2013].

118 Independent adoptions are only permitted under special circumstances, with the permission of the Danish Central Authority. In such a case, the Central Authority will play an active part in the adoption procedure – parents cannot carry out an adoption single-handed.

119 According to the responses of these states to the Hague Convention Trafficking Questionnaire (Hague Conference, *Responses to Questionnaire of April 2010 on the abduction, sale of, or traffic in children and some aspects of the practical operation of the 1993 Hague Intercountry Adoption Convention* (2010) <www.hcch.net/index_en.php?act=publications.details&pid=5451&dtid=33> [11 January 2012]).

120 Hague Conference, *Responses to Questionnaire of April 2010 on the abduction, sale of, or traffic in children and some aspects of the practical operation of the 1993 Hague Intercountry Adoption Convention: Austria* (2010) <www.hcch.net/index_en.php?act=publications.details&pid=5451&dtid=33> [14 January 2012]; Hague Conference, *Responses to Questionnaire of April 2010 on the abduction, sale of, or traffic in children and some aspects of the practical operation of the 1993 Hague Intercountry Adoption Convention: Cyprus* (2010) <www.hcch.net/index_en.php?act=publications.details&pid=5451&dtid=33> [14 January 2012]; Hague Conference, *Responses to Questionnaire of April 2010 on the abduction, sale of, or traffic in children and some aspects of the practical operation of the 1993 Hague Intercountry Adoption Convention: France* (2010) <www.hcch.net/index_en.php?act=publications.details&pid=5451&dtid=33> [14 January 2012]; Hague Conference, *Responses to Questionnaire of April 2010 on the abduction, sale of, or traffic in children and some aspects of the practical operation of the 1993 Hague Intercountry Adoption Convention: Germany* (2010) <www.hcch.net/index_en.php?act=publications.details&pid=5451&dtid=33> [14 January 2012].

particularly troubling as direct arrangements between birth and adoptive parents allow for the possibility of unacceptable pressure being placed on birth parents for their consent, or improper payments being made for this purpose. It can result in children being placed for adoption who would not otherwise have been, and although permission for the adoption will still have to be granted by the court, such retrospective examination will by virtue of process be more limited than participation of, and supervision by, the authorities from the beginning.

Further, independent adoptions have the potential to undermine the principle of subsidiarity by removing intercountry adoption from the scope of the wider child protection system. In advocating a greater role for independent adoption, Peter Hayes submits:

> "The Hague Convention takes as its starting point a child already within the system and does not consider how to reach out to more children in need ... Those involved in independent adoption see things differently. They act as they must to get a child out of chaotic conditions. They do not wait until a child is in the system, they work with the situation of the child as they find it. If this involves paying bribes, it is seen as adapting pragmatically to corruption that is already in place."[121]

By allowing such actions, independent adoption has the potential to bring children into intercountry adoption who would otherwise stay with their families, as was seen vividly in a UNICEF study that showed a significant drop in adoptions of children younger than three months where independent adoptions were restricted.[122] While it is true that the Hague Convention only works with children for whom intercountry has been deemed the best option, and does not itself reach out further into the community to assist other children in need, to suggest that this is a failing is to misrepresent the nature of the instrument. As discussed in Chapter Three, the Convention intends intercountry adoption to act as an extension of the domestic child protection system, as a last resort once family reunification and domestic placements have already been attempted and been found to be inappropriate. For parents to be sought out by independent agencies and facilitators, who have no obligation to offer assistance, short-term care options, or domestic solutions, fundamentally undermines both the rights of the child and of the family.[123] It should be the state authorities, who

---

121 Peter Hayes, "The Legality and Ethics of Independent Intercountry Adoption under the Hague Convention" (2011) 25(3) *International Journal of Law, Policy and the Family* 288, 300. It is not only independent adoption agencies that provide bribes, however, and the states report that even accredited bodies offer "incentives" to "expedite" placements (Hague Conference, *Guide to Good Practice No 1* (2008) [236]–[237]).

122 As quoted by the Hague Conference, *Report of the Special Commission on the Practical Operation of the 1993 Hague Intercountry Adoption Convention (17–25 June 2010)* (2011) [56] <www.hcch.net/upload/wop/adop2010_rpt_en.pdf> [8 February 2013].

123 The United Nations Special Rapporteur reported that in Guatemala, "[t]he recruiters use middlemen to seek out pregnant women who, because of poverty or prostitution, might be

(in principle) are impartial as to the outcome, who decide whether a child is in need of an adoptive placement, and when such a placement should be sought with foreign parents.[124]

5.5. CONCLUSION

As can be seen, while the rules regarding free consent are relatively clear (if not always adequately enforced), the regulation of inducement of consent is far from straightforward. The Hague Convention's failure to adequately regulate expenses, and make clear the appropriate circumstances in which payments can be made, makes it difficult to determine when and if there has been an inducement of consent by improper payment. Terms such as "reasonable" and "legitimate" expenses continue to be (perhaps purposefully) misunderstood by those involved in intercountry adoption, and many European states have insufficient controls to properly regulate such payments. This is a lost opportunity, and one that would have greatly added to the efficacy of the Convention, and the protection of children involved in intercountry adoption.

A further area in which the Hague Convention has fallen short is the regulation of "improper financial gain", and thus the implicit permission for "proper" gain within the intercountry adoption system. This same failing is seen in the permission given to states to delegate the powers of the Central Authority to profit-making non-accredited bodies. Where facilitation of intercountry adoption is delegated away from child welfare authorities, and to specialised agencies who operate solely in the field of intercountry adoption, this practice is removed from the child protection system and its primary role as a protection mechanism of last resort.

To adequately protect the rights of children in intercountry adoption, all payments or compensation must be prohibited, notwithstanding whether the prospective adoptive parents intended to induce consent, or whether the birth parents claim that it played no part in their decision. To allow payments opens the door for the emergence of a market in children, where children are treated as objects, rather than subjects of rights. Further, it may encourage children to be placed in alternative care where they would have otherwise stayed with their families, in violation of their rights under international law.

---

willing to give up their children or to sell them." (United Nations Committee on Human Rights, *Report of the Special Rapporteur on the Sale of Children, Child Prostitution and Child Pornography, Addendum: Report on the Mission to Guatemala* (27 January 2000, United Nations) E/CN.4/2000/73/Add/2, [13]).

124 This is not to suggest that state authorities are not themselves subject to allegations of corruption and improprieties in relation to adoption (see Chapter Three), but these are breaches of the law. The problems that arise in relation to independent adoption are a direct consequence of this practice, even if it is carried out completely legally.

CHAPTER 6

COMPULSORY ADOPTION: ADOPTION WITHOUT CONSENT

While the previous chapters have discussed the mechanisms by which parents may give their consent to adoption, and the safeguards necessary to preserve the child's rights in this respect, this section will examine the circumstances in which parental consent can be overridden or dispensed with.

Nearly every country in Europe has a mechanism for dispensing with the need for parental consent or overriding a refusal to give consent in certain circumstances, with the sole exception of Italy, where the consent of parents is not needed for adoption in the first place. This is an extremely important area, particularly as it relates to parental "abandonment", which is a common way in which many children pass into intercountry adoption.[1] In addition, conditions for dispensing with consent display the potential conflict or confluence between parental rights and children's rights, manifesting the weight that authorities give to family autonomy and protection from state interference. On the other hand, it is a testing ground for tensions between different aspects of the child's rights in the adoption process, challenging the state to find the appropriate balance between maintaining family ties and ensuring a safe and stable environment for the child.

As discussed previously, the Hague Convention and UNCRC leave many issues regarding consent to the discretion of member states, giving little guidance as to who must give consent, and none at all concerning when this can be dispensed with, or on what grounds. Article 5(3) of the Revised European Convention on the Adoption of Children of 2008 provides somewhat more content to this area, requiring that consent only be overruled or dispensed with on "exceptional grounds".[2] No guidance is given as to what may constitute "exceptional grounds", however, or the rights and interests to be taken into account when deciding these. As a result, it is not surprising that the mechanisms

1 See Hague Conference, *The Implementation and Operation of the 1993 Hague Intercountry Adoption Convention: Guide to Good Practice: Guide No 1* (2008) <www.hcch.net/upload/adoguide_e.pdf> [7 February 2013].

2 This test somewhat reflects the seminal decision of the ECtHR in *Johansen v Norway*, although in this case the court also required that the decision was motivated by an overriding requirement pertaining to the child's best interests ([1996] ECHR 31, [78]).

for dispensing with or overriding parental refusal to consent to adoption differ greatly between European states.

6.1. LOSS OF PARENTAL RIGHTS AND PARENTAL MISCONDUCT

The most common way in which consent is dispensed with is where the parents have been deprived of parental rights. This is the case in Armenia,[3] Belgium,[4] Croatia,[5] Denmark,[6] Estonia,[7] Greece,[8] Latvia,[9] Liechtenstein,[10] Lithuania,[11] Luxembourg,[12] Moldova,[13] Monaco,[14] Montenegro,[15] Norway,[16] Poland,[17] Serbia,[18] Slovakia,[19] Spain,[20] and Russia.[21] It is not possible in this book to go into detail concerning the mechanisms by which, and the substantive grounds for which, parental rights are deprived in these states. There are several countries, however, that refer in the legislation to the specific conduct of the parents when dispensing with consent. These vary from neglect or persistent mistreatment in Cyprus[22] and Malta,[23] to abuse of parental authority in the Netherlands,[24] risk of compromising the child's health or morals in France[25] and Monaco,[26] persistently grossly violating parental duties in

3 Article 119(c) Family Code.
4 A loss of parental authority will only carry with it a loss of the right to consent to adoption if the judge expressly stipulates this (Article 8 of the Law of April 24, 2003 modifying article 33 of the Law of Protection of Youth).
5 Petar Sarcevic et al, *Family Law in Croatia* (2011, Kluwer Law) 146.
6 Article 7 Adoption (Consolidation) Act.
7 Section 152(5) Family Law Act 2009.
8 Article 1552(b) Civil Code.
9 Section 169(3) Civil Law.
10 Article 179 Civil Code.
11 Article 3.214 Civil Code.
12 Article 351–2 Civil Code.
13 Article 125(a) Family Code.
14 Article 256 Civil Code.
15 Article 126(1) Family Law.
16 Section 7 Act of 28 February 1986, No 8 relating to Adoption.
17 Article 119(1) Family Code.
18 Article 99(1) Family Act.
19 Article 181(2) Act No 99/1963 Code of Civil Procedure.
20 Article 177(2)(ii) Civil Code, article 1827 Civil Procedural Law.
21 Article 130 Family Law 1995.
22 Section 5(1)(a) Adoption Act 1995.
23 Article 117(1)(a)(ii) Civil Code.
24 Or where the parent has grossly neglected his or her parental duties (article 1:228(2)(b) Civil Code).
25 Article 384–6 Civil Code.
26 Article 256 Civil Code. Portugal also has a similar condition, where the parent has put the child's safety, health, development or education in danger (article 1981 Civil Code).

Germany,[27] and not caring for the child to any meaningful degree in Switzerland.[28]

In some countries, the deprivation of rights must have lasted for a set period of time before an adoption can be granted. For example, in Russia, parents must have been deprived of their rights for longer than six months;[29] in Azerbaijan,[30] Georgia[31] and Slovenia,[32] this is extended to one year. Similarly in Ireland, consent can only be dispensed with where the parents have failed in their duties towards the child for one year.[33]

As will be discussed below in relation to determinations of "abandonment" by parents, setting time limits can help promote children's rights, but can also hinder them, depending on the length and flexibility of the time limit in question. On the one hand, it can give parents time to rectify their situation to admit the best chance at family reunification, and it can also allow time for authorities to search for kinship carers before an order is made for a non-relative or intercountry adoption. As was seen in Chapter Three, time limits are often used by countries in relation to placement for intercountry adoption, permitting this only once domestic solutions have been investigated for a certain time, ensuring that a child is only placed outside his or her country of birth where this is the only available solution.

On the other hand, inflexible time limits may also result in a child staying in institutional or foster care longer than he or she needs to, delaying an adoptive placement to his or her detriment. For example, where a child has been sexually abused, family reunification will often be undesirable, and if this is the case the best solution may be to allow an adoption as soon as possible. Long delays may also be extremely detrimental for a child. As noted above, in Georgia parents must have been deprived of their parental rights for one year before the child can be adopted. In addition, an intercountry adoption can only be considered if after six months a domestic placement has not been found. As a result, by the time the child is placed in a permanent home, 18 months may have passed. If this time is

27 It must also be the case that it would be disproportionately disadvantageous to the child if the adoption did not take place (section 1748(1) Civil Code). Parental consent may also be substituted if the violation of this duty, although not persistent, is particularly serious and it is probable that it will permanently not be possible to entrust the child to the care of the parent.

28 Article 265c(2) Civil Code.

29 Article 130 Family Law 1995.

30 Article 123.2 Family Code.

31 Article 1254(2) Civil Code.

32 Article 141(1) Marriage and Family Relations Act; Yves Brulard and Letitia Dumont, *Comparative Study Relating to Procedures for Adoption Among the Member States of the European Union, Practical Difficulties Encountered in this Field by European Citizens within the Context of the European Pillar of Justice and Civil Matters and Means of Solving these Problems and of Protecting Children's Rights* (2007, European Union).

33 Section 3(1)(I)(A) Adoption Act 1988. Consent can only be dispensed with if the court considers that the parents will continue to fail in their duties until the child reaches 18.

spent in an institution, his or her physical and emotional health will most likely be damaged, and development severely delayed.

6.2. OVERRIDING A REFUSAL TO CONSENT

Another common mechanism for allowing adoption without consent is where the parent's refusal is overridden in certain circumstances. In Cyprus[34] and Malta,[35] this is permitted if the court adjudges the consent to be "unreasonably" withheld, while in Austria[36] and Liechtenstein,[37] the standard is "refusal without legitimate grounds". The question arises: when is withholding consent unreasonable, or without justification? While the length of this book does not permit an in-depth examination of the application of these principles in all countries, the English experience can shed light on one possible interpretation.

Prior to the Adoption and Children Act 2002 (the provisions of which will be discussed in more detail below), English adoption legislation permitted parental consent to be dispensed with if it was withheld unreasonably, as well as on a range of other lesser used grounds.[38] The English courts took an objective approach to the test, considering the decision to refuse consent from the position of the hypothetical reasonable parent "with a mind and temperament capable of making reasonable decisions after having had regard to the totality of the relevant circumstances."[39] Such a parent would consider the welfare of the child, the nature of the current placement, the prospect of rehabilitation, the extent and regularity of contact, the age of the child, and the length of time in care.[40]

Most importantly, however, the courts made clear that they were not judging whether the parent had made the "right" or "wrong" decision, but whether it fell within a band of reasonable decisions that a parent could take.[41] As Lord Hailsham found in the seminal case of *Re W*, "[t]wo reasonable parents can perfectly reasonably come to opposite conclusions on the same set of facts without forfeiting the title to be regarded as reasonable."[42] This is similar to the margin of appreciation given to domestic governments under the ECHR – the ECtHR will not dictate the way in which a state must legislate, but will only

34 Section 5(1)(c) Adoption Act 1995.
35 Article 117(1)(a)(iii) Civil Code.
36 Article 181(3) Civil Code.
37 Article 181(3) Civil Code.
38 Section 3(1)(c) Adoption Act 1949; section 16(2)(b) Adoption Act 1976.
39 *Re M (Adoption or Residence)* [1998] 1 FLR 570, 598, per Ward LJ.
40 Justice Higgins, "Freeing for Adoption – the Legal Context" (1999) 5(3) *Child Care in Practice* 232, 239. Although Justice Higgins is a Northern Ireland Lord Justice of Appeal, these comments apply equally to the English context.
41 *Re W* [1971] AC 682.
42 Ibid.

decide whether it falls within a reasonable range of ways in which to respect the rights in question.

These laws that base dispensing of consent on "reasonableness" and "justification" retain their focus on parental rights and the autonomy of the family from state interference. Although the welfare of the child is a consideration in determining whether the parent is considered "reasonable" or not,[43] it will not dictate the outcome, and considerable discretion is still afforded to birth parents.[44] Parental rights are even more firmly entrenched in the consent laws of Andorra[45] and France,[46] which only allow refusal of consent to be overridden if that refusal is "abusive",[47] and in Romania, where even if parents are deprived of parental rights, their consent is still needed.[48]

On the contrary, some jurisdictions have shifted to a process that is more explicitly based on the welfare of the child, which is arguably more in accordance with the requirement under international law that children's rights be the paramount consideration in the adoption decision. In Poland, if the parents' refusal of consent is clearly contradictory to the child's welfare, consent can be dispensed with,[49] as it can be in Finland if there are not sufficient grounds for the denial of consent.[50] In Denmark consent can be dispensed with if it is of decisive importance to the welfare of the child,[51] whereas Malta goes even further, allowing consent to be dispensed with if it is in the best interests of the child.[52]

England made a similar shift from the "unreasonable" test under the Adoption Act 1976, to one that allowed consent to be dispensed with if the welfare of the child required it in the Adoption and Children Act 2002.[53] This is a significant change in approach, which can be seen as moving away from a position in which the wishes and interests of the birth parents are important considerations, to one in which the child's welfare is the paramount factor throughout the adoption process.[54]

---

43 In *Re L (An Infant)*, Lord Denning made clear that "in considering whether [the mother] is reasonable or unreasonable we must take into account the welfare of the child. A reasonable mother surely gives great weight to what is best for the child." ((1962) 106 SJ 611, CA).

44 *Re M (Adoption or Residence)* [1998] 1 FLR 570, 594.

45 Article 13 Qualified Law on Adoption of 21 March 1996.

46 Article 384-6 Civil Code.

47 Similarly in Greece refusal of consent can be overridden where this is abusively denied, on the condition the child has been living with the prospective adoptive family for one year (Article 1552(e) Civil Code).

48 This can be dispensed with if the refusal of consent is abusive, and the adoption order is in the child's best interests (articles 12(2), 13 Law No 273/2004).

49 Article 119(2) Family Code.

50 Section 11 Adoption Act 22/2012.

51 Article 9(2) Adoption (Consolidation) Act.

52 Article 117(1)(a)(vii) Civil Code.

53 Section 52 Adoption and Children Act 2002.

54 See Shazia Choudhry, "The Adoption and Children Act 2002, the Welfare Principle and the Human Rights Act 1998 – A Missed Opportunity?" (2003) 15(2) *Child and Family Law*

This shift can also be seen in the jurisprudence of the ECtHR in recent years. Traditionally, the Court approached the rights of children in the area of alternative care and adoption in a cautious manner, holding that they could, depending on their nature and seriousness, override the interests of biological parents.[55] This reflected the balancing approach inherent in article 8 – the Court must first examine the rights of the applicant, then determine whether any interference was proportionate to a legitimate aim pursued. However, in recent cases the Court has been taking a significantly more child-centred approach, and importantly in the decision of *R and H v United Kingdom*, it held that "[i]f it is in the child's interests to be adopted, and if the chances of a successful adoption would be maximised by [the relevant order], then the interests of the biological parents must inevitably give way to that of the child".[56] However, although the Court consistently states that strict scrutiny will be placed on domestic decisions that authorise adoption, this has not so far limited the wide range of systems in place in Europe to override or dispense with parental consent.[57] Scrutiny has instead focused on procedural aspects of adoption, access to information, inclusion in decision-making processes, and length of proceedings, rather than substantive challenges to the weight placed on parental or children's rights.[58]

In this way, it appears that few states have implemented the requirement under article 21 UNCRC that the best interests of the child be the paramount consideration in adoption in the area of parental consent. Parental rights are still very strongly represented in this field, and although several states have moved towards a more child-oriented approach, they are still very much in the minority.

6.3. ABANDONMENT, LACK OF CONTACT AND DISINTEREST

One of the major sources for intercountry adoptees is children who have been deemed abandoned by their parents. The precise grounds for dispensing with consent in this area vary significantly. While some states simply refer to

---

Quarterly 119. Parental rights are still maintained to a certain extent in light of the fact that the threshold conditions for removing a child from parental care (suffering or likely to suffer significant harm (section 31(2) Children Act 1989)) must still be met for a placement order to be made.

55 See *Johansen v Norway* [1996] ECHR 31.

56 [2011] ECHR 844, [77].

57 The jurisprudence surrounding unmarried fathers, which was discussed in Chapter Four, is an exception.

58 See, for example, *P, C and S v the United Kingdom* [2002] ECHR 604. For a further discussion of the change in approach by the ECtHR, see Claire Simmonds (Fenton-Glynn), "Paramountcy and the ECHR: A Conflict Resolved?" (2012) 71(3) *Cambridge Law Journal* 498.

"abandonment",[59] others use definitions such as not contacting the child,[60] being manifestly disinterested,[61] or not participating in his or her upbringing.[62] Others still dispense with consent where the parents' whereabouts or residence is unknown,[63] where the parents do not live with the child and have neglected their parental duties,[64] or where the child has been placed in an institution.[65] Different time limits are also placed on authorities before they can dispense with consent for these reasons, ranging from three months,[66] to six,[67] twelve,[68] or eighteen,[69] to "an extended period of time".[70]

Dispensing with parental consent on the grounds of abandonment requires a balancing act, which should not be characterised as a tension between parental rights and the rights of children,[71] but as one between different aspects of children's welfare. The ECtHR in the case of *Neulinger and Shuruk v Switzerland* outlined two considerations that must be balanced when determining the child's best interests: first, the maintenance of family ties except in cases where the family has proved particularly unfit; and second, the development of the child in

59 Cyprus: section 5(1)(a) Adoption Act 1995; Albania: article 250 Family Code; Andorra: article 14 Qualified Law on Adoption of 21 March 1996.

60 Hungary: section 48A Family Act 1952; Malta: article 117(1)(a)(vi) Civil Code.

61 France: article 350 Civil Code; Luxembourg: article 352 Civil Code.

62 Azerbaijan: article 123.1 Family Code; the Czech Republic: section 68(1)(a) Act No 94/1963 Sb on Family.

63 Slovenia: article 141(1) Marriage and Family Relations Act; Austria: article 181(2) Civil Code; Hungary: section 48A Family Act 1952; Montenegro: article 126(4) Family Law; Estonia: section 152(5) Family Law Act 2009; Switzerland: article 265c(1) Civil Code.

64 Moldova: article 125(e) Family Code; Montenegro: article 126(2) Family Law; Russia: article 130 Family Law 1995; Ukraine: article 219(2) Family Code.

65 Serbia: article 99 Family Act.

66 Montenegro (not living with a child and neglecting his or her care: article 126(2) Family Law); Portugal (not showing interest: article 1978(1) Civil Code).

67 Austria (whereabouts unknown: article 181(2) Civil Code); Azerbaijan (not participating in upbringing: article 123.1 Family Code); the Czech Republic (not manifested proper interest: section 68(1)(a) Act No 94/1963 Sb on Family); Hungary (whereabouts unknown: section 48A Family Act 1952); Moldova (not living with the child and evaded maintenance and education: article 125(e) Family Code); Montenegro (permanent residence unknown: article 126(4) Family Law); Ukraine (not live together: article 219(2) Family Code).

68 Albania (have not expressed concern: article 250 Family Code); Andorra (manifestly disinterested: article 14 Qualified Law on Adoption of 21 March 1996); Armenia (unjustifiably do not live with child for a year: article 119(d) Family Code); France: (manifestly disinterested: article 350 Civil Code); Hungary (not contacted: section 48A Family Act 1952) Luxembourg (manifestly disinterested: article 352 Civil Code); Slovenia (residence unknown: article 141(1) Marriage and Family Relations Act).

69 Malta (unjustifiably not having had contact: article 117(1)(a)(vi) Civil Code).

70 Estonia (whereabouts unknown: section 152(5) Family Law Act 2009). Switzerland similarly allows dispensing of consent when the parents' whereabouts are unknown for "some length of time" (article 265c(1) Civil Code).

71 As will be seen below, creating an automatic dichotomy between children's rights and parental rights is illogical, and presents a false conception of the relationship between parents and children. It is often through strengthening parental rights that children's rights are indirectly achieved.

a safe and secure environment.[72] In other words, states must choose between allowing greater time for family reunification, and minimising the time children spend in state care. There is no clear-cut answer to this dilemma, and in relation to intercountry adoption, the debate in this area is inexorably intertwined with that concerning institutional care.

As was discussed in Chapter Three, the use of institutional care as a temporary child-care facility is a common feature in many developing countries, especially where there is limited financial and social support available for families. A study of "abandoned" children in Romania found that the majority had been placed as a temporary measure while their parents had attempted to address their difficulties, and that the parents had not intended to relinquish them permanently.[73] Further, UNICEF reports that of 5,064 children left without parental care in Hungary in 2009, 4,962 of these were the result of the temporary inability of parents to care for the child. Similarly, in Moldova, such temporary inability was the cause of 993 placements of a total of 2,722, and Bosnia and Herzegovina 896 of 2,834.[74]

A declaration that a child has been "abandoned", however, has proved an easy way to provide more children for intercountry adoption. While proceedings for depriving a parent of parental rights can be time-consuming and expensive, requiring expert evidence and consideration of difficult issues of proof and attribution, many countries allow "abandonment" to be declared once a set period of time has passed since the child entered into care, or since the parent last visited the child.

This was particularly problematic in Romania, where the previous law on abandonment led to systemic abuses in order to free children more easily for lucrative intercountry adoption.[75] A team from Nottingham University found that during this time, often parents' visits to their children were not registered, so that abandonment could be more easily declared, and children placed with foreign families.[76] In addition, the Council of Europe have suggested that in more than 70 per cent of cases where parents had not visited the child, it was because of lack of money to travel to the institution, or because it was too far away.[77] As a result of this, the current Romanian law makes no provision for dispensing of consent for children who have been "abandoned", and the consent

72 [2010] ECHR 1053, [136].

73 University of Nottingham, *Legislation Relating to Child Abandonment in Romania* (2012) <www.nottingham.ac.uk/iwho/documents/childabandonment/romania/legislation-relating-to-child-abandonment.pdf> [7 February 2013].

74 UNICEF, *TransMONEE Database* (2012) <www.transmonee.org/> [22 May 2013].

75 Law No 47/1993.

76 University of Nottingham, *Legislation Relating to Child Abandonment in Romania*, above n 73.

77 Michael Hancock (Rapporteur, Council of Europe Parliamentary Assembly), *The Rights of Children in Institutions: follow-up to Recommendation 1601 (2003) of the Parliamentary Assembly* (8 February 2005) <http://assembly.coe.int/ASP/Doc/XrefViewHTML.asp?FileID=10786&Language=en> [7 February 2013].

of parents can only be dispensed with if they are unknown, deceased, declared missing in accordance with the law, or if it is proven that they are abusively refusing to give their consent,[78] thus substantially strengthening the rights of parents in this respect.

Russia has also addressed this issue, by limiting the circumstances in which parental consent can be dispensed with for intercountry adoption. Although for domestic adoptions, consent can be dispensed with if the parents do not live with the child and neglect their parental duties in relation to upbringing and maintenance for over six months, if the child is to be placed in an intercountry adoption, consent cannot be replaced by a court decision on abandonment.[79]

Where parents are deemed to have abandoned their child by operation of law, rather than a decision on the part of the parent, the rights of parents are significantly undermined. This is especially the case where parents place their children for economic reasons, with the intention of returning at a later date when their situation is improved. Where parental consent can be dispensed with after only three months of not living with, or showing interest in, the child,[80] there will often be insufficient time to allow parents to address the difficulties that have led to the child's placement in the first place, whether they be economic, social or behavioural. In this context, there is often a commonality of interest between parental rights and the needs of children, by which strengthening the rights of parents to care for their children can also benefit the child. Where parental rights are easily put aside, children who might otherwise return to their families may then be placed in intercountry adoption instead, depriving them of their right to family reunification, to retain their identity, and to not be placed away from their country, culture, language and environment unless this is necessary.

6.4. LEGAL ASSISTANCE TO PARENTS

When parental responsibility is being taken away from a parent, or the child is being placed for adoption against the parents' wishes, it is vital that they receive appropriate assistance to be able to challenge these decisions. While in Chapter Four the provision of emotional and psychological support was discussed for voluntary adoption, for adoption without consent the more crucial need is often legal assistance.

---

78 Articles 12, 13 Law No 273/2004.

79 Article 165 Family Law 1995 (see Olga Khazova, "Russia: Inter-country Adoption: Through a Large Amount of Law, Still a Lot of Uncertainty", in Andrew Bainham (ed), *The International Survey of Family Law* (2005, Jordans) 433, 444).

80 Such as Portugal and Montenegro, above n 66.

Article 9(2) of the UNCRC makes clear that in any proceedings that consider the separation of a child from his or her parents, all interested parties must be given an opportunity to participate. While it does not give any further guidance as to how this should be achieved, and on what grounds, it is clear that this right must be implemented in such a way that it is not theoretical, but effective in practice.

This has been an issue taken up by the ECtHR from a very early stage of its jurisprudence. In the seminal case of *Airey v Ireland*, the Court recognised the existence of positive obligations on states under article 6 to ensure a fair trial.[81] This case was brought by a woman seeking a divorce in Ireland, who had been denied legal aid and had to represent herself before the High Court. The ECtHR found that in litigation of this kind, involving complicated points of law, establishing facts, calling expert witnesses, and entailing a degree of emotional involvement inherent to marital disputes, a person in the applicant's position could not effectively present her own case.[82]

This principle was extended to cases involving taking a child into alternative care and freeing for adoption in *P, C and S v the United Kingdom*.[83] In this case, the mother of a child removed at birth alleged that her rights under article 6 had been violated because she had not been legally represented during the proceedings. The Court held that legal assistance will not always be indispensable, and in light of financial constraints on states, article 6 does not automatically provide the right to a lawyer. However, the Court went on to find that proceedings concerning care and adoption of children are of "exceptional complexity", and where the applicant's fitness as a parent is at the heart of the case, it will be especially difficult for her to conduct her own case.[84] As a result, to receive a fair trial, the applicant must be provided with appropriate assistance.

As such, it appears clear that for contested adoption decisions at least, biological parents will have a strong argument under the ECHR to be provided with legal support to assist them to fight against their separation from their child. While this may require an additional outlay of resources, as with many areas in the field of child protection, this is necessary to protect the rights of both the parents and, more importantly, the child to stay together wherever possible.

6.5. CONCLUSION

The involuntary severance of all legal ties between a child and his or her parents is an irreversible step, which should be accompanied by appropriate legal

81 [1979] ECHR 3.
82 Ibid., [24].
83 [2002] ECHR 604.
84 Ibid., [95].

safeguards, but no more. Too little deference to parental rights, and the rights of both the child and parent may be violated by unnecessary separation. Too great, and the child's mental and physical health may be damaged by institutional or other inappropriate alternative care. This is a fine line, which must be walked with the best interests of the child as the paramount consideration. The strength of parental rights should reflect the welfare interests of the child, protecting family ties, but yielding where the stability and security of the child is threatened.

A similar balancing act must be performed in terms of waiting periods for dispensing with parental consent, be it through abandonment or parental misconduct. The imposition of long and inflexible waiting periods before a child can be permanently placed for adoption in many European countries is worrying, as it can condemn children to long and potentially unnecessary stays in unsatisfactory placements. On the other hand, where this period is too short, family reunification may be unjustifiably curtailed.

No one solution exists to this dilemma, but its impact can be lessened by the establishment of appropriate domestic care alternatives, and parallel planning to ensure the minimum delay in placing the child permanently if necessary, with the maximum stability and care in the meantime. Furthermore, adequate focus on family reunification, and resources directed towards this, will help ensure that children are not in alternative care because of financial difficulties or temporary issues, and that the family can stay together wherever possible.

CHAPTER 7

CHILD PARTICIPATION: AUTONOMY AND PROTECTION

While the procedure by which parents can give consent, or have their consent dispensed with, is of great importance in protecting the rights of children in intercountry adoption, of equal importance is the right of the child himself or herself to be involved in the decision-making process, and to be adequately represented when doing so.

The participation of the child in the adoption process is important for three key reasons. First, it is of substantive value, as it enables decision-makers to come to better decisions. Without hearing the views of the child where it is possible to do so, and taking them into consideration, it is not possible to determine the content of the child's best interests.[1] As such, there can be no correct application of the welfare principle under article 3 UNCRC if the child's right to participate in the decision-making process is not respected.[2]

Second, hearing the voice of the child has procedural value. As Baroness Hale has emphasised, where the child is heard, he or she "will feel respected, valued and involved".[3] The child will be more likely to respect a decision where this is the case, which is of particular importance with respect to adoption. The success of an adoption depends heavily on the attitude of the child, and his or her willingness to integrate into a new environment. This is particularly the case in intercountry adoption, where the child will be integrated not only into a new family, but also into a new country, culture and society. Where the child is unhappy with the decision taken, he or she may cause difficulties in the placement, and pose a bar to its success. Even where the decision taken is against

1 United Nations Committee on the Rights of the Child, *General Comment 12* (20 July 2009) CRC/C/GC/12, [56].

2 Ibid., [74]. The connection between the child's participation and his or her welfare is made clear in the drafting of the UNCRC, in which the obligation to hear the child and take due consideration of his or her views (now contained in article 12) was originally part of article 3 on the best interests of the child (see Lothar Krappmann, "The Weight of the Child's View (Article 12 of the Convention on the Rights of the Child)" (2010) 18 *International Journal of Children's Rights* 501, 503–504).

3 Baroness Hale of Richmond, "Can You Hear Me, Your Honour?" (2012) 1 *Family Law* 30, 35. See also Sir Mark Potter, "The Voice of the Child: Children's 'Rights' in Family Proceedings" (2008) 3 *International Family Law* 140.

the child's wishes, the participation of the child can help him or her understand the process, and why that particular decision has been made.[4]

Third, there is symbolic value attached to the participation of the child.[5] The recognition of the autonomy of children was one of the most important features of the UNCRC, which will be discussed in more detail below. Previous international conventions and declarations of children's rights had focused on the need to protect children rather than empower them, and as such, the right of a child to participate was a landmark change in the way in which children were viewed before the law.[6] Only when children are permitted to participate in the decision-making process are they fully recognised as rights-holders, rather than passive recipients of rights. Such participation recognises that children are not only entitled to protection, but also to be viewed as individuals in their own right, capable of making decisions concerning their lives. As Katherine Hunt Federle suggested, "[t]he value of rights for children … lies in their potential to remedy powerlessness."[7] Children's views should not be listened to simply because it helps a decision be made, but because they come from someone who has a right to be heard.

7.1. INTERNATIONAL INSTRUMENTS

Since its inclusion in the UNCRC, the right to participation has fast become one of the cornerstones of children's rights law. Article 12 was designated by the Committee on the Rights of the Child as one of the four fundamental rights underpinning the UNCRC, reflecting the fact that it is not only a right in itself, but that it should also be considered in the interpretation and implementation of the other rights in the Convention.[8]

It reads:

> "1. States Parties shall assure to the child who is capable of forming his or her own views the right to express those views freely in all matters affecting the child, the views of the child being given due weight in accordance with the age and maturity of the child.

---

4 This was discussed in a Hague Abduction Convention case of *Re J (Abduction: Children's Objections)* [2011] EWCA Civ 1448; [2012] 1 FLR 457.

5 United Nations Committee on the Rights of the Child, *Day of General Discussion on the Right of the Child to be Heard* (29 September 2006) <www2.ohchr.org/english/bodies/crc/docs/discussion/Final_Recommendations_after_DGD.doc> [15 June 2012].

6 See League of Nations Geneva Declaration on the Rights of the Child (1924); United Nations Declaration of the Rights of the Child (1959).

7 Katherine Hunt Federle, "Children's Rights and the Need for Protection" (2000) 34(3) *Family Law Quarterly* 421, 439.

8 United Nations Committee on the Rights of the Child, *General Comment 12* (20 July 2009) CRC/C/GC/12, [2].

> 2. For this purpose, the child shall in particular be provided the opportunity to be heard in any judicial and administrative proceedings affecting the child, either directly, or through a representative or an appropriate body, in a manner consistent with the procedural rules of national law."[9]

Article 12(1) creates a two-fold obligation: first, that the child's wishes and opinions are ascertained; and second, that they are taken into consideration having regard to the age and maturity of the child. This is particularly important as many children who fall below the threshold of maturity required to make a determinative decision about their future will nonetheless have opinions and views that should be taken into consideration. Such a two-step approach ensures, at least in principle, that children are not ignored simply because they have not reached full maturity and decision-making capacity.[10]

Article 12 is an enabling provision, facilitating the exercise of the child's rights in other areas. Some articles, however, also make the requirement of participation explicit, reflecting the fundamental importance of the child's voice in certain decisions. This can be seen particularly in the case of state intervention in the family, and with regard to adoption. Article 9(2) requires that in cases concerning the separation of a child from his or her parents against their will, "all interested parties shall be given an opportunity to participate in the proceedings and make their views known", with children being an obvious "interested party".

Article 21(a), on the other hand, requires that before an adoption order is granted, "if required, the persons concerned have given their informed consent to adoption". This provision gives considerable scope to the domestic authorities, allowing them to determine whether a child's consent will be necessary. Even where the child's views are not determinative and the child does not have the right of consent under domestic law and article 21, adoption proceedings will still fall within the ambit of article 12 thus requiring the child to be consulted. This is further emphasised by the umbrella clause of article 21, which requires that the best interests of the child be the paramount consideration. As discussed above, without hearing the views of the child, and taking them into consideration, it is not possible to determine the content of the child's best interests.

It is important to note that the views of the child referred to in this chapter relate not to whether the child should be removed from his or her family – although this is of course another important issue in which the child's views

9 There have been declarations placed by three states in relation to this article. The governments of Kiribati, Poland, and Singapore all emphasised that the rights of the child as defined in UNCRC should be exercised with respect for parental authority, and in particular in accordance with customs and traditions regarding the place of the child within and outside the family.

10 However, this right is predicated on the ability of the child to form an opinion, which will be discussed in detail below.

should be considered[11] – but to the most appropriate form of long-term alternative care. The views of the child relate not to the choice between remaining with his or her family or being adopted, but rather whether he or she would prefer to be placed in kinship care, long-term foster care, domestic adoption, intercountry adoption or another form of alternative care.

The provisions of the Hague Convention do not place as much importance on the participation of the child as does the UNCRC. Under article 4(d), the competent authorities must ensure, having regard to the age and degree of maturity of the child, that consideration has been given to the child's wishes and opinions. This wording is particularly ambiguous. It does not make clear whether a young child's views must be sought, and then weighed according to age and maturity, or whether the state may take into account the child's age and maturity in order to determine whether or not to seek the child's views in the first place. These interpretations have vastly differing results, as will be discussed in detail below.

When it comes to determinative consent, the Hague Convention, like the UNCRC, leaves it to the discretion of states whether this will be required. Where such consent is deemed necessary according to domestic law, the Hague Convention places additional requirements on the authorities.[12] Under article 4(d) they are obliged, having regard to the age and maturity of the child, to ensure that: (1) he or she has been counselled and duly informed of the effects of the adoption and of his or her consent to the adoption;[13] (2) his or her consent has been given freely;[14] and (3) that the consent has not been induced by payment or compensation of any kind.[15]

The European Convention on Adoption 2008 provides greater guidance concerning the age of consent to adoption for children, requiring the consent of a child who has sufficient understanding, based on a set age limit prescribed by law, which must be no more than 14 years of age.[16] Further, it requires that a child whose consent is not necessary shall nonetheless be consulted and his or her views and wishes taken into account, having regard to his or her degree of

---

11 As is required under article 9(2) UNCRC. This right is particularly important as by the time the question of adoption arises, the child's choices may be severely limited by the decisions that have been made previously.

12 It is interesting to note the difference between a parent's consent, which is given "for adoption", and the child's consent "to the adoption". This move from the indefinite to the definite reflects the requirement that a child be permitted to express their views on, and objections to, specific adoptive placements or parents. In intercountry adoption, this is particularly important, as it allows the child to decide that he or she wishes to be adopted, but not outside his or her country, or to express his or her concerns about a certain placement option.

13 Article 4(d)(1) Hague Convention.

14 Article 4(d)(3).

15 Article 4(d)(4).

16 Article 5(1)(b) ECA 2008.

maturity.[17] This consultation may be dispensed with if it would be manifestly contrary to the child's best interests.[18]

7.2. ADOPTION IN EUROPE

The central theme that runs throughout these conventions is that the participation of the child – what form this takes, and the weight attached to it – will necessarily depend on the age, and maturity, of the child being adopted.

The age at which children are placed in intercountry adoption in Europe varies from country to country, and while in some it is predominantly infants who are adopted, in others, older children form the majority. Accurate statistics on intercountry adoption are difficult to compile, as they are not easily accessible in many countries of origin. Where they are, they are often not differentiated according to age.

Age of children placed in intercountry adoption in European states of origin: 2009[19]

	Total number	<1	1–4	5–9	>10
Albania	15	0%	33%	33%	33%
Czech Republic	28	7%	64%	29%	0%
Estonia	21	0%	29%	43%	29%
Hungary	122	6%	20%	54%	20%
Latvia	141	0%	37%	40%	23%
Lithuania	146	0%	21%	56%	23%
Slovakia	49	0%	63%	37%	0%

These statistics are somewhat surprising, given the common perception that predominantly infants are placed in intercountry adoption. The lack of children under one year old may reflect in part the amount of time that an adoption order takes to process, but is more likely to be accounted for by the requirement of subsidiarity of intercountry adoption to domestic alternatives, which has been implemented in many countries of origin (see Chapter Three). It is also acknowledged that these statistics are limited, not including major sending states such as Russia and Ukraine. However, confined though they are, they do indicate that in some countries at least, there are a non-negligible number of children being adopted who will have started to form opinions and the ability to express them.

17 Article 6.
18 Ibid.
19 Hague Conference, *Statistics* (2010) <www.hcch.net/index_en.php?act=conventions.publications&dtid=32&cid=69> [14 January 2013].

The following sections will discuss the participation of all ages of children, starting with situations in which children are deemed able to make autonomous and binding decisions, then discussing the role of the child where he or she is not of sufficient maturity to make a determinative choice. Finally, the participation of children who cannot formulate their own opinions will be discussed, and the way in which children's best interests can be protected through individual representation.

In undertaking this analysis, it is important to note the concerns expressed by the UN Committee on the Rights of the Child as to the significant differences in states between legislation and implementation.[20] In particular, children may not be heard independently, or their views may not be genuinely taken into account, despite legal requirements.[21] While this book will only look at the legislation in place in European jurisdictions, these problems with implementation must nevertheless be kept in mind.

7.3. AUTONOMOUS DECISION-MAKING

The right of the child to determine whether or not he or she will be adopted is not mandated by the international instruments; however, in all but a few European states this is a feature of the adoption legislation. The way this is regulated varies greatly from state to state, as will be outlined below.

7.3.1. STRICT AGE LIMITS

The most popular system for determining whether a child's consent is needed for adoption is the imposition of a strict age limit. Under such laws, once the child reaches a certain age, his or her consent is a necessary condition for

---

20 United Nations Committee on the Rights of the Child, *Concluding Observations: Azerbaijan* (12 March 2012) CRC/C/AZE/CO/3–4; *Concluding Observations: Czech Republic* (4 August 2011) CRC/C/CZE/CO/3–4; *Concluding Observations: Hungary* (17 March 2006) CRC/C/HUN/CO/2; *Concluding Observations: Lithuania* (17 March 2006) CRC/C/LTU/CO/2.

21 For example, in Russian child protection hearings (n.b. not adoption as this operates under different provisions), although the court must hear the child if he or she is eligible and asks to do so, there no obligation on the judge to take the initiative himself or herself, nor is the judge obliged to inform the child that he or she has a right to be heard. The content of the right is thus undermined, predicated on the child's prior knowledge of what he or she is entitled to under the law. For this reason, it is crucial that states go beyond legislation giving the child *permission* to be involved in proceedings, to *requiring* their opinions before an adoption goes ahead (see Masha Antokolskaia, *National Report: Russia* (date unknown, Commission on European Family Law) <http://ceflonline.net/wp-content/uploads/Russia-Parental-Responsibilities.pdf> [27 February 2013]).

granting the adoption order. This approach is in line with the ECA 2008, which requires

> "the consent of the child considered by law as having sufficient understanding; a child shall be considered as having sufficient understanding on attaining an age which shall be prescribed by law and shall not be more than 14 years."[22]

However, the Committee on the Rights of the Child has rejected the use of age barriers to the participation of children, arguing instead that age on its own should not be the criterion for deciding the weight to give a child's views.[23] As Hodgkin and Newell have emphasised, age should be a factor that is considered in conjunction with the maturity of the child, and the ability to understand and assess the implications of the decision that he or she is being asked to make.[24] In contrast to this, although the drafters of the Hague Convention refused calls to set a specific age limit upon which the consent of the child would be necessary, they anticipated that such age limits would be implemented by states of origin.[25]

The majority of European countries use binding age barriers for determining whether a child is capable of making an autonomous decision concerning adoption, although the age is set at widely different levels, from ten (Armenia,[26] Azerbaijan,[27] Estonia,[28] Georgia,[29] Lithuania,[30] Moldova,[31] Russia[32] and Slovenia)[33] to 11 (Malta),[34] 12 (Albania,[35] Andorra,[36] Belgium,[37] Croatia,[38] Latvia,[39] FYR

22 Article 5(1)(b).

23 United Nations Committee on the Rights of the Child, *General Comment 12* (2009) [20]–[21]. See also Rachel Hodgkin and Peter Newell *Implementation Handbook for the Convention on the Rights of the Child* (3rd ed, 2007, UNICEF) 183.

24 Hodgkin and Newell, ibid.

25 Gonzalo Parra-Aranguren, *Explanatory Report on the Convention on Protection of Children and Co-operation in Respect of Intercountry Adoption* (1993) [157] <www.hcch.net/index_en.php?act=publications.details&pid=918> [7 February 2013].

26 Article 24 Family Code.

27 Article 124.5 Family Code.

28 Section 151 Family Law Act 2009.

29 Article 1255 Civil Code.

30 Article 3.215 Civil Code.

31 Article 127 Family Code.

32 Article 132(1) Family Law 1995.

33 Article 137(2) Marriage and Family Relations Act 1976.

34 Article 115(3)(d) Civil Code.

35 Article 15(2) Law No 9695 of 19 March 2007.

36 Article 9 Qualified Law on Adoption of 21 March 1996.

37 Article 348-1 Civil Code.

38 Petar Sarcevic et al, *Family Law in Croatia* (2011, Kluwer Law) 146.

39 Section 169 Civil Law.

Macedonia,[40] Norway,[41] Portugal[42] and Spain[43]),[44] 13 (Poland[45] and France),[46] 14 (Bulgaria,[47] Germany,[48] and Italy)[49] and 15 (Luxembourg[50] and Monaco[51]).[52]

In none of these countries is it possible to displace the requirement, or for a child to be deemed mature enough to give consent at an earlier age. In many, however, the child's wishes will be taken into account even though they are not determinative, as will be discussed below.

The inflexibility of such a system fails to respond to the evolving capacities of the child, where the capability, understanding and intelligence of the child are acknowledged as working on a spectrum, not as a dichotomy. It also encourages authorities to place less weight on the views and opinions of those children under the age limit, regardless of their maturity. As Lansdown suggests, systems with fixed age limits usually reflect the economic and social priorities of the state, and promote traditional assumptions about the need for the protection of children.[53] It re-affirms patriarchal assumptions of children as lacking in competence, and is contrary to the spirit of the UNCRC.[54]

Furthermore Lansdown rightly argues that the development of children can depend significantly on environmental factors, and as such, children cannot be conceptualised as a homogenous group.[55] Factors such as social and economic status, ethnicity, family and age of siblings will also influence the child's

40 Article 123 Family Law (FYR Macedonia, *State Party Report to the UN Committee on the Rights of the Child* (12 November 2009) CRC/C/MKD/2, [43]).

41 Section 6 Law of 28 February 1986, No 8 relating to Adoption.

42 Article 1981 Civil Code.

43 Article 177(1) Civil Code.

44 Finland, the Netherlands, Denmark, Iceland and Sweden also set their age of consent at 12, but allow qualifications to this, and as such will be discussed in the next section. When reviewing its adoption law in the 1990s, England also considered setting 12 as the minimum age at which a child's consent would be needed, but did not include this in the final act, as it was considered that any age limit would place an unnecessary burden on the child (United Kingdom: Report to Ministers of an Interdepartmental Working Group, *Review of Adoption Law* (1992, Department of Health and Welsh Office) [9.5]).

45 Article 118(1) Family Code. The Guardianship court may exceptionally declare that consent is unnecessary if the child is not capable of giving consent. I have not included this in the category of age limit with exceptions, as it is intended to deal with situations of mental incapacity, not age related incapacity.

46 Article 345 Civil Code.

47 Article 89(4) Family Code.

48 Section 1746 Civil Code.

49 Article 7 Law 184/1983.

50 Article 356 Civil Code.

51 Article 249 Civil Code.

52 Note that these two countries fall beyond the range of age limits deemed acceptable under the ECA 2008 (although neither are parties to the Convention).

53 Gerison Lansdown, *The Evolving Capacities of the Child* (2005, UNICEF) 49 <www.unicef-irc.org/publications/pdf/evolving-eng.pdf> [7 February 2013].

54 See also Lansdown, ibid., 50.

55 Ibid., 26.

capacity,[56] and in particular, he argues that gender will greatly affect the development, and consequently the competency, of the child.[57] Any limit will as a consequence be necessarily arbitrary, and will deny some clearly competent children the opportunity to decide their own future.

It also may be that by setting an inflexible age limit, in addition to some children being denied the chance to make a decision when they are clearly capable, some children conversely may be forced to make decisions that they are not ready for. Taylor, Tapp and Henaghan have argued that

> "it is unethical to give the child the opportunity to express their views in the form of a choice or preference between the options before the Court *unless* the child is able to understand the Court process, the role they are being offered in the process and the potential consequences of expressing a choice or preference."[58]

Forcing children to make determinative decisions beyond their capacities may not only result in a decision which runs counter to his or her best interests, but may also be psychologically harmful. Article 5 of the UNCRC emphasises that the capabilities of the child evolve over time, and that it is necessary that those responsible for caring for him or her provide assistance and guidance in the exercise of his or her rights. This necessarily involves ensuring that too great a burden is not put on the child too early in a manner that would be detrimental.[59]

The Committee on the Rights of the Child has also made clear that the child must be permitted to choose not to exercise his or her right of participation. For every child, expressing an opinion should be a choice, and not an obligation.[60] This is especially the case where the child is being adopted through the public child protection system, and does not want to be *seen* to be making a choice between the prospective adopters and his or her biological family – even if this is not the choice that the child is being asked to make. In particular, young children cannot, and should not, be expected to make such decisions.

Nevertheless, a system of inflexible age limits is attractive to many countries as it is simple to implement, and does not involve complex assessments of

---

56 Ibid.

57 As Lansdown put it: "Attitudes towards girls inform their development. Subservient roles, constraints on personal autonomy, sexual exploitation, lower wages, domestic work and lower status within the family all affect girls' self-perception and realisation of their capacities and abilities." (ibid.).

58 Nicola Taylor, Pauline Tapp, Mark Henaghan, "Respecting Children's Participation in Family Law Proceedings" (2007) 15 *International Journal of Children's Rights* 61, 74 (original emphasis).

59 This was one of the major concerns in the drafting of the English law (see United Kingdom, *Review of Adoption Law*, above n 45). It was also central to the decision of the European Court of Human Rights in the case of *Sahin v Germany*, as will be discussed below.

60 United Nations Committee on the Rights of the Child, *General Comment 12* (2009) [16].

capacity by professionals, which many states do not have the financial or human resources to undertake.[61] Such a system is practical and easily accessible, and gives both adults and children a clear understanding of when the child's rights can be exercised.[62] Age limits are an accepted feature of other aspects of everyday life, including electoral rights, obtaining a driving licence, or buying alcohol, which would pose insurmountable difficulties if regulated in any other manner. However, prospective adoptive children are a much smaller subset of the population, and the potential impact on their lives of an adoption order is far greater. Although it may be easier and cheaper for states to use an inflexible limit, it clearly disregards the requirements of the UNCRC, and more nuanced systems should be implemented.

7.3.2. AGE LIMITS WITH EXCEPTIONS FOR CAPABLE CHILDREN

A second system of consent laws also sets age restrictions, but allows these to be lowered if the child is of sufficient maturity. In Finland, Hungary and the Netherlands, the legislation makes provision for the child under the age of consent to refuse an adoption order. In the Netherlands, if the child is under 12, but deemed to be able to make reasonable evaluation of his or her interests, he or she can veto the adoption.[63] Likewise in Finland, adoption cannot be granted against the will of a child younger than 12 if he or she is so mature that his or her will can be taken into consideration.[64] On the other hand, in Hungary, where a child under the age of 14 "bears full judgment", he or she must give consent.[65]

While such systems are preferable to fixed and immovable age limits, they nonetheless still have significant drawbacks. In particular, they place the burden of proof on the child to lower the age limit, relying on him or her to overturn an assumption of incapacity, clearly contrary to the UNCRC. As the Committee on the Rights of the Child suggested in its General Comment on article 12, domestic authorities

> "cannot begin with the assumption that a child is incapable of expressing her or his own views. On the contrary, States parties should presume that a child has the

---

61 Lansdown, above n 54, 50.

62 Ibid., 49.

63 Article 1:222.8(1)a Civil Code.

64 Section 10 Adoption Act 22/2012.

65 Yves Brulard and Letitia Dumont, *Comparative Study Relating to Procedures for Adoption Among the Member States of the European Union, Practical Difficulties Encountered in this Field by European Citizens within the Context of the European Pillar of Justice and Civil Matters and Means of Solving these Problems and of Protecting Children's Rights* (2007, European Union) 211.

capacity to form her or his own views and recognize that she or he has the right to express them; it is not up to the child to first prove her or his capacity."[66]

As Lansdown suggests, "poor and marginalized children are less likely to have access to opportunities for challenging the legal age-limits."[67] This is particularly problematic when considering intercountry adoption, as it is predominantly these children who are placed for adoption, as was discussed in Chapter Three.

Furthermore, while in the Netherlands there is a clear articulation of the degree of maturity which the child must show in order to be deemed capable of making a determinative decision – that is, able to make a reasonable evaluation of his or her interests – in Finland the standard set is much more opaque. The phrase "so mature that his or her will can be taken into consideration" does not provide a concrete level against which to judge capacity, and leaves much to the discretion of individual decision-makers. This is not necessarily a fatal flaw, as it is a determination that the UNCRC itself anticipates decision-makers making; however, it does require careful monitoring to ensure that it is not a *de facto* bar to recognition of the child's evolving capacity.

7.3.3. AGE LIMITS WITH EXCEPTIONS FOR BEST INTERESTS

The third system identified also allows for a variation from the required age of consent. Instead of allowing younger children to consent, however, it limits the ability of children who otherwise meet the age requirement to consent, by placing additional conditions on the right.[68] In Denmark, consent must be obtained for a child over 12 unless obtaining consent would be detrimental to the child,[69] whereas in Sweden, children can be denied the right to participate if it can be presumed that it would be to the child's detriment if he or she were asked.[70] Iceland, on the other hand, determines that the child's consent will not be sought where it is deemed questionable to seek approval due to his or her interests.[71] The Czech law is similar, allowing consent to be dispensed with where it "would frustrate the purpose of adoption",[72] which has been interpreted to apply to cases where a child has already been living with the

66 United Nations Committee on the Rights of the Child, *General Comment 12* (2009) [20].
67 Lansdown, above n 54, 51.
68 Many countries also have an exception to consent where the child is mentally incapacitated or disabled, but this will not be discussed in this book.
69 Article 6(1) Adoption (Consolidation) Act.
70 Section 5:5 Children and Parents Code (1949:381).
71 Article 6 Adoption Act No 130/1999.
72 Section 67 Act No 94/1963 Sb on Family.

prospective adopters and already considers them his or her parents – for example where the child is not aware that the adopters are not his or her natural parents.[73]

The compatibility of such provisions with the rights of the child depends on their individual application. The UNCRC does not require that the child's decision be determinative at any stage, only that his or her views are given weight according to age and maturity, and that the child's best interests are respected. Further, the ECA 2008 explicitly permits consultation with the child to be dispensed with if it is manifestly contrary to his or her interests.[74]

However, these European domestic laws appear not to be tailored to the welfare of the child, but to hiding the circumstances of his or her birth, and protecting adult interests. The importance of providing the child with information concerning his or her origins and identity will be discussed in detail in Chapter Nine with relation to access to birth records, and should apply equally in these circumstances. Although such provisions are unlikely to be applied to intercountry adoptions, they should nonetheless be treated with caution.

On the other hand, an example of good practice can be seen in Greece, where the legislation requires the child's consent to adoption if he or she is over the age of 12, unless this is refused abusively, that is, against his or her best interests.[75] There is an important distinction between overriding a *refusal* to consent, and the authorities deciding not to seek the child's views in the first place. While there may be situations in which it will not be in the child's best interests *to follow* the child's views, it is clear that it will never be in the child's interests not to attempt to gauge what these are.[76]

7.3.4. NO AGE LIMIT OR LAWS ON CONSENT

The final system considered is that under which there is no fixed age of consent. This system operates in Cyprus,[77] the Czech Republic,[78] Slovakia,[79]

73 Milana Hrusakova and Lenka Westpahlova, *Family Law in the Czech Republic* (2011, Kluwer Law) 119.

74 Article 6.

75 Ismene Androulidakis-Dimitriadis, *Family Law in Greece* (2011, Kluwer Law) 102.

76 As will be discussed below, there are mechanisms for obtaining the child's views without direct participation, or even discussing the issue directly with the child (see *Sahin v Germany* [2001] ECHR 266, [47]).

77 If his or her age and maturity permits (section 4c Adoption Law 1995).

78 If he or she is able to understand and consider the effects and consequences of the adoption, except in cases where it would frustrate the purpose of adoption (section 67 Act No 94/1963 Sb on Family).

79 When, having regard to age and maturity, he or she is able to assess the impact of the adoption (Act No 36/2005 on Family; Act No 305/2005 on Social and Legal Protection of Children and Social Nurture; Act No 99/1963 Code of Civil Procedure. See Hague Conference, *Country*

Switzerland,[80] Turkey[81] and Ukraine.[82] In each of these countries, the child's consent is required for adoption if he or she has the capacity, or is of sufficient maturity, to understand and consider the decision being made.

Such flexibility has considerable advantages for the child's right to make important decisions about his or her life. Without an arbitrary age barrier, the child can choose whether or not he or she wishes to make a decision regarding adoption, and the focus on the child's age and maturity is in line with the provisions of the UNCRC. It allows for individual determinations to be made regarding the child's capacity on a case-by-case basis.

However, it can pose considerable difficulties for children trying to assert their rights by placing the onus of proof on children to prove their capacity, assessments of which can be influenced by prejudice and discrimination, especially for girls, children from ethnic minorities, and children with disabilities.[83] In order to fully comply with the UNCRC, a child should not be required to prove his or her capacity, but rather the state should start with the assumption that he or she is capable.[84]

Furthermore, without strong safeguards, such an approach can allow a large degree of institutional paternalism. As can be seen in cases concerning consent to medical care in England, the determination of whether a child has the maturity to make a decision often comes down to whether it corresponds with the decision-maker's view of what is in the child's best interests.[85]

In a similar way, several European countries have intercountry adoption laws that do not require the child's consent at any stage of the legal process. This is the case in England, where although the court or adoption agency must have regard to the child's ascertainable wishes and feelings regarding the decision, considered in light of the child's age and understanding, at no time are the child's wishes legally determinative.[86] A similar requirement exists in Ireland.[87]

Profile: Slovakia (2010) <www.hcch.net/index_en.php?act=publications.details&pid=5095&dtid=42> [14 January 2012]).

80 If the child has the capacity to consent (article 265 Civil Code).

81 If the child has capacity to act on his or her own behalf (articles 305–320 Civil Code).

82 Article 218(1) Family Code. The child's consent is not required if, because of his or her age or state of health, he or she does not have sufficient understanding of the adoption (article 218(3)). There is also an exception if the child lives in the adopters' family and considers them as his or her parents (article 218(4)).

83 See Lansdown, above n 54, 50.

84 United Nations Committee on the Rights of the Child, *General Comment 12* (2009) [20].

85 See in particular *S v S* [1992] 2 FLR 31 and *Re E (A Minor) (Wardship: Medical Treatment)* [1993] 1 FLR 386. See also David Archard and Marit Skivenes, "Balancing a Child's Best Interests and a Child's Views" (2009) 17 *International Journal of Children's Rights* 1; Michael Freeman, "Why It Remains Important to Take Children's Rights Seriously" (2007) 15 *International Journal of Children's Rights* 5; Michael Freeman, "Rethinking *Gillick*" (2005) 13 *International Journal of Children's Rights* 201.

86 Section 1(4)(a) Adoption and Children Act 2002.

87 Section 3(2) Adoption Act 1964.

Likewise in Liechtenstein[88] and Austria[89] the Court has an obligation to hear the child from the age of five, but there is no legislative guidance as to the weight or consideration that will be given, and the child's determinative consent is not discussed by the legislation.

The problems that arise in relation to such laws are similar to those jurisdictions in which there is no fixed age of consent. In this case, however, the problems are exacerbated by the fact that on the face of the legislation, at no stage can the child expect his or her decisions to determine the outcome of the adoption, no matter what his or her age or level of maturity.

However, these last two categories are clearly most closely aligned with article 12 and the spirit of the UNCRC, if applied appropriately. To do so, states should put in place institutional structures to be able to expertly and impartially determine the maturity of the child, and the weight to be given to his or her views. This should not be based on a predetermined age, but on the understanding and intelligence that the child has shown, and his or her capacity to make autonomous decisions. All children should be deemed capable of doing so, unless proven otherwise.

7.3.5. EUROPEAN CONVENTION ON HUMAN RIGHTS

The participation of the child in decision-making processes has been one of the slowest areas of the ECtHR jurisprudence to develop, and is one in which there are still very few guiding principles. The Court has traditionally taken a paternalistic view of children's rights, focusing on the protection of the family unit and parental rights rather than recognising the child's evolving autonomy. A similar trend has emerged in relation to the relationship between the child and the state. As Fortin suggests, article 8 is drafted in such a way that it "appears to assume that as long as families are adequately protected from undue state interference, the regulation of family life can be entrusted to its adult members."[90]

There has been very little ECtHR jurisprudence concerning the participation of the child, and even less regarding when his or her decision will be treated as determinative.[91] Twenty-five years ago, in the seminal case of *Nielsen v Denmark*, the European Commission made the first tentative steps towards ensuring children's autonomous decision-making as part of their Convention rights. This case involved an allegation of deprivation of liberty under article 5 of the ECHR by a 12-year-old child detained in a psychiatric ward against his will. In coming

88 Article 181a Civil Code.
89 Article 181a Civil Code.
90 Jane Fortin, "Rights Brought Home for Children" (1999) 62 *Modern Law Review* 350, 357.
91 As Jane Fortin points out, children's rights are better protected by the ECtHR in some areas than others, such as juvenile justice and education, as opposed to family law decisions (ibid).

to its decision, the Commission considered the relationship between his mother's decision to place him in the facility and the child's own autonomy, and found that "the result will have to depend on a concrete assessment of the maturity of the applicant and his ability to understand his situation and to come to a decision".[92] It went on to hold:

> "The Commission does not find it necessary in this case to set out any fixed age-limit below which the opinion of a minor is of no importance. However, it is evident that the wishes of very young children regarding the question of hospitalisation and treatment in psychiatric wards cannot be decisive. On the other hand a system under which for example a 17-year-old minor could be placed in a closed ward with the consent of the holder of the parental rights and against his own wishes could hardly as such be considered a voluntary placement which would not raise any question of deprivation of liberty."[93]

This decision was, however, overturned by the full Court, in what has remained the principal case in determining the extent of a child's decision-making autonomy. The Court held that the child's admission against his will was not a deprivation of liberty, as his hospitalisation was a responsible exercise by his mother of her custodial rights in the interests of the child.[94] This was despite the fact that the child, who was described as a normally developed 12-year-old who was capable of understanding his situation and expressing his opinions clearly, objected to his admission. The Court considered that the child "was still of an age at which it would be normal for a decision to be made by the parent even against the wishes of the child".[95] Whether or not the decision was correct in the individual circumstances of the case, the Court thus stepped away from the recognition of the evolving capacity of the child, and instead retained the language of parental rights and protectionism.

MacDonald has suggested that the ECHR is not an effective instrument for the enforcement of children's rights, as it does not contain an explicit reference to this concept of evolving capacities.[96] While it is true that there has been inadequate consideration of this principle, and in particular the *Nielsen* judgment has held back children's rights before the Court, in the area of alternative care for children and the formation of family ties there has been some limited recognition of the importance of allowing the child to be the principal decision-maker.[97]

---

92 (Appl. No. 10929/84) Decision of 12 March 1987, [125].

93 Ibid., [126].

94 *Nielsen v Denmark* [1988] ECHR 23, [73].

95 Ibid., [72].

96 See Alistair MacDonald, "Bringing Rights Home for Children: Arguing the UNCRC" (2009) 39 *Family Law* 1073.

97 Criminal cases involving children have also paid heed to the evolving nature of the child's maturity and understanding by way of special protections in criminal proceedings (see *T v United Kingdom* [1999] ECHR 170).

An early example of this can be seen in *Hokkanen v Finland*.[98] In this case, the Court found that Finland was in violation of its obligations under article 8, as it had not adequately enforced a father's right to contact with his daughter. However, it emphasised that from the time at which the child expressed her opinions, and decided she did not wish to see her father, there was no longer any positive obligation on the part of the state under the ECHR. As such, the Court recognised that the child's capacity for decision-making would evolve, and that her opinions should be given greater weight as she matured, before finally becoming determinative.

The most important case in relation to intercountry adoption, however, is that of *Pini v Romania*, where the Court found that where the child had reached an age where his or her personality was sufficiently formed and had attained the necessary maturity to express an opinion as to the surroundings in which he or she wished to be brought up, this should be respected.[99] This case concerned two nine-and-a-half year old Romanian girls who were adopted by Italian citizens, but who resisted attempts to enforce the adoption order. Under the law in place at the time the adoption was made, the consent of children over ten was needed for adoption.[100] The ECtHR found that such a threshold age was reasonable, given the discretion given to national authorities by the international instruments.[101] However, the children were between ten and 12 years old when the adoption order was being enforced, and the Court considered that by then the children "had reached an age at which it could reasonably be considered that their personality was sufficiently formed and they had attained the necessary maturity to express their opinion as to the surroundings in which they wished to be brought up."[102] As such, their interests dictated that their opinions be taken into account, and they should not be forced to act against their will in forming an alternative family.

While this decision is to be commended for its recognition that children should be able to make autonomous decisions about their care when they are sufficiently mature, its passive acceptance of a minimum age of ten is highly problematic. By allowing the age limit without any further examination, the Court gave a significant amount of discretion to domestic authorities, and allowed an inappropriate constraint on the interpretation of the child's evolving capacity.

The difficulties that led to this case being brought before the ECtHR arose largely from the lack of participation of the children in the decision-making

98 [1994] ECHR 32.

99 [2005] ECHR 275, [157].

100 Government Emergency Ordinance No 25/1997 on the rules governing adoption (published in the Official Gazette on 12 June 1997), approved by article 7(1)(c) Law No 87/1998), as cited by the court in *Pini v Romania*, ibid.

101 Ibid., [145].

102 Ibid., [157].

process, and in the overall adoption proceedings. The girls were not consulted before the order was made, nor were they adequately prepared for its enforcement. As Judges Thomasson and Jungwiert suggest in their dissenting opinion,

> "[i]t does not appear from the evidence that they were ever asked for their opinion, either directly in an interview with a judge or a counsellor or indirectly through expert assessments which would have provided an opportunity to ascertain their views and feelings about the adoption in practical terms."

They also raised "very serious doubts" as to whether the requirements of article 4(d) of the Hague Convention had been met.

Although the ultimate decision in this case was the right one, the methodology was flawed, and reinforced the practice of states in operating on the presumption that children under a certain age lack capacity. Thus this is an area in which the ECHR has undermined the implementation of the UNCRC, allowing states to continue to maintain patriarchal assumptions of children as lacking in capacity and needing protection, rather than autonomy.

7.4. PARTICIPATION OF YOUNGER CHILDREN

In addition to setting age limits for when the child's views on adoption become determinative, many European states make provision for the opinions of younger children to be heard during the adoption proceedings. This is in line with the UNCRC, which makes clear that the child's participation should not be limited to the time when he or she can make determinative decisions, but that states must ensure that children of all ages are able to participate in decision-making processes concerning adoption. The age and maturity of the child have no relevance to whether or not the child should be included in the decision-making process, only to how this can be achieved, and the weight that is given to his or her views.

There is a wide divergence between European states as to the way in which children's views and opinions are sought and taken into consideration in adoption proceedings. Indeed, not all countries have laws allowing the child to participate under the age at which he or she is deemed competent to make a determinative decision – for example, in Armenia, Azerbaijan, Georgia, Malta, Moldova, Serbia, Slovakia and Turkey, there is no legislative requirement that the child be heard in adoption proceedings, except once he or she has reached the age of consent.

Even in states that make provision for participation, practices vary significantly. Examples of good practice can be seen in Denmark,[103] Estonia,[104]

[103] Article 6(3) Adoption (Consolidation) Act.
[104] Section 151 Family Law Act 2009.

Iceland[105] and Ireland,[106] where every child has the right to participate in proceedings concerning them, if he or she so wishes. The wishes and opinions of the child will then be weighed according to his or her age and maturity, accurately reflecting the requirements of article 12 UNCRC.[107]

On the other hand, in Albania,[108] Andorra,[109] Austria[110] and Liechtenstein,[111] a child will only be heard once he or she reaches a particular age (ranging from five to ten). Once that age is reached, the child's views and opinions must be taken into consideration. Such restrictions on the right to be heard disempower younger children, and prevent the child's exercise of autonomy in line with his or her evolving capacity. Especially where the age barrier for participation is set at ten – the age at which children in other countries are deemed capable of making a determinative decision – such barriers reflect arbitrary determinations on competence.

In Poland, Slovenia and Spain, children are only permitted to participate in the decision-making process once they prove they are of sufficient maturity (Slovenia[112] and Spain),[113] or able to understand the significance of adoption (Poland).[114] This is contrary to the two-step approach to article 12 – maturity and understanding should only be considered in giving weight to the child's opinions, not whether he or she is permitted to express them in the first place.[115] It also fails to recognise that it is not always the child's opinion or decision itself that is important, but rather the reasons expressed behind it. Explanations of a child's reasons can often shed light on issues that are important to the child, and are especially important where the court is attempting to determine whether an adoption would be in his or her best interests, or if another long-term placement option would be more appropriate. Much more can be learnt than a simple "yes" or "no".

---

105 Article 6 Adoption Act No 130/1999.

106 Section 3(2) Adoption Act 1964.

107 It is not clear, however, the extent to which the authorities will act positively to ascertain the child's views when he or she is unable to clearly express them. As discussed below, this is an integral part of the ability of younger children to participate, without which the right loses some of its content.

108 Over ten (article 15 Law No 9695 (19 March 2007), Hague Conference, *Country Profile: Albania* (2010) <www.hcch.net/index_en.php?act=publications.details&pid=5081&dtid=42> [14 January 2012]).

109 Over ten (Article 9 Qualified Law on Adoption of 21 March 1996).

110 Over five (article 181a Civil Code).

111 Over five (article 181a Civil Code).

112 Brulard and Dumont, above n 66.

113 Article 177(1) Civil Code.

114 Article 118 Family Code.

115 Norway operates on a combination of these previous two approaches. When over the age of seven, the child is given the opportunity to voice his or her opinion, and it is given weight in accordance with his or her age and maturity. However, younger children are also given the opportunity to participate, if they are capable of forming their own opinions (section 6 Act of 28 February 1986, No 8 relating to Adoption).

This is reflected in the new Finnish legislation. Under the 2012 Adoption Act, the social worker responsible for adoption counselling must discuss the adoption with the child, if this is possible considering his or her age and degree of maturity. He or she will seek to determine the child's attitude towards the adoption by consulting the child for his or her views discretely and sensitively.[116]

On the other hand, in Italy, Lithuania, Switzerland and Russia, although in principle all children have the right to be heard, legislation makes exceptions to this, allowing this to be derogated from where it is deemed to be in his or her best interests.[117] In England, the child's best interests can likewise override any requirement that the child be heard. The Adoption and Children Act 2002 makes the child's welfare throughout his or her life the paramount consideration in making a decision on adoption, and although courts are directed to take into account "the child's ascertainable wishes and feelings", this will be subject to the overall welfare consideration.[118] The Revised European Convention on the Adoption of Children of 2008 also allows such an exception, with article 6 providing that consultation with a child "may be dispensed with if it would be manifestly contrary to the child's best interests." The use of the term "manifestly" should be noted, however, setting a significantly higher threshold than the domestic states in question.

Article 12 of the UNCRC makes no similar exception for the best interests of the child. Although article 3 directs that in all actions concerning children, the best interests of the child shall be a primary consideration, as discussed above, the Committee on the Rights of the Child has made clear that the only way to determine the child's interests is through the participation of the child. Broad exceptions to participation rely on a paternalistic interpretation of the child's welfare, reflecting an outdated approach to the place of the child in relation to the state and his or her family. State authorities should be clear that participation is a fundamental right of the child, and there must be pressing and serious reasons for it to be limited in any way, which should be explained and justified to the child and to other parties involved, with the opportunity for appeal.

There has only been one case before the ECtHR that has directly considered the participation of a young child in family law judicial decision-making, and

---

116 Section 26 Adoption Act 22/2012.

117 Italy: article 7 Law 184/1983; Lithuania: article 3.164(1) Civil Code; Russia: article 57 Family Law 1995; Switzerland: article 314(1) Civil Code. Italy is a particularly interesting example: the authority of the courts to override the child's right to be heard can only be exercised until the child reaches the age of 12. After that, he or she has a right to be heard, no matter what the opinion of the court as to his or her interests; at 14, his or her opinion is determinative.

118 Although dealing with a case in private law under the Children Act 1989, rather than under the Adoption and Children Act 2002, see the case of *Mabon v Mabon*, where the court found that direct participation could be curtailed if it "would pose an obvious risk of harm to the child, arising out of the nature of the continuing proceedings", although indirect participation was still permitted ([2005] EWCA Civ 634; [2005] 2 FLR 1011, [29]). This case will be discussed in more detail below.

this involved a challenge by an adult, rather than a child himself or herself. The case of *Sahin v Germany* was brought before the Court by an unmarried father who had been denied access to his child by the mother. Under German law, fathers of children born out of wedlock could only have access to the child if the mother agreed, or if a court ruled that contact was in the child's best interests. The father challenged this law, alleging it violated his right to respect for family life under article 8, and was discriminatory under article 14 in conjunction with article 8. In coming to its decision concerning the child's best interests, the domestic court did not hear the views of the child (who was five years old), but relied on the findings of a psychological expert, who advised against hearing the child in court. She concluded that the very process of questioning entailed a risk for the child, which could not be avoided by special arrangements. Her findings on the child's best interests, presented to the court, had been ascertained not by asking the child directly about her father (as this would have been damaging according to the expert) but by exploring the feelings of the child through the course of various games. The father challenged this, claiming that the failure of the court to hear the child directly constituted a procedural violation of the ECHR.

The Fourth Chamber of the Court found in favour of the applicant, holding that:

> "[T]he German courts' failure to hear the child reveals an insufficient involvement of the applicant in the access proceedings. It is essential that the competent courts give careful consideration to what lies in the best interests of the child after having had direct contact with the child. The Regional Court should not have been satisfied with the expert's vague statements about the risks inherent in questioning the child without even contemplating the possibility to take special arrangements in view of the child's young age."[119]

It is interesting to note that the problem identified by the Chamber was not insufficient involvement of the *child* in the decision-making process, but of the *father*. While this in part reflects the fact that it was the father who had taken the case before the Court, the failure to even mention the rights of the child in this regard is extremely problematic. In a precedent-setting case concerning the requisite participation needed for procedural fairness, the child's rights should have been mentioned, either as a contribution to the best interests determination, or even in passing for sake of recognition. The failure to do so shows a lack of awareness, and reinforces the view that the Court is often an inadequate instrument for enforcing children's rights.

The Chamber focused only on *direct* participation, not making allowance for the need for *indirect* participation for some children. While the procedural rights

119 *Sahin v Germany* [2001] ECHR 594, [47].

of the father may be best protected by the child appearing before the decision-maker in person, this may not always be the wish, or in the best interests, of the child. This was the approach of the Grand Chamber, which overturned the Fourth Chamber decision on appeal. It paid considerable deference to the margin of appreciation given to member states to ascertain all the relevant facts, and assess the evidence before them, and thus decide what form of participation best suited the child. It found that:

> "It would be going too far to say that domestic courts are always required to hear a child in court on the issue of access to a parent not having custody, but this issue depends on the specific circumstances of each case, having due regard to the age and maturity of the child concerned."[120]

The Court found that direct participation of the child was unnecessary, as long as the wishes of the child were presented to the courts in some manner. This reflects the provision in article 12 of the UNCRC that the child has the opportunity to be heard "either directly, or through a representative or an appropriate body".

The way in which children's views are conveyed to the decision-maker has been a much-debated issue in recent years, and for this reason, this chapter will not go into great depth in this area.[121] However, it is important to briefly discuss the different ways in which a child's views can be elicited and received.

First, the child can be heard by direct participation in the proceedings, through an interview with the decision-maker himself or herself (usually a judge). This was the system that the father in *Sahin* was arguing for, as it has significant advantages for both the child and the decision-making process. It enables the child to feel more fully involved in the process, and allows him or her to know that the person who will be making such an important decision about

---

120 [2003] ECHR 340, [73].

121 See Jane Fortin, "Children's Representation Through the Looking Glass" (2007) 37 *Family Law* 500; American Bar Association Child Custody and Adoption Pro Bono Project, "Hearing Children's Voices and Interests in Adoption and Guardianship Proceedings" (2007) 41(2) *Family Law Quarterly* 365; Mark Henaghan, "What Does a Child's Right to be Heard in Legal Proceedings Really Mean? ABA Custody Standards Do Not Go Far Enough" (2008) 42(1) *Family Law Quarterly* 117; Nicola Taylor, Pauline Tapp and Mark Henaghan, "Respecting Children's Participation in Family Law Proceedings" (2007) 15(1) *International Journal of Children's Rights* 61; Donald N Duquette, "Legal Representation for Children in Protection Proceedings: Two Distinct Lawyer Roles are Required" (2000) 34(3) *Family Law Quarterly* 441; Judy Cashmore and Patrick Parkinson, "What Responsibility Do Courts Have to Hear Children's Voices?" (2007) 15(1) *International Journal of Children's Rights* 43; David Archard and Marit Skivenes, "Balancing a Child's Best Interests and a Child's Views" (2009) 17(1) *International Journal of Children's Rights* 1; Judith Masson, "Representation of Children in England: Protecting Children in Child Protection Proceedings" (2000) 34(3) *Family Law Quarterly* 467; E Kay, M Tisdall, R Bray, K Marshall et al, "Children's Participation in Family Law Proceedings: A Step Too Far or a Step Too Small?" (2004) 26(1) *Journal of Social Welfare and Family Law* 17.

his or her life has taken the time to listen to what he or she has to say. Where the child feels respected and involved in the process, he or she is more likely to accept the decision of the judge, whatever that decision may be.

However, in England an interview of a child by a judge poses several problems, the most serious of which being that the child cannot be offered confidentiality for the things he or she imparts. If the judge hears anything in the interview that may influence his or her decision, the parents and counsel must be informed of this, so that they have an opportunity of addressing it. For this reason, any judicial interview with a child in England is strictly for the purposes of enabling the child to gain an understanding of the decision-making process, and will not involve evidence gathering.[122] The judge will also make clear to the child that anything he or she says will be communicated to the other parties.[123]

This tension between natural justice and the child's best interests is resolved in a different manner in Belgium, where a child under the age of consent will – if he or she so wishes – be heard alone by the court, save for the presence of the clerk and an expert. The hearing will explore the child's opinion on adoption and its consequences, and there will be a hearing report drawn up, instead of an official transcript, to more accurately reflect the outcome of the hearing.[124] Similarly, in Norway, the child's opinion can be given to a judge in a closed session without either the parties or their lawyers present.[125] These systems acknowledge that the interests of parents to access all information may sometimes be overridden by the paramount interests of the child in being able to express his or her opinion while maintaining confidentiality.

The second option for hearing the child is through indirect participation, where a social worker or psychologist is appointed to present the child's views to the court. This is particularly advantageous to young children, who may be unsuited to direct participation, or indeed unable to do so.[126] This method ensures that the views and opinions have been elicited in a professional manner, where the child is interviewed in a safe environment without the pressure that a court appearance may bring. A judge's life experiences are often far away from those of the child, and the judge may feel uncomfortable interviewing him or her, or unable to do this effectively and appropriately.[127] Professionals who work with children have the skills and training to be able to make the child feel at

---

122 United Kingdom: Family Justice Division, *Guidelines for Judges Meeting Children Who are Subject to Family Proceedings* [2010] 2 FLR 1872.

123 Ibid.

124 Brulard and Dumont, above n 66, 20.

125 Section 61(4) Act of 8 April 1981, No 7 relating to Children and Parents.

126 It must be differentiated from a best interests analysis, however, which will be discussed in detail below.

127 See, for example, Judge Ian Mill, "Conversations with Children: A Judge's Perspective on Meeting the Patient before Operating on the Family" (2008) 6 *New Zealand Family Law Journal* 72.

ease, ensure that the child's pronouncements are not taken at face value, and that the reasons behind them are explored, so that his or her views can be accurately represented. Furthermore, they are able to interpret non-verbal communication from both young and older children, so may widen the scope of the ability of the child to participate. Unlike judges, who are restricted to a strict judicial timetable and scheduling, a professional has the opportunity to spend considerable periods of time with the child, getting to know him or her and gaining his or her trust, which allows the child to express his or her true wishes more freely.

Indirect participation may not satisfy some children, however. In 2010, Ursula Kilkelly, through the Council of Europe, undertook a wide-ranging study into participation of children in decisions concerning them. Answers were collected from over 25 countries,[128] and 3,721 children. Children were asked about a decision that had been made about them – who made the decision, what was it about, and whether they had been involved in it.[129] 92 per cent of those who responded said they would like to express their views to the decision-maker directly,[130] and when asked about alternative representatives, 61 per cent children rejected the use of parents, and 63 per cent rejected lawyers, to speak for them.

In deciding whether to allow the child direct or indirect participation, the guiding principle must be the wishes of the child unless there is a manifest reason for disregarding these. Where the child wishes to speak to the judge directly, his or her welfare will be greatly damaged if this is not permitted, meaning equally strong reasons would be needed to decide otherwise. In any case, it is of paramount importance that children are able to be heard in one way or another in proceedings, no matter their age or level of maturity.

7.5. PARTICIPATION AND THE PROTECTION OF THE CHILD'S WELFARE

Despite the increasing age of children placed in intercountry adoption, there remain a substantial number of children under the age of five who are being adopted in Europe. In many circumstances, these children will be too young to form decisive views and opinions on their situation, nor express them if they do.

---

128 Azerbaijan, Belgium, Bosnia and Herzegovina, Croatia, Cyprus, Finland, France, Georgia, Hungary, Ireland, Italy, Latvia, Lithuania, Malta, Moldova, the Netherlands, Poland, Romania, Russia, Serbia, Slovakia, Spain, Sweden, Ukraine, and the United Kingdom. Responses were not evenly spread over the countries with some only returning a few responses (such as Sweden, with five), while others many (such as Serbia with 872).

129 The answers returned related to decisions concerning divorce, residence, contact, care admission, and adoption, but also education, health, custody and immigration.

130 Ursula Kilkelly, *Listening to Children About Justice: Report of the Council of Europe Consultation with Children on Child-Friendly Justice* (2010, Council of Europe) 29 <www.coe.int/childjustice> [4 April 2012].

This does not mean that they should not be given the opportunity to participate in the decision-making processes, although states may need to find different ways of accommodating this.

Children are able to demonstrate understanding, choices and preferences from a very young age,[131] and for this reason article 12 UNCRC is not restricted to verbal expression: a child's views can be expressed in a myriad of ways, including through play, body language, facial expressions, emotions, or art.[132] In these cases, indirect participation will be the most appropriate way for the child to be heard, and it is up to the state to provide independent, trained professionals to be able to elicit or interpret these preferences. For children in this position, however, although ensuring their participation is important, the key consideration must be the protection of their best interests.

Throughout Europe, different emphasis is placed on the welfare of the child in adoption proceedings, despite the requirement that his or her best interests be paramount under article 21 of the UNCRC. In the Czech Republic,[133] England[134] and Finland,[135] for example, this article is accurately reflected, including the use of the term "paramount", while in Spain, the requirement that "the best interests of the child shall take precedence over any other competing interest" conveys the same effect.[136] Similarly, the Romanian child protection law requires that "the best interests of the child … take priority over the rights and duties of the child's parents, legal guardians, or other persons legally responsible for him or her."[137] On the other hand, in Monaco the adoption "must be justified, above all else, by the interests of the child",[138] and in the Netherlands, the adoption must be "manifestly in the best interests of the

131 For example, Pugh and Selleck suggest that "[a]lthough most infants do not learn to talk until their second year, their 'voices' are there to hear from birth." (Gillian Pugh and Dorothy Rouse Selleck, "Listening to and Communicating with Young Children", in Ron Davie, Graham Upton and Ved Varma (eds), *The Voice of the Child: A Handbook for Professionals* (1996, Falmer)).

132 United Nations Committee on the Rights of the Child, *General Comment 12* (2009) [21]. See also Lansdown, above n 54, 4. This has been acknowledged by the High Court of New Zealand where Randerson J suggested that "[a] child may 'express' views in non-verbal ways and observations by a suitably skilled or experienced person of a child's behaviour in the company of a parent or caregiver may give valuable insights into the child's preferences. That can be a useful alternative approach [where a child is non-verbal] as well as providing a supplementary means of ascertaining the views of a child who is able to express views verbally." (*C v S and W* (2006) High Court Napier, CIV-2005-441-776, [31(c)]).

133 Section 5 Act No 359/1999 Sb on Social Legal Protection of a Child.

134 Section 1(2) Adoption and Children Act 2002.

135 Section 2 Adoption Act 22/2012.

136 Article 2 Organic Law 1/1996 for the Legal Protection of Minors. See also article 2(1) of Organic Law 54/2007 on Intercountry Adoption, which reads: "This law establishes the legal framework and instruments essential to ensure that all intercountry adoptions take place with a view to the best interests of the child".

137 Article 2(2), Law 272/2004.

138 Article 240 Civil Code.

child";[139] these are lower standards, but still place the welfare of the child above other considerations.

In many other jurisdictions, however, reference is made to the child's "best interests" needing to be served by the adoption, but not whether these take paramount place over the rights and interests of others. This is the case in Albania,[140] Belgium,[141] Germany,[142] Greece,[143] Iceland,[144] Montenegro,[145] Norway,[146] Poland,[147] Portugal,[148] Serbia,[149] Switzerland[150] and Ukraine.[151] More worrying still is the fact that in several more jurisdictions, including Armenia,[152] Bulgaria,[153] Georgia,[154] Latvia,[155] Lithuania[156] and Russia,[157] reference is only made to the child's "interests" or "welfare", rather than his or her "best interests".

The problem with the legislation in these latter jurisdictions that refer to the need to serve the child's "interests" is that they do not specify the weight that these interests will be given. The UNCRC requires that in matters of adoption the child's interests be given paramount importance, meaning that no other rights or interests should be considered equal to those of the child,[158] but in the majority of states across Europe this is not adequately implemented in legislation.

Ensuring that the child's welfare is taken into consideration by the court is an important step towards protecting his or her best interests as required under international law. To do so, it is important that children, and their interests, are represented in a professional and independent manner before decision-makers. This is not just an issue for young children – although it will become of lesser importance as the child is able to express his or her opinions clearly, as will be discussed below – however, it is of particular importance for those for whom protection is more important than autonomy.

---

139 Article 1:227(3) Civil Code.

140 Article 240 Family Code.

141 Article 344-1 Civil Code.

142 Section 1741 Civil Code.

143 Article 1542 Civil Code.

144 Article 4 Adoption Act No 130/1999.

145 Article 123 Family Law.

146 Section 2 Act of 28 February 1986, No 8 relating to Adoption.

147 Article 113 Family Code.

148 Article 1974(1) Civil Code. The legislation also requires that the adoption would not be inequitable to the other children of the adoptive parents.

149 Article 92 Family Act.

150 Article 264 Civil Code. The legislation also requires that the adoption would not be inequitable to the other children of the adoptive parents.

151 Article 207(2) Family Code.

152 Article 122(2) Family Code.

153 Article 97(2) Family Code.

154 Article 1239 Civil Code.

155 Section 162 Civil Law.

156 Article 3.209(1) Civil Code.

157 Article 124(2) Family Law 1995.

158 United Nations Commission on Human Rights, *Report of the Working Group on a Draft Convention on the Rights of the Child* (2 March 1989, United Nations) E/CN.4/1989/48, [359]–[364].

This can be seen in the European Convention on the Exercise of Children's Rights 1996,[159] which provides that in proceedings affecting a child in which his or her parents are precluded from representing him or her as a result of a conflict of interest, the judicial authority shall have the power to appoint a special representative for the child.[160] The role of this representative is to provide information to the child if he or she is of sufficient understanding, to provide explanations to a child of sufficient understanding as to the possible consequences of compliance with his or her views, and importantly, to determine the views of the child and present these views to the judicial authority unless this would be manifestly contrary to the best interests of the child.[161]

The circumstances in which a representative may be appointed for the child in adoption proceedings, if one may be appointed at all, very greatly throughout Europe. An example of good practice can be seen in Belgium[162] and Cyprus,[163] where a "guardian" is automatically appointed in all adoption proceedings, with the duty of safeguarding the interests of the child before the court. Similarly, in Spain, the Ministerio Fiscal is party to any judicial procedure involving a child, although it is generally acknowledged that it lacks the resources to adequately carry out this function.[164]

In other jurisdictions, however, a guardian is only appointed where this is needed to protect the child's interests; this is the case in Hungary[165] and Slovenia.[166] In Finland[167] and Greece,[168] on the other hand, a "special guardian"

159 This Convention has been ratified by 17 European states (Albania, Austria, Croatia, Cyprus, the Czech Republic, Finland, France, FYR Macedonia, Germany, Greece, Italy, Latvia, Montenegro, Poland, Slovenia, Turkey, Ukraine) and signed by a further 11 (Hungary, Iceland, Ireland, Luxembourg, Malta, Portugal, Russia, Serbia, Slovakia, Spain, Sweden).

160 Article 9(1) European Convention on the Exercise of Children's Rights 1996. In addition, article 4 of this Convention provides a right to the child to apply for the appointment of such a representative where the holders of parental responsibility are precluded from representing him or her. This is of relevance to older children only, who are capable of submitting such an application.

161 Article 10.

162 Walter Pintens and Dominique Pignolet, *National Report: Belgium* (date unknown, Commission on European Family Law) <http://ceflonline.net/wp-content/uploads/Belgium-Parental-Responsibilities.pdf> [27 February 2013].

163 Section 9(3) Adoption Law 1995.

164 Cristina Gonzalez Beilfuss, *National Report: Spain* (date unknown, Commission for European Family Law) <http://ceflonline.net/wp-content/uploads/Spain-Parental-Responsibilities.pdf> [27 February 2013].

165 Emilia Weiss and Orsolya Szeibert, *National Report: Hungary* (date unknown, Commission on European Family Law) <http://ceflonline.net/wp-content/uploads/Hungary-Parental-Responsibilities.pdf> [27 February 2013].

166 Civil Procedure Act (Slovenia, *State Party Report to the UN Committee on the Rights of the Child* (18 June 2003) CRC/C/70/Add.19).

167 Section 55 Adoption Act 22/2012.

168 Articles 1517 and 1627–1628 Civil Code; Achilles G Koutsouradis, *National Report: Greece* (date unknown, Commission on European Family Law) <http://ceflonline.net/wp-content/uploads/Greece-Parental-Responsibilities.pdf> [27 February 2013].

is appointed in cases where the interests of the child are in conflict with those of his or her parent or guardian, while in the Netherlands, not only must the interests of the child and parents be in conflict, but the court must consider a special guardian necessary in the best interests of the child.[169] In Switzerland, at the request of an interested party or of its own accord, the guardianship authority will appoint a welfare advocate where the legal representative of a child has interests that conflict with him or her.[170]

A further example of good practice can be seen in England, Italy and France, where the child is provided not only with a welfare representative, but also with a lawyer. While in France, the lawyer is appointed on a discretionary basis by the "special administrator" whose role is to protect the child's welfare,[171] in Italy, the court *must* appoint both a welfare representative and a lawyer, regardless of the ability and understanding of the child.[172] In England, the court can appoint a solicitor for the child, whose role will be to represent him or her, acting through the children's guardian (also appointed by the court).[173] The guardian's task is to be the independent representative of the child, informing the court of his or her views, but also presenting an objective professional judgment of what is in the child's best interests.[174]

The individual representation of children has been an issue that has also been raised by judges of the ECtHR concerning cases that come before them. In his dissenting opinion in *Kroon and Others v the Netherlands*, Judge Bonnici condemned the approach of the majority in the fact that "[t]he interests of the child were never looked after by an independent person, a 'curator ad litem', and in fact they are not mentioned in the judgment. The 'interests' of the mother and of the other applicant are the only interests which have really been considered."[175] Judge Pettiti has also made similar comments, and suggested that lawyers should be instructed specifically to represent the interests of the children in cases before the ECtHR that also involve their parents.[176] The problems that can arise are most vividly seen in cases concerning international child abduction, where the

---

169 Article 1:250 Civil Code.

170 Article 392 Civil Code.

171 Article 388(2) Civil Code; *TGI La Roche-sur-Yon* (29 July 1993) BICC 1 March 1994, No 302. See Frédérique Ferrand, *National Report: France* (date unknown, Commission on European Family Law) <http://ceflonline.net/wp-content/uploads/France-Parental-Responsibilities.pdf> [27 February 2013].

172 Article 8 Law 149/2001 on Adoption and Child Custody (Amendments to Law 184 of 4 May 1983 on the "Regulation of child adoption and custody"); Italy, *State Party Report to the UN Committee on the Rights of the Child* (5 July 2010) CRC/C/ITA/3–4, [151].

173 In the majority of cases, the solicitor will in fact be appointed in the initial care proceedings, and continue to represent the child through to the adoption stage.

174 This has been described as the "Rolls Royce" model of child representation: *Mabon v Mabon* [2005] EWCA Civ 634; [2005] 2 FLR 1011, [25].

175 (Appl. No. 18535/91) Judgment of 27 October 1994.

176 See, for example, *X, Y and Z v United Kingdom* [1997] ECHR 20; *Olsson v Sweden (No 2)* [1992] ECHR 75.

parent with parental responsibility can bring a claim before the Court on behalf of his or her children, despite the fact that the children themselves might in fact be fighting against the outcome that that parent desires.[177]

As can be seen, the role of a welfare representative is an extremely important safeguard for children who are unable to express their own views, or who cannot participate in the adoption proceedings without assistance. Where the birth parents and adoptive parents are each advocating for their own interests and their own desired outcome, it is crucial that there is someone appointed to ensure that the expert opinion concerning the welfare of the child is presented to the court.

However, for older children, it is important that the child's rights, and in particular the right to be heard, are not infringed upon by focusing purely on welfare considerations. This is a criticism that has arisen in relation to the German system, where the court may appoint a representative in proceedings concerning a child if it is necessary to safeguard his or her interests.[178] However, Stötzel and Fegert point out that there is no indication whether the guardian should concentrate on the *welfare* or *wishes* of the child, only stating that he or she should represent the child's interests, which includes both aspects.[179] Thus, if these two aspects of the child's interests conflict, it is unclear which should take precedence.

This problem has also arisen in England, most famously in a private law case concerning residence orders for three boys aged 13, 15 and 17. In *Mabon v Mabon*, the children were joined as parties to the action and represented by the court-appointed guardian. They wished to appoint separate representation to convey their wishes to the court, but this was refused on the grounds that it would be contrary to their welfare to be involved in the litigation process, and that their interests were being advocated for by the guardian. This was overturned by the Court of Appeal, who emphasised the importance of the child's welfare being promoted, but also the equal importance of ensuring respect for the autonomy of the child and the right to be heard under article 12 UNCRC.[180]

Thus while a guardian can be an important role for a young child, as children grow older it may be seen as a tool of disenfranchisement.[181] In terms of

---

177 See, for example, *Raw and Others v France* [2013] ECHR 199.

178 Section 50 Act on Voluntary Jurisdiction.

179 Manuela Stötzel and Jörg M Fegert, "The Children's Guardian from a Child's Perspective" (2006) 20 *International Journal of Law, Policy and the Family* 201, 202.

180 *Mabon v Mabon* [2005] EWCA Civ 634; [2005] 2 FLR 1011.

181 As Herring suggests, there is a vast practical and theoretical distinction between these two concepts. The "interests" and "needs" of the child are defined by others, making the decision essentially paternalistic and emphasising the child's dependence, rather than the autonomy that individual participation provides. The children's guardian must act in the child's best interests, even if this means acting in contravention of, or advocating in opposition to, the child's wishes (Jonathan Herring, "The Human Rights Act and the Welfare Principle in

procedural and symbolic benefits flowing from the participation of an older child, participation through a guardian focusing on welfare singularly fails to meet these objectives. The child fails to reap the benefit of *knowing* that his or her voice has been listened to, and the symbolic message that is sent through indirect participation through a welfare evaluation is that of continuing dependency, rather than evolving autonomy. As Henaghan suggests, "[a] child's wishes are the child's voice; a child's needs are determined by others."[182] Even where the representative also presents the child's views and wishes to the court, where this is followed by a professional opinion that these should not be followed, it can be detrimental to the child's belief in the integrity of the process.

For this reason, the difference between protecting the child's interests and hearing his or her views must be clearly demarcated. This can only adequately be done by separating the role of welfare advocate from the role of presenting the child's views to the court. Employing a guardian to advocate for the welfare of the child presents the epitome of child protection, and is a mechanism that should be emulated to ensure the best interests of all children are protected in adoption proceedings. Nevertheless, it has the potential to conflict with the procedural and symbolic aspects of the child's right to be heard and should be regarded as a separate, albeit interrelated, aspect of the child's participation in proceedings.

7.6. CONCLUSION

The right to participate in decision-making processes is one of the fundamental principles of children's rights; however it has been slow to implement in many European countries. Despite the clear requirement in the UNCRC that all children be heard and have the opportunity to participate in judicial proceedings, no matter their age or maturity, in the field of adoption few states in Europe have adequately legislated in this regard. There is a lack of integrated approach for children of different ages and maturity in many states, and too often limitations are placed on participation, including restrictive age limits, or requiring the child to prove capacity before voicing his or her opinion. Almost 25 years on from the UNCRC, protectionist policies still dominate most of Europe, and child agency is still slow to be recognised.

Perhaps as a result of this, legislation promoting the welfare of the child before adoption decision-makers is somewhat more uniform, with many states making admirable steps in that direction. However, despite this legislation, there

---

Family Law – Conflicting or Complementary?" (1999) 11(3) *Child and Family Law Quarterly* 223).

182 Mark Henaghan, "What Does a Child's Right to Be Heard in Legal Proceedings Really Mean? ABA Custody Standards Do Not Go Far Enough" (2008) 42(1) *Family Law Quarterly* 117, 120.

is still a long way to go to ensure that the welfare of the child is presented to the decision-maker in an objective manner, by an independent representative. In many states, there continues to be the expectation that children's rights will be protected by their parents, despite the potential conflict of interest in adoption cases. The ECtHR has done little to rectify this, and has in fact entrenched parental rights at the expense of the autonomy of children. While the Court has begun to slowly recognise the evolving capacity of the child, it continues to take a very traditional approach to the place of children in relation to the family and the state, as well as to individual representation before the Court.

The voice of the child in intercountry adoption proceedings will become of greater importance as the years progress, with trends indicating a growing number of older children being placed in this system. It is important that states begin to address this issue, to ensure that all the rights of the child, both to be protected and to be heard, are respected.

CHAPTER 8

ADOPTIVE PARENTS: ELIGIBILITY, PREPARATION, AND SUPPORT

While the first sections of this book have considered how to determine whether a child is eligible and suited to be placed in intercountry adoption, and the necessary consents before this can occur, this chapter will concentrate on the position of adoptive parents. Despite this change of focus, the guiding principle for analysis continues to be the rights of the child, and how appropriate selection and preparation of, and support for, prospective adoptive parents can promote this.

This chapter will be divided into three parts. The first will address whether there exists a "right to adoption", both from the point of view of the prospective adoptive parents, and from the view of the child. It will analyse the factors driving intercountry adoption, and whether there is an obligation on either sending or receiving states to practise intercountry adoption.

The second part of this chapter will focus on the criteria used to determine whether a prospective adoptive parent is eligible and suitable to adopt. Determining who should be eligible to adopt has, as Jane Lewis put it, "always been something of a litmus test in respect of much larger issues: what 'the family' should look like".[1] Societal preconceptions concerning the ability of certain groups to bring up children are laid bare in adoption legislation, and the criteria of age, marital status and sexual orientation will be discussed.

Finally, the support provided to prospective adoptive parents will be analysed. This will consider pre-adoption counselling and preparation, and the establishment of a relationship between the parents and child before the adoption order, as well as post-adoption monitoring and the services provided to the family to ensure that the adoptive placement thrives.

---

1 Jane Lewis, "Adoption: The Nature of Policy Shifts in England and Wales, 1972–2002" (2004) 18 *International Journal of Law Policy and the Family* 235, 236.

8.1. ADOPTIVE PARENTS AND THE RIGHTS OF CHILDREN: COMPLEMENTARY OR CONTRADICTORY?

8.1.1. INTERCOUNTRY ADOPTION: AN EMERGING MARKET

The inception of intercountry adoption came from the need to care for children in the aftermath of global conflict; however, these roots have been long left behind.[2] Its evolution into an industry capable of producing large profits begs the question: to what extent does intercountry adoption continue to address the needs of children, and to what extent is it now driven by the desires of prospective adoptive parents?

The number of babies available for adoption in developed countries is declining, with women having greater control over their fertility, and social changes making it increasingly acceptable for unmarried women to bring up a child on their own. In England, the number of children adopted domestically from care per year has dropped from more than 16,000 in 1968,[3] to just over 3,980 in the year ending March 2013.[4] As a result, the demand for "desirable" domestic children often outstrips supply:[5] for example, in Italy, there are 15 couples wishing to adopt for every one local child eligible for adoption.[6] For this reason, many wanting to become parents have started to look to other jurisdictions to fulfil this aim.

Intercountry adoption is not only attractive because of the (perceived) number of children available for adoption,[7] but because of the characteristics of the children available. Adoptive parents are usually seeking a very young child with no attachments who can be easily integrated into their own family.[8] Although we saw from the statistics in Chapter Eight that many of the children leaving Albania, the Czech Republic, Estonia, Hungary, Latvia, Lithuania and

---

2 Indeed, intercountry adoption is specifically discouraged in such situations. See UNHCR, *Policy on Adoption of Refugee Children* (1995) <www.unhcr.org/cgi-bin/texis/vtx/home/opendocPDF.pdf?docid=3bd035d14> [19 February 2013]; International Social Service, *Earthquake in Haiti: Intercountry Adoption Cases* (2009, ISS/IRC) <www.iss-ssi.org/2009/assets/files/news/haiti_position%20CIR_ENG.pdf> [19 February 2013].

3 24,831 children were adopted in 1968, but 8,517 were adopted by parents or step-parents.

4 This number excludes step-parent adoptions (United Kingdom: Department for Education, *Children looked after in England, including adoption* (2013) <https://www.gov.uk/government/publications/children-looked-after-in-england-including-adoption> [19 May 2014]).

5 The characteristics of "desirable" adoptive children are discussed below.

6 United Nations Department of Economic and Social Affairs: Population Division, *Child Adoption: Trends and Policies* (2009) ST/ESA/SER.A/292, 108.

7 As was discussed in Chapter Three, often the children who are in institutions are not in need of a new family.

8 See United Nations Department of Economic and Social Affairs, above n 6, 98–135.

Slovakia are in fact older, the statistics in receiving countries tell a different story of the children entering Europe.[9] In 2009 in Norway, the average age of a child adopted domestically was 12.2 years, whereas for a child brought into the country through intercountry adoption, the average age was 2.2 years.[10] In Ireland, these figures were 8.2 years and 1.8 years respectively, in Denmark 15.8 years and 4.0 years, Switzerland 11.9 and 6.8 years.[11] This, in part, explains the preference for Russia as a country of origin for intercountry adoption: 32 per cent of children in institutional care are under the age of one.[12]

In addition to seeking children with certain "desirable" qualities, adoptive parents often seek intercountry adoption because the restrictions on parenting are lower than in their own country[13] – this is particularly true where parents have been deemed too old to adopt a child domestically, but can still seek a foreign child in a jurisdiction that does not have upper age limits.

The desire for parents to adopt – to have a child of their own, to form a family – is not an unnatural one and is most certainly not one that should be discouraged. There are many children who are genuinely in need of a loving family environment that only adoption will provide. However, this desire should not override the best interests of the child. As adoption is the only issue concerning which the best interests of the child is required to be the *paramount* consideration under the UNCRC, it clearly demands a purely child-centred approach that focuses not on the wishes of parents, but on the rights of the children. Shopping around for a jurisdiction that provides "desirable" children with low qualification criteria for adoptive parents is not in itself unethical, nor is it inconsistent with a genuine desire to care for a destitute child. However, it can become problematic where the desire for such children outpaces supply.

In 2006 in Spain there were 9,235 couples or individuals approved as intercountry adopters, but only 4,472 adoptions occurred,[14] whereas in Italy that figure was 6,309 approvals to 2,534 adoptions.[15] In 2007 in Denmark there were 1,500 prospective adopters waiting for children, with only 427 adoptions during

9 Table 1 in Chapter One shows that only four per cent of children entering Norway for intercountry adoption are from other European jurisdictions, while in Denmark that figure is ten per cent, Switzerland 28 per cent. Ireland is significantly higher with 65 per cent.

10 United Nations Department of Economic and Social Affairs, above n 6, 92. However, it should be noted that the statistics on domestic adoption may be driven up due to the number of step-parent adoptions, which make up 18.2 per cent of all adoptions (ibid., 103).

11 Ibid., 92. As above, this may be driven up by step-parent adoption: In Denmark, step-parent adoptions make up 46.4 per cent of all adoptions, while in Switzerland, they make up 25.6 per cent (ibid., 103). Statistics are not available for Ireland.

12 In 2004, this amounted to 19,962 children (ibid., 123–124).

13 See, for example, the English case of *Re C (Adoption: Legality)* [1999] 1 FLR 370 as discussed in Chapter Five.

14 European Union, *International Adoption in the European Union* (2009, European Parliament) 41 <www.childoneurope.org/issues/adoption/Report%20EP%20international%20adoption_EN.pdf> [7 February 2013].

15 Ibid., 42.

that year,[16] while in France, most dramatically, as of 2009 between 25,000 and 30,000 French applicants were certified as "fit to adopt" a foreign child, but only 4,000 children are brought into the country in intercountry adoption each year.[17]

The generation of such a large number of certificates of "eligibility to adopt" – as approval is known under the Hague Convention – is a threat to the systems of sending countries that are faced with a level of applications that is well above the number of children who are available for adoption.[18] Lammerant and Hofstetter report that Central Authorities and accredited bodies from sending countries vie with each other for certain "target" countries of origin, while other countries are ignored.[19] This means a considerable amount of pressure on sending countries, particularly when receiving countries are pushing to increase the number of children made available.[20] In this way, intercountry adoption becomes a market, regulated according to the laws of supply and demand.[21]

One way in which certain sending countries maintain control over intercountry adoption is to create a system of quotas under which each receiving state is allocated a number of applications that can be submitted by their citizens during a certain time period. However, this is not without its own problems. The greatest problem, as UNICEF suggests, is that it sends out the message that the country of origin will be "sending" a pre-determined number of children, which is neither constructive nor ethical.[22] Such a system also opens the door for corruption and abuse, where receiving state governments may lobby for higher quotas, rather than allowing these to be based purely on the needs and interests of children. Further, children should be matched according to their best interests, finding the best family for the individual child no matter which receiving country the parents are from. Where all places under the quota for a

---

16 Ibid., 41.

17 UNICEF Guidance Note on Intercountry Adoption in the CEE/CIS Region (September 2009) <www.unicef.org/ceecis/UNICEF_ICA_CEE_Guidance_WEB.pdf> [16 November 2012].

18 Ibid.

19 Isabelle Lammerant and Marlene Hofstetter, *Adoption: at what cost?* (2007, Terre des Hommes) 7, <www.terredeshommes.org/pdf/publication/adoption_embargo.pdf> [7 February 2013].

20 For example, the French Minister for Protection has advocated an increase in the number of adoptable foreign children for the benefit of prospective adoptive parents (ibid., 6). This can also be seen in the push from US Congress on Romania to lift its moratorium on intercountry adoption (see United States House of Representatives, *House Resolution 578* (109th Congress 2005–2006) (18 November 2005)).

21 In 2000, the Parliamentary Assembly of the Council of Europe expressed deep concern regarding "the current transformation of international adoption into nothing short of a market regulated by the capitalist laws of supply and demand, and characterised by a one-way flow of children from poor states or states in transition to developed countries" (*Recommendation 1443(2000): International Adoption: Respecting children's rights* (2000) <http://assembly.coe.int/Main.asp?link=/Documents/AdoptedText/ta00/EREC1443.htm> [21 May 2013]).

22 UNICEF, *Guidance Note on Intercountry Adoption in the CEE/CIS Region* (2009, UNICEF) <www.unicef.org/ceecis/UNICEF_ICA_CEE_Guidance_WEB.pdf> [16 November 2012].

particular country are taken, it may be that the child is sent to whichever country happens to have places still available. In the same way, there may be more children that need placement than are permitted under the quota, meaning that children are left in inadequate care where they may otherwise find a permanent family home.[23]

The solution to all of these problems is to reverse the system of intercountry adoption to one that is driven by sending countries, and by the needs of children, rather than by adoptive parents and their desires. UNICEF advocates such an approach, suggesting that sending states should contact receiving states when there is a child that needs placement, not vice versa.[24] However, in a world where intercountry adoption is increasingly seen by individuals and couples desirous to be parents as a logical step after infertility treatment and domestic adoption, this is easier said than done.

8.1.2. A RIGHT TO A CHILD?

Although it appears that intercountry adoption is now predominantly driven by the desires of adoptive parents, this does not mean that at any stage these parents have the *right* to adopt.[25] While this proposition is fairly uncontroversial when taken in the abstract, when applied in practice, it becomes more problematic. This is particularly the case when a Central Authority from a receiving state has issued a certificate under the Hague Convention that an individual or couple is "eligible and suited" to adopt, giving rise to an expectation – at least in the mind of that parent or parents – that they will be matched with a child.

This was challenged in the English case of *R (Thomson) v Minister of State for Children*,[26] in which prospective adoptive parents who were in various stages of the process to adopt children from Cambodia – including some for whom the certificate had been sent to the Cambodian authorities – disputed the decision of the Secretary of State to impose a moratorium on adoptions from that country due to numerous documented abuses. The prospective parents argued that there were undoubtedly orphans in Cambodia for whom an intercountry adoption would be a better option than a childhood spent in an institution; they suggested that there were less restrictive measures that should have been imposed that could have equally achieved the aim of preventing trafficking in children, and as such the moratorium was unjustified. Further, they argued that there was a

---

23 Ibid.

24 Ibid.

25 This is part of a wider debate concerning the "right to a child" driven in part by reproductive advancements. In the European context, see, for example, *Evans v United Kingdom* [2007] ECHR 264.

26 [2005] EWHC 1378 (Admin).

breach of the legitimate expectation that once they were approved as adopters, their application would continue to progress in the usual way.[27]

The High Court found that there was a pressing public interest that justified the suspension of intercountry adoptions from Cambodia without prior warning. The Secretary of State was entitled to conclude that there were no reasonably feasible safeguards that would have been sufficiently effective to address the real and urgent problems in that country,[28] and thus the adopters' applications could be halted, regardless of the current state of their application.

This decision was predicated on the fact that adoption is not a fundamental right analogous to an individual freedom, which would oblige the state to provide it to all citizens, but rather a privilege voluntarily extended, that can also be legitimately restricted. This has been confirmed in the European system by the European Commission on Human Rights in *X v Belgium and the Netherlands*, which in 1975 decided that

> "a State cannot separate two persons united by an adoption contract, or forbid them to meet, without engaging its responsibility under Article 8 of the Convention. But one should not deduce from this a positive obligation on the State to grant a particular status – that of adoption – to the applicant and the person in his care."[29]

As will be seen below, however, if the state does decide to voluntarily extend this privilege to its citizens, this must be extended equally, with any differentiation in treatment justified on reasonable and objective grounds.

The European Court of Human Rights has also made clear that even if an intercountry adoption has taken place, this should not be enforced against the interests of the children. In *Pini v Romania*, the adoption order had been made between two Romanian girls and Italian adoptive parents, but this was not enforced due to the obstruction of the institution that the girls were living in. On application to the ECtHR, the Court found that the interference with the adoptive family life was justified under article 8, as the girls did not want to join the parents, and that adoption must be about the interests of the children.[30]

These principles are relatively settled in international and regional human rights law. The more interesting question is whether the *sending state* has an obligation to make children available for intercountry adoption when they cannot be cared for in a suitable manner within the jurisdiction.

---

27 This is different from claiming that they had a right to adopt once the certificate had been issued – they acknowledged that there were various legitimate issues that may have arisen that would have prevented this, such as not being matched with a suitable child. But they argued that a moratorium was outside of such "normal" reasons for an adoption not to take place.

28 *R (Thomson) v Minister of State for Children* [2005] EWHC 1378 (Admin), [161].

29 (Appl. No. 6482/74) Decision of 10 July 1975.

30 [2005] ECHR 275. The Court did find a violation of article 6 as a result of the failure of the Romanian authorities to execute the adoption order in a timely manner.

There is clearly no obligation to permit intercountry adoption under article 21 of the UNCRC. This article states in its chapeau that it applies only to those states "that recognise and/or permit the system of adoption", allowing states to decide whether or not to undertake this practice. Further, article 21(b) provides that even for those states that do practise adoption, "intercountry adoption *may* be considered as an alternative means of child's care".[31] As was discussed in Chapter Two, the original drafting of this article required states to "facilitate the process of adoption", but this was revised following the objection of certain states who were philosophically opposed to intercountry adoption and did not want it mandated, or even encouraged.[32]

Further, the Hague Convention does not commit a state to placing children in intercountry adoption – it is up to the state of origin to decide what level of involvement with this practice is consistent with the best interests of the child.[33] As the Hague Guide to Good Practice makes clear, even the placing of a moratorium on intercountry adoption is not necessarily inconsistent with the obligations under the Convention.[34] Especially in cases of widespread corruption or other abuses, or where the system of intercountry adoption is undermining the domestic child welfare system – as was seen in Chapter Three – the domestic authorities may decide that there is too much danger in allowing the practice to continue.

Some authors, such as Sara Dillon, have criticised moratoria on intercountry adoption on the grounds that they deny children living in institutions the right to grow up in a family environment.[35] This argument is based on article 27 of the UNCRC, which recognises the right to a standard of living adequate for the child's physical, mental, spiritual, moral and social development and places an obligation on states to secure this, within their abilities and financial capacities. However, while leaving a child in an inadequate environment is clearly not optimal, the situation cannot be resolved that easily. As was discussed previously, where intercountry adoption is not strictly regulated, it can lead to children being separated from their families improperly, and others being placed in the welfare system – and institutions – who would not otherwise be there. Moreover, where intercountry adoption is undermining domestic care options, this can

31 My emphasis.

32 David Johnson, "Cultural and Regional Pluralism in the Drafting of the UN Convention on the Rights of the Child", in Michael Freeman and Philip Veerman (eds), *The Ideologies of Children's Rights* (1992, Kluwer Law) 105.

33 See Hague Conference, *The Implementation and Operation of the 1993 Hague Intercountry Adoption Convention: Guide to Good Practice: Guide No 1* (2008) [448] <www.hcch.net/upload/adoguide_e.pdf> [7 February 2013].

34 Ibid., [458].

35 Sara Dillon, "Making Legal Regimes for Intercountry Adoption Reflect Human Rights Principles: Transforming the United Nations Convention on the Rights of the Child with the Hague Convention on Intercountry Adoption" (2003) 21 *Boston University International Law Journal* 179.

violate the rights of not only the children currently in need of placement, but those of years to come. Thus although the best interests of the individual child must be a primary consideration in deciding whether to permit the practice of intercountry adoption,[36] this can be overridden in the interests of the regulation of the system as a whole, in order to prevent further violations of the rights of other children.

As such, it is clear that there is neither a right to adopt, nor a right to be adopted. Where intercountry adoption is permitted, however, and such a placement has been determined to be in the best interests of the individual child, the question that must be answered is how, and on what criteria, prospective adoptive parents should be chosen.

8.2. QUALIFICATIONS OF ADOPTIVE PARENTS

8.2.1. INTERNATIONAL INSTRUMENTS

The selection of prospective adoptive parents is an area in which the international conventions provide little guidance. The UNCRC does not contain any reference to the identity or attributes of adopters, nor has the Committee on the Rights of the Child shed any light on the issue.

The Hague Convention provides little more in the way of criteria, requiring only that the competent authorities of the receiving state have determined that the adoptive parents "are eligible and suited to adopt", meaning that they have fulfilled all the legal requirements (eligible) and meet the social-psychological criteria (suited).[37] As a result of the (intentional) imprecision of this requirement, it is up to the receiving state to decide how it will determine whether an applicant is eligible and suitable to adopt a foreign child. While some states may adopt the same criteria as those which apply to prospective domestic adoptive parents, others place additional, or fewer, requirements on intercountry adoptions, despite this being contrary to the requirement under the UNCRC that children concerned by intercountry adoption enjoy safeguards and standards equivalent to those in domestic adoption.[38]

The Hague Convention also requires the Central Authority in the receiving state to prepare a report with information on adopters including their "identity,

---

36 When deciding on the adoptability of the child and whether or not he or she should be adopted, the child's best interests will be paramount. When deciding the organisation of the child welfare system and the possible mechanisms for alternative care, article 3 of the UNCRC and the requirement of "primary" consideration applies.

37 Gonzalo Parra-Aranguren, *Explanatory Report on the Convention on Protection of Children and Co-operation in Respect of Intercountry Adoption* (1993) [180] <www.hcch.net/index_en.php?act=publications.details&pid=918> [7 February 2013].

38 Article 21(c) UNCRC.

eligibility and suitability to adopt, background, family and medical history, social environment, reasons for adoption, ability to undertake an intercountry adoption, as well as the characteristics of the children for whom they would be qualified to care."[39] There is no guidance given on how such factors are to be determined, leaving it to the domestic authorities to decide whether they have been fulfilled.

The authorities of the sending state will also play a role in determining whether or not prospective parents may adopt a child from within their jurisdiction. Sending states must agree that the adoption may proceed under article 17(c) of the Convention, leaving it within their power to refuse adoptive parents who do not meet the eligibility and suitability requirements within their own domestic law. This means that prospective adoptive parents often have to meet two sets of criteria, one in the receiving, one in the sending, state. Although when assessing *suitability*, sending states predominantly adopt a flexible approach and accept the assessment of the receiving state,[40] on issues of *eligibility*, particularly concerning age, marital status and sexual orientation, much stricter scrutiny applies.

Of course, not all states are party to the Hague Convention, including major sending states such as Russia and Ukraine. In such cases, different rules may apply in the receiving state, although the adoptive parents will still have to meet the adoption requirements in the country of origin. In England, for example, no matter where the child is to be adopted from, the prospective adoptive parents must be approved by the local authorities or a registered adoption agency, and be issued with a certificate of eligibility. The only difference between a Hague Convention adoption and one that involves a child from a non-designated country is whether or not an adoption order will have to be issued by English courts, or whether the foreign adoption is accepted.[41] However, as was discussed in Chapter Five, in other states non-Hague adoptions can be undertaken without any oversight by local authorities or registered agencies, leaving children adopted under such situations without the benefit of official regulation of their placement.

8.2.2. THE AGE OF ADOPTERS: HOW OLD IS TOO OLD?

Age is a criterion used by every jurisdiction to determine the eligibility of prospective parents to adopt. This can take the form of a maximum or

39 Article 15(1) Hague Convention.

40 Parra-Aranguren, above n 37, [505].

41 See Adoption with a Foreign Element Regulations 2005. Adoptions from certain countries that are not parties to the Hague Convention, but are deemed "designated countries" (according to the Adoption (Designation of Overseas Adoptions) Order 1973) are also recognised directly in England.

minimum age for the parents, and/or a maximum or minimum age difference between the parents and the child, determined either by judicial practice or legislation.

Despite the lack of clarity in the international instruments, the Revised European Convention on the Adoption of Children of 2008 contains some guidance in this area, although it takes a very loose approach, leaving a large degree of leeway for national authorities.

Article 9 of the Convention reads:

> "1. A child may be adopted only if the adopter has attained the minimum age prescribed by law for this purpose, this minimum age being neither less than 18 nor more than 30 years. There shall be an appropriate age difference between the adopter and the child, having regard to the best interests of the child, preferably a difference of at least 16 years.
> 2. The law may, however, permit the requirement as to the minimum age or the age difference to be waived in the best interests of the child:
> (a) when the adopter is the spouse or registered partner of the child's father or mother; or
> (b) by reason of exceptional circumstances."

Nearly all European jurisdictions require a minimum age difference between the adoptive parents and child.[42] This ranges from 14 years (Spain),[43] 15 years (Andorra,[44] Belgium,[45] Bulgaria,[46] France,[47] Luxembourg,[48] Moldova,[49] Monaco,[50] Ukraine),[51] 16 years (Azerbaijan,[52] Georgia,[53] Russia,[54]

42 England, Estonia, Germany, Iceland, Ireland, Norway and Sweden are the exceptions. However, although there is no legislation in place regarding this issue, it is often practice to ensure that there is a reasonable age difference between the child and adoptive parent.

43 Article 175(2) Civil Code.

44 Article 4 Qualified Law on Adoption of 21 March 1996. This is reduced to ten years if the adoptee is the child of a spouse.

45 Article 345 Civil Code. If the child is that of a spouse or cohabitant, or a descendant of the first degree, then the age difference only need be ten years.

46 Article 79 Family Code. The age difference need only be between the child and one of the couple adopting, and is waived if the adoptee is the child of a spouse.

47 Article 344 Civil Code. This is reduced to ten years if the adoptee is the child of a spouse. The age requirement can also be dispensed with if a court sees fit.

48 Article 334 Act of 13 June 1989. This may be reduced if the adoptee is the child of a spouse, but there must still be at least ten years difference.

49 Article 123 Family Code. This does not apply if the adoptee is the child of a spouse. The age difference may be reduced for good reasons, but there must remain at least five years' difference.

50 Article 266 Civil Code. This can be reduced to ten years if the adoptee is the child of a spouse.

51 Article 211 Family Code.

52 Article 121.1 Family Code. This age difference is only required if the child is being adopted by a single person, and the court may reduce this for significant reasons.

53 Article 1250 Civil Code. The court can dispense with this requirement for legitimate reasons.

54 Article 128 Family Law 1995. This requirement is only for a single adopter, and can be reduced for valid reasons by the courts.

Switzerland),[55] and 18 years (Albania,[56] Armenia,[57] Austria,[58] Bosnia and Herzegovina,[59] Croatia,[60] Cyprus,[61] Finland,[62] Greece,[63] Italy,[64] Latvia,[65] Liechtenstein,[66] Lithuania,[67] FYR Macedonia,[68] Montenegro,[69] the Netherlands,[70] Romania,[71] San Marino,[72] Serbia,[73] Slovenia,[74] Turkey)[75] to 21 years (Malta).[76] In the Czech Republic,[77] Poland[78] and Slovakia,[79] there is no age restriction defined by legislation, and it is up to the courts to decide whether the age difference is adequate, in light of the usual age difference between a parent and child.

---

55 Article 265 Civil Code.

56 Article 241 Family Code. This can be reduced to 15 years if the adoptee is the child of a spouse.

57 Article 117 Family Code. This age difference is only required if the child is being adopted by a single person.

58 Article 180 Civil Code. This can be waived if the adoptee is the child of a spouse, or related to one of the parents.

59 United States: Department of State, *Country Information* <http://adoption.state.gov/country_information.php> [21 December 2012].

60 Petar Sarcevic et al, *Family Law in Croatia* (2011, Kluwer Law) 147.

61 Section 4 Adoption Law 1995. Only one of the spouses must meet this age requirement.

62 Section 7 Adoption Act 22/2012. An exception can be made if the adoptee is the child of a spouse, a relationship comparable with that between a parent and child has already been established, or there are other justified grounds.

63 Article 1544 Civil Code. If there is good reason, or if the adoptee is the child of a spouse, the courts may authorise the reduction of this limit, but there must remain at least 15 years' difference.

64 Article 6(3) Law 184/1983.

65 Section 163 Civil Law. This may be reduced if the adoptee is the child of a spouse, but there must still be at least 16 years' difference.

66 Article 180 Civil Code. This may be reduced if the adoptee is the child of a spouse, but there must still be at least 16 years' difference.

67 Article 3.210 Civil Code. This may be reduced if the adoptee is the child of a spouse, but there must still be at least 15 years' difference.

68 Article 118 Family Law (FYR Macedonia, *State Party Report to the UN Committee on the Rights of the Child* (12 November 2009) CRC/C/MKD/2, [141]).

69 Article 126 Family Law. This only needs to be met by one of the adopters.

70 Article 1:228(1)(c) Civil Code.

71 Article 9 Law No 273/2004. This can be reduced to 15 years for well-founded reasons.

72 Section 7 Law No 49/1986 (San Marino, *State Party Report to the UN Committee on the Rights of the Child* (17 March 2003) CRC/C/8/Add.46, [66]).

73 Article 103 Family Act. This can be reduced for exceptional reasons.

74 Hague Conference, *Country Profile: Slovenia* (2010) <www.hcch.net/index_en.php?act=publications.details&pid=5096&dtid=42> [14 January 2012]. The Centre for Social Work can waive this requirement if it is in the adoptee's interests.

75 Turkey, *State Party Report to the UN Committee on the Rights of the Child* (18 July 2011) CRC/C/TUR/2–3, [97].

76 Article 115 Civil Code.

77 Section 65(1) Act No 94/1963 Sb on Family.

78 Article 114(2) Family Code.

79 Hague Conference, *Country Profile: Slovakia* (2010) <www.hcch.net/index_en.php?act=publications.details&pid=5095&dtid=42> [14 January 2012].

Several states prescribe a maximum age difference between a child and a prospective adoptive parent, either instead of, or in conjunction with, the minimum age difference. This is set at 40 years in Denmark[80] and the Netherlands,[81] 45 years in Finland,[82] Italy,[83] Malta,[84] FYR Macedonia[85] and San Marino,[86] and 50 years in Greece,[87] Montenegro,[88] Portugal[89] and Serbia.[90]

The purpose of such laws is to ensure that there is an appropriate difference between the parents and child to resemble a traditional family. However, notions of what constitutes a "traditional family" are rapidly changing, as will be seen below in relation to single parent adoption, as well as homosexual parenting.

Maximum age differences are often further justified on the grounds that children need parents who are emotionally and physically fit to parent them until they achieve independence, which is increasingly later in life.[91] Concerns have also been expressed about older parents placing a burden on their children later in their own lives, with health problems that need support and assistance, and surveys suggest that children of older adoptive parents feel that their parents are less likely to understand them, as there are often two generation gaps, rather than simply one.[92]

While definite limits may be easier from an administrative point of view for receiving countries, it is important that children are not denied loving homes

---

80 This is not set in legislation, but as a general rule the courts will not accept a prospective adoptive parent over 40 years older than the child (see Hague Conference, *Country Profile: Denmark* (2010) <www.hcch.net/index_en.php?act=publications.details&pid=5128&dtid=42> [14 January 2012]).

81 This is not contained in legislation, but permission to adopt will be refused by the responsible Minister if the age difference of one of the prospective adopters and the child exceeds 40 years, unless there are special circumstances (see Hague Conference, *Country Profile: Netherlands* (2010) <www.hcch.net/index_en.php?act=publications.details&pid=5429&dtid=42> [14 January 2012]).

82 Section 7 Adoption Act 22/2012.

83 Articles 6(3), 6(6) Law 184/1983. The difference may be over 45 years for one of the adoptive couple, as long as it does not exceed 55 years.

84 Article 115 Civil Code.

85 Article 118 Family Law (FYR Macedonia, *State Party Report to the UN Committee on the Rights of the Child* (12 November 2009) CRC/C/MKD/2, [141]).

86 Section 7 Law No 49/1986 (San Marino, *State Party Report to the UN Committee on the Rights of the Child* (17 March 2003) CRC/C/8/Add.46, [66]).

87 Article 1544 Civil Code.

88 Article 126 Family Law.

89 Article 1979(3), (4) Civil Code. The adopter's age can exceed 50 years if exceptionally strong reasons justify it.

90 Article 103 Family Act. This can be extended in exceptional circumstances.

91 Australia: Western Australia Department for Child Protection, *Excerpts from Submissions to the Parliamentary Legislative Review Committee* (undated) <www.dcp.wa.gov.au/FosteringandAdoption/AdoptionAndHomeForLife/Documents/PlacementCriteriaAgeRestrictions.pdf> [16 November 2012].

92 Ibid.

based on arbitrary numbers. All parents will have strengths and weaknesses, which should be considered on an individual basis rather than according to assumptions concerning certain types of applicants.

Nevertheless, in addition to minimum and maximum age differences for parents, many states require a prospective adoptive parent to be of a minimum age before they adopt. While some set this at 18, or the age of full legal capacity (Armenia,[93] Bulgaria,[94] the Czech Republic,[95] Georgia,[96] Lithuania,[97] Romania,[98] Slovakia,[99] Slovenia),[100] others set higher age minimums of 21 (Croatia,[101] England,[102] Ireland,[103] Italy,[104] Serbia,[105] Ukraine),[106] 25 (Andorra,[107] Belgium,[108] Bosnia and Herzegovina,[109] Cyprus,[110] Estonia,[111] Finland,[112] Germany,[113] Iceland,[114] Latvia,[115]

93 Hague Conference, *Country Profile: Armenia* (2010) <www.hcch.net/index_en.php?act=publications.details&pid=5115&dtid=42> [14 January 2012].

94 Article 79 Family Code. This is only required for one of the couple, and an exception may be made if the adoptee is the child of a spouse.

95 Hague Conference, *Country Profile: Czech Republic* (2010) <www.hcch.net/index_en.php?act=publications.details&pid=5116&dtid=42> [14 January 2012].

96 Article 1245 Civil Code.

97 Article 3.210 Civil Code.

98 Article 9(1) Law No 273/2004.

99 Hague Conference, *Country Profile: Slovakia* (2010) <www.hcch.net/index_en.php?act=publications.details&pid=5095&dtid=42> [14 January 2012].

100 Hague Conference, *Country Profile: Slovenia* (2010) <www.hcch.net/index_en.php?act=publications.details&pid=5096&dtid=42> [14 January 2012].

101 Petar Sarcevic et al, *Family Law in Croatia* (2011, Kluwer Law) 147. When siblings are being adopted, only one parent must meet this condition.

102 Section 50(1), (2) Adoption and Children Act 2002. Where one of the couple is the mother or father of the adoptee, it is sufficient if that parent is 18, and the other member of the couple 21.

103 Section 10(5)(a) Adoption Act 1991. Only one spouse must be over 21 if the adoptee is the child or relative of one of the spouses.

104 Hague Conference, *Country Profile: Italy* (2012) <www.hcch.net/index_en.php?act=publications.details&pid=5153&dtid=42> [14 January 2012].

105 Article 103(1) Family Act.

106 Article 211 Family Code.

107 Or the average age of the couple cannot be less than 25 (Hague Conference, *Country Profile: Andorra* (2010) <www.hcch.net/index_en.php?act=publications.details&pid=5082&dtid=42> [14 January 2012]).

108 Article 345 Civil Code. The minimum age can be reduced to 18 if the adoptee is the child of a spouse.

109 United States: Department of State, *Country Information* <http://adoption.state.gov/country_information.php> [21 December 2012].

110 Section 4 Adoption Law 1995. Only one parent must meet this requirement.

111 Section 150 Family Law Act 2009. A younger person may be permitted to adopt if the court deems there is a good reason.

112 Section 6 Adoption Act 22/2012. This can be lowered to 18 if the adoptee is the child of a spouse, or if there are exceptional grounds.

113 Section 1743 Civil Code. This is reduced to 21 if the adopter is single, or when spouses are adopting, only one must be 25 and the other must be 21.

114 Article 5 Adoption Act No 130/1999. This can be reduced to 20 if special circumstances apply.

115 Section 163 Civil Law.

Luxembourg,[116] Moldova,[117] Norway,[118] Portugal,[119] San Marino,[120] Spain,[121] Sweden),[122] 28 (France,[123] Malta,[124] Monaco),[125] 30 (Greece,[126] Montenegro,[127] Turkey),[128] and exceptionally, 35 (Switzerland).[129]

The situation in Austria and Liechtenstein is unusual, as it differentiates between female and male applicants. While females need only be 28 years of age, males must be 30.[130] The reason for this difference in treatment on the basis of gender is unclear, as there appears to be no objective reason why women would be suited to adopt at an earlier age than men.

Several states also place maximum age limits on prospective adoptive parents, either in law or in practice. These vary from 35 in Croatia,[131] to 41 in the Netherlands,[132] 45 in Andorra,[133] Bosnia and Herzegovina,[134] FYR Macedonia,[135]

---

116 Article 334 Act of 13 June 1989. Where spouses are adopting, only one must be older than 25, as long as the other is older than 21.

117 Article 121 Family Code.

118 Section 3 Act of 28 February 1986, No 8 relating to Adoption. If there are strong reasons for doing so, the Ministry may issue an order to a person who has reached 20 years of age.

119 Article 1979 Civil Code. If the adopter is single, he or she must be over 30 years.

120 Section 7 Law No 49/1986 (San Marino, *State Party Report to the UN Committee on the Rights of the Child* (17 March 2003) CRC/C/8/Add.46, [66]).

121 Article 175(1) Civil Code. Only one spouse need be over the age of 25, and exceptions can be made for a sole applicant who is adopting a relative.

122 Section 5:1 Children and Parents Code (1949:381). This can be reduced to 18 if the adoptee is the child of a spouse.

123 Article 343-1 Civil Code. Only one of a couple must be over 28.

124 Article 115 Civil Code.

125 Article 242 Civil Code. Only one of the adopters must be of this age.

126 Article 1543 Civil Code.

127 Article 126 Family Law. If spouses are adopting, only one must be over 30.

128 Turkey, *State Party Report to the UN Committee on the Rights of the Child* (18 July 2011) CRC/C/TUR/2-3, [98]. If the parent(s) wish to adopt a child under one year old, they must be under 40 years of age.

129 Articles 264–265 Civil Code. This is only for single persons – married couples adopting must have been married for five years.

130 Austria: article 180 Civil Code; Liechtenstein: article 180 Civil Code. An exception can be made in each of these jurisdictions if the adoptee is the child of a spouse or a relative.

131 Petar Sarcevic et al, *Family Law in Croatia* (2011, Kluwer Law) 147. In cases where there are particularly justifiable reasons, the adopters may be over 35, but the age difference may not be more than 45 years. When siblings are being adopted, only one parent must meet this condition.

132 Hague Conference, *Country Profile: Netherlands* (2010) <www.hcch.net/index_en.php?act=publications.details&pid=5429&dtid=42> [14 January 2012]. Once the prospective adoptive parent reaches the age of 42, the Minister may grant an exception if he or she considers it appropriate in the particular circumstances.

133 This is only if the child is less than 12 months old, in which case the average age of the couple must be less than 45 (Hague Conference, *Country Profile: Andorra* (2010) <www.hcch.net/index_en.php?act=publications.details&pid=5082&dtid=42> [14 January 2012]).

134 United States: Department of State, *Country Information*, <http://adoption.state.gov/country_information.php> [21 December 2012].

135 Article 118 Family Law (FYR Macedonia, *State Party Report to the UN Committee on the Rights of the Child* (12 November 2009) CRC/C/MKD/2, [141]).

Norway[136] and Serbia,[137] 50 in Finland,[138] Lithuania,[139] Moldova,[140] Montenegro,[141] and Slovakia,[142] and 60 in Greece[143] and Portugal.[144]

The requirement for prospective adopters to be of a certain age can be attributed to the need for a parent to be stable and settled, both financially and emotionally; however, as with age differences, this is something that could be better judged by an individual examination of the prospective adopter's circumstances and personal attributes, rather than an arbitrary number.[145] It is interesting to note in this respect that the minimum age for a prospective adoptive parent in Switzerland – 35 – is the maximum age for a prospective adoptive parent in Croatia.

In light of this, the Polish and Czech approach seems especially suitable, having no age set in legislation, with the decision being left to the courts as to whether the ages of the parents, and the age difference between them and the child, are appropriate. However, such an approach could cause difficulties in intercountry adoptions, where prospective adopters may be matched with a child and travel to the country, only to find that at the last judicial hearing they are deemed too old or young. While some assurance will of course be given by studying judicial practice, it could create considerable uncertainty in the mind of prospective adopters who are on the borderline of what might be deemed an acceptable age difference, and discourage them from adopting children in that jurisdiction.

Many states have legislative exceptions for the welfare of the child, if an adoption would be in his or her best interests, as is contemplated by the ECA 2008.[146] Where there is no such exception, however, it raises the question of whether an age restriction promotes the welfare of children, or whether it simply narrows the pool of prospective adopters unnecessarily and denies children the chance to be placed in appropriate and loving homes. This is a question that will

136 Hague Conference, *Country Profile: Norway* (2010) <www.hcch.net/index_en.php?act=publications.details&pid=5090&dtid=42> [14 January 2012]. Exceptions to this can be made.

137 Article 103(1) Family Act. The Minister may allow a person who is older than 45 to adopt exceptionally.

138 Section 6 Adoption Act 22/2012.

139 Article 3.210 Civil Code. An adopter may be permitted who is older than 50 in exceptional cases.

140 Article 121 Family Code.

141 Article 126 Family Law. If there are particularly justified reasons, an adopter may be older than 50, but the age difference must not be more than 50 years.

142 Hague Conference, *Country Profile: Slovakia* (2010) <www.hcch.net/index_en.php?act=publications.details&pid=5095&dtid=42> [14 January 2012].

143 Article 1543 Civil Code.

144 Article 1979 Civil Code.

145 While some states permit 18- and 21-year-olds to adopt, this is usually a matter of law and not practice, and adoption is almost never granted to people this young except in cases of relative adoption.

146 As can be seen above, the majority of states also allow exceptions to these rules where the adoptee is the child of the spouse of the adopter, removing the restriction completely or adjusting the age or age difference required. However, relative adoptions will not be discussed in this book.

arise in relation to all restrictions on adoptive parents, whether it be age, marital status or sexual orientation, and it is one which the ECtHR has dealt with on a number of occasions.

Although, as established above, there is no right to adopt under international law or the ECHR, where the state extends a privilege falling within the scope of one of the Convention rights, it must do so in a non-discriminatory manner.[147] As such, if adoption is permitted by the state, the restrictions on eligibility and suitability of prospective adopters must comply with article 14 ECHR. To withstand scrutiny under this article, any difference in treatment must have an objective and reasonable justification (that is, pursue a legitimate aim), and there must be a reasonable relationship of proportionality between this aim and the means employed to pursue it.[148] This is a less strict level of scrutiny than that imposed by the principle of proportionality under article 8, discussed in Chapter Three. The means employed do not have to cause the least interference possible, merely be a reasonable response to the objective pursued.

In the case of *X v Netherlands*,[149] a couple complained that the Dutch authorities had discriminated against them because their suitability to act as adoptive parents in an intercountry adoption was measured in terms of age. At the time, the Dutch law required that the age difference be less than 40 years for a foreign child, but 50 years for a Dutch child. The Commission noted that "it is left to national law to determine whether, or subject to what conditions, the exercise of the right should be permitted", subject to the "reasonable relationship" test outlined above. Although the Commission did not come to a decision on this issue, as the case was concluded on other grounds, this test has formed the basis of decisions concerning the qualifications of adopters for the last 30 years.

For this reason, except in the cases of Austria and Liechtenstein, which differentiate on the basis of sex, it would appear unlikely that any challenge to the age requirements on prospective adoptive parents would be upheld by the ECtHR. The wide range of practices throughout Europe, and the child-welfare-based reasons for the restrictions, would mean that the Court would be likely to afford states a wide margin of appreciation in this area. Nevertheless, given the

147 In *Fretté v France* [2002] ECHR 156, the Court held that the desire to adopt fell within the scope of article 8, and thus could be examined for compliance with article 14. However, the partly concurring opinion of Judge Costa joined by Judges Jungwiert and Traja disagreed with this analysis. They argued that because there is no right to adopt or form a family under international law or the ECHR, there was no interference by the state in the applicant's private or family life, and there could be no link between article 14 and article 8. This was reiterated by Judge Zupančič in the case of *EB v France* [2008] ECHR 55, which will be discussed below. While these judges made a valid point that the reasoning behind the majority's decision that the matter fell within the scope of article 8 was lacking, their own argument relied too greatly on whether there had been a *violation* of article 8, rather than whether the desire to found a family could fall within its scope.

148 See, for example, *Fretté v France* [2002] ECHR 156, [34].

149 (Appl. No. 8896/80) Decision of 10 March 1981.

lack of consideration given to this issue by the international instruments, and the permissive nature of the ECA 2008, the ECHR is potentially the most effective instrument in this area in Europe.

It is clear that a flexible approach would be most appropriate to ensure that the best families are found for children placed in intercountry adoption, regardless of age. Although this necessarily involves substantially more resources, as an individual assessment must be carried out for each applicant, rather than relying on set age limits, in the majority of countries this is a payment that the adoptive parent is responsible for, rather than the authorities themselves. As such, a flexible approach would be more consistent with not only the rights of parents not to be discriminated against on the basis of their age alone, unconnected with personal attributes, but also the right of the child to be placed in the most suitable family.

8.2.3. MARITAL STATUS: SINGLE ADOPTION

While once adoption, like other forms of parenting, was seen as strictly the domain of married couples, it is now widely viewed as a legitimate mechanism by which a single person may form a family. In Finland, 14.3 per cent of adoptions are now ordered in favour of single parents, with 10.6 per cent in England, 10.3 per cent in Denmark and 6.8 per cent in France.[150]

The Revised European Convention on the Adoption of Children of 2008 requires that both single and married persons be permitted to adopt, with article 7(1) stating:

> "The law shall permit a child to be adopted:
> (a) by two persons of different sex
> (i) who are married to each other, or
> (ii) where such an institution exists, have entered into a registered partnership together;
> (b) by one person."

Although the ECA 2008 is still not widely ratified, the majority of European states do allow intercountry adoption by single persons; the only exception being Ukraine – which *is* a party to the ECA 2008 – which allows domestic adoption by single parents, but only permits married foreigners to adopt a Ukrainian child.[151]

---

150 It should be noted, however, that these figures vary from state to state, with only 3.9 per cent in Slovakia and 2.3 per cent in Switzerland (United Nations Department of Economic and Social Affairs: Population Division, *Child Adoption: Trends and Policies* (2009) ST/ESA/SER.A/292, 101; United Kingdom: Department for Education, *Children looked after in England, including adoption* (2013) <https://www.gov.uk/government/publications/children-looked-after-in-england-including-adoption> [19 May 2014].).

151 Article 212(1)(9) Family Code.

However, many other jurisdictions only permit single foreigners to adopt in exceptional circumstances, or for special reasons, for example in Cyprus,[152] Croatia,[153] Serbia[154] and Slovakia.[155] These conditions are often so restrictive that the possibility for single persons to adopt is illusory in practice. Further, in Lithuania, single persons are only permitted to adopt where the prospective parent has been the foster parent, where the child has extremely serious health problems and no married couple wish to adopt, or where the child is over eight years of age and unable to be placed with another family.[156]

While the purpose of these laws is clearly to protect the "traditional" family, in view of changing social conditions and the evolving face of families in Europe, it is important that such restrictions are carefully tailored to suit the best interests of children. In Montenegro and Luxembourg, single persons are only permitted to enter into a simple adoption,[157] which, as will be seen below in the case of *Wagner and JMWL v Luxembourg*, can mean that a child is left without the permanency of a full adoption despite the fact that his or her legal ties to the birth family have been completely severed.

Furthermore, in Georgia, Lithuania and Russia, if the child is adopted by a single person, he or she will retain the links with the birth parent of the opposite sex of the adopter, so he or she will continue to have one male and one female "parent".[158] This can create an uneasy covenant between the birth family and adoptive family, and although Chapter Nine will emphasise the importance for a child of the ability to obtain information concerning his or her origins and identity, it may be disruptive to the adoptive placement to continue to have such close ties immediately after the adoption takes place. It is important for the welfare of the child that the adoptive parent is secure in his or her role, and does not fear being displaced by a birth parent, or forced to share parenting decisions with someone otherwise uninvolved with the child's life in another country.

Further restrictions are in place in Malta, where a single person cannot adopt a female child,[159] and Cyprus, where a single male cannot adopt a female child, unless there are special circumstances.[160] The reasons for such prohibitions can

---

152 Yves Brulard and Letitia Dumont, *Comparative Study Relating to Procedures for Adoption Among the Member States of the European Union, Practical Difficulties Encountered in this Field by European Citizens within the Context of the European Pillar of Justice and Civil Matters and Means of Solving these Problems and of Protecting Children's Rights* (2007, European Union) 77.

153 Petar Sarcevic et al, *Family Law in Croatia* (2011, Kluwer Law) 147.

154 Article 105 Family Act.

155 Brulard and Dumont, above n 152, 433.

156 Article 3.210(2) Civil Code. See also United States: Department of State, *Country Information*, <http://adoption.state.gov/country_information.php> [21 December 2012].

157 Montenegro: article 134 Family Law; Luxembourg: article 367 Civil Code; but see *Wagner and JMWL v Luxembourg* (Appl. No. 76240/01) Judgment of 28 June 2007 below.

158 See *Wagner and JMWL v Luxembourg*, [69].

159 Ibid., [68].

160 Section 4(2) Adoption Law 1995.

be seen in the reports of sexual abuse of internationally adopted children.[161] On the other hand, Armenia prohibits single males from adopting under any circumstances, which is based not so much on the protection of the child from abuse, but on social stereotypes concerning the roles of men and women in caring for children.[162]

If single adopters are not to be granted equal status with adoptive couples, the Irish legislation best reflects the requirement of the best interests of the child, allowing single persons to adopt where the Adoption Authority considers it desirable, taking into account the child's welfare.[163] As with restrictions on the age of adopters, restrictions on single parenthood often fail to take into account the individual circumstances and aptitude of the adopter, focusing rather on his or her status. While studies show that children in two-parent families are less likely to experience cognitive, emotional and social problems, receive more effective parenting and are subjected to fewer stressful events and circumstances than children in one-parent households,[164] this should be merely one factor that is considered in an application from a prospective adoptive parent or parents. While it is legitimate to consider the impact that single parenthood may have on the individual applicant's ability to provide care for the child, it should not be the only consideration.

Contrary to this approach, however, the ECtHR has been reluctant to interfere with restrictions on adoptions by single persons. In the 1975 case of *X v Belgium and the Netherlands*,[165] the European Commission on Human Rights found that there had been no violation of an unmarried man's right to "marry and to found a family" in refusing his adoption application, as the existence of a couple was fundamental to the exercise of this right.

As discussed above, the Commission went on to find that article 8 did not place a "positive obligation on the State to grant a particular status – that of adoption – to the applicant and the person in his care". While it is true that the ECHR does not require adoption to be recognised within the jurisdiction, and therefore establishes no "right to adopt", recent jurisprudence suggests that where adoption *is* permitted, domestic authorities must grant sufficient legal safeguards to parent–child relationships that are already established.

This was seen in the seminal case of *Wagner and JMWL v Luxembourg*, which involved a single woman who was a Luxembourger citizen, who travelled to Peru to adopt a child. The adoption order was granted by the Peruvian provincial family court, but the mother's attempt to have this recognised as a full adoption in Luxembourg failed, as only simple adoptions were available to single persons.

161 See, for example, the case of Russian born adoptee Masha Allen.
162 See *Wagner and JMWL v Luxembourg*, above n 157, [68].
163 Section 10(2) Adoption Act 1991.
164 See, for example, Paul Amato, "The Impact of Family Formation Change on the Cognitive, Social and Emotional Well-Being of the Next Generation" (2005) 15(2) *The Future of Children* 75.
165 (Appl. No. 6482/74) Decision of 10 July 1975.

The applicant argued that the distinction between married and single adopters was discriminatory and thus in contravention of article 14 in conjunction with article 8 ECHR. The government, on the other hand, contended that the distinction had the legitimate aim of protecting the child, as two parents were better able to care for an adopted child, especially one who had come from abroad and had been uprooted from everything he or she knew.[166]

Interestingly, the Court based its findings under article 14 not on the claims of the *mother* not to be discriminated against, but focused on the situation of the *child* not to be treated differently from other children who had been the subject of a judgment of full adoption in Peru resulting in a complete break from the family of origin. It held that although these biological ties had been legally broken, because of the decision of the Luxembourg authorities, no alternative legal link had been forged with the adoptive mother, leaving the child in a legal vacuum. The Court found that there was no reason to justify such discrimination in this case, especially since other Peruvian children adopted by single mothers had previously obtained full adoptions in Luxembourg.[167]

While the focus of the Court on the position of the child is commendable, this was a rather contrived argument that seems designed to avoid the difficult issue of discrimination on the grounds of marital status in adoption, rather than to promote children's rights.[168] Although there appears to be near consensus in Europe that single people *should* be permitted to adopt, the question remains unanswered whether there is a right for a single person to adopt *on an equal basis* with a married couple.

8.2.4. MARITAL STATUS: UNMARRIED COUPLES

In light of the evolution of the form of the traditional family throughout Europe – although some states are evolving in this area faster than others – it is important to consider the position of unmarried couples in relation to intercountry adoption. While most of the academic discussion has focused on

---

166 *Wagner and JMWL v Luxembourg*, above n 157, [146]–[147].

167 This decision was partly aided by the fact that prior to the applicant's adoption application, all Peruvian adoptions, including those by single parents, were automatically approved. It was only at the time of her application that new rules were applied to strictly scrutinise judgments. The Court found that she had thus entered into the adoption in good faith, and was not trying to avoid Luxembourger laws, and had a legitimate expectation that the adoption would be approved.

168 This is hardly surprising, as the Court tends to avoid findings on the most difficult issues if it can base its decisions on more clear-cut grounds (for example, *X v Belgium and the Netherlands* (Appl. No. 6482/74) Decision of 10 July 1975).

the position of same-sex couples – which will be considered below – a growing number of states are permitting heterosexual cohabitants to adopt.

To ensure the stability of these relationships, states that allow unmarried couples to adopt usually require that they have lived together for a minimum length of time. While in some regions of Spain, this can be as low as one year,[169] in the Netherlands[170] and Belgium[171] this is raised to three, and Portugal sets the minimum at four years.[172] In Andorra[173] and Iceland,[174] five years of stable communal life or cohabitation is required respectively, while in Bosnia and Herzegovina, couples must show a common-law marriage lasting at least five years.[175] Montenegro also requires proof of a common-law marriage, but does not require a defined number of years, simply that it has lasted "a long time".[176] Likewise, in England unmarried couples must show an "enduring family relationship".[177]

However, it should be noted that married couples do not escape scrutiny, and in many countries couples must have been married or living together for a certain number of years to ensure the stability of their relationship. While in France only two years is required,[178] this is increased to two-and-a-half years in Denmark,[179] three years in the Czech Republic,[180] Malta[181] and Italy,[182] four

169 In Spain, requirements of adopters are set by regional authorities rather than by the central government so the age limit may also vary (Hague Conference, *Country Profile: Spain* (2010) <www.hcch.net/index_en.php?act=publications.details&pid=5107&dtid=42> [14 January 2012]).

170 Article 1:227 Civil Code.

171 Article 343 Civil Code.

172 Article 1979(1) Civil Code.

173 Article 2 Qualified Law on Adoption of 21 March 1996.

174 Article 2 Adoption Act No 130/1999.

175 United States: Department of State, *Country Information*, <http://adoption.state.gov/country_information.php> [21 December 2012]. For these purposes, I have included common-law marriage with the information on cohabitation, although in some circumstances it may be more akin to a legal marriage, and this categorisation may be contested.

176 Article 132 Family Law.

177 Section 144 Adoption and Children Act 2002 defines a "couple" as either a married couple or "two people (whether of different sexes or the same sex) living as partners in an enduring family relationship."

178 Alternatively, adoption is allowed if both partners are over the age of 28 (article 343 Civil Code).

179 Before an application for adoption is submitted (Hague Conference, *Country Profile: Denmark* (2010) <www.hcch.net/index_en.php?act=publications.details&pid=5128&dtid=42> [14 January 2012]).

180 The requirement is simply that the marriage is stable, which is usually interpreted by the courts to mean three years (Hague Conference, *Country Profile: Czech Republic* (2010) <www.hcch.net/index_en.php?act=publications.details&pid=5116&dtid=42> [14 January 2012]).

181 Article 114 Civil Code.

182 The couple cannot have been separated during this time, even *de facto* (article 6(1) Law 184/1983).

years in Portugal,[183] and five years in Andorra,[184] Monaco,[185] Poland,[186] Switzerland[187] and Turkey.[188]

In the United Kingdom, it has been found that it is unlawful to refuse the application of a prospective adoptive couple on the grounds that they are not married to each other. In a case arising in Northern Ireland, the House of Lords found that although the state was entitled to consider that it was generally better for children to be brought up by a married couple, there should not be a "bright line rule" and instead the interests of the child should be considered on an individual basis. The fact that the couple was not married could be considered as a factor in assessing the stability of their relationship, and whether this may have an impact on the welfare of the child, but it could not be a basis in and of itself for refusing an adoption application.[189] This approach, in line with that advocated for applications from single adopters, puts the child's welfare as the paramount consideration, as is required by the UNCRC and serves as an example of good practice to be emulated.

Despite this, the ECtHR has taken a somewhat more conservative approach, allowing states to differentiate between unmarried and married adopters if they so wish. The cases that have come before the Court on this issue have concerned second-parent adoptions, but the rules they lay down are equally applicable to non-relative intercountry placements. In *X v Austria*[190] and *Gas and Dubois v France*[191] the Court found that unmarried couples are not in a relevantly similar situation to married couples in forming a family under article 8, and thus are not discriminated against by differential treatment. As such, the state is free to refuse to allow heterosexual unmarried couples to adopt; however, where they do allow such applications, same-sex unmarried couples must be allowed to adopt on the same grounds, as will be discussed below.

---

183 The couple must have been living together for four years – this article applies to both married and unmarried joint adopters (article 1979(1) Civil Code).

184 Article 2 Qualified Law on Adoption of 21 March 1996.

185 Article 242 Civil Code.

186 This is not contained in legislation, but is required in practice for the courts to accept the couple as suitable adopters (Hague Conference, *Country Profile: Poland* (2010) <www.hcch.net/index_en.php?act=publications.details&pid=5093&dtid=42> [14 January 2012]).

187 Alternatively, adoption is allowed if both partners are over the age of 35 (article 264a(2) Civil Code).

188 Turkey, *State Party Report to the UN Committee on the Rights of the Child* (18 July 2011) CRC/C/TUR/2-3, [98].

189 *Re P (Adoption: Unmarried Couple)* [2008] UKHL 38.

190 [2013] ECHR 148.

191 (Appl. No. 25951/07) Judgment of 15 March 2012.

8.2.5. ADOPTION BY SAME-SEX COUPLES: CHANGING SOCIAL PERCEPTIONS?

With increasingly tolerant attitudes towards same-sex relationships in many European states, and the greater openness that comes with this, the issue of same-sex adoption has gained prominence over the last 15 years. While the 1967 European Convention on Adoption contemplated adoption by married couples or single persons only, a new provision was inserted into the 2008 Revised Convention, reading:

> "States are free to extend the scope of this Convention to same sex couples who are married to each other or who have entered into a registered partnership together. They are also free to extend the scope of this Convention to different sex couples and same sex couples who are living together in a stable relationship."[192]

However, the adoption of children by same-sex couples continues to be a controversial issue throughout Europe. Of the seven states that have ratified this Convention, two (Ukraine and Romania) have made a declaration stating that they will not apply this article.

Further, a 2006 EU study showed that although 69 per cent of respondents in the Netherlands supported the authorisation of adoption for same-sex couples throughout Europe,[193] and 51 per cent in Sweden, these were the only countries in which a majority were of that opinion. A very clear divide can be seen in the survey of the EU states, with western European jurisdictions showing significantly higher support than those in eastern Europe. Denmark and Austria both had 44 per cent in favour, with Belgium and Spain close behind at 43 per cent, and Germany at 42 per cent. On the other hand, in Estonia only 14 per cent of respondents were in favour, with 13 per cent in Hungary, 12 per cent in Bulgaria, Lithuania and Slovakia, 11 per cent in Greece, ten per cent in Cyprus, eight per cent in Latvia and Romania and seven per cent in Malta and Poland.[194]

Despite this lack of popular support, there has been a small, but growing, number of countries that have now permitted joint adoption by same-sex couples

---

192 Article 7(2) ECA 2008.

193 It should be emphasised that the respondents were asked whether "adoption of children should be authorised for homosexual couples throughout Europe", rather than simply whether they would support same-sex couples being authorised to adopt within their jurisdiction. As such, it is unclear whether respondents disagreed with the proposition because they were against adoption by same-sex couples, or because they did not feel this was an issue upon which there should be an EU-wide mandate.

194 European Commission, Eurobarometer 66: Public Opinion in the European Union (2006) 45 <http://ec.europa.eu/public_opinion/archives/eb/eb66/eb66_en.pdf> [14 November 2012].

on the same basis as heterosexual couples: Denmark,[195] England,[196] France,[197] Iceland,[198] Norway,[199] Spain[200] and Sweden.[201]

In two further jurisdictions, same-sex couples are permitted to adopt jointly, but have additional restrictions put on them that heterosexual couples do not.[202] In the Netherlands, same-sex couples are permitted to adopt domestically, but not undertake an intercountry adoption.[203] The reason for this difference in treatment is unclear, but may be due to the practical consideration that there are no sending countries that accept applications from same-sex couples. Despite this, such a restriction only for intercountry adoptions goes against the requirement in article 21(c) of the UNCRC that children in intercountry adoption enjoy equivalent safeguards and standards to those in domestic adoption. As such, each should be afforded the same quality of adoptive parents, and there is no reason to allow same-sex adopters for one form of adoption but not the other.

On the other hand, in Belgium, same-sex couples are permitted to adopt jointly if they are married or legal cohabitants,[204] but joint adoption by unmarried partners who have not entered into a legal cohabitation agreement is only permitted for heterosexual couples. While a legal cohabitation agreement is relatively simple to enter into, it is unclear why there should be this initial hurdle for same-sex couples that does not exist for their heterosexual counterparts.

The distinction between unmarried heterosexual couples and same-sex couples is particularly important in this context. In the 2013 ECtHR case of *X v Austria* the Court found that Austria could not prohibit second-parent adoptions by same-sex couples if they were permitted by unmarried heterosexual couples.[205] As a result, Belgium's differentiated laws would be unlikely to survive a legal challenge, but more importantly, jurisdictions such as Andorra and Portugal, which allow unmarried heterosexual couples to adopt after living together for a certain period of time, would be required to extend the same

195 Hague Conference, *Country Profile: Denmark* (2010) <www.hcch.net/index_en.php?act=publications.details&pid=5128&dtid=42> [14 January 2012].

196 Sections 49, 50, 144 Adoption and Children Act 2002.

197 Law 2013/404.

198 Law of 27 June 2006.

199 Hague Conference, *Country Profile: Norway* (2010) <www.hcch.net/index_en.php?act=publications.details&pid=5090&dtid=42> [14 January 2012].

200 See article 44 Civil Code, which allows same-sex couples to marry.

201 Section 5:3 Children and Parents Code (1949:381).

202 It is interesting to note in this respect that Portugal permits same-sex marriage, but not same-sex adoption.

203 Brulard and Dumont, above n 152, 111.

204 Same-sex marriage is permitted under article 143 Civil Code. Legal cohabitation can be undertaken by any two persons who are of a legal age if they form a household at the same address, and are not bound by marriage or another legal cohabitation to anyone else. All that is required is a written statement signed at the Registry Office (see articles 1475–1479 Civil Code).

205 [2013] ECHR 148.

permission to same-sex couples. This is an important shift in the law, although as this is a very recent decision, it is yet to be seen whether the Court will continue in this direction, or take a more cautious approach in future.

However, it must be noted that already in relation to homosexual adoptions the Court has been particularly influential through its decisions regarding single adopters, allowing prospective homosexual parents a route to form a family even before joint adoption has been possible. The European Court of Human Rights has examined the right of single homosexuals to adopt on two principal occasions, coming to vastly different results in each. In the first case, *Fretté v France* in 2002, the Court upheld the decision of the French authorities to refuse permission to adopt based on questions raised concerning the applicant's "particular circumstances as a homosexual man."[206] It found that the scientific community, and particularly experts on childhood, psychiatrists and psychologists, was divided on the consequences for a child of being adopted by one or more homosexual parent, and that the French authorities were legitimately allowed to limit the right to adopt in the interests of children.[207]

This view was strongly challenged by the joint partly dissenting opinion of Judge Sir Nicholas Bratza and Judges Fuhrmann and Tulkens, who found no evidence to suggest that homosexual parents would be harmful to children, and suggested that where single persons were permitted to adopt, any rejection of an application based solely on the grounds of sexual orientation was in breach of article 14 ECHR in conjunction with article 8.

It was this view that was endorsed six years later in the case of *EB v France*, when in a short section, with very little explanation, the Court found that the arguments of the French government regarding the consequences of a child being brought up by a homosexual parent were not convincing or weighty enough to justify refusing to accept a homosexual's application.[208] It held that "in rejecting the applicant's application for authorization to adopt, the domestic authorities made a distinction based on considerations regarding her sexual orientation, a distinction which is not acceptable under the Convention."[209]

This case demonstrates a marked shift in attitudes towards homosexual parenting in Europe. While *Fretté* allowed the government to focus on the aim of "protecting" children from homosexual parents, such arguments were not given

---

206 [2002] ECHR 156, [10].

207 Ibid., [42].

208 [2008] ECHR 55. This case has been extensively criticised for its reasoning, and for its position on the so-called "contamination" of the decision-making process. In this case, the French government claimed that the refusal to adopt was based on two distinct grounds: a lack of paternal referrant; and the ambivalence of the applicant's partner's commitment to her adoption plans. The majority decided that where two grounds were relied on to reject the applicant, it was sufficient for one to be invalid to find the decision in violation of article 14 in conjunction with article 8. For commentary on this issue, see, for example, Andrew Bainham, "Homosexual Adoption" (2008) 67(3) *Cambridge Law Journal* 479.

209 *EB v France*, ibid., [96] (footnotes omitted).

any weight by the Court six years later. Only one of the dissenting judges relied on the "negative" role that the "erotic relationship with its inevitable manifestations and the couple's conduct towards each other" would have on the personality of the child,[210] while the rest of the dissenting judges considered that a refusal of adoption on the grounds of sexual orientation alone would have violated article 14, had not other legitimate reasons been put forward for refusing the application.[211]

8.2.6. CONCLUSION

The guiding principle in all criteria for choosing prospective adoptive parents must be the best interests of the child. As the saying goes, adoption is about finding a family for a child, not a child for a family, and for that reason, conditions for prospective parents should not follow bright line rules but instead take a flexible approach that takes into account the individual attributes of the adopter.

Restrictions on single parents, same-sex adopters, and on older or younger applicants should only relate to the individual applicant, rather than assumptions made about the group as a whole. In this way, it is also important that societal prejudices concerning certain groups, for example homosexuals, or traditional family models such as a "two-parent family", do not prevent those who would otherwise be capable of providing a safe and loving environment for a child from doing so. A parent's ability to care for the child should be the paramount consideration, and should not be obscured by prejudice and preconceptions.

8.3. FACILITATING THE ADOPTION: COUNSELLING, CONTACT, MONITORING AND SUPPORT

The success of an adoptive placement does not rely simply on the eligibility and suitability of the adoptive parent alone, however. Of equal, if not of more, importance, is adequate preparation and support for the child and parents in the adoptive relationship, which can be achieved through pre-adoption counselling and contact, as well as the provision of post-adoption services.

---

210 Dissenting opinion of Judge Loucaides.

211 Judge Zupančič argued that adoption was a privilege, and not a right, and therefore distinctions could be made on grounds that were not affected by arbitrariness, prejudice or frivolity. He held that a decision is arbitrary when it is not based on reasonable grounds and reasonable decision-making, but instead rests on prejudice, such as prejudice against homosexuals. However, he did not subscribe to the 'contamination' theory of the majority, and found that it was sufficient that one ground was valid for the refusal to adopt to be legitimate.

This area is of particular importance in light of the changing demographic of intercountry adoption. Many countries of origin are increasingly allowing intercountry adoption primarily or exclusively of children who have special needs, are older, or are in sibling groups, and it is important that parents are able to respond to these challenges. As such, we must reshape good practice to ensure that parents are prepared for adoption, and given the support that is needed to be able to provide a stable and loving family.

This is an area in which law itself cannot provide all the answers: any legal changes must work together with, and be supported by, appropriate training, funding and professional standards for the social welfare authorities and others carrying out such work. There can be little benefit in requiring counselling of prospective adoptive parents, for example, if there are not enough professionals available to provide quality assistance. As such, this must be an evolutionary process, in which legal requirements work hand in hand with good practice, education, and investment.

8.3.1. COUNSELLING OF PROSPECTIVE ADOPTIVE PARENTS

Counselling is a crucial aspect of the adoption process for all parties involved. It provides a safe and open space for participants to discuss with professionals a variety of issues and feelings relating to the adoption, and work through any problems that may arise. However, although counselling is often advocated for biological parents and the children themselves, prospective adoptive parents are often overlooked in this vital area.

Counselling for prospective adoptive parents was included in the Hague Convention as one of the preconditions to an adoption taking place. However, as with counselling of biological parents under that instrument, the wording of the obligation is weak, requiring only that the competent authorities have "ensured that the prospective adoptive parents have been counselled as may be necessary".[212] This leaves the decision solely in the hands of the domestic authorities, despite the fact that pre-adoption counselling for prospective parents has been shown to be a critically important protective factor in preventing the breakdown of adoptions.[213]

Notwithstanding the lack of imperative in the international instruments, some form of counselling is mandatory for prospective adoptive parents in

212 Article 5(b) Hague Convention.

213 Marianne Berry, R Barth and B Needell, "Preparation, support, and satisfaction of adoptive families in agency and independent adoptions" (1996) 13(2) *Child and Adolescent Social Work Journal* 157. Although this study concerned domestic adoptions (in California), it is arguable that it is equally applicable to intercountry placements.

Albania,[214] Andorra,[215] Austria,[216] Belgium,[217] the Czech Republic,[218] Denmark,[219] Estonia,[220] Georgia,[221] Italy,[222] Latvia,[223] Lithuania,[224] Malta,[225] Netherlands,[226] Portugal,[227] Slovakia,[228] Spain[229] and Sweden.[230]

---

214 Hague Conference, *Country Profile: Albania* (2010) <www.hcch.net/index_en.php?act=publications.details&pid=5081&dtid=42> [14 January 2012].

215 Five mandatory sessions before initiating the evaluation process (Hague Conference, *Country Profile: Andorra* (2010) <www.hcch.net/index_en.php?act=publications.details&pid=5082&dtid=42> [14 January 2012]).

216 In most federal states, counselling courses are mandatory. They are required after the first counselling interview by either the youth welfare authorities or registered agencies. These vary between three weekend courses, or courses for two months (Hague Conference, *Country Profile: Austria* (2010) <www.hcch.net/index_en.php?act=publications.details&pid=5083&dtid=42> [14 January 2012]).

217 Counselling is organised by the Central Authority, and must be undertaken before the assessment of the aptitude of the parent(s) as adopter(s) (Hague Conference, *Country Profile: Belgium* (2012) <www.hcch.net/index_en.php?act=publications.details&pid=5084&dtid=42> [14 January 2012]).

218 Hague Conference, *Country Profile: Czech Republic* (2010) <www.hcch.net/index_en.php?act=publications.details&pid=5116&dtid=42> [14 January 2012].

219 This is mandatory for two full weekends, but those who have adopted before are excused (Hague Conference, *Country Profile: Denmark* (2010) <www.hcch.net/index_en.php?act=publications.details&pid=5128&dtid=42> [14 January 2012]).

220 Hague Conference, *Country Profile: Estonia* (2010) <www.hcch.net/index_en.php?act=publications.details&pid=5242&dtid=42> [14 January 2012].

221 Hague Conference, *Country Profile: Georgia* (2010) <www.hcch.net/index_en.php?act=publications.details&pid=5118&dtid=42> [14 January 2012].

222 Counselling must be undertaken either before or after the evaluation process (Hague Conference, *Country Profile: Italy* (2012) <www.hcch.net/index_en.php?act=publications.details&pid=5153&dtid=42> [14 January 2012]).

223 Hague Conference, *Country Profile: Latvia* (2010) <www.hcch.net/index_en.php?act=publications.details&pid=5087&dtid=42> [14 January 2012].

224 Article 3.210 Civil Code. Prospective adoptive parents must be adults who are "properly prepared for adoption".

225 Counselling is provided by the delegated agency some time after the prospective adoptive parents apply for consideration. This lasts for seven weeks (Hague Conference, *Country Profile: Malta* (2010) <www.hcch.net/index_en.php?act=publications.details&pid=5088&dtid=42> [14 January 2012]).

226 Counselling is mandatory after the submission of an application for permission to adopt. This is conducted for three months by the Dutch Foundation for Adoption Services (Hague Conference, *Country Profile: Netherlands* (2010) <www.hcch.net/index_en.php?act=publications.details&pid=5429&dtid=42> [14 January 2012]).

227 Nine sessions are required in all, through different stages of the adoption process, including two post-adoption. These are organised by the welfare services (Hague Conference, *Country Profile: Portugal* (2010) <www.hcch.net/index_en.php?act=publications.details&pid=5094&dtid=42> [14 January 2012]).

228 Hague Conference, *Country Profile: Slovakia* (2010) <www.hcch.net/index_en.php?act=publications.details&pid=5095&dtid=42> [14 January 2012].

229 This is regulated by the Autonomous Communities, but is obligatory in nearly all of these, usually before the evaluation of the prospective adoptive parents' eligibility to adopt. These average 14 hours in total, and are organised by the Central Authority or private entities contracted by them (Hague Conference, *Country Profile: Spain* (2010) <www.hcch.net/index_en.php?act=publications.details&pid=5107&dtid=42> [14 January 2012]).

230 The prospective adoptive parents must have participated in a parental course assigned by the municipality prior to the adoption. The course is seven sessions of three hours, or two

All these states require the counselling to be undertaken before the match is made between the parents and the child. Portugal is unique, however, in requiring under legislation ongoing counselling throughout the adoption process. One preliminary 90-minute session is required before the adoption process is started, followed by one 180-minute session during the evaluation of the adoption file. While waiting to be matched with a child, prospective parents have five sessions of 200 minutes each, while after the child has been placed with the parents but before the adoption order is made, there are two final 230-minute sessions.[231]

On the other hand, in Armenia,[232] Finland,[233] France,[234] Germany,[235] Greece,[236] Monaco,[237] Norway,[238] Poland,[239] Slovenia[240] and Switzerland,[241] counselling is purely optional, although in some of these jurisdictions it is strongly recommended and provided free of charge by social services or the Central Authority.[242] While the provision of free counselling if parents so wish is beneficial, the lack of mandatory counselling is worrying, especially since these states are among those that receive the largest number of children in Europe.

---

weekends (Hague Conference, *Country Profile: Sweden* (2010) <www.hcch.net/index_en.php?act=publications.details&pid=5097&dtid=42> [14 January 2012]).

231 Hague Conference, *Country Profile: Portugal* (2010) <www.hcch.net/index_en.php?act=publications.details&pid=5094&dtid=42> [14 January 2012].

232 Hague Conference, *Country Profile: Armenia* (2010) <www.hcch.net/index_en.php?act=publications.details&pid=5115&dtid=42> [14 January 2012].

233 Hague Conference, *Country Profile: Finland* (2010) <www.hcch.net/index_en.php?act=publications.details&pid=5243&dtid=42> [14 January 2012].

234 Hague Conference, *Country Profile: France* (2010) <www.hcch.net/index_en.php?act=publications.details&pid=5086&dtid=42> [14 January 2012].

235 Hague Conference, *Country Profile: Germany* (2010) <www.hcch.net/index_en.php?act=publications.details&pid=5156&dtid=42> [14 January 2012].

236 Hague Conference, *Country Profile: Greece* (2012) <www.hcch.net/index_en.php?act=publications.details&pid=5141&dtid=42> [14 January 2012].

237 Hague Conference, *Country Profile: Monaco* (2010) <www.hcch.net/index_en.php?act=publications.details&pid=5210&dtid=42> [14 January 2012].

238 Hague Conference, *Country Profile: Norway* (2010) <www.hcch.net/index_en.php?act=publications.details&pid=5090&dtid=42> [14 January 2012].

239 Hague Conference, *Country Profile: Poland* (2010) <www.hcch.net/index_en.php?act=publications.details&pid=5093&dtid=42> [14 January 2012].

240 Hague Conference, *Country Profile: Slovenia* (2010) <www.hcch.net/index_en.php?act=publications.details&pid=5096&dtid=42> [14 January 2012].

241 Hague Conference, *Country Profile: Switzerland* (2010) <www.hcch.net/index_en.php?act=publications.details&pid=5150&dtid=42> [14 January 2012].

242 For example, in Norway, although courses are not mandatory, most prospective adoptive parents choose to participate in any case. They are provided by the Norwegian Central Authority over two weekends (Hague Conference, *Country Profile: Norway* (2010) <www.hcch.net/index_en.php?act=publications.details&pid=5090&dtid=42> [14 January 2012]). In France courses are offered by the Aide Sociale a l'Enfance before authorisation (Hague, *Country Profile: France* (2010) <www.hcch.net/index_en.php?act=publications.details&pid=5086&dtid=42> [14 January 2012]), while in Germany, courses are offered by the Central Authority, accredited bodies and private providers (Hague Conference, *Country Profile: Germany* (2010) <www.hcch.net/index_en.php?act=publications.details&pid=5156&dtid=42> [14 January 2012]).

Counselling should not simply be about whether the parents themselves think they need it, but an essential step in preparing prospective adopters for some of the problems that they will inevitably face. Not all of these are things that the parents will themselves consider in making the decision to adopt, and for that reason, it is important that an outside expert draws their attention to a wide range of possible issues that may arise. In many cases, the child will also be going through the psychological trauma of losing his or her family, being separated from friends and siblings and everything that is safe and familiar. Counselling can help parents understand and explore what to expect, and possible ways to deal with these issues. This is particularly the case when the child's circumstances require special preparation, for example, where the child has been living in an institution, or has mental or physical disabilities. A study of internationally adopted children by the Donaldson Adoption Institute found that of a sample of 1,034 parents, 47 per cent adopted a child with special needs. Of these children, 50 per cent were diagnosed in the country of origin as special needs; however, the other 50 per cent were not diagnosed until they reached the country of destination. Among those who were diagnosed within the country of origin, an additional special need was identified once reaching the receiving state in 42 per cent of cases. Nearly 70 per cent of identified in the receiving state had mental or emotional problems, and 52 per cent of these had developmental delays.[243]

In addition, counselling for prospective adoptive parents benefits not only the parents and child themselves, but the adoption system as a whole. For example, it can help manage the expectations of prospective parents, who often enter into the adoption wishing for a child of a certain age, sex and racial background. However, as has been discussed previously, the number and profile of available adoptable children do not always correspond with such expectations.[244] As a result, counselling can diminish the pressure on states of origin to produce children with certain characteristics, and ensure that prospective parents are realistic about their expectations and do not feel that they have a right to a child.

As such, counselling provides a valuable resource for prospective adoptive parents to help them ensure that the best interests of the adopted child are protected, and that they are entering into the adoption process with their eyes open. Although it cannot guarantee the success of the placement, it can reduce subsequent difficulties and breakdown, and as a result, should be compulsory for all prospective parents.

---

243 Ellen Pinderhughes et al, *A Changing World: Shaping best practices through understanding of the new realities of intercountry adoption* (2013, Evan B Donaldson Adoption Institute) 32–33.

244 This has been argued by the Hague Convention Guide to Good Practice: Hague Conference, *The Implementation and Operation of the 1993 Hague Intercountry Adoption Convention: Guide to Good Practice: Guide No 1* (2008) [406]–[412] <www.hcch.net/upload/adoguide_e.pdf> [7 February 2013].

8.3.2. ESTABLISHING A PRE-ADOPTION RELATIONSHIP

Once a prospective adoptive parent has been approved as eligible and suitable for adoption, the next step will be to match them with a child. Under the Hague Convention, the matching is performed by the Central Authority in the state of origin, who will determine, on the basis of the reports relating to the child and the prospective adoptive parents, whether the placement is in the best interests of the child.[245] The prospective adoptive parents will then be asked to give consent to the match, before the legal adoption proceedings take place.

This section will address the contact permitted, or required, between the prospective adoptive parents and the child after the match is made, but before the adoption order. Contact between the parents and child is crucial to ensure that the placement is suitable for both parties. Especially if the adopted child is older or has special needs, it is essential to ensure that the parents can adequately undertake caring for the child, and that the child is happy with the placement and can adapt well with his or her prospective parents. This in turn leads to fewer adoption breakdowns.

This was exemplified in the ECtHR case of *Pini v Romania*, which has been discussed previously. In this case, two Italian couples adopted Romanian girls who were nine-and-a-half years old at the time of the adoption order. Both couples met their respective adoptive children once before the adoption order was made, but had sent them letters and presents since that time (in accordance with Romanian law). Nevertheless, the institution at which the girls were staying obstructed the enforcement of the adoption order and the girls objected to any attempt to force them to move to Italy to live with their adoptive parents. In coming to its decision, the ECtHR "deplored" the lack of real and effective contact between the adoptive parents and children before the adoption order, and held it up as an example of the problems that can occur when there is insufficient preparation of the parent and child for their life together.[246]

Nevertheless, several European states continue to allow only minimal contact between children and prospective adoptive parents before the adoption order itself. In Lithuania, for example, contact between the prospective parents and the child is not routine, and prospective parents may only meet with the child before the adoption if they obtain the consent of the welfare services.[247] Other states allow contact between the parties, but do not allow the prospective parents to take the child into their care. For example, Polish authorities allow the parents and child to meet after matching,[248] while Estonian authorities allow parents to

245 Article 16(1) Hague Convention.

246 [2005] ECHR 275, [163].

247 Hague Conference, *Country Profile: Lithuania* (2010) <www.hcch.net/index_en.php?act=publications.details&pid=5209&dtid=42> [14 January 2012].

248 Hague Conference, *Country Profile: Poland* (2010) <www.hcch.net/index_en.php?act=publications.details&pid=5093&dtid=42> [14 January 2012].

call, and send photos and emails, after the initial meeting.[249] In Georgia, authorities allow contact for the purposes of introduction and the establishment of a relationship between the parents and the child, as well as for the prospective parents to examine his or her health.[250]

While it is obviously a step in the right direction to have meetings between the prospective parents and children, these are usually only of short duration, an hour or two each time at most. Both adults and children can be on their best behaviour for a short visit, meaning that the parties do not really get to know each other. Longer visits, including overnight stays, allow all parties to become comfortable and be themselves, meaning that that they will see each other in the good and bad. This is particularly important as many intercountry adoptees will have had prolonged stays in institutional care, which can be harmful to development, behavioural patterns, and to attachment, where placement can initially be difficult.

For this reason, many states require that prospective adoptive parents take the child into their care for a period of time before the adoption order can be finalised. In Slovakia, this is set at two weeks for a child under three years of age, or three weeks for an older child.[251] Similarly, the Albanian authorities require a probationary period to test the parent–child relationship, which will last between two and six weeks depending on the circumstances of the child.[252] On the other hand, in Latvia, the parent–child relationship not only has to be *tested*, but must be shown to have been *established* before a final court order can be made. In practice, this means that prospective adoptive parents must share a household with the child in Latvia, and take care of him or her, for a period ranging from three weeks to six months.[253]

More lengthy periods are required in the Czech Republic, Cyprus, Portugal, Switzerland and Turkey, requiring prolonged stays in these countries on the part of the prospective adoptive parents. In Cyprus, the infant must have been continuously in the care and "possession" of the applicant for at least three consecutive months immediately preceding the date of the order,[254] whereas in Portugal, all children will have a "transition plan", which will differ according to the age of the child, and his or her needs and circumstances. After observing the first contacts between the child and the prospective parents, the adoption

249 Hague Conference, *Country Profile: Estonia* (2010) <www.hcch.net/index_en.php?act=publications.details&pid=5242&dtid=42> [14 January 2012].

250 Hague Conference *Country Profile: Georgia* (2010) <www.hcch.net/index_en.php?act=publications.details&pid=5118&dtid=42> [14 January 2012].

251 Hague Conference, *Country Profile: Slovakia* (2010) <www.hcch.net/index_en.php?act=publications.details&pid=5095&dtid=42> [14 January 2012].

252 Hague Conference, *Country Profile: Albania* (2010) <www.hcch.net/index_en.php?act=publications.details&pid=5081&dtid=42> [14 January 2012].

253 Hague Conference, *Country Profile: Latvia* (2010) <www.hcch.net/index_en.php?act=publications.details&pid=5087&dtid=42> [14 January 2012].

254 Section 4(6)(a) Adoption Law 1995.

authorities will apply to the competent tribunal to transfer custody to the parents for the "pre-adoption" period. They will then live together until the final court hearing, with the adoption order only granted when they have lived together for a period of time sufficient to enable the court to determine whether there is the possibility that a real tie of affection will be able to develop. This "pre-adoption" period will last for a maximum of six months.[255] On the other hand, the Czech Republic requires that the prospective parents care for the child for a *minimum* of six months, during which time three reports must be made concerning the progress of the placement.[256] The most lengthy placement procedures are in Switzerland[257] and Turkey,[258] however, where prospective parents must care for the child for a year before an adoption order can be made.

For prospective adoptive parents considering intercountry adoption, such lengthy periods of time in the sending country can be prohibitively difficult and expensive, especially for parents with jobs or other children. However, it does allow the children to transition into their new family slowly, and to be in a familiar environment despite the drastic change in their circumstances. Given the difficulties inherent in enforcing post-adoption monitoring, as will be discussed below, this is perhaps the most appropriate way to ensure that the match between the prospective parents and child is suitable, and that a relationship is able to form.

8.3.3. POST-ADOPTION SERVICES

The obligation on states in intercountry adoption does not cease once the adoption order has been made final. There is increasing recognition both in law and practice of the importance of post-adoption services in ensuring the ongoing stability of the adoptive placement, giving both parents and children the support they need for the newly formed family to thrive.

The situation in which families and children find themselves in the months and years following the adoption order is often incredibly difficult, and no matter how well prepared all parties are for the adoption, what comes afterwards can never be adequately predicted. Children who have been taken from everything familiar, and placed with people they do not know, far away from anywhere they have ever been before, can experience feelings of loss, and a lack of identity. They can feel rejected, not only by their biological family, but also by their previous

255 Hague Conference, *Country Profile: Portugal* (2010) <www.hcch.net/index_en.php?act=publications.details&pid=5094&dtid=42> [14 January 2012].

256 Hague Conference, *Country Profile: Czech Republic* (2010) <www.hcch.net/index_en.php?act=publications.details&pid=5116&dtid=42> [14 January 2012].

257 Article 264 Civil Code.

258 United States: Department of State, *Country Information* <http://adoption.state.gov/country_information.php> [21 December 2012].

foster family or institutional carers, who they may feel have sent them to live with strangers. Further, children may experience psychological and emotional difficulties, leaving them unable to form attachments, or to function as is expected of them by adoptive parents. While hopefully prospective adoptive parents will have been provided with pre-adoption counselling to familiarise them with such issues, as discussed above, it will be substantially different when they have to confront them face-to-face.

The problems that both adopted children and adoptive parents can experience were highlighted in the case of Artem Saveliev, who was adopted from a Russian orphanage at age six by a single American mother. This case came to the attention of the world one year later when the mother put Artem on a plane back to Moscow by himself, with a note in his backpack to telling officials "I no longer wish to parent this child". This is simply the latest in several highly publicised disruptions of intercountry adoption placements, where adoptive parents have been simply unable to cope with the realities of the adoptive placement.[259]

The issue of post-adoption services is touched on briefly in the Hague Convention, where it is required that Central Authorities take, "directly or through public authorities or other bodies duly accredited in their State, all appropriate measures, in particular to promote the development of adoption counselling and post-adoption services in their States."[260] This is a very weak provision, providing no real imperative, nor any way to measure its implementation. It is thus left up to states to decide on the extent to which services will be extended to children and families.

Concerns have been raised by some receiving countries over continued monitoring of the family situation, indicating that it sits somewhat uncomfortably with the notion of adoption as a complete legal transfer, as it may interfere with the parental autonomy of the adoptive parents. These countries have suggested that Central Authorities cannot interfere with the private lives of families, and that they do not have the power to oblige adoptive parents to provide ongoing reports, particularly for extended periods of time.[261] However, where such requirements are made clear to parents as a part of the adoption process, ongoing monitoring should be seen as simply a condition of engaging in an adoption. This is in line with the view of adoption as a child protection mechanism, with the welfare of children as the paramount consideration.

Furthermore, the provision of supportive services both before and after adoption has been found to be a protective factor in diminishing domestic

259 See also the 2005 case of Tristan Dowse, an Indonesian boy adopted by an Irish man and his Azerbaijani wife, and the 2000 case of Jesse and Crystal Money, who decided to dissolve their adoption of a nine-year-old girl from a Russian orphanage.

260 Article 9 Hague Convention.

261 Hague Conference, *The Implementation and Operation of the 1993 Hague Intercountry Adoption Convention: Guide to Good Practice: Guide No 1* (2008) 128 <www.hcch.net/upload/adoguide_e.pdf> [7 February 2013].

adoption breakdown,[262] especially if this is provided by specially qualified professionals.[263] There are no statistics available concerning the breakdown of intercountry adoptions, which is in itself a problem;[264] however, there are indications that counselling can provide valuable assistance to adoptive families in improving relationships between children and parents. From 2007 to 2010, the Danish Department of Family Affairs undertook a pilot project giving free counselling to all adoptive families within the first three years that the child was placed with them. 35 per cent of eligible families took up this offer, the vast majority of whom had undertaken an intercountry adoption.[265]

After counselling, 97 per cent of participants experienced progress in at least one of their problem areas, 40 per cent felt more secure in the things they did as parents, giving greater confidence and feeling better in their role, and 40 per cent also felt that they handled conflicts with their child in a more constructive way.[266] In addition, 43 per cent of parents felt that the child was more able to show he or she was afraid, indicating that he or she felt more secure in the relationship and had more confidence in the parents, and thus was able to show anxiety.[267] Importantly, 98 per cent of participants said that they would recommend post-adoption counselling to others in the same situation.[268]

Nevertheless, in many countries in Europe such as Andorra, the Czech Republic, Estonia, Finland, Greece, Ireland, Lithuania, Malta, Norway, Portugal, Slovenia and Sweden, there are no official services offered to parents who have entered into an intercountry adoption, outside ordinary social services offered to all families.[269] However, certain other jurisdictions are beginning to incorporate greater post-adoption support for adoptive parents and families, including monitoring, counselling and assistance.

---

262 DM Houston and LA Kramer, "Meeting the Long-Term Needs of Families who Adopt Children Out of Foster Care: A three year follow-up study" (2008) 87 *Child Welfare* 145; T Festinger, "After Adoption: Dissolution or Permanence?" (2002) 81(3) *Child Welfare* 515; International Social Service, *Adoption Breakdown* (2007, ISS/IRC) <www.iss-ssi.org/2009/assets/files/thematic-facts-sheet/eng/51.Adoption%20breakdown%20eng.pdf> [6 December 2012].

263 Judith S Rycus et al, "Confronting Barriers To Adoption Success" (2006) 44(2) *Family Court Review* 210.

264 By "breakdown", I refer to both temporary disruption and legal dissolution of intercountry adoption placements.

265 97.5 per cent of all Danish adoptions are through intercountry adoption (based on statistics from 2005 to 2009, submitted by the Danish authorities to the Hague Conference).

266 Denmark: Familiestyrelsen, *Evaluering af Forsøgsprojekt Med Tidlig Rådgivning Efter Adoptionen* (2010) 4 <www.familiestyrelsen.dk/fileadmin/user_upload/Adoption/Evalueringsrapport_PAS.pdf> [11 February 2013].

267 Ibid.

268 Ibid., 5.

269 Hague Conference, *Country Profiles* (2010) <www.hcch.net/index_en.php?act=conventions.publications&dtid=42&cid=69> [14 January 2012]. See also ChildONEurope, *Partners Experiences on Post Adoption Services' Best Practices* (date unknown) <www.childoneurope.org/issues/adoption2.htm#post_adoption> [13 December 2012].

In some countries, this is general. For example, the German authorities require that the adoption placement office consults with the child and family during the familiarisation period and offers them support.[270] In Italy, on the other hand, social service authorities monitor the situation for a year after the adoption, while in France, this monitoring continues for three years.[271]

In others, however, there are much more specific requirements. In Belgium, there is an obligation on the adoption authorities to undertake at least one home visit in the three months after the arrival of the child, and to provide support through a multi-disciplinary team to achieve the integration of the child into the family. The authorities must organise to make services constantly available to the parents and the child for any help and guidance they may need.[272] Meanwhile, in Switzerland, when a child arrives in the country as the result of an intercountry adoption, the Guardianship Authority must appoint a guardian for that child without delay, whose role it is to assist the adoptive parents with advice and support regarding the care of the child. The guardian will continue in this function for 18 months, during which time he or she must produce a report on the development of the adoptive relationship.[273]

The International Social Service suggests that child protection services in receiving states should address and respond to difficulties encountered by adoptive families in accordance with general principles of child protection – seek to offer assistance and support first, through counselling, financial support, or time away from caring, then look for short-term temporary placements to allow the family time to address whatever problems they are having. However, in following these principles, it is important that states remember that adopted children, and particularly those who have been through an intercountry adoption, are not simply the same as every other child. More support is needed to ensure that these families are able to establish strong parent–child relationships, and be able to cope with the difficulties that attend such placements. For this reason, states cannot simply rely on the standard services available to all families, but should offer additional, specialised services to these families who face additional, and different, difficulties. The Belgian and Swiss approaches are particularly positive examples of good practice, providing monitoring, guidance and support on an ongoing basis. There is no data available on the levels of adoption breakdown in these jurisdictions as compared to others,

---

270 Hague Conference, *Country Profile: Germany* (2010) <www.hcch.net/index_en.php?act=publications.details&pid=5156&dtid=42> [14 January 2012].

271 Hague Conference, *Country Profile: France* (2010) <www.hcch.net/index_en.php?act=publications.details&pid=5086&dtid=42> [14 January 2012]; Hague Conference, *Country Profile: Italy* (2012) <www.hcch.net/index_en.php?act=publications.details&pid=5153&dtid=42> [14 January 2012].

272 Hague Conference, *Country Profile: Belgium* (2012) <www.hcch.net/index_en.php?act=publications.details&pid=5084&dtid=42> [14 January 2012].

273 Article 17 Federal Law relative to the Hague Convention on adoption and of protection of children in cases of intercountry adoption.

or in the strength of the adopted parent–child relationships there, indicative of the need for research in this area. However, the pilot programme in Denmark indicates that there are great benefits to the provision of counselling and support, which should not be underestimated.

8.4. CONCLUSION

As can be seen from this chapter, the areas of selecting and assisting adoptive parents are among the least regulated in the field of intercountry adoption, and there is little coherence among the European jurisdictions. While the reasons for the lack of regulation are clear, given the wide range of societal norms relating to the most appropriate form of family life and the most conducive environment for bringing up a child, it is an area in which international guidance and uniformity would be of great assistance, and is sadly lacking.

Services to facilitate the development of a stable and strong relationship between an adoptive child and his or her parents, and to subsequently monitor this, are not well regulated under the international treaties, and are underdeveloped in many European jurisdictions. While there are some examples of good practice, in many states services are not targeted, nor provided by professionals, and too much latitude is granted to parents to decide whether they will participate or not.

This is an area of adoption practice that is still developing, and there is a great deal of research to be undertaken to fully understand the benefits that various types of counselling and support can provide. In the meantime, however, states cannot avoid the obligation to provide services on the basis of the best available research, which indicates that adoption breakdown is greatly diminished by the provision of pre-adoption counselling, appropriate matching, and post-adoption services.

CHAPTER 9

WHO AM I? THE CHILD'S RIGHT TO IDENTITY

The last substantive chapter in this book moves from procedures concerning the adoption process, to a wider issue concerning the welfare of adoptive children in their later life. One of the most prominent debates regarding adoption currently concerns the issue of access to birth records and information concerning an adoptee's origins. This is an issue that arises both in relation to domestic and to intercountry adoption, and raises questions of the balancing of rights between the adopted child and his or her birth parents, adoptive parents, and public policy. However, in many instances, the fact that the child has come from a different country will pose additional burdens that may not be present in a domestic setting, and must also be addressed.

When discussing the child's right to know his or her biological origins, two issues arise: one, whether the information is collected in the first place; and two, whether the child is permitted to access this information. This chapter will thus discuss not only the *negative* obligation on states not to prevent a child from accessing details regarding his or her parents, but also the *positive* obligation to ensure that these details are collected and retained.

It is important to note at this stage that the desire of adopted children to access information on their origins can vary dramatically across individuals, and across different periods of their life. Some adoptees might yearn for information, while others have no interest at all. This chapter does not suggest that all people must know their origins, rather that all should be given the opportunity to do so if they so wish.

9.1. INTERNATIONAL INSTRUMENTS

9.1.1. UNITED NATIONS CONVENTION ON THE RIGHTS OF THE CHILD

The right of a child to have access to his or her origins was first addressed by the United Nations in the 1986 Declaration on Social and Legal Principles relating to the Protection and Welfare of Children. Article 9 of this Declaration proclaims:

> "The need of a foster or an adopted child to know about his or her background should be recognized by persons responsible for the child's care unless this is contrary to the child's best interests."

This requirement, clearly articulating the needs of the child and placing his or her interests at the centre of any decision, was unfortunately not echoed in the UNCRC three years later. Although similar sentiments remain, lack of clarity and the potential for differing interpretations somewhat hinder the rights of children in this area.

The principal article to address this issue in the UNCRC is article 7, which reads:

> "The child shall be registered immediately after birth and shall have the right from birth to a name, the right to acquire a nationality and, as far as possible, the right to know and be cared for by his or her parents."

Under this article, the right to "know and be cared for" by parents is arguably joint and severable, with the right to "know" being seen as the basis for a claim of a child to access to information on his or her origins.[1] However, the drafting is somewhat ambiguous. The term "parent" is not defined in the Convention, and thus there has been some contention as to whether this article refers to the right of a child to know his or her *biological* parents, or his or her *legal* (e.g. adoptive) parents. In this respect, the United Kingdom lodged a declaration when ratifying the Convention, stating that: "The United Kingdom interprets the references in the Convention to 'parents' to mean only those persons who, as a matter of national law, are treated as parents".[2]

It has also been argued that the use of the qualifying phrase "as far as possible" indicates that children were not intended to have unimpeded access to information on their origins. The US delegation, whose wording was adopted in the final article, argued that particularly in the case of adopted children, it is not always possible or desirable for a child to know such information.[3] However, Van Beuren rightly argues that this phrase should be read as relating to the practicalities of providing the information, not the legality.[4] As will be seen

1 The English courts, for example, have made clear that this encompasses two separate rights: one to know, and the other to be cared for by, one's parents (see *Re H (Paternity: Blood Test)* [1996] 2 FLR 65).

2 While the Committee on the Rights of the Child have indicated, albeit indirectly, that biological as well as legal parents are included under this article, and have used it as a basis for recommending that states ensure that a child can have access to information on his or her birth parents (see, for example, *Concluding Observations: France* (30 June 2004) CRC/C/15/Add.240, [23]), states have been slow to accept that this is an obligation under article 7 as is discussed below.

3 Geraldine Van Bueren, "Children's Access to Adoption Records: State Discretion or an Enforceable International Right?" (1995) 58(1) *Modern Law Review* 37, 48.

4 Ibid.

below, information is not always available concerning the child's origins, which makes realisation of the right under article 7 sometimes impossible in practice.

Perhaps as a result of this uncertainty, several states have felt the need to lodge reservations in relation to article 7, to the effect that a failure to provide adopted children with information does not violate the Convention. For example, Poland states that:

> "With respect to article 7 of the Convention, the Republic of Poland stipulates that the right of an adopted child to know its natural parents shall be subject to the limitations imposed by binding legal arrangements that enable adoptive parents to maintain the confidentiality of the child's origin."

The Czech Republic also placed such a reservation, providing that "the non-communication of a natural parent's name or natural parents' names to the child is not in contradiction with this provision".

It is therefore clear that there are many different interpretations of the implications and scope of the rights contained within article 7, and, as will be seen below, there are still wide divergences in practice between different states. However, there is another article of the Convention that has also been used to make a claim for the child's right to access information on his or her origins. Article 8 states:

> "1. States Parties undertake to respect the right of the child to preserve his or her identity, including nationality, name and family relations as recognized by law and without unlawful interference.
> 2. Where a child is illegally deprived of some or all of the elements of his or her identity, States Parties shall provide appropriate assistance and protection, with a view to re-establishing speedily his or her identity."

This article was proposed by Argentina, in response to the military junta in that country, under which approximately 500 children were taken from prisoners and brought up by childless military couples.[5] While some delegates regarded this article as superfluous in light of the rights contained in article 7,[6] Argentina argued that it was important as it made the distinction between the child's "true and genuine identity and his or her legal one."[7]

Like article 7, however, the interpretation of this article is ambiguous. The key phrase in subparagraph 1 is "without unlawful interference", yet there is no guidance whether this covers the situation of adopted children searching for their origins.

---

5 United Nations Commission on Human Rights, *Report of the Working Group on a Draft Convention on the Rights of the Child* (3 April 1985, United Nations) E/CN.4/1985/64.

6 Norway, the Netherlands, Austria, the USA, Canada and Brazil (United Nations Commission on Human Rights, *Report of the Working Group on a Draft Convention on the Rights of the Child* (13 March 1986, United Nations) E/CN.4/1986/39).

7 Ibid.

As such, while the UNCRC purports to protect the right of the child to identity and to know his or her parents, the exact import of these rights in relation to adoptive children remains unclear. No guidance is provided as to when, and under what circumstances, an adopted child should be able to access information, or what competing interests could limit this right.

9.1.2. HAGUE CONVENTION ON INTERCOUNTRY ADOPTION

Unfortunately, no more than the UNCRC does the Hague Convention attempt to deal with these more intricate and difficult aspects of the right to identity, instead leaving this question to domestic law.[8] However, the search for information concerning an intercountry adoptee's origins will necessarily involve administrative procedures spanning across several countries, and it is in the area of procedural cooperation that the Hague Convention excels.

Article 30 of the Hague Convention governs access to information concerning a child's origin and identity, and reads:

> "1. The competent authorities of a Contracting State shall ensure that information held by them concerning the child's origin, in particular information concerning the identity of his or her parents, as well as the medical history, is preserved.
> 2. They shall ensure that the child or his or her representative has access to such information, under appropriate guidance, in so far as is permitted by the law of that State."

In addition, article 16 of the Hague Convention provides that the sending state must prepare a report on the child for the receiving state which includes information about the child's identity, background, family history, and the medical history of both the child and his or her family. When transmitting this report to the receiving state, however, article 16(2) explicitly allows for the withholding of the identity of the mother and father of the child if, in the state of origin, their identity may not be disclosed.

As such, procedurally the Hague Convention simplifies a child's search for information on his or her origins, by ensuring that any information is preserved and centrally held. This is of key importance for a child who is searching for his or her origins across several jurisdictions, and ensures that it is relatively simple for that child to know who to contact to gain access to information.

---

8 Gonzalo Parra-Aranguren, *Explanatory Report on the Convention on Protection of Children and Co-operation in Respect of Intercountry Adoption* (1993) [512] <www.hcch.net/index_en.php?act=publications.details&pid=918> [7 February 2013].

However, substantively there are restrictions on both ends on the process, allowing both the sending and receiving state to limit access to information in accordance with national laws. While these domestic laws are nominally guided by the UNCRC,[9] as was seen above, this Convention fails to provide concrete guidance in this area, leaving intercountry adopted children in a somewhat tenuous position.

9.1.3. REVISED EUROPEAN CONVENTION ON THE ADOPTION OF CHILDREN

The Revised European Convention on the Adoption of Children of 2008 is perhaps the most comprehensive instrument on the preservation of the child's origins. Article 22, entitled "Access to and disclosure of information" was a new addition to the Revised Convention, showing the shift in understanding of a child's rights in this area since the original 1967 Convention. In this original version, article 20 provided that the parties should have access to a document stating the date and place of birth of the child, but nothing "expressly revealing the fact of adoption or the identity of his former parents", reflecting the emphasis on adoption as a complete break from the birth family, and a "new start" into the adoptive one.

In the years since this Convention was drafted, however, attitudes have changed towards both adoption, and the rights of children, and the Revised Convention reflects this. Article 22 of the ECA 2008 contains subparagraphs ensuring, *inter alia*, that adoption is concealed from third parties and that records are preserved for 50 years after the adoption takes place. However, the most important provision in relation to the right of a child to information is subparagraph (3), which states:

> "The adopted child shall have access to information held by the competent authorities concerning his or her origins. Where his or her parents of origin have a legal right not to disclose their identity, it shall remain open to the competent authority, to the extent permitted by law, to determine whether to override that right and disclose identifying information, having regard to the circumstances and to the respective rights of the child and his or her parents of origin. Appropriate guidance may be given to an adopted child not having reached the age of majority."

While this article still does not give the child an absolute right to access to information, the inclusion of even the possibility for authorities to override parental refusal to disclose their identity is an important step forward for children's rights, and hopefully the start of a change in thinking in this area.

9 Save in the case of the United States, Somalia and South Sudan.

9.2. THE RIGHT TO ACCESS INFORMATION?

9.2.1. WHY IS ACCESS TO INFORMATION IMPORTANT FOR A CHILD?

The right of the child to access information on his or her origins flows from his or her psychological, social and medical interests, although it is important to note that each individual adoptee will have his or her own combination of reasons for wishing to know this information, or may not even wish to access it at all. This chapter will not argue that children should know who their birth parents are, rather that they should have the right to choose whether or not they do so.[10]

The importance of information on a child's origins in the formation of his or her identity has been the subject of much academic research. Studies suggest that without this information, where it is desired, the child may have difficulty forming his or her own identity, and the ensuing state of uncertainty fundamentally undermines the child's security and mental health.[11] It is an important element in a child's psychological balance,[12] as evidence suggests a manifest need in adoptive children "to know about their background, their genealogy, and their personal history if they are to grow up feeling complete and whole."[13] The less information concerning his or her origins that the child knows, the greater the problems.[14]

Further, as Fried has pointed out, control over knowledge about oneself is inherent in the right to privacy. While others control access to that knowledge, the child is denied the opportunity to dictate important aspects of his or her

---

10 Although there are limited statistics available concerning the number of children who have sought access to their birth records, in was reported that in England there are approximately 3,500–4,000 applications per year (Rupert Rushbrooke, *The Proportion of Adoptees Who Have Received Their Birth Records in England and Wales* (2001, Office of National Statistics) <www.ons.gov.uk/ons/taxonomy/search/index.html?newquery=*&nscl=Adoptions&nscl-orig=Adoptions&content-type=publicationContentTypes&sortDirection=DESCENDING&sortBy=pubdate> [19 February 2013]). Although this figure comes from 2001, it had remained within this range for the approximately 15 years before this date.

11 HJ Sants, "Genealogical Bewilderment in Children with Substitute Parents" (1964) 37(2) *British Journal of Medical Psychology* 133, 133.

12 Samantha Besson, "Enforcing the Child's Right to Know Her Origins: Contrasting Approaches Under the Convention on the Rights of the Child and the European Convention on Human Rights" (2007) 21 *International Journal of Law, Policy and the Family* 137, 140.

13 John Triseliotis, "Obtaining Birth Certificates" in Philip Bean (ed), *Adoption: Essays in Social Policy, Law, and Sociology* (1984, Tavistock) 38.

14 John Triseliotis, *In Search of Origins: The Experiences of Adopted People* (1973, London, Routledge & Kegan Paul) 54–55. It is acknowledged that this need may be a socially constructed phenomenon that may not be present in children brought up in societies where the nuclear biological family is not the established norm. The nuclear biological family is, however, the model that adoption attempts to emulate, and for the purposes of this book, there will be no further consideration of the social impetus behind this need.

private life, and his or her autonomy is impinged upon.[15] This situation can be exacerbated in intercountry adoption as the child may seek information not only concerning his or her biological parents and extended family, but national, cultural, religious and ethnic elements may also be present. Denying the child information on these issues affects his or her identity, dignity, autonomy and liberty, and puts him or her at a distinct disadvantage vis-à-vis other children.

This issue of disadvantage is also taken up by Van Beuren, who argues that a denial of access to identifying information constitutes discrimination against adoptive children and

> "goes to the very heart of child-to-child equality, child autonomy and participation. Autonomy requires not only the skills to use knowledge but also, as a necessary precondition, access to the knowledge. Secrecy in adoption, however, excludes the adopted child from access to the knowledge, thereby limiting the child's moral choice."[16]

Finally, with the increasing significance of genetics in prevention, diagnosis and treatment of disease, knowledge concerning a child's family medical history can be of particular importance. However, for adopted children without access to information regarding their origins, this benefit is denied them. Unlike the social and psychological needs of the child, this can largely be provided by releasing non-identifying information, which maintains the anonymity of the birth parents while ensuring that the child is not disadvantaged due to his or her adoptive status. Nevertheless, this can only provide information available to the parents at the time of birth, so will be incomplete. In addition, this still requires the cooperation of the adoptive parents, who must inform the child that he or she is adopted in the first place: something that is not always guaranteed.

9.2.2. THE CHILD'S ACCESS TO INFORMATION IN EUROPE

Unfortunately, there are only a handful of countries in Europe that fully recognise the importance to a child of knowing his or her origins and thus require adoptive parents to tell their child that he or she is adopted: for example, Croatia,[17] Iceland,[18] Italy,[19] Montenegro[20] and Norway.[21] Croatia and Montenegro require

---

15 Charles Fried, "Privacy" (1968) 77 *Yale Law Journal* 475, 482.
16 Van Bueren, above n 3, 43.
17 Petar Sarcevic et al, *Family Law in Croatia* (2011, Kluwer Law) 150–151.
18 Article 26 Adoption Act No 130/1999.
19 Article 24 Law 149/2001.
20 Article 122 Family Law.
21 Section 12 Act of 28 February 1986, No 8 relating to Adoption.

that this be done before the child reaches the age of seven, while the other states rely on the discretion of parents to choose when this is advisable, or when the child is mature enough.[22] This approach is consistent with research by Triseliotis that suggests that the longer the secret of adoption was kept from the child, the more serious the consequences when this was subsequently revealed.[23]

On the other end of the scale in Ukraine, however, a child has the right *not* to have his or her adoption disclosed, even to himself or herself.[24] Similarly, in the FYR Macedonia, legislation permits adopted children to be registered with the names of the adoptive parents in place of the biological parents, and does not require the preservation of information concerning the child's origins,[25] and in Russia, even if a child is informed of his or her adoptive status, there is no legal mechanism for obtaining access to information about his or her origins.[26] Furthermore, Russian law allows the date of the child's birth to be changed by up to three months, as may the place of birth on the birth certificate, in order to ensure the secret of the adoption.[27]

These approaches are at odds not only with the current research, but also with the rights of the child under the UNCRC, and Russia in particular has been criticised by the Committee on the Rights of the Child for not protecting the right of the adopted child to know his or her original identity.[28] Such secrecy protects the interests of the stronger parties, namely the birth and adoptive parents, at the expense of the best interests of the child.[29] It also perpetuates the myth that adoption is somehow shameful, and something that children should be protected from knowing about, raising considerable psychological difficulties if and when the child does find out.

In all other European countries, however, the child's right to know his or her origins is accepted, although the extent to which this is restricted by age or circumstances varies greatly from state to state. The most common restriction is that of age. The majority of countries allow an unrestricted right to access information once the child reaches 18 (the Czech Republic,[30] England,[31]

---

22 Although the Icelandic legislation advises that, as a rule, this should be done before the child reaches six years of age.

23 John Triseliotis, above n 14, 36. This is in line with the current English jurisprudence on establishing paternity: see *Re R (A Minor) (Contact)* [1993] 2 FLR 762.

24 Article 226(2) Family Code.

25 United Nations Committee on the Rights of the Child, *Concluding Observations: FYR of Macedonia* (11 June 2010) CRC/C/MKD/CO/2, [34].

26 See Family Law 1995.

27 Article 135(1) Family Law 1995. This may only be done in the child is less than 12 months old when adopted.

28 United Nations Committee on the Rights of the Child, *Concluding Observations: Russian Federation* (23 November 2005) CRC/C/RUS/CO/3, [40]-[41].

29 See Van Bueren, above n 3, 43–44.

30 Hague Conference, *Country Profile: Czech Republic* (2010) <www.hcch.net/index_en.php?act=publications.details&pid=5116&dtid=42> [14 January 2012].

31 Section 60 Adoption and Children Act 2002.

Greece,[32] Hungary,[33] Iceland,[34] Lithuania,[35] Norway,[36] Poland,[37] Slovakia,[38] Spain,[39] Switzerland),[40] although this is lowered to 15 in Serbia,[41] 14 in Austria[42] and Ukraine,[43] and 12 in the Netherlands.[44] On the other hand, Italy requires the adopted person to be 25 before he or she can apply to access official files, and even then permission must be granted by the Juvenile Court after listening to the interested parties.[45]

In some of these countries, however, exceptions are made for younger children who meet certain criteria. In Italy and Lithuania, younger children can apply for access to their records if this is required for reasons of health or other important reasons (Lithuania),[46] or if there are serious and proven reasons concerning the psychological or physical health of the adopted child (Italy).[47] Switzerland has a similar exception, but phrased more generally, requiring that a "legitimate interest" be shown.[48] These exceptions recognise the potentially serious psychological implications that can result from denying a child information concerning his or her identity, and the growing importance of genetics in diagnosing and treating illness. However, asking the child to show a "good cause" or a specific reason why he or she should be allowed to access birth records places

32 Article 1559 Civil Code.

33 ChildONEurope, *Extracts of the Legislation on Adoption: Hungary* (date unknown) <www.childoneurope.org/issues/adoption/adoption_legislation/hungary.pdf> [8 June 2012].

34 Article 27 Adoption Act No 130/1999.

35 Article 3.221 Civil Code.

36 Section 12 Act of 28 February 1986, No 8 relating to Adoption.

37 Hague Conference, *Country Profile: Poland* (2010) <www.hcch.net/index_en.php?act=publications.details&pid=5093&dtid=42> [14 January 2012].

38 Hague Conference, *Country Profile: Slovakia* (2010) <www.hcch.net/index_en.php?act=publications.details&pid=5095&dtid=42> [14 January 2012].

39 Article 180(5) Civil Code.

40 Article 268c Civil Code.

41 The child must also be "able to reason" (article 59 Family Act).

42 Hague Conference, *Country Profile: Austria* (2010) <www.hcch.net/index_en.php?act=publications.details&pid=5083&dtid=42> [14 January 2012].

43 Article 226(3) Family Code. Although as discussed above, under Ukrainian law the child has a right *not* to know about his or her adoption, so may not know that there are files to access.

44 Article 17d Act on the Adoption of Foreign Children. It is interesting to note that this legislation covers only children adopted into the Netherlands through intercountry adoption. In the Netherlands, in contrast to many other European countries, domestic adoption is not conducted in secret and it is standard practice for the child to be informed about his or her natural parents (see United Nations Committee on the Rights of the Child, *Concluding Observations: Netherlands* (24 July 1997) CRC/C/51/Add.1, [76]; MJ Vonk, "Tensions Between Legal, Biological and Social Conceptions of Parenthood in Dutch Family Law" (May 2007) 11(1) *Electronic Journal of Comparative Law*, 18).

45 Article 28 Law 184/1983. However, where the mother has refused to be named, this cannot be overturned (see discussion below).

46 Article 3.221 Civil Code.

47 Above n 45. However, the child must be over 18 for this exception to be granted, and it will have to be approved by the Juvenile Court, having considered the interests of all the parties. Additionally, if the biological parent refuses, he or she cannot be identified.

48 Article 268c Civil Code.

a discriminatory burden on access to his or her rights. What other children are granted without restrictions by right, adopted children must show reason for.[49]

A different kind of exception is made in the Netherlands, where access is granted to any intercountry adoptee under 12 (the age at which the right is automatic) who is considered able to reasonably assess his or her own interests.[50] This confirms that in the Netherlands at least, access to information is considered the absolute right of the child, rather than being weighed against other competing interests. The only limiting factor is the competency of the child to determine whether he or she wishes to know. This is the only country that does not balance to some extent the rights of the biological and adoptive parents with those of the child. This follows the domestic adoption practice, where adoption is open and a child must know that he or she is adopted, and can gain information on his or her biological mother by a simple application to the Council for the Protection of Children. The approach relies on the Dutch Supreme Court decision that "fundamental rights such as the right of respect for one's private life, the right to freedom of thought, conscience and religion and the right of free speech are based on a general personality right that amongst other things includes the right to know who one's biological parents are."[51]

In other countries where access to the right is predicated on attaining a certain age, there is an inevitable balancing of interests. Especially where the age is set at majority, this can be seen to allow the birth parent qualified privacy, and more importantly, to allow the adoptive family time to bond together to attain security and stability. The public policy objective of protecting the adoption process and ensuring that adoptive parents still want to adopt is very influential in maintaining these barriers to information for children. The importance to adoptive families of having their "own" child should not be underestimated, and is associated with the exclusive model of adoption described by Lowe, which both *de facto* and *de jure* transplants the child exclusively to the adoptive family.[52] The wish of adoptive parents for their adoption to conform to this model has in large

---

49 See Caroline B Fleming, "The Open-Records Debate: Balancing the Interests of Birth Parents and Adult Adoptees" (2004–2005) 11 *William and Mary Journal of Women and the Law* 461, 470–1; Van Bueren, above n 3, 43. This line of argument was briefly examined by the European Court of Human Rights in the case of *Odièvre v France* [2003] ECHR 86, where the applicant had claimed that she could not access the same inheritance rights as other children because she could not know the identity of her birth parents. The Court found that her situation with regard to her natural mother was not comparable to that of children who enjoy established parental ties with their natural parents, and in any case, she could inherit from her adoptive parents. The Court dealt with this issue summarily though, and did not discuss in depth the issue from the perspective of the right to identity, only inheritance.

50 Article 17d Act on the Adoption of Foreign Children.

51 Vonk, above n 44, 18. See *Valkenhorst II* (HR 15 April 1994) *NJ* 1994, 608. In this case, an institution in which the child's biological mother was living was obliged to divulge the adoption documentation it held, despite the fact that the mother had not given her consent.

52 Nigel Lowe, "The Changing Face of Adoption – the Gift/Donation Model Versus the Contract/Services Model" (1997) 9 *Child and Family Law Quarterly* 371.

part driven the increase of intercountry adoptions in recent years. As was seen in Chapter Eight, fewer eligible infants have become available in developed countries, and prospective adopters have started to look across national borders for young children in other parts of the world. Indeed, a recent study found that 35% of prospective adoptive parents chose intercountry adoption specifically because it follows this model, and does not require ongoing contact with families of origin.[53] Unlike children in western Europe in need of adoption, who are now predominantly older when they are adopted and have significant ties already to their birth families, intercountry adoption is seen as a quicker process that allows adoption of younger children with no pre-existing ties.[54]

The desire for security and stability of their family is not an unreasonable wish, and care should be taken not to alienate prospective adopters by putting unreasonable demands on them. However, it should also be considered that secrecy in adoption may not be *necessary* for stability and security of adoptive parents, but is instead a socially created phenomenon that relies on the traditional form of adoption that was practiced throughout the 20th century. In current times, where more pluralistic family forms are acceptable, and there is no longer so great an emphasis on the nuclear family comprising two parents only, such preconceptions should be challenged.[55]

In contrast to this, several countries have gone further and placed the child's ability to access information solely in the hands of the adoptive parents. In Armenia[56] and Azerbaijan,[57] the child cannot access any information regarding his or her origins without the permission of the adoptive parents, and as stated above, in Russia, Ukraine and FYR Macedonia, it is entirely up to the adoptive parents whether the child will be informed if he or she is adopted at all. The power is also placed in the adoptive parents' hands in Estonia,[58] Hungary,[59] Latvia,[60] Portugal[61] and Spain,[62] where legislation requires that if the child is

53 Ellen Pinderhughes et al, *A Changing World: Shaping best practices through understanding of the new realities of intercountry adoption* (2013, Evan B Donaldson Adoption Institute) 53.

54 See Table 4 in Chapter Seven, which sets out the ages of children adopted in intercountry adoption from sending states in Europe. Although a higher proportion of infants are adopted than in England, for example, children older than five are increasingly likely to make up a high proportion of children sent abroad for adoption.

55 This is already operating in domestic adoption practice in England, with open adoption and post-adoption contact being ordered with increasing frequency.

56 Article 169 Family Code. The Committee on the Rights of the Child has criticised this approach (*Concluding Observations: Armenia* (26 February 2004) CRC/C/15/Add.225, [38]).

57 Article 130 Family Code.

58 Section 164(7) Family Law Act 2009. Even then, the birth parents must also have consented to their information being revealed.

59 The child must be over 14, and this may still be refused in the interests of the child (ChildONEurope, *Extracts of the Legislation on Adoption: Hungary* (date unknown) <www.childoneurope.org/issues/adoption/adoption_legislation/hungary.pdf> [8 June 2012]).

60 Section 162 Civil Law.

61 Article 1985 Civil Code.

62 Article 180(5) Civil Code.

younger than 18, access is granted only with the adoptive parents' consent.[63] While in such cases, adoptive parents may act as a safeguard to ensure that the child does not find out information before he or she is sufficiently mature to understand and cope with it, the same power can also be used to protect the adoptive parents' position, to the detriment of mature and capable children.

In Denmark and Germany the adoptive parents' rights must also be considered. In Germany, access to the information may be denied if there is overriding opposition from one of the other parties to the adoption;[64] and Danish authorities will decide whether to allow access to records on an individual assessment, balancing individual privacy with securing access for any party with a legitimate interest.[65] Although these laws are an improvement on those that allow an automatic veto by one of the other parties to the adoption, it is essential that the balancing of rights be conducted with the best interests of the child as the primary consideration, and that the needs and desires of the adoptive parents are not permitted to dictate the outcome of the procedure.

The best interests principle has itself been used to place restrictions on the access of children to information. In Albania, access to records may be restricted or rejected on "special occasions" where there are reasons to believe that it will bring about grave consequences.[66] Finnish authorities may also deny access where this would be dangerous to the health or development of the adoptee, or if access would otherwise be manifestly contrary to his or her best interests, or other private interests; although where the identity of the birth parent is known, it must always be disclosed to an adoptee who has achieved the age of 12, notwithstanding these objections.[67] In addition, in Croatia, all children have the right to examine their adoption files and birth register, if the social welfare authorities establish that this would be in their interests.[68]

It is not clear in these countries on what grounds the authorities may decide that the knowledge would be contrary to the child's best interests if he or she wished to access it. In such circumstances, any denial would have to be founded on particularly serious projected consequences for these to outweigh the damage to the child at having the request refused. The drafters of the UNCRC itself considered including a best-interests consideration in determining whether a child should be able to know and be cared for by his or her parents.[69] However, in the end, delegates opted for the much stricter "as far as possible test". As

---

63 Note that in Portugal and Estonia, the birth parents' consent is also needed.

64 Section 9b Act on Adoption Agency and the Prohibition of Agency for Surrogate Mothers.

65 Hague Conference, *Country Profile: Denmark* (2010) <www.hcch.net/index_en.php?act=publications.details&pid=5128&dtid=42> [14 January 2012].

66 Article 37 Law No 9695 (19 March 2007); Hague Conference, *Country Profile: Albania* (2010) <www.hcch.net/index_en.php?act=publications.details&pid=5081&dtid=42> [14 January 2012].

67 Section 93 Adoption Act 22/2012.

68 Article 142 Family Act (Petar Sarcevic et al, *Family Law in Croatia* (2011, Kluwer Law)).

69 See United Nations Commission on Human Rights, *Report of the Working Group on a Draft Convention on the Rights of the Child* (2 March 1989, United Nations) E/CN.4/1989/48.

UNICEF suggests, this test is less subjective than a best-interests determination, and implies that children are entitled to know about their origins if they so wish, even where others consider that this is against their interests.[70]

This does not mean that best interests should be totally outside a consideration of whether a child should receive information about his or her origins, as it is one of the underlying principles of all articles of the UNCRC. However, it suggests that there would have to be a decided indication that detrimental consequences would follow for this to override the substantive rights in articles 7 and 8 of the Convention.

9.3. SECRECY AND BIRTH PARENTS

While the rights of adoptive parents and the interests of the child are important factors in most domestic laws, the principal interests invoked to qualify the right of the child to access information on his or her origins are those of the birth parents. More accurately, it is the interests of the biological mother that have been most persuasive in this debate, due to the traditional prevalence of single mothers giving up their children for adoption or asking for anonymous birth. In this respect, the request for privacy arises at two different stages: first, when the child is born and information is being entered onto the birth certificate; and second, when the child is seeking access to the information.

9.3.1. MUST INFORMATION BE RECORDED?

The debate concerning access to information for adopted children is inextricably linked with the debate regarding anonymous birth, and state practices that permit the anonymous relinquishment of children (i.e. "baby-boxes", "baby hatches", and "incubators"). Anonymous birth and relinquishment, as they preclude information being recorded concerning the child's parents, interfere with the very essence of this right of a child to know his or her origins, making it a virtual impossibility that this will ever be achieved. This goes beyond whether adoption records should be sealed or not, to whether or not there will be a record to access in the first place.

Anonymous birth is the practice by which mothers can give birth in a hospital without stating their identity, and the child is then placed for adoption. While France is the most prominent exponent of this practice,[71] it is also legal in

70 Rachel Hodgkin and Peter Newell, *Implementation Handbook for the Convention on the Rights of the Child* (3rd ed, 2007, UNICEF) 107.

71 Provided for in article 341 Civil Code.

Luxembourg, Germany and Austria.[72] Other European countries also incorporate secrecy not simply as a facet of the adoption process, when files are sealed, but at the time of birth. In Italy there is no requirement that the mother be entered onto the birth certificate of the child,[73] and in the Czech Republic[74] and Greece,[75] although the mother's identity is recorded, the birth records can be kept secret.

In addition to anonymous birth, in the last 15 years there has been an increasing trend towards the creation of "baby-boxes" throughout central and eastern Europe, which allow parents to leave their child in the care of the state anonymously. In France, this practice dates back to the time of St Vincent de Paul, who introduced the use of a revolving crib in the wall of a charitable institution.[76] The baby could be placed in the crib, and a bell rung, at which time the crib would pivot and the child would be taken into the institution without the identity of the mother being revealed.[77] In recent times, such boxes have spread dramatically across Europe, and can now be found in Austria, Belgium,[78] the Czech Republic, Germany, Hungary, Italy, Latvia, Lithuania, Poland, Portugal, Russia, Slovakia and Switzerland.[79] The number of boxes in each country varies: while only one box exists in Belgium, 45 can be found in Poland, 47 in the Czech Republic, and around 80 in Germany.[80]

While statistics are not available for all these countries, in 2009/2010 13 infants were left in Lithuania, 11 in the Czech Republic, seven in Slovakia, and six in both Austria and Latvia. In Hungary, 40 children were placed in incubators from 2000 to 2010,[81] and in Poland, 31 infants were placed from 2006 to 2010.[82] The largest numbers of children are placed in Germany, where 500

72 In Austria, the practice is somewhat different however, as while the mother is not required to provide proof of her identity or register with the health services, she must leave her details to be accessible to the child at the age of 14. This provides a compromise between the two sets of interests, and will be discussed below.

73 Article 250 of the Civil Code does not make it mandatory for parents to recognise an illegitimate child, and if they choose not to do so, they will not be named on the birth certificate. If the child searches for information on his or her parents at a later date, this will not be disclosed if the parent wished for anonymity.

74 Section 67 Act No 20/1966 Sb on Care for Populace Health (as amended by Act No 422/2004).

75 Kevin Browne, Shihning Chou, and Kate Whitfield, *Child Abandonment and its Prevention in Europe* (2012, University of Nottingham) 21 <http://resourcecentre.savethechildren.se/content/library/documents/child-abandonment-and-its-prevention-europe> [7 February 2013].

76 Although only introduced to France in the 17th century, there is record of "foundling wheels" used in Italy from 1198.

77 *Odièvre v France* [2003] ECHR 86, [15].

78 It should be noted that although the baby-box is legal in Belgium, abandoning a baby in it is illegal.

79 Browne, Chou and Whitfield, above n 75, 4. There is also an initiative to set up a baby-box in the Netherlands (Radio Netherlands Worldwide, *Controversial Plan to Help Dutch Foundlings* (2011) <www.rnw.nl/english/video/controversial-plan-help-dutch-foundlings> [22 October 2012]).

80 Browne, Chou and Whitfield, ibid., 20.

81 Hungarian Department of Child and Youth Protection, 2010 (ibid.).

82 Ibid., 9. Since there are 45 incubators placed in this country, this means that almost one-third of them have not been used during this time.

children were left in baby-boxes between 2000–2011.[83] These numbers are minimal in comparison to anonymous births in France, however, with approximately 600 women per year requesting anonymity under this legislation.[84]

Although the provision of anonymous birth and anonymous relinquishment is spreading throughout Europe, and is popular among citizens – a Swiss poll in 2011 found that 87 per cent of participants thought baby-boxes were "very useful or useful", and more than a quarter thought that every hospital should have one[85] – it remains a contentious issue. Indeed, in many cases, the state itself has not set up the baby-boxes, and may in fact be officially opposed to them (for example in Belgium, Austria and the Czech Republic). However, where they have been established by non-governmental organisations, states are often reluctant to intervene, perhaps for political reasons as they fear the consequences if they shut down these facilities, and a child is found abandoned elsewhere. This was particularly obvious in Austria's discussions with the Committee on the Rights of the Child in September 2012.[86]

Whether the state has provided the service itself, or simply allowed the establishment of baby-boxes by other entities within its jurisdiction, it is effectively sanctioning a mechanism under which children cannot know and be cared for by their own parents, in violation of article 7 of the UNCRC. This was acknowledged by the Spanish Supreme Court in 1999, when it found that allowing the words "mother unknown" to be entered in the official register was unconstitutional as it contradicted the constitutional principles of equality and knowledge of one's paternity, as the child completely loses the link that would allow, in due course, knowledge of his or her true parentage.

Anonymous birth and relinquishment allow the mother to decide whether the child will be able to access his or her rights, not only in relation to information on origins, but also concerning the right to stay with his or her wider family group where possible. It gives no opportunity to the authorities to determine whether there is a chance for the child to stay with other members of

---

83 Ibid., 20.

84 *Odièvre v France* [2003] ECHR 86, [36]. A similar situation exists in Austria, where in 2010 six newborns were placed in baby flaps, but 40 children were born anonymously (National Coalition for the Implementation of the UN Convention on the Rights of the Child: Austria, *Supplementary Report on the 3rd and 4th Report of Federal Republic of Austria to the United Nations, Pursuant to Article 44, paragraph 1B of the UN Convention on the Rights of the Child* (2012) <www.crin.org/docs/Austria_NCICRCA_CRC,OPAC,OPSC%20Report.pdf> [7 October 2012]).

85 Randeep Ramesh, *Spread of 'baby boxes' in Europe alarms United Nations* (10 June 2012, The Guardian) <www.guardian.co.uk/world/2012/jun/10/unitednations-europe-news> [22 September 2012]. Further, the Committee on the Rights of the Child's recommendations to the Czech Republic with regard to baby-boxes created a furore of media attention and criticism, which spread over state borders to neighbouring Slovakia and Hungary, and drew recriminations from Members of the European Parliament.

86 The author was present for these discussions.

the birth family through kinship care, and in particular, deprives the child and his or her father from establishing any relationship.

In France, the father of a child born under anonymous birth is denied any right to establish a relationship with his child. Even if he is aware of the child's birth, he cannot legally recognise him or her, and cannot establish paternity. This was seen in *Association Enfance et Familles v F et A*,[87] where the father legally recognised the child prior to birth. The mother told him that the child was stillborn, but eventually confessed that the child had been born anonymously. The father sought to establish paternity and custody of the child, but in the meantime, an adoption order had been made. The Court of Appeal held that the father's recognition of the child was not valid, since it related to a child who was legally deemed not to have been born to the mother.[88] As such, the mother has the opportunity to unilaterally prevent the father from establishing paternity or caring for the child, and deny the child the right to know and be cared for by his or her father.

While the French courts have accepted this situation, the Spanish Supreme Court was not similarly permissive. When declaring anonymous birth unconstitutional, the Court also noted the incongruity of the fact that while paternity can be coercively imposed on the father, the mother is free to decide whether to continue the pregnancy, or completely cut any ties with the child, and has a clear path to avoid any obligations.[89]

The right of the mother to unilaterally decide whether a child is placed for adoption, and to control the relationship between him or her and the father, has been argued to be part of the reproductive autonomy of women. Lori Chambers in particular has suggested that an unfettered right to release a newborn child for adoption is an essential component of a mother's autonomy and dignity, which should be exercised exclusively. She argues that if obliged to notify the father and allow him a chance to care for the child, the mother might instead choose abortion.[90] Relinquishment, in her view, should be seen as an act of caring for the child, not as an act of abandonment,[91] and thus the mother should be permitted to decide how and where the child gets placed, and whether the father is involved.

The right of a child to be cared for by his or her parents is not predicated on the sex of that parent, and there is no reason why the mother should be permitted to choose the involvement of the father in the child's life, even if she has been the

---

87 Court of Appeal of Riom, 16 December 1997 (1998) JCP II 10147.

88 The mother is deemed under French law never to have given birth, so the father could not claim paternity of her child.

89 Recurso de Casacion num. 2854/1994, Sentencia del TS de 21 septiembre 1999.

90 Lori Chambers, "Newborn Adoption: Birth Mothers, Genetic Fathers, and Reproductive Autonomy" (2010) 26 *Canadian Journal of Family Law* 339, 343–345.

91 In this respect, see the English case of *Watson v Nikolaisen* [1955] 2 QB 286, in which the High Court held that where a mother had given a child to an adoptive family she had not abandoned the child, as she had made provision for its care by placing her with people who desired to adopt her and in whom she had confidence.

one who has given birth. If the mother fears that the father would harm the child, this could be dealt with by the child welfare and criminal justice systems; in all other cases, it should not be for the mother to decide the extent to which the child's right to know and be cared for by his or her parents should be exercised.

Further, in relation to a woman's reproductive autonomy, where abortion is *not* permitted, or only permitted under very limited circumstances,[92] it has been argued that anonymous birth and baby-boxes are mechanisms that can allow a woman to take back control of her body, in line with her individual rights.[93] The problem with this argument is that while abortion allows a woman the right to control her own body, once the child is born, it is not a question of the mother's reproductive rights but of her right to refuse motherhood, and to escape defined societal roles and the moral and legal obligations imposed on parents. However, these latter rights are not predicated on anonymity, but can be achieved simply through placing the child for adoption in a conventional manner.

The Committee on the Rights of the Child has made clear that the state has a responsibility under the UNCRC to gather and conserve information concerning a child's identity,[94] and as such has taken a strong stance against anonymous relinquishment and the use of baby-boxes, stating that they are in contravention of articles 6 (right to survival and development), 7 and 8 (as discussed above), 9 (right not to be separated from parents except in accordance with the law) and 19 (right to protection of the child and support of parents) of the Convention.[95] In its Concluding Observations on the Czech Republic in 2011, the Committee strongly urged the government to end the programme as soon as possible, and instead address the root causes of child abandonment, including providing family planning, adequate counselling, social support and the prevention of risk pregnancies.[96] The Committee had previously expressed concern over the existence of such programmes in Slovakia and Austria.[97]

Anonymous birth has also been criticised, with the Committee telling France that it "remains concerned that … the right to conceal the identity of the mother if she so wishes is not in conformity with the provisions of the Convention,"[98]

---

92 See, for example, Andorra, Cyprus, Ireland, Malta, Monaco and Poland.

93 Nadine Lefaucheur, "The French 'Tradition' of Anonymous Birth: The Lines of Argument" (2004) 18 *International Journal of Law, Policy and the Family* 319, 331.

94 United Nations Committee on the Rights of the Child, *Concluding Observations: Belgium* (18 June 2010) CRC/C/BEL/CO/3–4, [52].

95 United Nations Committee on the Rights of the Child, *Concluding Observations: Austria* (5 October 2012) CRC/C/AUT/CO/3–4, [29].

96 United Nations Committee on the Rights of the Child, *Concluding Observations: Czech Republic* (4 August 2011) CRC/C/CZE/CO/3–4, [50].

97 United Nations Committee on the Rights of the Child, *Concluding Observations: Slovakia* (10 July 2007) CRC/C/SVK/CO/2, [41]; *Concluding Observations: Austria* (31 March 2005) CRC/C/15/Add.251, [29].

98 United Nations Committee on the Rights of the Child, *Concluding Observations: France* (30 June 2004) CRC/C/15/Add.240, [23].

and recommending that it "take all appropriate measures to fully enforce the child's right to know his or her biological parents and siblings, as enshrined in article 7 of the Convention and in the light of the principles of non-discrimination (art. 2) and the best interests of the child (art. 3)."[99] Similarly, in relation to Luxembourg, the Committee urged the state to take all necessary measures to eliminate anonymous birth and ensure that information on a child's parents is registered and kept on file to allow the child to know his or her origins at an appropriate time.[100]

In contrast to these pronouncements by the Committee on the Rights of the Child, the ECtHR in the case of *Odièvre v France* found that anonymous birth, as practiced in France, was not in violation of the European Convention on Human Rights. Interestingly, it came to this decision without mentioning the UNCRC at any stage. This case has far-reaching implications not just for anonymous birth and relinquishment, but for the wider question of a child's access to origins in general in Europe.

The application was brought by a French woman, born in 1965, whose mother had requested that her birth be kept secret. She was thus placed for adoption anonymously. In 1990, the applicant was able to obtain non-identifying information about her natural family, but her applications for further identifying information about her parents and natural siblings were refused. She made an application to the ECtHR, complaining that her inability to obtain this information prevented her from finding out her personal history, in violation of article 8 of the Convention.

In presenting her case, the applicant argued that mothers who asked for their identity to be kept secret did so through lack of autonomy related to social and economic issues. She contended that anonymous birth thus constituted an act of violence that was easily avoidable, and that concerns for the mother could be addressed by providing her with the necessary assistance and support, rather than promising anonymity.[101]

This argument is supported by research by Bilson and Markova, who found that in the majority of cases, women openly abandoning their babies did not want to relinquish the child, but felt that they could not care for him or her.[102] It also appears to be reinforced by the submissions of the French Government itself

---

99 United Nations Committee on the Rights of the Child, *Concluding Observations: France* (11 June 2009) CRC/C/FRA/CO/4, [44].

100 United Nations Committee on the Rights of the Child, *Concluding Observations: Luxembourg* (31 March 2005) CRC/C/15/Add.250, [28]–[29]. However, Luxembourg has submitted a reservation in relation to article 7 of the Convention, stating that it believes that this "presents no obstacle to the legal process in respect of anonymous births, which is deemed to be in the interest of the child, as provided under article 3 of the Convention."

101 *Odièvre v France* [2003] ECHR 86, [31].

102 Andy Bilson and Galina Markova, "But You Should See Their Families: Preventing Child Abandonment and Promoting Social Inclusion in Countries in Transition" (2007) 12(3) *Social Work & Social Sciences Review* 29.

in *Odièvre*, which stated that there were three main categories of women who chose to give birth anonymously:

(1) young women who were not yet independent;
(2) young women still living with their parents in Muslim families originating from North African or sub-Saharan African societies in which pregnancy outside marriage was a great dishonour; and
(3) isolated women with financial difficulties (the youngest, many of whom were under 25, were single mothers; many of the older women were over 35 and for the most part separated or divorced or had been abandoned, some being victims of domestic violence, with several children to look after).[103]

Regarding the circumstances that led the women to seek the confidentiality of anonymous birth, the Government suggested that "the stated reasons sometimes concealed more serious problems, such as rape or incest, which were not always revealed by those concerned."[104] The Government argued that protecting these women justified the practice of anonymous birth, allowing them to give birth in a controlled and safe environment, while preventing abortion or child abandonment. This was accepted by the majority of the Court, with Judge Greve in his concurring opinion arguing that at the prenatal stage, the rights and interests of the mother and child converge: in these circumstances, he held that it is in the best interests of the child to be born in a safe environment, without putting either the child's or the mother's life in jeopardy, no matter what the future consequences.

Such considerations were also characterised as a balance between the competing rights of the child himself or herself, with Judge Greve arguing that "[t]he primary interest of the child is to be born and born under circumstances where its health is not unnecessarily put at risk by birth in circumstances in which its mother tries to secure secrecy even when that means that she will be deprived of professional assistance when in labour."[105]

These arguments do little to address the true issues at stake, which are the underlying social, economic and cultural circumstances that lead women to feel that they have no other option but to take such a step. It should not be a dichotomy between the child's safety and knowing his or her identity, but instead states should institute measures to ensure that mothers are not put in the position to have to make this choice.

The principal argument in favour of baby-boxes relies on the same justifications; that is, the right of the child to life. Those in favour argue that if baby-boxes did not exist, children would be killed by mothers unable to cope or

103 *Odièvre v France* [2003] ECHR 86, [36].
104 Ibid.
105 Ibid.

be abandoned in unsafe places.[106] However, there is no indication that either anonymous birth or baby-boxes have had any effect on the number of abortions or children illegally abandoned or killed. Danner et al found that despite the provision of anonymous birth in Austria, there are still cases of abandonment and infanticide, and suggest that the women who give birth anonymously are not in fact those who are in crisis, or would otherwise kill their babies.[107] Similarly, a German study found that the number of infants abandoned illegally has not dropped since baby-boxes were introduced.[108]

Furthermore, in the Czech Republic, children can be placed in a baby-box up to one year of age.[109] In such cases, there appears little reason to allow a child to be placed in this manner, rather than through social services. It is no longer an issue of "women in specific situations who unfortunately keep their pregnancy a secret and fear to approach official institutions" – as put by Members of the European Parliament[110] – but a kind of officially sanctioned alternative to traditional adoption.[111] This was confirmed by the auditor of the Foundation for Abandoned Children (Statim) in the Czech Republic, who said that the boxes were needed to solve the problem of abandoned children, as "it quickens the adoption process, which is very slow in our country."[112]

The use of baby-boxes for such a purpose, effectively bypassing alternative care procedures, is in clear violation of the UNCRC.[113] Under article 19(1) of the Convention, states have a duty to take all steps to protect the child from neglect or negligent treatment, and by facilitating the separation of a child from his or her parents through placement in a baby-box, prior to there having been a bona fide attempt to take all reasonable measures to fulfil the rights of the child to

---

106 Director of the NGO "Our Children Foundation" as quoted by Robert Tait, *Baby boxes in Czech Republic: 'the first thing should be the child's right to life'* (10 June 2012, The Guardian) <www.guardian.co.uk/world/2012/jun/10/czech-republic-baby-box> [15 October 2012]; Representative of Hamburg's SterniPark, as quoted by Kathleen Moore, *Europe: Controversial 'Baby Box' Lets Mothers Abandon Infants Safely* (4 June 2005, Radio Free Europe Radio Liberty) <www.rferl.org/content/article/1059124.html> [22 September 2012].

107 C Danner et al, "Anonymous Birth and Neonaticide in Tyrol" (2005) 209(5) *Z Geburtshilfe Neonatol* 192.

108 Deutscher Ethikrat, *Anonymous Relinquishment of Infants* (2009) 25. A study by Terre des Hommes in Germany found that from 1999 to 2009, over 30 infants were found abandoned in places other than baby-boxes each year (with the exception of 2005, where 29 infants were found abandoned) (Terre des Hommes, *Hilfe Für Kinder in Not* (2012) <www.tdh.de/was-wir-tun/themen-a-z/babyklappe-und-anonyme-geburt/statistik.html> [15 June 2012]).

109 Browne, Chou and Whitfield, above n 75, 18.

110 Zuzana Roithova, *Letter to Professor Yanghee Lee, Chairwoman, Committee on the Rights of the Child* (14 July 2011) <www.eppgroup.eu/press/pdoc11/110714letter-to-un-chairwoman.pdf> [30 September 2012].

111 This was also noted in the report by Deutscher Ethikrat, *Anonymous Relinquishment of Infants* (2009) 31.

112 Tait, above n 106.

113 United Nations Committee on the Rights of the Child, *Concluding Observations: Austria* (5 October 2012) CRC/C/AUT/CO/3–4, [29].

know and be cared for by his or her parents, the state is allowing the violation of this right. The child also has the right to be placed with relatives where that is possible, and not to be placed in alternative care without assistance being provided to help prevent this. Under article 9 of the UNCRC, there is an obligation on states to undertake a fully informed determination of a child's specific situation prior to undertaking measures that would deprive him or her of these rights, a determination which anonymous relinquishment diverts and effectively prevents.

This fast track into adoption also raises serious ethical considerations where children are subsequently placed for intercountry adoption. If there has been no attempt to address the issues behind the relinquishment, including the provision of adequate support and assistance, it raises the possibility that impoverished and vulnerable families are giving up their children because they cannot cope, to be taken in by wealthy foreign families. Such a transfer of children from poor to rich was discussed in Chapter Five on inducement of consent, and should be considered very carefully.

It may also be that anonymous relinquishment actually creates a new market for legal abandonment, rather than solving problems for mothers who are actually in distress. In particular, the availability of this simple procedure, without any associated checks or assistance, may cause pressure to be placed on mothers to abandon their child, similar to the pressure that may be placed on mothers to have abortions. Although for obvious reasons little is known about the demographic of persons placing children in baby-boxes, the University of Nottingham's report on child abandonment cites anecdotal evidence provided by porters from one hospital in Hungary, in which 15 out of the 16 children placed in incubators in that hospital were placed by men, not women.[114] Similarly, reports are now emerging about abuse of the system of anonymous birth in Spain throughout the regime of Franco, when mothers were told that their children had died, only to find later that the child had been registered as an anonymous birth and subsequently adopted.[115] In these circumstances, such mechanisms may well be failing the mother, as well as the child.

In this area, anonymous birth has considerable advantages over baby-boxes, as it allows women to go anonymously to hospital and receive adequate medical care, rather than giving birth in unsafe conditions, trying to continue to conceal the pregnancy. As Maria Herczog, a member of the UN Committee on the Rights of the Child, argues, the baby-box programme "sends out the mistaken message to pregnant women in crisis that they are right to continue with hiding their pregnancies, giving birth under uncontrolled circumstances, and then

114 Browne, Chou and Whitfield, above n 75, 29.

115 Katya Adler, *Spain's stolen babies and the families who lived a lie* (15 November 2012, BBC News) <www.bbc.co.uk/news/magazine-15335899> [15 November 2012].

abandoning their babies anonymously, losing the possibility to connect with them again."[116]

Anonymous birth also provides the possibility that counselling can be given to the mother, thus ensuring that her decision is not made under pressure from others, and that it is adequately informed. As was discussed in Chapter Four, figures from Germany suggest that between 50 and 75 per cent of women who sought anonymity on birth changed their minds once counselling was provided,[117] further supporting the argument that anonymous birth and relinquishment stem from a failure of the state to address social, cultural and economic issues. As Simon Wright, head of Child Survival at Save the Children, stated: "[b]aby boxes are a short-cut response to a much bigger problem, and do not deal with any of the underlying reasons why babies are abandoned. Instead of setting them up, governments should concentrate on giving women choice and control over having children ... In the long run, they are not good for mothers or children."[118]

In the case of anonymous birth, the mother can also be encouraged to leave some details for her child, so that the child has some future opportunity of gaining at least limited information about his or her parent(s). Even if this practice is still not in conformity with the UNCRC, it is better than the child receiving no information at all. This was acknowledged by the Committee on the Rights of the Child in its 2012 Concluding Observations on Austria, when it urged the government

> "to undertake all measures necessary to end the practice of anonymous abandonment and expeditiously strengthen and promote alternatives such as the possibility of anonymous births at hospitals as a measure of last resort to avoid abandonment and or death of the child, and to keep a confidential record of the parents to which the child could access at a later stage, taking into account the duty to fully comply with all provisions of the Convention."[119]

This recommendation rests on the unique nature of Austrian anonymous birth, where the mother does not have to leave her name with the hospital, but must leave identifying information with the child welfare authorities for the child to access when he or she reaches 14 years of age. A similar law was passed in 2013 in Germany, allowing women to give a false name to give birth in

---

116 Anna Szoboszlay, *Baby Boxes' Polarise Hungary* (11 June 2012, The Guardian) <www.guardian.co.uk/world/2012/jun/11/baby-boxes-polarise-hungary> [19 August 2012].

117 Deutscher Ethikrat, *Anonymous Relinquishment of Infants* (2009) 28.

118 Edna Fernandes, *Abandoned... in a postbox for babies: The shocking rise of newborns being left in 'adoption hatches' by mothers unable to cope* (7 July 2012, Daily Mail) <www.dailymail.co.uk/femail/article-2170150/Babywiege-Newborns-abandoned-baby-boxes-German-hospital.html> [22 September 2012].

119 United Nations Committee on the Rights of the Child, *Concluding Observations: Austria* (5 October 2012) CRC/C/AUT/CO/3–4, [30].

hospital and for the birth certificate, but requiring that their correct personal data be sealed and stored in a central agency for access by the child once he or she turns 16.[120]

These solutions provide a more nuanced approach to the balancing of rights in this area, allowing qualified privacy for the mother, while ensuring the child can have access to information at a later date. It is by no means satisfactory that women continue to feel the need to hide their pregnancy and motherhood, and it would be optimal if anonymous birth of any kind was not required; however, until these issues can be addressed at a deeper social, cultural and economic level, it is necessary to provide a mechanism to ensure that the rights of both women and the children they bear are protected.

9.3.2. BALANCING THE RIGHTS OF BIOLOGICAL PARENTS AND CHILDREN

Even in situations where the information has been collected upon the child's birth, and retained by the authorities, in some countries the birth parents can veto the release of this information if the child searches for it at a later date. In Portugal,[121] Estonia,[122] France,[123] Georgia,[124] Italy[125] and Slovenia[126] the identity of a birth parent cannot be revealed to the child if he or she opposes it, leaving the child in the same situation as if no records had been collected at all. These countries do not engage in a balancing process, and simply leave all the power in the hands of the birth parents to decide what rights a child can have access to.

The balance between parental rights, public policy considerations and the right of the child to information concerning his or her identity has been central to the jurisprudence of the European Court of Human Rights in this area, and in particular the issue was at the heart of the dissenting opinion in the case of *Odièvre*. The judges argued that no balancing of interests is possible where a birth had been registered anonymously, and suggested that French law allowed the mother's decision to constitute an absolute defence to any request for information, irrespective of the reasons for, or legitimacy of, that decision. In an (in)famously emotive judgment, they stated that: "The mother thus has a

120 Act on the expansion of assistance for pregnant women and for regulating confidential birth.
121 Article 1985 Civil Code.
122 Section 164(7) Family Law Act 2009.
123 Article 147-6 Law No 2002/93.
124 Hague Conference, *Country Profile: Georgia* (2010) <www.hcch.net/index_en.php?act=publications.details&pid=5118&dtid=42> [14 January 2012].
125 Article 28 Law 184/1983 (but see decision of *Godelli v Italy* (Appl. No. 33783/09) 25 September 2012, as discussed below).
126 Hague Conference, *Country Profile: Slovenia* (2010) <www.hcch.net/index_en.php?act=publications.details&pid=5096&dtid=42> [14 January 2012].

discretionary right to bring a suffering child into the world and to condemn it to lifelong ignorance."[127]

The solution of the minority was to create an independent body that could consider the reasons for, and legitimacy of, the decision of the mother to maintain her anonymity, in line with the previous jurisprudence, and particularly the 1989 case of *Gaskin v United Kingdom*.[128] The question that must be raised, however, is what a justifiable reason for refusing consent could be? In *Gaskin*, this could be seen as an acceptable solution because the information was coming from professionals who on occasions required anonymity to be able to perform their duties in the best interests of the children they were caring for. In cases involving parents though, what reasons could be accepted for withholding information?

It is easy in considering such questions for the line between knowledge of origins and post-adoption contact to become blurred. Many arguments invoked by biological parents for not releasing information involve a wish not to be contacted by the child at a later date. For this reason, England, and some states and provinces within the United States and Canada, have established adoption registers, which allow information to be provided to children and parents, while limiting the right of contact.

In England, a passive adoption register has been created for adoptive children and birth relatives to indicate whether they wish to have a relationship with one another. While an adopted child can have access to his or her birth certificate through simply filling out a form when he or she reaches 18, information on the current whereabouts of the birth parents is strictly controlled.[129] To access this information, the child must sign up to the Adoption Contact Register. If the birth parents are also on the register as willing to have contact with him or her, then the information will be provided to the child.[130] Such a system allows for information to be provided, but for contact to be controlled where one party is unwilling.

While statistics are only available to 2001, these indicate that in the ten years since the inception of this register in 1991, 19,683 adoptees and 8,492 relatives had placed themselves on the register. During that time, only 539 pairs of records were matched.[131] One disadvantage of such a passive register, perhaps linked to

---

127 Joint dissenting opinion of Judges Wildhaber, Sir Nicholas Bratza, Bonello, Loucaides, Cabral Barreto, Tulkens and Pellonpää, *Odièvre v France*, [7].

128 [1989] ECHR 13.

129 It should be noted that although access to this information from the register is controlled, parties to the adoption are increasingly using other mechanisms, such as social media, to locate other members of the adoption triad.

130 See United Kingdom, *Adoption Records* (31 January 2013) <https://www.gov.uk/adoption-records> [7 February 2013].

131 John Haskey, *Adoptees and Relatives Who Wish to Contact One Another Using the Adoption Contact Register: Trends, Relationships and Proportions of Records Matched* (2001, Office for National Statistics) <www.ons.gov.uk/ons/taxonomy/search/index.html?newquery=*&nscl=

the low number of matches, is the lack of awareness about this service, meaning that the other party might have no objection to contact, or actively wish it, but does not know of the existence of the service. To combat this problem, certain jurisdictions in the United States and Canada have active contact registers, meaning that if *either* the child or the parent signs up, the agency in charge will actively seek out the other party to see if they wish for contact. However, it also permits a party to place a contact veto on the file, making any attempt to personally contact them a misdemeanour.[132]

Such registers provide a balance between the rights of the child to information, and the privacy of the biological parents. However, the majority of the ECtHR in *Odièvre* took a more restrictive balancing approach, deeming that it was sufficient that non-identifying information be provided to the child which would enable her to trace some of her roots. While this concession may allow a child's medical interest in finding information on his or her origins to be satisfied, it does not address the psychological and social interests of the child in obtaining full and detailed information concerning the identity of his or her parents. There is no balance in such a system, as the mother's wishes continue to be paramount.

The majority of the Court further relied on the fact that the French system permitted the mother to change her mind and decide to release her information at a later date, claiming that this introduced an element of balance. The importance of this element was once again confirmed in the most recent case on anonymous birth before the ECtHR, *Godelli v Italy*, decided in September 2012. In this case, the Court found that the Italian system was in violation of the ECHR as a child whose mother had claimed anonymity is neither provided with non-identifying information, nor may the mother's identity be disclosed, even with her later consent. The Court found that such restrictions prevented any balancing of interests, giving blind preference to the birth mother, in contrast to the French system endorsed by *Odièvre*.[133] It is difficult to see how the mother's ability to change her mind creates a balance between the mother's and child's rights; instead, it appears simply to continue to leave the decision as to whether the child's rights will be respected to the mother herself. However, this appears now to be the settled approach of the ECtHR.

While the decision of *Godelli* is a step in the right direction, the Court nevertheless continues to judicially approve a system that denies the child the right to know and be cared for by his or her birth parents, and the right to preserve his or her identity. As a result, the European Convention on Human Rights, which in principle should be an optimal instrument for dealing with an issue involving the balancing of competing rights, has failed to evolve in line

---

Adoptions&nscl-orig=Adoptions&content-type=publicationContentTypes&sortDirection=DESCENDING&sortBy=pubdate> [19 February 2013].

132 This system is in place in Tennessee, for example.

133 (Appl. No. 33783/09) Judgment of 25 September 2012.

with current understandings of the importance of knowledge concerning biological origins to an adopted child, and allowed states to sidestep obligations to both mothers and children to deal with the underlying social and economic issues that drive the wish to remain anonymous, both before and after birth. This in turn has undermined the correct application of the rights of the child under the UNCRC in European jurisdictions.

9.4. CONCLUSION

The right of the child to access biological information in order to form his or her own identity has now been clearly recognised in theory, but is slow to be implemented in practice. Adoption in the minds of many still rests on the traditional concepts of secrecy and exclusivity, which is unfortunately reflected in the legislation of many European states. While some few states have legislated to ensure that all children have the right to know they are adopted and to access information on their origins, restrictive provisions still exist in many jurisdictions, putting the right of the child at the mercy of the wishes of biological and/or adoptive parents.

This problem is exacerbated by the growing trend of anonymous relinquishment across Europe, which effectively denies the child any chance of obtaining the necessary information. This practice is particularly problematic as it by-passes the child protection system, which is in place to ensure that the child can stay with his or her family or kin wherever possible, and as it enables the child to be fast-tracked into adoption, perhaps unnecessarily. Anonymous birth raises similar ethical issues, but has advantages for both the mother and the child, in that the mother can be provided with counselling and appropriate medical attention, and can be encouraged to leave some information, to the benefit of the child.

Although this discussion has not specifically focused on intercountry adoption, the implications of denying the child the right to access information are equally weighty, if not more so, in such a situation. In such a case, it is not only information on the parents themselves that is important, but also nationality, ethnicity and religion enter into the equation. While the Hague Convention has put in place strong procedural structures to enable the child's search for origins, without the cooperation of domestic authorities to collect and retain this information, it is of little assistance.

This is an area where there needs to be a radical change of perspective among national legislators as well as the European Court of Human Rights. As it currently stands, the interests of biological and adoptive parents are being given preference over those of adopted children, which are not being given the full weight they deserve. There needs to be a re-evaluation of the approach in this area, focusing on the rights of children, with less deference given to domestic authorities and a stronger stance at regional and international levels.

CHAPTER 10
CONCLUSION

The purpose of this book has been relatively simple: it has sought to determine how best to protect the rights of children in intercountry adoption in Europe by providing content to the principles set out in international law. In doing so, it has provided practical examples from European jurisdictions of the issues that can arise in establishing appropriate legislation for intercountry adoption, and how these can be improved upon by using a children's rights framework.

It has not been the intent to advocate uniform rules across Europe, but to expand on international human rights law principles to provide more detailed guidelines for conducting the intercountry adoption system in conformity with the best interests of the child. There are many areas in which uniform laws would not be beneficial; an example of this was seen in Chapter Three in the discussion of the in-country waiting periods for children before placement in intercountry adoption – the length of time that domestic alternative care is considered will necessarily depend on the individual situation in the jurisdiction in question. Where domestic foster care and alternative accommodation is well developed, then longer periods are justified in order to give the child the highest chance of a placement that ensures continuity of culture, ethnicity, language and religion, subject to difficulties for young children concerning attachment. On the other hand, where there are few domestic foster care or adoptive placements available, and the child will otherwise be living in substandard institutional care, shorter time periods must be advocated. In this situation, this book has proposed general guidelines that states must consider when developing their legislation, and when deciding what length of waiting period best suits their particular situation.

There are other issues discussed in this book that are more conducive to a prescriptive approach, for example services for adoptive parents such as pre-adoption counselling, post-adoption services, and psychological and legal assistance for birth parents. While the implementation of such services will depend on the financial resources of the state, the aim of the system and the principles behind it will remain unchanged.

Comparative research in this area is important, not only to highlight areas in which children's rights are not being protected, but also to provide examples of good practice so states can learn from one another when implementing adoption and child protection laws. However, the gaps in this research highlight how difficult it is to access reliable information on intercountry adoption law and practice. This has not been solely a matter of language – information about intercountry adoption in any language is often scarce, especially when it comes to the number of children involved in this practice. For example, when the European Union enquired of its member states how many children were sent or received in intercountry adoption, Cyprus and Slovenia had no annual data, Germany admitted that their data was not very reliable and the United Kingdom could only supply information on the number of prospective parents who had been approved, rather than the number of actual adoptions taking place.[1] Similar issues arise in relation to intercountry adoption breakdown, as well as the costs of adoption. In this light, greater transparency and accountability are needed to be able to effectively regulate intercountry adoption. The Hague Convention has tried to rectify this with numerous questionnaires and requests for information. However, compliance is voluntary, and many states provide limited information, if any.

A large gap can also be seen in information regarding the relationship between domestic adoption and intercountry adoption. There is scarce information available concerning the number of domestic parents waiting to adopt in various jurisdictions, and information on the domestic alternative care mechanisms is often limited. This is particularly troubling as, to protect children's rights, this book has aimed to place intercountry adoption firmly back into the sphere of child protection, as an integral part of domestic care procedures. Many of the difficulties that have arisen in relation to intercountry adoption have resulted from it being treated as a distinct and separate practice, rather than integrated with wider domestic child protection mechanisms. This involves ensuring that the intercountry adoption system is operated solely according to child welfare principles, and not influenced by market forces, and moreover, that it is not viewed as a panacea for all children in state care.

This is the importance of the subsidiarity principle as set out in international law, which was demonstrated in Chapter Three, but has also bound together all subsequent chapters. As has been shown, subsidiarity goes beyond preferring domestic care to intercountry adoption, and extends to ensuring that the child is able to stay with his or her family wherever possible, and that all efforts towards family reunification are made. For this reason, this book has focused on making sure that when a parent gives consent to adoption, it is free, informed, and made with all the legal and psychological assistance necessary. Similarly, where consent is overridden or dispensed with, this cannot be achieved without appropriate safeguards. This aim has also driven the discussion on anonymous birth and relinquishment, as well as that on the identification and involvement of fathers; it is only possible to consider family reunification and seek kinship care if both parents are identified.

---

1 European Union, *International Adoption in the European Union* (2009) 11.

While the UNCRC and the Hague Convention make clear the importance of the family unit, and maintaining it wherever possible, neither instrument makes explicit the aim of family reunification, and it is in this area that we have seen the ECHR offer a distinctive contribution. The principle of proportionality, as interpreted by the ECHR, offers more concrete guidelines to states when deciding on the most appropriate alternative care for a particular child, and sets limitations on the extent to which the state can intervene.

The impact of the ECHR on intercountry adoption law and practice is significant, although unfortunately not always fully realised. As a highly influential instrument across Europe, it has the ability to effectively protect children's rights in this area, but can equally undermine them when it fails to implement them in line with international principles. Throughout the book, we have seen examples of both, although instances of the former primarily appear when parental rights are enforced, and thus children's rights are consequentially preserved as a by-product.

This was seen in particular with the child's right to stay within his or her family wherever possible, which can be effectively enforced through ensuring that parental rights are respected at the pre-adoption stage, especially since it is parents who can, and do, take cases before national and regional courts. Parental rights in this area have been defended fiercely by the ECtHR, which has established significant safeguards to ensure that children cannot be placed in alternative care without due process. However, this is a dangerous mechanism for ensuring the enforcement of children's rights, and must be treated with caution, for although there is a potential commonality of interests between the child and birth parents to stay with the family wherever possible, this must be balanced by the corresponding right of the child to be promptly placed in secure and stable alternative care if this is necessary. As was seen in Chapter Six with regard to overriding or dispensing with parental consent, this is a balance that states have found difficult to achieve, with many jurisdictions failing to give adequate weight to the child's rights in decision-making in this area.

The failure of states to put the child at the centre of the decision-making processes regarding intercountry adoption is a problem that arises on a consistent basis throughout this book. Despite the international imperative, in very few jurisdictions are the best interests of the child required to be a paramount consideration in adoption decisions, and restrictions are still placed on children's rights in many areas of the law. Perhaps the most pertinent example of the failure of the majority of European jurisdictions to fully engage with the rights of children was seen in the conditions put on the participation of the child in the adoption process. While a limited number of states allow the full participation of the child in line with UNCRC requirements, the majority place restrictions on the child's opportunity to convey his or her view to the decision-maker based on age and what is considered to be in his or her "interests".

The lack of emphasis on children's rights is perhaps unsurprising, however, given the approach of the European Court of Human Rights. The rights of children have been consistently overlooked by the Court in its decision-making, and it has failed to come to terms with the autonomy of children and their evolving capacities in the field of family law. This is an area in which the ECtHR has emerged as a substantial stumbling block in effectively protecting and developing the rights of children in Europe. In the battles between children's and parents' rights, despite the insistence that children's best interests be of paramount importance, it is the latter that have achieved greater prominence.

In this respect, this book has shown that there is a need for greater representation of children in adoption decision-making, both for the purposes of conveying the child's views to the decision-maker, and in order to advocate for his or her best interests. An adoption case deals with many competing interests, with the state, prospective adoptive parents, birth parents and birth family all having an interest. For this reason, it is vital that the child is independently represented by a guardian, to make sure that his or her views and interests are put forward and not drowned out by stronger adult voices. While some states have provided for this in their legislation, many still rely on others to define and protect the child's interests, conveying an outdated, conservative view of the relationship between a child, the family and the state.

Conservative notions remain in certain parts of Europe concerning not only family relations, but also concerning the status of adoption itself. It was seen that in some states, adoption continues to be treated as something that should be hidden, something to be ashamed of; for example, in Ukraine, where the child has the right *not* to have the adoption revealed, even to himself or herself. Although this is an extreme example, it is important that these vestiges of stigma be eliminated, so that the rights of the child in adoption can be fully implemented. This can be achieved through the development of a stronger culture of familial alternative care, of fostering and adoption, and for these to be brought into the mainstream as legitimate family forms.

The focus on the "traditional" family can be seen in two additional respects: the place of the father in the adoption process, and the criteria for the selection of prospective adoptive parents. The identification and involvement of the biological father has been an often overlooked aspect of the adoption debate, and is one in which conservative notions concerning the roles of men and women in rearing children can be seen throughout much of Europe. In particular, stereotypes concerning unmarried fathers are present in a number of jurisdictions, and often undermine the right of the child to know and be cared for by both his or her parents. This is especially problematic in intercountry adoption, where identification of a father opens the door to further options for kinship care.

This has been an area in which ECtHR jurisprudence has been especially influential, particularly in enforcing procedural rights for fathers to be involved in the adoption process. This continues to predominantly rest on the extent of involvement of the father in the mother or child's life, although recent decisions have indicated a shift towards greater rights for fathers whose involvement is prevented by the birth mother. While this is an important step in the right direction, such a right can only be enforced where the father *knows* about the child, and tries to establish a relationship. Where the child is kept secret from the father, for example in cases of anonymous birth, the rights of the father, and the child to have a relationship with him, continue to be severely compromised both under Strasbourg case-law, and throughout the majority of European jurisdictions. As such, a more inclusive approach to fathers is needed, based on mutual recognition of the role of both parents, as was shown in some Nordic and Balkan states; however, these remain outliers in practice rather than the norm.

A further example of the continuation of adherence to conservative family models can be seen in the selection of prospective adoptive parents. While nearly all states allow single persons to enter into an intercountry adoption, the restrictions and reservations put on this show that a two-parent family is still the highly preferred family form. Meanwhile, adoption by same-sex couples is available in only a minority of jurisdictions. It is understandable that international instruments have shied away from such contentious areas, but when adopting a child rights based approach, it is important that restrictions on a parent's eligibility are not arbitrarily imposed, and suitability to adopt is based purely on whether the individual in question could provide a safe and loving home.

There are a number of areas that have emerged in which the international instruments have been insufficient in their protection of children's rights. This was seen most vividly in relation to "improper" financial gain under the UNCRC, as well as the permission given to authorised non-accredited bodies to facilitate adoption under the Hague Convention. While it is clear that the latter was a compromise intended to ensure the participation of the United States in the Convention regime, the introduction of profit-making activities removes intercountry adoption from what should be its primary, and indeed only, function: as an alternative care mechanism.

Likewise, the right of the child to access his or her origins under the UNCRC has been compromised by a lack of clarity, leading to interpretations that give precedence to the interests of adults. While article 7 gives to a child the right to know and be cared for by his or her parents as far as possible, there is uncertainty among states as to the intended meaning of this provision, and the extent to which it applies to adopted children. As with child representation, this is an area in which the true status of children's rights in domestic law becomes apparent, and without clear international guidance, there is a risk that the focus of legislation will be towards child protection, instead of respecting and promoting the autonomy of children.

The largest gap in the international instruments, however, lies in the facilitation and oversight of the adoptive placement through the preparation of adoptive parents and post-adoption services. With more and more so-called "special needs" children being adopted – those in sibling groups, who are older, or who have mental or physical disabilities – greater attention must be paid to ensuring that prospective parents are given assistance, both in preparing for the adoption, and coping with the difficulties that may arise afterwards. International guidance on these issues is conspicuous in its absence, especially in the field of post-adoption monitoring where effective coordination is required between sending and receiving countries.

Despite the great influx of intercountry adoption in recent decades, there is still a large degree of uncertainty surrounding this practice, and the best way to regulate it. Time and again, reports have come from all corners of the globe of parental consent being obtained inappropriately, children not being consulted over their placement, and adoption breakdown through lack of support and adequate monitoring. This is an area of law that is in vital need of greater clarification from authoritative sources; there needs to be a better understanding of the content of children's rights, and how these apply in specific situations. Twenty-five years after the UNCRC entered into force, and despite its almost universal ratification, the fundamental principles that underpin children's rights are not always well understood, or fully accepted, and where substantial scope is given to domestic authorities, adult-centred legislation is often the result. While uniformity between jurisdictions is not recommended, this book has attempted to give content to the fundamental principles of the international instruments by proposing a child-focused framework within which they can be applied. It can now only be hoped that domestic laws will continue to develop in this direction.

LIST OF LEGISLATION

INTERNATIONAL AND REGIONAL INSTRUMENTS

COUNCIL OF EUROPE

European Convention for the Protection of Human Rights and Fundamental Freedoms (1950) (Council of Europe, ETS 5)
European Convention on the Adoption of Children (1967) (Council of Europe, ETS 58)
European Convention on the Exercise of Children's Rights (1996) (Council of Europe, ETS 160)
European Convention on the Adoption of Children (Revised) (2008) (Council of Europe, ETS 202)

HAGUE CONFERENCE ON PRIVATE INTERNATIONAL LAW

Hague Convention on Jurisdiction, Applicable Law and Recognition of Decrees Relating to Adoptions (1965)
Hague Convention on Protection of Children and Cooperation in Respect of Intercountry Adoption (1993)

UNITED NATIONS

League of Nations Geneva Declaration on the Rights of the Child (1924)
United Nations Declaration of the Rights of the Child (1959)
United Nations Convention on the Rights of the Child (1989) 1577 UNTS 3
Optional Protocol to the United Nations Convention on the Rights of the Child on the Sale of Children, Child Prostitution and Child Pornography (2000) 2171 UNTS 227
Protocol to Prevent, Suppress and Punish Trafficking in Persons, especially Women and Children, supplementing the United Nations Convention against Transnational Organized Crime (2000) 2237 UNTS 319
United Nations Human Rights Council, Draft Resolution to the General Assembly: Guidelines for the Alternative Care of Children (15 June 2009) A/HRC/11/L.13

DOMESTIC LEGISLATION

ALBANIA

Family Code
Criminal Code

ANDORRA

Qualified Law on Adoption of 21 March 1996

ARMENIA

Family Code

AUSTRIA

Civil Code

AZERBAIJAN

Family Code

BELGIUM

Civil Code
Law of April 24, 2003 modifying article 33 of the Law of Protection of Youth

BULGARIA

Family Code

CYPRUS

Adoption Act 1995

CZECH REPUBLIC

Act No 94/1963 Sb on Family
Act No 20/1966 Sb on Care for Populace Health (as amended by Act No 422/2004)
Act No 359/1999 Sb on Social Legal Protection of a Child

DENMARK

Children Act
Adoption (Consolidation) Act
Act on Parental Responsibility

ENGLAND AND WALES

Adoption Act 1949
Adoption Act 1976
Children Act 1989
Human Rights Act 1998
Adoption and Children Act 2002
Mental Capacity Act 2005
Welfare Reform Act 2009
Children and Families Act 2014
Adoption (Designation of Overseas Adoptions) Order 1973
Adoption with a Foreign Element Regulations 2005
Family Procedure Rules 2010

ESTONIA

Family Law Act 2009

FINLAND

Paternity Act 1975
Adoption Act 22/2012

FRANCE

Civil Code
Law No 2002/93
Law No 2013/404

GEORGIA

Civil Code

GERMANY

Civil Code
Act on Adoption Agency and the Prohibition of Agency for Surrogate Mothers
Act on Voluntary Jurisdiction
Act on the Expansion of Assistance for Pregnant Women and for Regulating Confidential Birth

GREECE

Civil Code

HUNGARY

Family Act 1952

ICELAND

Adoption Act No 130/1999
Act in Respect of Children No 76/2003
Law of 27 June 2006

IRELAND

Births and Deaths Registration Act 1880
Adoption Act 1949
Adoption Act 1964
Guardianship of Children Act 1964
Adoption Act 1976
Adoption Act 1988

ITALY

Civil Code
Law 184/1983
Law 149/2001
Law 54/2006

LATVIA

Civil Law

LIECHTENSTEIN

Civil Code

LITHUANIA

Civil Code

LUXEMBOURG

Civil Code
Act of 13 June 1989

MALTA

Civil Code

MOLDOVA

Family Code

MONACO

Civil Code
Montenegro
Family Law

NETHERLANDS

Civil Code
Act on the Adoption of Foreign Children

NORWAY

Act of 8 April 1981, No 7 relating to Children and Parents
Act of 28 February 1986, No 8 relating to Adoption

POLAND

Family Code

PORTUGAL

Civil Code

ROMANIA

Law No 47/1993
Law No 272/2004
Law No 273/2004

RUSSIA

Family Law 1995

SERBIA

Family Act

SLOVAKIA

Act No 99/1963 Code of Civil Procedure
Act No 36/2005 on Family
Act No 305/2005 on Social and Legal Protection of Children and Social Nurture

SLOVENIA

Civil Procedure Act
Marriage and Family Relations Act 1976

SPAIN

Civil Code
Civil Procedure Law
Organic Law 1/1996 for the Legal Protection of Minors
Organic Law 54/2007 on Intercountry Adoption

SWEDEN

Children and Parents Code (1949:381)
Penal Code (1962:700)
Welfare Act (1996:1030)

SWITZERLAND

Civil Code
Federal Law relative to the Hague Convention on adoption and of protection of children in cases of intercountry adoption

TURKEY

Civil Code

UKRAINE

Family Code

UNITED STATES

Illinois Compiled Statutes
Florida Statute
Utah Code (2005)
Virginia Code (2007)

LITERATURE

Adler, Katya, *Spain's stolen babies and the families who lived a lie* (15 November 2012, BBC News) <www.bbc.co.uk/news/magazine-15335899> [15 November 2012].

Aldgate, Jane and McIntosh, Miranda, *Looking After the Family: A study of children looked after in kinship care in Scotland* (2006, Social Work Inspection Agency: Scotland) <www.scotland.gov.uk/Publications/2006/06/07132800/0> [20 November 2012].

Alston, Philip, "The Best Interests Principle: Towards a Reconciliation of Culture and Human Rights" (1994) 8(1) *International Journal of Law, Policy and the Family* 1.

Amato, Paul, "The Impact of Family Formation Change on the Cognitive, Social and Emotional Well Being of the Next Generation" (2005) 15(2) *The Future of Children* 75.

Ambrose, Michael W and Coburn, Anna Mary, *Report on Intercountry Adoption in Romania* (2001) <http://pdf.usaid.gov/pdf_docs/PNACW989.pdf> [30 January 2012].

American Bar Association Child Custody and Adoption Pro Bono Project, "Hearing Children's Voices and Interests in Adoption and Guardianship Proceedings" (2007) 41(2) *Family Law Quarterly* 365.

Ames, Elinor, *The Development of Romanian Orphanage Children Adopted to Canada* (1997, Simon Fraser University).

Androulidakis-Dimitriadis, Ismene, *Family Law in Greece* (2011, Kluwer Law).

Antokolskaia, Masha, *National Report: Russia* (date unknown, Commission on European Family Law) <http://ceflonline.net/wp-content/uploads/Russia-Parental-Responsibilities.pdf> [27 February 2013].

Archard, David and Skivenes, Marit, "Balancing a Child's Best Interests and a Child's Views" (2009) 17 *International Journal of Children's* Rights 1.

Australia: Western Australia Department for Child Protection, *Excerpts from Submissions to the Parliamentary Legislative Review Committee* (undated) <www.dcp.wa.gov.au/FosteringandAdoption/AdoptionAndHomeForLife/Documents/PlacementCriteriaAgeRestrictions.pdf> [16 November 2012].

Australian Intercountry Adoption Network, *International Adoption Statistics* (2010) <www.aican.org/statistics.php?region=0&type=birth> [26 February 2013].

Bainham, Andrew, "When is a Parent Not a Parent? Reflections on the Unmarried Father and his Child in English Law" (1989) 3 *International Journal of Law, Policy and the Family* 208.

Bainham, Andrew, "Can We Protect Children and Protect Their Rights" (2002) 32 *Family Law* 279.

Bainham, Andrew, "Homosexual Adoption" (2008) 67(3) *Cambridge Law Journal* 479.

Bainham, Andrew, "What is the Point of Birth Registration?" (2008) 20(4) *Child and Family Law Quarterly* 449.

Bainham, Andrew, "The Politics of Child Protection in Romania" (2009) 17 *International Journal of Children's Rights* 527.

Bartholet, Elizabeth, "International Adoption: Current Status and Future Prospects" (1993) 3(1) *The Future of Children* 89.

Bartholet, Elizabeth, "International Adoption: Propriety, Prospects and Pragmatics" (1995) 13 *Journal of the American Academy of Matrimonial Law* 181.

Bartholet, Elizabeth, "What's Wrong with Adoption Law?" (1996) 4 *International Journal of Children's Rights* 263.

Bartholet, Elizabeth, *Nobody's Children: Abuse and Neglect, Foster Drift, and the Adoption Alternative* (1999, Beacon Press).

Bartholet, Elizabeth, "International Adoption: Thoughts on the Human Rights Issues" (2007) 13 Buffalo Human Rights Law Review 151.

BBC News, *Germany to Allow Hospital Births Under False Name* (14 March 2013, BBC News) <www.bbc.co.uk/news/world-europe-21774845> [17 March 2013].

Bell, Thomas, *Nepal comes to terms with foreign adoption tragedy* (28 September 2011, BBC News) <www.bbc.co.uk/news/world-south-asia-15066220> [16 February 2012].

Bennett Woodhouse, Barbara, "'Are You My Mother?': Conceptualizing Children's Identity Rights in Transracial Adoptions" (1995) 2 *Duke Journal of Gender Law and Policy* 107.

Berry, Marianne, Barth, R and Needell, B, "Preparation, support, and satisfaction of adoptive families in agency and independent adoptions" (1996) 13(2) *Child and Adolescent Social Work Journal* 157.

Besson, Samantha, "Enforcing the Child's Right to Know Her Origins: Contrasting Approaches Under the Convention on the Rights of the Child and the European Convention on Human Rights" (2007) 21 *International Journal of Law, Policy and the Family* 137.

Bilson, Andy and Markova, Galina, "But You Should See Their Families: Preventing Child Abandonment and Promoting Social Inclusion in Countries in Transition" (2007) 12(3) *Social Work & Social Sciences Review* 29.

Bilson, Andy, *The Development of Gate-Keeping functions in Central and Eastern Europe and the CIS: Lessons from Bulgaria, Kazakhstan and Ukraine* (2010) <www.unicef.org/ceecis/overview_Report_20_August_preface.doc> [7 June 2012].

Boele-Woelki, Katharina, Braat, Bente and Curry-Sumner, Ian (eds), *European Family Law in Action: Volume III – Parental Responsibilities* (2005, Intersentia).

Brazier, Margaret, "Can You Buy Children?" (1999) 11(4) *Child and Family Law Quarterly* 345.

Browne, Kevin, *The Risk of Harm to Young Children in Institutional Care* (2009, Save the Children) <http://resourcecentre.savethechildren.se/content/library/documents/risk-harm-young-people-institutional-care> [16 May 2012].

Browne, Kevin and Hamilton-Giachritsis, Catherine, *Mapping the Number and Characteristics of Children under Three in Institutions Across Europe at Risk of Harm* (2005, University of Birmingham).

Browne, Kevin, Chou, Shihning and Whitfield, Kate, *Child Abandonment and its Prevention in Europe* (2012, University of Nottingham) <http://resourcecentre.savethechildren.se/content/library/documents/child-abandonment-and-its-prevention-europe> [7 February 2013].

Browne, Kevin, Hamilton-Giachritsis, Catherine, Johnson, Rebecca and Ostergren, Mikael, "Overuse of Institutional Care for Children in Europe" (2006) 332 *British Medical Journal* 485.

Brulard, Yves and Dumont, Letitia, *Comparative Study Relating to Procedures for Adoption Among the Member States of the European Union, Practical Difficulties Encountered in this Field by European Citizens within the Context of the European Pillar of Justice and Civil Matters and Means of Solving these Problems and of Protecting Children's Rights* (2007, European Union).

Carter, Richard, *Family Matters: A Study of Institutional Childcare in Central and Eastern European and the Former Soviet Union* (2005, Everychild) <http://p-ced.com/reference/Family_Matters_summary.pdf> [7 February 2013]

Cashmore, Judy and Parkinson, Patrick, "What Responsibility Do Courts Have to Hear Children's Voices?" (2007) 15(1) *International Journal of Children's Rights* 43.

Cerderblad, Marianne, Hook, Borje, Irhammar, Malin and Mercke, Ann-Mari, "Mental Health in International Adoptees as Teenagers and Young Adults: An epidemiological study" (1999) 40 *Journal of Child Psychology and Psychiatry and Allied Disciplines* 1239.

Chai, Jolie, *Forced Removal of Romani Children from the Care of their Families* (2005, European Roma Rights Centre) <www.errc.org/article/forced-removal-of-romani-children-from-the-care-of-their-families/2290> [3 February 2012].

Chambers, Lori, "Newborn Adoption: Birth Mothers, Genetic Fathers, and Reproductive Autonomy" (2010) 26 *Canadian Journal of Family Law* 339.

ChildONEurope, *Extracts of the Legislation on Adoption: Hungary* (date unknown) <www.childoneurope.org/issues/adoption/adoption_legislation/hungary.pdf> [8 June 2012].

ChildONEurope, *Partners Experiences on Post Adoption Services' Best Practices* (date unknown) <www.childoneurope.org/issues/adoption2.htm#post_adoption> [13 December 2012].

Children's Human Rights Centre of Albania et al, *Albania Alternative Report to the Optional Protocol of the Convention on the Rights of the Child on the Sale of Children, Child Prostitution, and Child Pornography* (2012) <www2.ohchr.org/english/bodies/crc/docs/ngos/Albania_AlbanianCoalitionAgainstChildTrafficking SexualExploitationofChildren_CRC61OPSC%20Report.pdf> [10 January 2013].

Chisholm, Kim, "A Three Year Follow-up of Attachment and Indiscriminate Friendliness in Children Adopted from Romanian Orphanages" (1998) 69(4) *Child Development* 1092.

Chou, Shihning and Browne, Kevin "The Relationship Between Institutional Care and the International Adoption of Children in Europe" (2008) 32(1) *Adoption and Fostering* 40.

Choudhry, Shazia and Fenwick, Helen, "Taking the Rights of Parents and Children Seriously: Confronting the Welfare Principle under the Human Rights Act" (2005) 25(3) *Oxford Journal of Legal Studies* 453.

Choudhry, Shazia and Herring, Jonathan, *European Human Rights and Family Law* (2010, Hart).

Choudhry, Shazia, "The Adoption and Children Act 2002, the Welfare Principle and the Human Rights Act 1998 – A Missed Opportunity?" (2003) 15(2) *Child and Family Law Quarterly* 119.

Cody, Claire, *Count Every Child: The Right to Birth Registration* (2009, Plan) <http://plan-international.org/birthregistration/files/count-every-child-2009> [21 December 2011].

Condon, John, "Psychological Disability in Women Who Relinquish a Baby for Adoption" (1986) 144 *Medical Journal of Australia* 117.

Conway, Helen, "Parental Responsibility and the Unmarried Father" (1996) 146 *New Law Journal* 782.

Cooper, Andrew, "International Perspectives on Child Protection" in Malcolm Hill, Anne Stafford and Pam Green Lister (eds), *International Perspectives on Child Protection* (2002) <www.scotland.gov.uk/Resource/Doc/1181/0009926.pdf> [9 March 2011].

Council of Europe, *Explanatory Report to the European Convention on the Adoption of Children (Revised)* (2008) <http://conventions.coe.int/Treaty/en/Reports/Html/202.htm> [18 January 2013].

Council of Europe: Parliamentary Assembly, *Recommendation 1443(2000): International Adoption: Respecting children's rights* (2000).

Coupet, Sasha, "Swimming Upstream Against the Great Adoption Tide: Making the Case for 'Impermanence'" (2005) 34 *Capital University Law Review* 405.

Danner, C, Pacher, M, Ambach, E and Brezinka, C, "Anonymous Birth and Neonaticide in Tyrol" (2005) 209(5) *Z Geburtshilfe Neonatol* 192.

de Oliveira, Guilherme and Martins, Rosa, *National Report: Portugal* (date unknown, Commission on European Family Law) <http://ceflonline.net/wp-content/uploads/Portugal-Parental-Responsibilities.pdf> [27 February 2013].

Denmark: Familiestyrelsen, *Evaluering af Forsøgsprojekt Med Tidlig Rådgivning Efter Adoptionen* (2010) <www.familiestyrelsen.dk/fileadmin/user_upload/Adoption/Evalueringsrapport_PAS.pdf> [11 February 2013].

Deutscher Ethikrat, *Anonymous Relinquishment of Infants: Tackling the Problem* (2009, German Ethics Council) <www.ethikrat.org/files/der_opinion_anonymous-relinquishment-of-infants.pdf> [15 June 2012].

Dickens, Jonathan, "The Paradox of Inter-Country Adoption: Analysing Romania's Experience as a Sending Country" (2002) 11 *International Journal of Social Welfare* 76.

Dillon, Sara, "Making Legal Regimes for Intercountry Adoption Reflect Human rights Principles: Transforming the United Nations Convention on the Rights of the Child with the Hague Convention on Intercountry Adoption" (2003) 21 *Boston University International Law Journal* 179.

Dillon, Sara, "The Missing Link: A Social Orphan Protocol to the United Nations Convention on the Rights of the Child" (2007) 1 *Human Rights and Globalization Law Review* 39.

Dolgin, Janet L, "Just a Gene: Judicial Assumptions About Parenthood" (1992–1993) 40 *UCLA Law Review* 637.

Duerr Berrick, Jill, "When Children Cannot Remain Home: Foster Family Care and Kinship Care" (1998) 8(1) *The Future of Children* 72.

Duquette, Donald N, "Legal Representation for Children in Protection Proceedings: Two Distinct Lawyer Roles are Required" (2000) 34(3) *Family Law Quarterly* 441.

Eekelaar, John and Dingwall, Robert, *Human Rights: Report on the Replies of Governments to the Enquiry under Article 57 of the European Convention on Human Rights* (1987, Council of Europe).

Eekelaar, John, "The Interests of the Child and the Child's Wishes: The Role of Dynamic Self-Determinism" (1994) 8 *International Journal of Law, Policy and the Family* 48.

Eekelaar, John, "Beyond the Welfare Principle" (2002) 14(3) *Child and Family Law Quarterly* 237.

Eekelaar, John, "Contact and the Adoption Reform" in Bainham, Andrew, Lindley, Bridget, Richards, Martin and Trinder, Liz (eds), *Children and Their Families; Contact Rights and Welfare* (2003, Hart).

England: Law Commission, *Working Paper No 74: Family Law: Illegitimacy* (1979).

European Commission, *Eurobarometer 66: Public Opinion in the European Union* (2006) <http://ec.europa.eu/public_opinion/archives/eb/eb66/eb66_en.pdf> [14 November 2012].

European Union, *International Adoption in the European Union* (2009, European Parliament) <www.childoneurope.org/issues/adoption/Report%20EP%20international%20adoption_EN.pdf> [7 February 2013].

Eurostat, *Total population having completed at least upper secondary education* (2012) <http://epp.eurostat.ec.europa.eu/tgm/table.do?tab=table&init=1&language=en&pcode=tps00065&plugin=1> [23 November 2012].

Feigelman, W, "Adjustments of transracially and inracially adopted young adults" (2000) 17 *Child and Adolescent Social Work Journal* 165

Fenwick, Helen, "Clashing Rights, the Welfare of the Child and the Human Rights Act" (2004) 67(6) *Modern Law Review* 889.

Fernandes, Edna, *Abandoned... in a postbox for babies: The shocking rise of newborns being left in 'adoption hatches' by mothers unable to cope* (7 July 2012, Daily Mail) <www.dailymail.co.uk/femail/article-2170150/Babywiege-Newborns-abandoned-baby-boxes-German-hospital.html> [22 September 2012].

Ferrand, Frédérique, *National Report: France* (date unknown, Commission on European Family Law) <http://ceflonline.net/wp-content/uploads/France-Parental-Responsibilities.pdf> [27 February 2013].

Festinger, T, "After Adoption: Dissolution or Permanence?" (2002) 81(3) *Child Welfare* 515.

Fleming, Caroline B, "The Open-Records Debate: Balancing the Interests of Birth Parents and Adult Adoptees" (2004–2005) 11 *William and Mary Journal of Women and the Law* 461.

Fortin, Jane, "Children's Representation Through the Looking Glass" (2007) 37 *Family Law* 500.

Fortin, Jane, "Children's Rights: Are the Courts Now Taking Them More Seriously?" (2004) 15 *King's College Law Journal* 253.

Fortin, Jane, "Rights Brought Home for Children" (1999) 62 *Modern Law Review* 350.

France: Ministère des Affaires Étrangeres et Européennes, *Intercountry Adoption in France* (2010) <www.diplomatie.gouv.fr/fr/IMG/pdf/Adoption_FinaleAng_BD.pdf> [9 March 2011].

Freeman, Michael, "Taking Children's Rights More Seriously" (1992) 6 *International Journal of Law, Policy and the Family* 52.

Freeman, Michael, "Rethinking *Gillick*" (2005) 13 *International Journal of Children's Rights* 201.

Freeman, Michael, "Why It Remains Important to Take Children's Rights Seriously" (2007) 15 *International Journal of Children's Rights* 5.

Fried, Charles, "Privacy" (1968) 77 *Yale Law Journal* 475.

FYR Macedonia, *State Party Report to the UN Committee on the Rights of the Child* (12 November 2009) CRC/C/MKD/2.

George, Melisa C, "Tossed Salad: Diversity Considerations in Adoption" (1997) 21 *Law and Psychology Review* 197.

Godsk Pedersen, Hans Viggo and Lund-Andersen, Ingrid, *Family Law in Denmark* (2011, Kluwer Law).

Gonzalez Beilfuss, Cristina, *National Report: Spain* (date unknown, Commission for European Family Law) <http://ceflonline.net/wp-content/uploads/Spain-Parental-Responsibilities.pdf> [27 February 2013].

Graff, EJ, *The Seamier Side of International Adoption* (10 May 2009, New York Times) <http://roomfordebate.blogs.nytimes.com/2009/05/10/celebrity-adoptions-and-the-real-world/> [19 April 2011].

Graff, EJ, *Adopting new standards on adoption* (10 September 2010, The Guardian) <www.guardian.co.uk/commentisfree/cifamerica/2010/sep/10/adoption-parents-and-parenting> [16 February 2012].

Graff, EJ, *Anatomy of an Adoption Crisis* (12 September 2010, Foreign Policy) <www.foreignpolicy.com/articles/2010/09/07/anatomy_of_an_adoption_crisis?page=0,0> [4 February 2012].

Graff, EJ, *The Makeni Children* (9 August 2011, Slate) <www.slate.com/articles/double_x/doublex/features/2011/the_makeni_children/that_was_the_last_time_we_ever_saw_these_children.html> [16 February 2012].

Guggenheim, Martin, "Ratify the UN Convention on the Rights of the Child, But Don't Expect Any Miracles" (2006) 20 *Emory International Law Review* 43.

Hague Conference on Private International Law, *The Implementation and Operation of the 1993 Hague Intercountry Adoption Convention: Guide to Good Practice: Guide No 1* (2008) <www.hcch.net/upload/adoguide_e.pdf> [7 February 2013].

Hague Conference on Private International Law, *The Implementation and Operation of the 1993 Hague Intercountry Adoption Convention: Guide to Good Practice: Guide No 2* (2012) <www.hcch.net/upload/adoguide2en.pdf> [22 February 2013].

Hague Conference on Private International Law, *Report and Conclusions of the Special Commission on the Practical Operation of the Hague Convention of 29 May 1993 on Protection of Children and Co-operation in Respect of Intercountry Adoption 28 November–1 December 2000* (2001) <www.hcch.net/upload/scrpt33e2000.pdf> [7 February 2013].

Hague Conference on Private International Law, *Report of the Special Commission on the Practical Operation of the 1993 Hague Intercountry Adoption Convention (17–25 June 2010)* (2011) <www.hcch.net/upload/wop/adop2010_rpt_en.pdf> [8 February 2013].

Hague Conference on Private International Law, *A Discussion Paper on the Financial Aspects of Intercountry Adoption* (2012) <www.hcch.net/index_en.php?act=events.details&year=2012&varevent=284> [14 January 2013].

Hague Conference on Private International Law, *Statistics* (2010) <www.hcch.net/index_en.php?act=conventions.publications&dtid=32&cid=69> [14 January 2013].

Hague Conference on Private International Law, *Country Profiles* (2010) <www.hcch.net/index_en.php?act=conventions.publications&dtid=42&cid=69> [14 January 2012].

Hague Conference on Private International Law, *Country Profile: Albania* (2010) <www.hcch.net/index_en.php?act=publications.details&pid=5081&dtid=42> [14 January 2012].

Hague Conference on Private International Law, *Country Profile: Andorra* (2010) <www.hcch.net/index_en.php?act=publications.details&pid=5082&dtid=42> [14 January 2012].

Hague Conference on Private International Law, *Country Profile: Armenia* (2010) <www.hcch.net/index_en.php?act=publications.details&pid=5115&dtid=42> [14 January 2012].

Hague Conference on Private International Law, *Country Profile: Austria* (2010) <www.hcch.net/index_en.php?act=publications.details&pid=5083&dtid=42> [14 January 2012].

Hague Conference on Private International Law, *Country Profile: Belgium* (2012) <www.hcch.net/index_en.php?act=publications.details&pid=5084&dtid=42> [14 January 2012].

Hague Conference on Private International Law, *Country Profile: Czech Republic* (2010) <www.hcch.net/index_en.php?act=publications.details&pid=5116&dtid=42> [14 January 2012].

Hague Conference on Private International Law, *Country Profile: Denmark* (2010) <www.hcch.net/index_en.php?act=publications.details&pid=5128&dtid=42> [14 January 2012].

Hague Conference on Private International Law, *Country Profile: Estonia* (2010) <www.hcch.net/index_en.php?act=publications.details&pid=5242&dtid=42> [14 January 2012].

Hague Conference on Private International Law, *Country Profile: Finland* (2010) <www.hcch.net/index_en.php?act=publications.details&pid=5243&dtid=42> [14 January 2012].

Hague Conference on Private International Law, *Country Profile: France* (2010) <www.hcch.net/index_en.php?act=publications.details&pid=5086&dtid=42> [14 January 2012].

Hague Conference on Private International Law, *Country Profile: Georgia* (2010) <www.hcch.net/index_en.php?act=publications.details&pid=5118&dtid=42> [14 January 2012].

Hague Conference on Private International Law, *Country Profile: Germany* (2010) <www.hcch.net/index_en.php?act=publications.details&pid=5156&dtid=42> [14 January 2012].

Hague Conference on Private International Law, *Country Profile: Greece* (2012) <www.hcch.net/index_en.php?act=publications.details&pid=5141&dtid=42> [14 January 2012].

Hague Conference on Private International Law, *Country Profile: Italy* (2012) <www.hcch.net/index_en.php?act=publications.details&pid=5153&dtid=42> [14 January 2012].

Hague Conference on Private International Law, *Country Profile: Latvia* (2010) <www.hcch.net/index_en.php?act=publications.details&pid=5087&dtid=42> [14 January 2012].

Hague Conference on Private International Law, *Country Profile: Lithuania* (2010) <www.hcch.net/index_en.php?act=publications.details&pid=5209&dtid=42> [14 January 2012].

Hague Conference on Private International Law, *Country Profile: Malta* (2010) <www.hcch.net/index_en.php?act=publications.details&pid=5088&dtid=42> [14 January 2012].

Hague Conference on Private International Law, *Country Profile: Monaco* (2010) <www.hcch.net/index_en.php?act=publications.details&pid=5210&dtid=42> [14 January 2012].

Hague Conference on Private International Law, *Country Profile: Netherlands* (2010) <www.hcch.net/index_en.php?act=publications.details&pid=5429&dtid=42> [14 January 2012].

Hague Conference on Private International Law, *Country Profile: Norway* (2010) <www.hcch.net/index_en.php?act=publications.details&pid=5090&dtid=42> [14 January 2012].

Hague Conference on Private International Law, *Country Profile: Poland* (2010) <www.hcch.net/index_en.php?act=publications.details&pid=5093&dtid=42> [14 January 2012].

Hague Conference on Private International Law, *Country Profile: Portugal* (2010) <www.hcch.net/index_en.php?act=publications.details&pid=5094&dtid=42> [14 January 2012].

Hague Conference on Private International Law, *Country Profile: Slovakia* (2010) <www.hcch.net/index_en.php?act=publications.details&pid=5095&dtid=42> [14 January 2012].

Hague Conference on Private International Law, *Country Profile: Slovenia* (2010) <www.hcch.net/index_en.php?act=publications.details&pid=5096&dtid=42> [14 January 2012].

Hague Conference on Private International Law, *Country Profile: Spain* (2010) <www.hcch.net/index_en.php?act=publications.details&pid=5107&dtid=42> [14 January 2012].

Hague Conference on Private International Law, *Country Profile: Sweden* (2010) <www.hcch.net/index_en.php?act=publications.details&pid=5097&dtid=42> [14 January 2012].

Hague Conference on Private International Law, *Country Profile: Switzerland* (2010) <www.hcch.net/index_en.php?act=publications.details&pid=5150&dtid=42> [14 January 2012].

Hague Conference on Private International Law, *Questionnaire on Accredited Bodies in the Framework of the Hague Convention of 29 May 1993 on Protection of Children and Co-operation in Respect of Intercountry Adoption: Norway* (2009) <www.hcch.net/upload/wop/adop2010_no.pdf> [21 February 2013].

Hague Conference on Private International Law, *Responses to Questionnaire of April 2010 on the abduction, sale of, or traffic in children and some aspects of the practical operation of the 1993 Hague Intercountry Adoption Convention* (2010) <www.hcch.net/index_en.php?act=publications.details&pid=5451&dtid=33> [11 January 2012]).

Hague Conference on Private International Law, *Responses to Questionnaire of April 2010 on the abduction, sale of, or traffic in children and some aspects of the practical operation of the 1993 Hague Intercountry Adoption Convention: Albania* (2010) <www.hcch.net/index_en.php?act=publications.details&pid=5451&dtid=33> [14 January 2012].

Hague Conference on Private International Law, *Responses to Questionnaire of April 2010 on the abduction, sale of, or traffic in children and some aspects of the practical operation of the 1993 Hague Intercountry Adoption Convention: Andorra* (2010) <www.hcch.net/index_en.php?act=publications.details&pid=5451&dtid=33> [14 January 2012].

Hague Conference on Private International Law, *Responses to Questionnaire of April 2010 on the abduction, sale of, or traffic in children and some aspects of the practical operation of the 1993 Hague Intercountry Adoption Convention: Armenia* (2010) <www.hcch.net/index_en.php?act=publications.details&pid=5451&dtid=33> [14 January 2012].

Hague Conference on Private International Law, *Responses to Questionnaire of April 2010 on the abduction, sale of, or traffic in children and some aspects of the practical operation of the 1993 Hague Intercountry Adoption Convention: Austria* (2010) <www.hcch.net/index_en.php?act=publications.details&pid=5451&dtid=33> [14 January 2012].

Hague Conference on Private International Law, *Responses to Questionnaire of April 2010 on the abduction, sale of, or traffic in children and some aspects of the practical operation of the 1993 Hague Intercountry Adoption Convention: Belgium* (2010) <www.hcch.net/index_en.php?act=publications.details&pid=5451&dtid=33> [14 January 2012].

Hague Conference on Private International Law, *Responses to Questionnaire of April 2010 on the abduction, sale of, or traffic in children and some aspects of the practical operation of the 1993 Hague Intercountry Adoption Convention: Cyprus* (2010) <www.hcch.net/index_en.php?act=publications.details&pid=5451&dtid=33> [14 January 2012].

Hague Conference on Private International Law, *Responses to Questionnaire of April 2010 on the abduction, sale of, or traffic in children and some aspects of the practical operation of the 1993 Hague Intercountry Adoption Convention: Czech Republic* (2010) <www.hcch.net/index_en.php?act=publications.details&pid=5451&dtid=33> [14 January 2012].

Hague Conference on Private International Law, *Responses to Questionnaire of April 2010 on the abduction, sale of, or traffic in children and some aspects of the practical operation of the 1993 Hague Intercountry Adoption Convention: Denmark* (2010) <www.hcch.net/index_en.php?act=publications.details&pid=5451&dtid=33> [14 January 2012].

Hague Conference on Private International Law, *Responses to Questionnaire of April 2010 on the abduction, sale of, or traffic in children and some aspects of the practical operation of the 1993 Hague Intercountry Adoption Convention: Finland* (2010) <www.hcch.net/index_en.php?act=publications.details&pid=5451&dtid=33> [14 January 2012].

Hague Conference on Private International Law, *Responses to Questionnaire of April 2010 on the abduction, sale of, or traffic in children and some aspects of the practical operation of the 1993 Hague Intercountry Adoption Convention: France* (2010) <www.hcch.net/index_en.php?act=publications.details&pid=5451&dtid=33> [14 January 2012].

Hague Conference on Private International Law, *Responses to Questionnaire of April 2010 on the abduction, sale of, or traffic in children and some aspects of the practical operation of the 1993 Hague Intercountry Adoption Convention: Georgia* (2010) <www.hcch.net/index_en.php?act=publications.details&pid=5451&dtid=33> [14 January 2012].
Hague Conference on Private International Law, *Responses to Questionnaire of April 2010 on the abduction, sale of, or traffic in children and some aspects of the practical operation of the 1993 Hague Intercountry Adoption Convention: Germany* (2010) <www.hcch.net/index_en.php?act=publications.details&pid=5451&dtid=33> [14 January 2012].
Hague Conference on Private International Law, *Responses to Questionnaire of April 2010 on the abduction, sale of, or traffic in children and some aspects of the practical operation of the 1993 Hague Intercountry Adoption Convention: Greece* (2010) <www.hcch.net/index_en.php?act=publications.details&pid=5451&dtid=33> [14 January 2012].
Hague Conference on Private International Law, *Responses to Questionnaire of April 2010 on the abduction, sale of, or traffic in children and some aspects of the practical operation of the 1993 Hague Intercountry Adoption Convention: Hungary* (2010) <www.hcch.net/index_en.php?act=publications.details&pid=5451&dtid=33> [14 January 2012].
Hague Conference on Private International Law, *Responses to Questionnaire of April 2010 on the abduction, sale of, or traffic in children and some aspects of the practical operation of the 1993 Hague Intercountry Adoption Convention: Italy* (2010) <www.hcch.net/index_en.php?act=publications.details&pid=5451&dtid=33> [14 January 2012].
Hague Conference on Private International Law, *Responses to Questionnaire of April 2010 on the abduction, sale of, or traffic in children and some aspects of the practical operation of the 1993 Hague Intercountry Adoption Convention: Latvia* (2010) <www.hcch.net/index_en.php?act=publications.details&pid=5451&dtid=33> [14 January 2012].
Hague Conference on Private International Law, *Responses to Questionnaire of April 2010 on the abduction, sale of, or traffic in children and some aspects of the practical operation of the 1993 Hague Intercountry Adoption Convention: Lithuania* (2010) <www.hcch.net/index_en.php?act=publications.details&pid=5451&dtid=33> [14 January 2012].
Hague Conference on Private International Law, *Responses to Questionnaire of April 2010 on the abduction, sale of, or traffic in children and some aspects of the practical operation of the 1993 Hague Intercountry Adoption Convention: Malta* (2010) <www.hcch.net/index_en.php?act=publications.details&pid=5451&dtid=33> [14 January 2012].
Hague Conference on Private International Law, *Responses to Questionnaire of April 2010 on the abduction, sale of, or traffic in children and some aspects of the practical operation of the 1993 Hague Intercountry Adoption Convention: Norway* (2010) <www.hcch.net/index_en.php?act=publications.details&pid=5451&dtid=33> [14 January 2012].
Hague Conference on Private International Law, *Responses to Questionnaire of April 2010 on the abduction, sale of, or traffic in children and some aspects of the practical operation of the 1993 Hague Intercountry Adoption Convention: Portugal* (2010) <www.hcch.net/index_en.php?act=publications.details&pid=5451&dtid=33> [14 January 2012].
Hague Conference on Private International Law, *Responses to Questionnaire of April 2010 on the abduction, sale of, or traffic in children and some aspects of the practical operation of the 1993 Hague Intercountry Adoption Convention: Romania* (2010) <www.hcch.net/index_en.php?act=publications.details&pid=5451&dtid=33> [14 January 2012].
Hague Conference on Private International Law, *Responses to Questionnaire of April 2010 on the abduction, sale of, or traffic in children and some aspects of the practical operation*

of the 1993 Hague Intercountry Adoption Convention: Slovakia (2010) <www.hcch.net/index_en.php?act=publications.details&pid=5451&dtid=33> [14 January 2012].

Hague Conference on Private International Law, *Responses to Questionnaire of April 2010 on the abduction, sale of, or traffic in children and some aspects of the practical operation of the 1993 Hague Intercountry Adoption Convention: Slovenia* (2010) <www.hcch.net/index_en.php?act=publications.details&pid=5451&dtid=33> [14 January 2012].

Hague Conference on Private International Law, *Responses to Questionnaire of April 2010 on the abduction, sale of, or traffic in children and some aspects of the practical operation of the 1993 Hague Intercountry Adoption Convention: Spain* (2010) <www.hcch.net/index_en.php?act=publications.details&pid=5451&dtid=33> [14 January 2012].

Hague Conference on Private International Law, *Responses to Questionnaire of April 2010 on the abduction, sale of, or traffic in children and some aspects of the practical operation of the 1993 Hague Intercountry Adoption Convention: Sweden* (2010) <www.hcch.net/index_en.php?act=publications.details&pid=5451&dtid=33> [14 January 2012].

Hague Conference on Private International Law, *Responses to Questionnaire of April 2010 on the abduction, sale of, or traffic in children and some aspects of the practical operation of the 1993 Hague Intercountry Adoption Convention: Switzerland* (2010) <www.hcch.net/index_en.php?act=publications.details&pid=5451&dtid=33> [14 January 2012].

Hale, Baroness of Richmond, "Can You Hear Me, Your Honour?" (2012) 1 *Family Law* 30.

Hamilton-Giachritsis, Catherine and Browne, Kevin, *Identifying Good Practices in the Deinstitutionalisation of Children under 5 Years from European Institutions* (2005) <http://ec.europa.eu/justice_home/daphnetoolkit/html/projects/dpt_2003_046_c_en.html> [16 May 2012].

Hancock, Michael (Rapporteur, Council of Europe Parliamentary Assembly), *The Rights of Children in Institutions: follow-up to Recommendation 1601 (2003) of the Parliamentary Assembly* (8 February 2005) <http://assembly.coe.int/ASP/Doc/XrefViewHTML.asp?FileID=10786&Language=en> [7 February 2013].

Haskey, John, *Adoptees and Relatives Who Wish to Contact One Another Using the Adoption Contact Register: Trends, Relationships and Proportions of Records Matched* (2001, Office for National Statistics) <www.ons.gov.uk/ons/taxonomy/search/index.html?newquery=*&nscl=Adoptions&nscl-orig=Adoptions&content-type=publicationContentTypes&sortDirection=DESCENDING&sortBy=pubdate> [19 February 2013].

Hawkins-Leon, Cynthia G and Bradley, Carla, "Race and Transracial Adoption: The answer is neither simply black or white nor right or wrong" (2002) 51 *Catholic University Law Review* 1227.

Hayes, Peter, "The Legality and Ethics of Independent Intercountry Adoption under the Hague Convention" (2011) 25(3) *International Journal of Law, Policy and the Family* 288.

Heifetz Hollinger, Joan, "Adoption Law" (Spring 1993) 3(1) *The Future of Children* 43.

Henaghan, Mark, "Respecting Children's Participation in Family Law Proceedings" (2007) 15(1) *International Journal of Children's Rights* 61.

Henaghan, Mark, "What Does a Child's Right to be Heard in Legal Proceedings Really Mean? ABA Custody Standards Do Not Go Far Enough" (2008) 42(1) *Family Law Quarterly* 117.

Herring, Jonathan, "The Human Rights Act and the Welfare Principle in Family Law – Conflicting or Complementary?" (1999) 11(3) *Child and Family Law Quarterly* 223.

Higgins, Justice, "Freeing for Adoption – the Legal Context" (1999) 5(3) *Child Care in Practice* 232.

Hodgkin, Rachel and Newell, Peter, *Implementation Handbook for the Convention on the Rights of the Child* (3rd ed, 2007, UNICEF).

Hollingsworth, Leslie Doty, "Effect of Transracial/Transethnic Adoption on Children's Racial and Ethnic Identity and Self-Esteem: A Meta-Analytic Review" (1997) 25(1–2) *Marriage and Family Review* 99.

Holt International, *Cambodia Orphanage Survey* (2005, USAID) <http://pdf.usaid.gov/pdf_docs/PNADI624.pdf> [5 February 2012].

Houston, DM and Kramer, LA, "Meeting the Long-Term Needs of Families who Adopt Children Out of Foster Care: A three year follow-up study" (2008) 87 *Child Welfare* 145.

Howe, Ruth-Arlene W, "Race Matters in Adoption" (2009) 42(3) *Family Law Quarterly* 465.

Hrusakova, Milana and Westpahlova, Lenka, *Family Law in the Czech Republic* (2011, Kluwer Law)

Hunt Federle, Katherine, "Children's Rights and the Need for Protection" (2000) 34(3) *Family Law Quarterly* 421.

ILPEC Guatemala, *Adoption and the Rights of the Child in Guatemala* (2000) <www.iss-ssi.org/Resource_Centre/Tronc_DI/ilpec-unicef_english_report_2000.pdf> [5 September 2011].

Independent Group for International Adoption Analysis, *Re-organising the International Adoption and Child Protection System* (2002) <www.afaener.org/Rapport_FINAL_ang.doc> [30 January 2012].

International Social Service and UNICEF, *Improving Protection for Children Without Parental Care: Kinship Care: An Issue for International Standards* (2004, UNICEF) <www.unicef.org/french/videoaudio/PDFs/kinship_note.pdf> [5 April 2012].

International Social Service, *Adoption Breakdown* (2007, ISS/IRC) <www.iss-ssi.org/2009/assets/files/thematic-facts-sheet/eng/51.Adoption%20breakdown%20eng.pdf> [6 December 2012].

International Social Service, *Earthquake in Haiti: Intercountry Adoption Cases* (2009, ISS/IRC) <www.iss-ssi.org/2009/assets/files/news/haiti_position%20CIR_ENG.pdf> [19 February 2013].

International Social Service, *Fact Sheet No. 29: 'Simple Adoption' versus 'Full Adoption': The Effects of Adoption* (2007, ISS/IRC) <www.iss-ssi.org/2009/assets/files/thematic-facts-sheet/eng/29.Adoption%20simple-full.%20eng.pdf> [1 March 2011].

International Social Service, *Fact Sheet No. 51: Kafalah* (2007, ISS/IRC) <www.crin.org/docs/Kafalah.BCN.doc> [7 April 2011].

International Social Service, *Is Intercountry Adoption Linked with Trafficking for Exploitation?* (2005, ISS/IRC) <www.iss-ssi.org/2009/assets/files/editorial-monthly-review/Editorials/2005/Edito%202005%2011%2012eng.pdf> [31 January 2012].

Italy, *State Party Report to the UN Committee on the Rights of the Child* (5 July 2010) CRC/C/ITA/3–4.

Iusmen, Ingi, "The EU and International Adoption from Romania" (2013) 27(1) *International Journal of Law, Policy and the Family* 1, 14.

Jagland, Thorbjørn (Council of Europe Commissioner for Human Rights), *Adoption and Children: A Human Rights Perspective* (28 April 2011) <https://wcd.coe.int/wcd/ViewDoc.jsp?id=1780157> [30 May 2011].

Johnson, Angella, *Madonna's Adopted Baby's Father Tells How He Was Powerless to Stop Her* (15 October 2006, Daily Mail) <www.dailymail.co.uk/news/article-410451/Madonnas-adopted-babys-father-tells-powerless-stop-her.html> [7 April 2011].

Johnson, David, "Cultural and Regional Pluralism in the Drafting of the UN Convention on the Rights of the Child", in Freeman, Michael and Veerman, Philip (eds), *The Ideologies of Children's Rights* (1992, Kluwer Law).

Jones, ED and McCurdy, R, "The Links Between Types of Maltreatment and Demographic Characteristics of Children" (1992) 16(2) *Child Abuse and Neglect* 201.

Joyce, Kathryn, *How Ethiopia's Adoption Industry Dupes Families and Bullies Activists* (21 December 2011, The Atlantic) <www.theatlantic.com/international/archive/2011/12/how-ethiopias-adoption-industry-dupes-families-and-bullies-activists/250296/?single_page=true> [8 February 2013].

Juffer, Femmie, "Children's Awareness of Adoption and Their Problem Behaviour in Families with 7-Year-Old Internationally Adopted Children" (2006) 9 *Adoption Quarterly* 1.

Kalus, Stanislawa and Habdas, Magdalena, *Family Law in Poland* (2011, Kluwer Law).

Kay, E, Tisdall, M, Bray, R, Marshall, K, and Cleland, A, "Children's Participation in Family Law Proceedings: A Step Too Far or a Step Too Small?" (2004) 26(1) *Journal of Social Welfare and Family Law* 17.

Keller, Helen and Stone-Sweet, Alex (eds), *A Europe of Rights* (2008, Oxford University Press).

Kennard, Holly C, "Curtailing the Sale and Trafficking of Children: A Discussion of the Hague Conference Convention in Respect of Intercountry Adoptions" (1994) 14(4) *University of Pennsylvania Journal of International Business Law* 623.

Kennedy, Randall L, "Interracial Adoption: Is the Multiethnic Placement Act Flawed? Yes: Race-Matching Is Horrendous" (1995) 81 *American Bar Association Journal* 44.

Khazova, Olga, "Russia: Inter-country Adoption: Through a Large Amount of Law, Still a Lot of Uncertainty", in Bainham, Andrew (ed), *The International Survey of Family Law* (2005, Jordans).

Kilkelly, Ursula, "The Best of Both Worlds for Children's Rights? Interpreting the European Convention on Human Rights in the Light of the UN Convention on the Rights of the Child" (2001) 23 *Human Rights Quarterly* 308.

Kilkelly, Ursula, *Listening to Children About Justice: Report of the Council of Europe Consultation with Children on Child-Friendly Justice* (2010, Council of Europe) <www.coe.int/childjustice> [4 April 2012].

Kilkelly, Ursula, *The Child and the European Convention on Human Rights* (1999, Ashgate).

Kitsantonis, Niki and Brunwasser, Matthew, *Baby Trafficking is thriving in Greece* (18 December 2006, New York Times) <www.nytimes.com/2006/12/18/world/europe/18iht-babies.3939121.html> [3 February 2012].

Koutsouradis, Achilles G, *National Report: Greece* (date unknown, Commission on European Family Law) <http://ceflonline.net/wp-content/uploads/Greece-Parental-Responsibilities.pdf> [27 February 2013].

Krappmann, Lothar, "The Weight of the Child's View (Article 12 of the Convention on the Rights of the Child)" (2010) 18 *International Journal of Children's Rights* 501.

Krawiec, Kimberly D, "Altruism and Intermediation in the Market for Babies" (2009) 66 *Washington and Lee Law Review* 203.

Lammerant, Isabelle and Hofstetter, Marlene, *Adoption: at what cost?* (2007, Terre des Hommes) <www.terredeshommes.org/pdf/publication/adoption_embargo.pdf> [7 February 2013].

Landes, Elisabeth M and Posner, Richard A, "The Economics of the Baby Shortage" (1978) *Journal of Legal Studies* 323.

Lansdown, Gerison, *The Evolving Capacities of the Child* (2005, UNICEF) <www.unicef-irc.org/publications/pdf/evolving-eng.pdf> [7 February 2013].

Lefaucheur, Nadine, "The French 'Tradition' of Anonymous Birth: The Lines of Argument" (2004) 18 *International Journal of Law, Policy and the Family* 319.

Lewis, Jane, "Adoption: The Nature of Policy Shifts in England and Wales, 1972–2002" (2004) 18 *International Journal of Law Policy and the Family* 235.

Lindsay, Duncan, *The Welfare of Children* (1994, Oxford University Press).

Lithuania: Institute for Social Research, *Every Child Counts* (2005) <www.sociologija.eu/media/file/every%20child%20counts.pdf> [6 June 2012].

Louw, Anne, "The Constitutionality of a Biological Father's Recognition as a Parent" (2010) 13(3) *Potchefstroomse Elektroniese Regsblad* 156.

Lowe, Nigel, "The Changing Face of Adoption – the Gift/Donation Model Versus the Contract/Services Model" (1997) 9 *Child and Family Law Quarterly* 371.

Lozinski, Vladimir, *Ending Child Abandonment in Romania* (2006, UNICEF) <www.unicef.org/infobycountry/romania_37375.html> [22 February 2012].

MacDonald, Alistair, "Bringing Rights Home for Children: Arguing the UNCRC" (2009) 39 *Family Law* 1073.

Maldonado, Solangel, "Discouraging Racial Preferences in Adoptions" (1996) 39 *University of California Davis Law Review* 1415.

Mann, L and Dolea, I, *OSCE Trial Observation Manual for the Republic of Moldova* (2006, OSCE/ODIHR).

Masson, Judith, "Representation of Children in England: Protecting Children in Child Protection Proceedings" (2000) 34(3) *Family Law Quarterly* 467.

Mathieu, B, *L'argent, premier écueil et dernier tabou de l'adoption* (1 October 2008, L'Expansion) <www.lexpansion.lexpress.fr> [14 January 2013].

Meulders-Klein, Marie-Thérèse, "The Status of the Father in European Legislation" (1996) 44(3) *The American Journal of Comparative Law* 487.

Mezmur, Benyam D, "From Angelina (to Madonna) to Zoe's Ark: What are the 'A-Z' Lessons for Intercountry Adoptions in Africa?" (2009) 23 *International Journal of Law, Policy and the Family* 145.

Mill, Ian, "Conversations with Children: A Judge's Perspective on Meeting the Patient before Operating on the Family" (2008) 6 *New Zealand family Law Journal* 72.

Minow, Martha, "Whatever Happened to Children's Rights?" (1995) 80 *Minnesota Law Review* 267.

Mnookin, Robert, "Child-Custody Adjudication: Judicial Functions in the Face of Indeterminacy" (1975) 39 *Law and Contemporary Problems* 226.

Moore, Kathleen, *Europe: Controversial 'Baby Box' Lets Mothers Abandon Infants Safely* (4 June 2005, Radio Free Europe Radio Liberty) <www.rferl.org/content/article/1059124.html> [22 September 2012].

Narey, Martin, *The Narey Report: A blueprint for the nation's lost children* (5 July 2011, The Times) <www.thetimes.co.uk/tto/life/families/article3083832.ece> [18 July 2011].

National Coalition for the Implementation of the UN Convention on the Rights of the Child: Austria, *Supplementary Report on the 3rd and 4th Report of Federal Republic of Austria to the United Nations, Pursuant to Article 44, paragraph 1B of the UN Convention on the Rights of the Child* (2012), <www.crin.org/docs/Austria_NCICRCA_CRC,OPAC,OPSC%20Report.pdf> [7 October 2012].

Netherlands: Ministerie van Justitie, *Adoptie: trends en analyse* (15 March 2010) <www.hcch.net/upload/wop/adop2010pd05_nl.pdf> [9 March 2011].

O Fatharta, Conall, *The Waiting Game* (1 November 2010, Irish Examiner) <www.irishexaminer.com/ireland/kfmhojkfcwmh/rss2/> [22 October 2011].

O'Donnell, Dan, *Child Protection: A Handbook for Parliamentarians* (2004, UNICEF) <www.unicef.org/ceecis/Guide_Enfants_OK.pdf> [7 February 2011].

OECD, *Better Life Index* (2012) <www.oecdbetterlifeindex.org/> [8 February 2013].

OECD, *Family Database* (2012) <www.oecd.org/els/familiesandchildren/41919586.pdf> [16 November 2012].

Office of the United Nations High Commissioner for Human Rights, *Legislative History of the Convention on the Rights of the Child* (2007, United Nations) HR/PUB/07/1.

Oren, Laura, "Unmarried Fathers and Adoption: 'Perfecting' or 'Abandoning' an Opportunity Interest" (2007) 36 *Capital University Law Review* 253.

Parness, Jeffrey, "Adoption Notices to Genetic Fathers: No to Scarlet Letters, Yes to Good-Faith Cooperation" (2005) 36(1) *Cumberland Law Review* 63.

Parra-Aranguren, Gonzalo, *Explanatory Report on the Convention on Protection of Children and Co-operation in Respect of Intercountry Adoption* (1993) <www.hcch.net/index_en.php?act=publications.details&pid=918> [7 February 2013].

Perera, Janaka, *Call for Re-Opening 'Prem Nivasa' Case* (23 January 2012, Asian Tribune) <www.asiantribune.com/news/2012/01/22/call-re-opening-'prem-nivasa'-case> [16 February 2012].

Pfund, Peter H, "Intercountry Adoption: The 1993 Hague Convention: Its Purpose, Implementation, and Promise" (1995) 28(1) *Family Law Quarterly* 53.

Pilotti, FJ, "Intercountry Adoption – Trends, Issues and Policy Implications for the 1990s", in *Childhood* (1993, Instituto Interamericano del Nino).

Pinderhughes, Ellen, Matthews, Jessica, Deoudes, Georgia and Pertman, Adam, *A Changing World: Shaping best practices through understanding of the new realities of intercountry adoption* (2013, Evan B Donaldson Adoption Institute).

Pintens, Walter and Pignolet, Dominique, *National Report: Belgium* (date unknown, Commission on European Family Law) <http://ceflonline.net/wp-content/uploads/Belgium-Parental-Responsibilities.pdf> [27 February 2013]).

Potter, Sir Mark, "The Voice of the Child: Children's 'Rights' in Family Proceedings" (2008) 3 *International Family Law* 140.

Pugh, Gillian and Selleck, Dorothy Rouse, "Listening to and Communicating with Young Children" in Ron Davie, Graham Upton and Ved Varma (eds) *The Voice of the Child: A Handbook for Professionals* (1996, Falmer).

Purdy, Laura, "Why Children Shouldn't Have Equal Rights" (1994) 2 *International Journal of Children's Rights* 223.

Radio Netherlands Worldwide, *Controversial Plan to Help Dutch Foundlings* (2011) <www.rnw.nl/english/video/controversial-plan-help-dutch-foundlings> [22 October 2012]).

Ramesh, Randeep, *Spread of 'baby boxes' in Europe alarms United Nations* (10 June 2012, The Guardian) <www.guardian.co.uk/world/2012/jun/10/unitednations-europe-news> [22 September 2012]).

Rankine, Carrie A, "Romania's New Child Protection Legislation: Change in Intercountry Adoption Law Results in a Human Rights Violation" (2007) 34 *Syracuse Journal of International Law and Commerce* 259.

Roberts, Dorothy E, *Shattered Bonds: The Color of Child Welfare* (2002, Basic Civitas Books).

Rodham, Hillary, "Children Under the Law" (1973) 43 *Harvard Educational Review* 487.

Roithová, Zuzana, *Letter to Professor Yanghee Lee, Chairwoman, Committee on the Rights of the Child* (14 July 2011) <www.eppgroup.eu/press/pdoc11/110714letter-to-un-chairwoman.pdf> [30 September 2012].

Romania: Ministry of Labour, Social Solidarity and Family, *"Children First" Human Rights in Child Protection: A Manual of Good Practice* (2005, European Union).

Rowe, J, Caine, M, Hundleby, M and Keene, A, *Long Term Foster Care* (1984, Batsford).

Rudolph Schaffer, H and Emerson, Peggy E "The Development of Social Attachments in Infancy" (1964) 29(3) *Monographs of the Society for Research in Child Development* 1.

Rule, Gwen, *Recruiting Black and Minority Ethnic Adopters/Foster Carers* (2006, British Association for Adoption and Fostering).

Rushbrooke, Rupert, *The Proportion of Adoptees Who Have Received Their Birth Records in England and Wales* (2001, Office of National Statistics) <www.ons.gov.uk/ons/taxonomy/search/index.html?newquery=*&nscl=Adoptions&nscl-orig=Adoptions&content-type=publicationContentTypes&sortDirection=DESCENDING&sortBy=pubdate> [19 February 2013].

Rushton, Alan, Grant, Margaret, Simmonds, John, Feast, Julia, "Assessing Community Connectedness and Self-Regard in a Mid-Life Follow-ip of British Chinese Adoptions" (2012) 36 *Adoption and Fostering* 62.

Rycus, Judith S, Freundlich, Madelyn, Hughes, Ronald C, Keefer, Betsy and Joyce Oakes, Emily, "Confronting Barriers To Adoption Success" (2006) 44(2) *Family Court Review* 210.

Sallnas, Marie, Vinnerljung, Bo and Westermark, Pia Kyhle, "Breakdown of Teenage Placements in Swedish Foster and Residential Care" (2004) 9(2) *Child and Family Social Work* 141.

Samuels, Elizabeth J, "Time to Decide? The Laws Governing Mothers' Consents to the Adoption of their Newborn Infants" (2005) 72 *Tennessee Law Review* 509.

San Marino, *State Party Report to the UN Committee on the Rights of the Child* (17 March 2003) CRC/C/8/Add.46.

Sants, HJ, "Genealogical Bewilderment in Children with Substitute Parents" (1964) 37(2) *British Journal of Medical Psychology* 133.

Sarcevic, Petar, Josipovic, Tatjana, Gliha Igor, Hlaca Nenad and Kunda, Ivana, *Family Law in Croatia* (2011, Kluwer Law).

Sarloos, Kees Jan, *Dissertation: European Private International Law on Legal Parentage?* (2010, Maastrict University).

Schuster Institute for Investigative Journalism, *Adoption: Vietnam* (22 February 2011) <www.brandeis.edu/investigate/adoption/vietnam.html> [5 February 2012].

Schuster Institute for Investigative Journalism, *News Reports of Adoption Irregularities in Cambodia* (22 February 2011) <www.brandeis.edu/investigate/gender/adoption/CambodiaNews.html> [4 February 2012].

Schuster Institute for Investigative Journalism, *News Reports of Adoption Irregularities in China* (22 February 2011) <www.brandeis.edu/investigate/adoption/ChinaNews.html> [5 February 2012].

Selman, Peter, *The Impact of Intercountry Adoption on the Well-Being of Children in Europe* (2007) <www.ciimu.org/webs/wellchi/conference_3/selman.pdf> [21 February 2013].

Selman, Peter, "Global Trends in Intercountry Adoption: 2001–2010" (2012) 44 *Adoption Advocate* 1.

Selman, Peter, "The Global Decline of Intercountry Adoption: What Lies Ahead?" (2012) 11(3) *Social Policy and Society* 381.

Semanchin Jones, Annette and LaLiberte, Traci, *Adoption Disruption and Dissolution Report* (2010, Centre for Advanced Studies in Child Welfare, University of Minnesota).

Shanley, Mary L, "Unwed Fathers' Rights, Adoption, and Sex Equality: Gender-Neutrality and the Perpetuation of Patriarchy" (1995) 95(1) *Columbia Law Review* 60.

Shook Slack, Kristen, "Understanding the Risks of Child Neglect: An Exploration of Poverty and Parenting Characteristics" (2004) 24(9) *Child Maltreatment* 395.

Shook, Kristen, "Does the Loss of Welfare Income Increase the Risk of Involvement with the Child Welfare System?" (1999) 21(9–10) *Children and Youth Services Review* 781.

Simmonds, Claire, "Paramountcy and the ECHR: A Conflict Resolved?" (2012) 71(3) *Cambridge Law Journal* 498.

Slovakia, *State Party Report to the UN Committee on the Rights of the Child* (21 September 2006) CRC/C/SVK/2.

Slovenia, *State Party Report to the UN Committee on the Rights of the Child* (18 June 2003) CRC/C/70/Add.19.

Smith Rotabi, Karen, *Guatemala City: Hunger Protests Amid Allegations of Child Kidnapping and Adoption Fraud* (22 August 2009, Socmag) <www.socmag.net/?p=540> [7 February 2013].

Smith Rotabi, Karen, *Inter-country Adoption: Steep Declines in International Adoptions by US Parents Reflect Mixed Record* (18 November 2011, RH Reality Check) <www.rhrealitycheck.org/article/2011/11/18/intercountry-adoption-steep-declines-in-the-us> [21 November 2011].

Smith, Carole, "Adoptive Parenthood as a 'Legal Fiction' – Its Consequences for Direct Post-Adoption Contact" (2002) 14(3) *Child and Family Law Quarterly* 281.

Smith, Susan, McRoy, Ruth, Freudlich, Madelyn and Kroll, Joe, *Finding Families for African American Children: The role of race and law in adoption from foster care* (2008, Evan B Donaldson Institute).

Smolin, David M, "Intercountry Adoption as Child Trafficking" (2004) 39(2) *Valparaiso University Law Review* 281.

Smolin, David M, "The Two Faces of Intercountry Adoption: The Significance of the Indian Adoption Scandals" (2005) 35 *Seton Hall Law Review* 403.

Smolin, David M, "Child Laundering: How the Intercountry Adoption System Legitimizes and Incentivizes the Practices of Buying, Trafficking, Kidnaping, and Stealing Children" (2006) 52 *Wayne Law Review* 113.

Smolin, David M, "Child Laundering as Exploitation: Applying Anti-Trafficking Norms to Intercountry Adoption under the Coming Hague Regime" (2007) 32 *Vermont Law Review* 1.

SOS Children's Villages: Canada, *Haitian Children Sold for only $1.20* (21 February 2011) <www.soschildrensvillages.ca/News/News/child-charity-news/Pages/Haitian-Children-Trafficked-611.aspx> [16 February 2012].

Statistics Netherlands, *Adoption* (2013) <www.cbs.nl/en-GB/menu/themas/veiligheid-recht/cijfers/extra/mappingworld-2-adoptie.htm> [9 March 2011].

Stativa, Ecaterina, Anghelescu, Carmen, Mitulescu, Rodica, Nanu, Mihaela and Stanciu, Nina, *The Situation of Child Abandonment in Romania* (2005, UNICEF) <www.ceecis.org/child_protection/PDF/child%20abandonment%20in%20Romania.pdf> [7 January 2013].

Stein, Jonathan G, "A Call to End Baby Selling: Why the Hague Convention on Intercountry Adoption Should be Modified to Include the Consent Provisions of the Uniform Adoption Act" (2002) 24 *Thomas Jefferson Law Review* 39.

Steiner, Eva, "Odièvre v France – Desperately seeker mother – anonymous births in the European Court of Human Rights" (2003) 15 *Child and Family Law* Quarterly 425.

Stötzel, Manuela and Fegert, Jörg M, "The Children's Guardian from a Child's Perspective" (2006) 20 *International Journal of Law, Policy and the Family* 201.

Sweden: Intercountry Adoptions Authority, *Annual Adoption Statistics* (2010) <www.hcch.net/upload/wop/adop2010pd05_se.pdf> [9 March 2011].

Szoboszlay, Anna, *Baby Boxes' Polarise Hungary* (11 June 2012, The Guardian) <www.guardian.co.uk/world/2012/jun/11/baby-boxes-polarise-hungary> [19 August 2012].

Tait, Robert, *Baby boxes in Czech Republic: 'the first thing should be the child's right to life'* (10 June 2012, The Guardian) <www.guardian.co.uk/world/2012/jun/10/czech-republic-baby-box> [15 October 2012].

Taylor, Nicola, Tapp, Pauline and Henaghan, Mark, "Respecting Children's Participation in Family Law Proceedings" (2007) 15 *International Journal of Children's Rights* 61.

Tenthani, Raphael, *Malawi Welcomes Madonna Adoption* (13 June 2009, BBC News) <http://news.bbc.co.uk/2/hi/entertainment/8098719.stm> [7 April 2011].

Terre des Hommes, *Hilfe Für Kinder in Not* (2012) <www.tdh.de/was-wir-tun/themen-a-z/babyklappe-und-anonyme-geburt/statistik.html>, [15 June 2012].

The Independent, *16 on Trial for Selling Babies for Adoption* (23 September 2009, The Independent) <www.independent.co.uk/news/world/asia/16-on-trial-for-selling-babies-for-adoption-1791716.html> [4 February 2012].

Thoburn, June, *Globalisation and Child Welfare: Some Lessons from a Cross-National Study of Children in Out-of-Home Care* (2007, University of East Anglia) <www.uea.ac.uk/polopoly_fs/1.103398!globalisation%201108.pdf> [4 April 2011].

Todorova, Velina, "Family Law in Bulgaria: Legal Norms and Social Norms" (2000) 13 *International Journal of Law, Policy and the Family* 148.

Todorova, Velina, "Children's Rights in Bulgaria after the End of Communism" (2009) 17(4) *International Journal of Children's Rights* 623.

Triseliotis, John, *In Search of Origins: The Experiences of Adopted People* (1973, Routledge & Kegan Paul).

Triseliotis, John, "Obtaining Birth Certificates" in Philip Bean (ed), *Adoption: Essays in Social Policy, Law, and Sociology* (1984, Tavistock).

Triseliotis, John, Shireman, Joan and Hundleby, Marion, *Adoption: Theory, Policy and Practice* (1997, Continuum International Publishing Group).

Turano, Margaret V, "Black Market Adoptions" (1976) 22(1) *Catholic Lawyer* 48.

Turkey, *State Party Report to the UN Committee on the Rights of the Child* (18 July 2011) CRC/C/TUR/2–3.

Ukraine, *State Party Report to the UN Committee on the Rights of the Child* (3 March 2010) CRC/C/UKR/3–4.

UNICEF, *Guidance Note on Intercountry Adoption in the CEE/CIS/Baltics Region* (2003, UNICEF) <www.unicef.org/ceecis/Guidance_note_Intercountry_adoption.pdf> [1 September 2011].

UNICEF, *Guidance Note on Intercountry Adoption in the CEE/CIS Region* (2009, UNICEF) <www.unicef.org/ceecis/UNICEF_ICA_CEE_Guidance_WEB.pdf> [16 November 2012].

UNICEF, *Innocenti Social Monitor 2009: Child Well-Being at a Crossroads: Evolving Challenges in Central and Eastern Europe and the Commonwealth of Independent States* (2009, UNICEF) <www.unicef.org/romania/ism_2009.pdf> [7 June 2012].

UNICEF, *ChildInfo: Monitoring the Situation of Children and Women* (2011) <www.childinfo.org/birth_registration_tables.php> [13 January 2012].

UNICEF, *TransMONEE Database* (2012) <www.transmonee.org/> [22 May 2013].

United Kingdom, *Report to Ministers of an Interdepartmental Working Group: Review of Adoption Law* (1992, Department of Health and Welsh Office).

United Kingdom: Secretary of State for Health, *Adoption: A New Approach* (2000, HM Stationary Office).

United Kingdom: CAFCASS, *Guidance for Witnessing Consent to the Making of an Adoption Order (in Partner and other Non-Agency Adoptions)* (2007) <www.cafcass.gov.uk/pdf/CONSENT%20TO%20THE%20MAKING%20OF%20AN%20ADOPTION%20ORDER%20FPR%200411v2.pdf> [6 January 2012].

United Kingdom: Office of National Statistics, *Historical Adoption Tables* (2011) <http://ons.gov.uk/ons/publications/re-reference-tables.html?edition=tcm%3A77-264215> [19 February 2013].

United Kingdom: Department for Education, *Statistical First Release: Children looked after in England (including adoption and care leavers) year ending 31 March 2011* (2011) <http://media.education.gov.uk/assets/files/pdf/s/main%20text%20sfr212011.pdf> [31 December 2012].

United Kingdom: Department for Education, *Consideration of the Children and Families Bill Provisions in Light of the European Convention on Human Rights and the United Nations Convention on the Rights of the Child* (2013) <http://media.education.gov.uk/assets/files/pdf/e/140213%20echr%20and%20uncr%20note%20for%20publication%20final%20lao.pdf> [2 May 2013].

United Kingdom: Department for Education, *Policy Statements: Children and Families Bill* (2013) <http://media.education.gov.uk/assets/files/pdf/a/adoption%20-%20policy%20statements.pdf> [2 May 2013].

United Kingdom, *Adoption Records* (31 January 2013) <https://www.gov.uk/adoption-records> [7 February 2013].

United Kingdom: Family Justice Council, *Guidelines for Judges Meeting Children Who are Subject to Family Proceedings* [2010] 2 FLR 1872.

United Nations Commission on Human Rights, *Report of the Working Group on a Draft Convention on the Rights of the Child* (3 April 1985, United Nations) E/CN.4/1985/64.

United Nations Commission on Human Rights, *Report of the Working Group on a Draft Convention on the Rights of the Child* (13 March 1986, United Nations) E/CN.4/1986/39.

United Nations Commission on Human Rights, *Report of the Working Group on a Draft Convention on the Rights of the Child* (2 March 1989, United Nations) E/CN.4/1989/48.

United Nations Committee on Human Rights, *Report of the Special Rapporteur on the Sale of Children, Child Prostitution and Child Pornography, Addendum: Report on the Mission to Guatemala* (27 January 2000, United Nations) E/CN.4/2000/73/Add/2.

United Nations Committee on the Rights of the Child, *Concluding Observations: Armenia* (26 February 2004) CRC/C/15/Add.225.

United Nations Committee on the Rights of the Child, *Concluding Observations: Austria* (31 March 2005) CRC/C/15/Add.251.

United Nations Committee on the Rights of the Child, *Concluding Observations: Austria* (5 October 2012) CRC/C/AUT/CO/3-4.

United Nations Committee on the Rights of the Child, *Concluding Observations: Azerbaijan* (12 March 2012) CRC/C/AZE/CO/3-4.

United Nations Committee on the Rights of the Child, *Concluding Observations: Belgium* (18 June 2010) CRC/C/BEL/CO/3-4.

United Nations Committee on the Rights of the Child, *Concluding Observations: Czech Republic* (4 August 2011) CRC/C/CZE/CO/3-4.

United Nations Committee on the Rights of the Child, *Concluding Observations: France* (11 June 2009) CRC/C/FRA/CO/4.

United Nations Committee on the Rights of the Child, *Concluding Observations: France* (30 June 2004) CRC/C/15/Add.240.

United Nations Committee on the Rights of the Child, *Concluding Observations: FYR of Macedonia* (11 June 2010) CRC/C/MKD/CO/2.

United Nations Committee on the Rights of the Child, *Concluding Observations: Hungary* (17 March 2006) CRC/C/HUN/CO/2.

United Nations Committee on the Rights of the Child, *Concluding Observations: Lithuania* (17 March 2006) CRC/C/LTU/CO/2.

United Nations Committee on the Rights of the Child, *Concluding Observations: Luxembourg* (31 March 2005) CRC/C/15/Add.250.

United Nations Committee on the Rights of the Child, *Concluding Observations: Netherlands* (24 July 1997) CRC/C/51/Add.1.

United Nations Committee on the Rights of the Child, *Concluding Observations: Russian Federation* (23 November 2005) CRC/C/RUS/CO/3.

United Nations Committee on the Rights of the Child, *Concluding Observations: Slovakia* (10 July 2007) CRC/C/SVK/CO/2.

United Nations Committee on the Rights of the Child, *Concluding Observations: United Kingdom* (20 October 2008) CRC/C/GBR/CO/4.

United Nations Committee on the Rights of the Child, *Concluding Observations – Optional Protocol: Albania* (5 October 2012) CRC/C/OPSC/ALB/CO/1.

United Nations Committee on the Rights of the Child, *Concluding Observations – Optional Protocol: Azerbaijan* (12 March 2012) CRC/C/OPSC/AZE/CO/1

United Nations Committee on the Rights of the Child, *Concluding Observations – Optional Protocol: Belgium* (11 June 2010) CRC/C/OPSC/BEL/CO/1.

United Nations Committee on the Rights of the Child, *Concluding Observations – Optional Protocol: Bosnia and Herzegovina* (1 October 2010) CRC/C/OPSC/BIH/CO/1.

United Nations Committee on the Rights of the Child, *Concluding Observations – Optional Protocol: FYR of Macedonia* (30 November 2012) CRC/C/OPSC/MKD/CO/1.

United Nations Committee on the Rights of the Child, *Concluding Observations – Optional Protocol: Greece* (20 July 2012) CRC/C/OPSC/GRC/CO/1.

United Nations Committee on the Rights of the Child, *Concluding Observations – Optional Protocol: Montenegro* (1 October 2010) CRC/C/OPSC/MNE/CO/1.

United Nations Committee on the Rights of the Child, *Concluding Observations – Optional Protocol: Serbia* (11 June 2010) CRC/C/OPSC/SRB/CO/1.

United Nations Committee on the Rights of the Child, *Day of General Discussion on the Right of the Child to be Heard* (29 September 2006) <www2.ohchr.org/english/bodies/crc/docs/discussion/Final_Recommendations_after_DGD.doc> [15 June 2012].

United Nations Committee on the Rights of the Child, *General Comment 7* (20 September 2006) CRC/C/GC/7/Rev.1.

United Nations Committee on the Rights of the Child, *General Comment 12* (20 July 2009) CRC/C/GC/12.

United Nations Department of Economic and Social Affairs: Population Division, *Child Adoption: Trends and Policies* (2009) ST/ESA/SER.A/292.

United Nations High Commissioner for Refugees, *Policy on Adoption of Refugee Children* (1995) <www.unhcr.org/cgi-bin/texis/vtx/home/opendocPDF.pdf?docid=3bd035d14> [19 February 2013].

United Nations International Commission Against Impunity in Guatemala (CICIG), *Report on Players Involved in the Illegal Adoption process in Guatemala since the Entry Into Force of the Adoption Law (Decree 77-2007)* (2010) <http://cicig.org/uploads/documents/informes/INFOR-TEMA_DOC05_20101201_EN.pdf> [7 February 2013].

United States Embassy: Hanoi, *Summary of Irregularities in Adoptions in Vietnam* (25 April 2008) <http://vietnam.usembassy.gov/irreg_adoptions042508.html> [22 October 2011].

United States House of Representatives, *House Resolution 578* (109th Congress 2005–2006) (18 November 2005).

United States: Department of Homeland Security, *Backgrounder: Operation Broken Hearts* (19 November 2004) <www.ethicanet.org/galindo_backgr.pdf> [5 February 2012].

United States: Department of State, *Country Information*, <http://adoption.state.gov/country_information.php> [21 December 2012].

United States: Department of State, *Summary of Irregularities in Adoptions in Vietnam* (25 April 2008) <http://vietnam.usembassy.gov/irreg_adoptions042508.html> [10 January 2012].

University of Nottingham, *Causes and Consequences of Child Abandonment: Bulgaria* (2012) <www.nottingham.ac.uk/iwho/documents/childabandonment/bulgaria/causes-and-consequences-of-child-abandonment.pdf> [3 June 2012].

University of Nottingham, *Child Abandonment in Slovakia* (2012) <www.nottingham.ac.uk/iwho/research/projects/childabandonment/slovakia.aspx> [25 October 2012].

University of Nottingham, *Child Abandonment in the Czech Republic* (2012) <www.nottingham.ac.uk/iwho/research/projects/childabandonment/czechrepublic.aspx> [22 October 2012].

University of Nottingham, *Data Collected from Maternity Units in Slovakia* (2012) <www.nottingham.ac.uk/iwho/documents/childabandonment/slovakia/data-collected-from-maternity-units.pdf> [14 January 2013].

University of Nottingham, *Legislation Relating to Child Abandonment in the Czech Republic* (2012) <www.nottingham.ac.uk/iwho/documents/childabandonment/czechrepublic/legislation-relating-to-child-abandonment.pdf> [3 June 2012].

University of Nottingham, *Legislation Relating to Child Abandonment in Poland* (2012) <www.nottingham.ac.uk/iwho/documents/childabandonment/poland/legislation-relating-to-child-abandonment.pdf> [3 June 2012].

University of Nottingham, *Legislation Relating to Child Abandonment in Slovakia* (2012) <www.nottingham.ac.uk/iwho/documents/childabandonment/slovakia/legislation-relating-to-child-abandonment.pdf> [3 June 2012].

University of Nottingham, *Legislation Relating to Child Abandonment in Romania* (2012) <www.nottingham.ac.uk/iwho/documents/childabandonment/romania/legislation-relating-to-child-abandonment.pdf> [7 February 2013].

University of Nottingham, *Preventing Child Abandonment in Slovakia* (2012) <www.nottingham.ac.uk/iwho/documents/childabandonment/slovakia/preventing-child-abandonment.pdf> [25 October 2012].

Van Bueren, Geraldine, "Children's Access to Adoption Records: State Discretion or an Enforceable International Right?" (1995) 58(1) *Modern Law Review* 37.

Vonk, MJ, "Tensions Between Legal, Biological and Social Conceptions of Parenthood in Dutch Family Law" (May 2007) 11(1) *Electronic Journal of Comparative Law* 18.

Wald, Michael S, "Children's Rights: A Framework for Analysis" (1979) 12 *University of California, Davis, Law Review* 255.

Warman, Andrea and Roberts, Ceridwen, *Adoption and Looked after Children – an International Comparison* (Working Paper 2003/1, Department of Social Policy and Social Work, University of Oxford).

Watkins, Dawn, "Intercountry Adoption and the Hague Convention: Article 22 and Limitations upon Safeguarding" (2012) 24(4) *Child and Family Law Quarterly* 389.

Weiss, Emilia and Szeibert, Orsolya, *National Report: Hungary* (date unknown, Commission on European Family Law) <http://ceflonline.net/wp-content/uploads/Hungary-Parental-Responsibilities.pdf> [27 February 2013].

Westhof, Dirk, *Flow Model Institutionalised Children in Romania and the Determining Variables* (2005) <www.crin.org/docs/resources/treaties/crc.40/GDD_2005_Flowstudy_children_in_residential_care_Romania.pdf> [15 May 2012].

Wilson, Tom, *Romania rethinks adoption ban despite child-trafficking concerns* (26 April 2011, Deutsche Welle) <www.dw.de/dw/article/0,,15029244,00.html> [13 February 2012].

World Bank, *GNI per Capita, Atlas Method (current US$)* (2011) <http://data.worldbank.org/indicator/NY.GNP.PCAP.CD> [6 February 2012].

Zermatten, Jean, "The Best Interests of the Child Principle: Literal Analysis and Function" (2010) 18 *International Journal of Children's Rights* 483.

Zweigert, Konrad and Siehr, Kurt, "Jhering's Influence on the Development of Comparative Legal Method" (1971) 19 *American Journal of Comparative Law* 215.

INDEX

A

adoption intermediaries 81, 83, 89, 90, 91, 92, 93, 95, 98, 100, 102, 103
adoption register 208, 209
adoptive parents 5, 9, 15, 17, 30, 32, 46, 60, 101, 103, 125, 128, 183, 194, 195, 196, 210, 214, 215
Albania 2, 6, 24, 26, 45, 48, 58, 71, 84, 94, 97, 121, 123, 134, 141, 148, 157, 174, 178, 196
Andorra 3, 58, 71, 84, 97, 109, 123, 134, 156, 159, 160, 167, 168, 170, 174, 181
anonymous birth 9, 197, 198, 199, 200, 201, 202, 203, 204, 205, 206, 207, 208, 210, 212, 215
anonymous relinquishment 9, 197, 198, 199, 201, 202, 203, 204, 205, 206, 210, 212
Argentina 187
Armenia 2, 6, 18, 24, 31, 36, 38, 42, 46, 48, 59, 71, 73, 84, 97, 106, 123, 133, 141, 157, 159, 165, 175, 195
Austria 3, 23, 68, 76, 101, 108, 130, 134, 157, 160, 162, 168, 169, 170, 174, 193, 198, 199, 201, 204, 206
Azerbaijan 2, 23, 36, 38, 48, 59, 71, 74, 75, 84, 107, 123, 133, 156, 195

B

Belgium 3, 18, 36, 56, 59, 62, 71, 74, 106, 123, 138, 141, 142, 152, 156, 159, 165, 167, 169, 170, 174, 182, 198, 199
best interests 4, 9, 15, 17, 19, 21, 30, 31, 33, 49, 58, 60, 82, 100, 109, 110, 115, 117, 119, 121, 122, 129, 135, 136, 137, 138, 140, 141, 142, 143, 145, 149, 150, 152, 154, 161, 172, 176, 177, 196, 197, 202, 203, 211, 213, 214
Bosnia and Herzegovina 2, 17, 23, 36, 38, 112, 157, 159, 160, 167
Bulgaria 2, 6, 24, 26, 27, 32, 36, 38, 40, 54, 56, 62, 71, 84, 92, 124, 141, 156, 159, 169

C

Cambodia 45, 85, 90, 151, 152
Canada 208, 209
Central Authority 17, 30, 96, 97, 98, 99, 101, 103, 150, 151, 154, 177, 180
children with disabilities 23, 38, 47, 48, 91, 129, 164, 173, 176, 177, 216
China 91
Committee on the Rights of the Child 32, 37, 95, 122, 123, 125, 126, 135, 154, 192, 199, 201, 202, 206
Council of Europe 112, 139
counselling
- for adoptive parents 9, 173, 176, 180, 181, 183, 211, 216
- for birth parents 52, 65, 86, 173, 206, 210, 211, 212
- for child 120

Croatia 2, 23, 36, 71, 73, 75, 106, 123, 157, 159, 160, 161, 164, 191, 196
Cyprus 3, 23, 56, 69, 84, 93, 101, 106, 108, 128, 142, 157, 159, 164, 169, 178, 212
Czech Republic 2, 24, 28, 36, 37, 38, 42, 46, 48, 56, 59, 71, 73, 82, 84, 97, 98, 101, 121, 127, 128, 140, 148, 157, 159, 161, 167, 174, 178, 179, 181, 187, 192, 198, 199, 201, 204

D

Declaration on Social and Legal Principles relating to the Protection and Welfare of Children 185
Denmark 3, 6, 18, 23, 36, 40, 56, 59, 60, 68, 76, 84, 93, 97, 101, 106, 109, 127, 130,

131, 133, 149, 158, 163, 167, 169, 170, 174, 181, 183, 196

E

ECA 1967 18, 169, 189
ECA 2008 7, 11, 18, 52, 55, 57, 61, 120, 123, 128, 135, 156, 161, 163, 169, 189
article 5 52, 105
article 7 163
article 9 156
article 22 189
England 23, 31, 36, 40, 41, 55, 56, 57, 63, 65, 66, 68, 74, 75, 78, 79, 86, 87, 93, 94, 100, 108, 109, 129, 135, 138, 140, 143, 144, 148, 151, 152, 155, 159, 163, 167, 170, 192, 208
Estonia 2, 6, 23, 31, 42, 46, 48, 56, 59, 71, 73, 93, 98, 106, 121, 123, 133, 148, 159, 169, 174, 177, 181, 195, 207
Ethiopia 90
ethnicity 13, 24, 34, 49, 124, 176, 191, 210, 211
European Commission on Human Rights 33, 70, 71, 130, 131, 152, 162, 165
European Convention on Human Rights 6, 7, 11, 12, 22, 108, 114, 133, 162, 163, 171, 202, 209, 213
article 2, Protocol 1 12
article 5 11, 130
article 6 12, 114
article 8 22, 27, 59, 60, 64, 65, 69, 70, 71, 110, 130, 136, 152, 162, 165, 166, 168, 171, 202
article 14 136, 162, 166, 171, 172
European Convention on the Exercise of Children's Rights 1996 142
European Court of Human Rights 4, 6, 11, 12, 18, 22, 27, 57, 59, 60, 64, 65, 69, 71, 108, 110, 111, 114, 133, 135, 136, 137, 143, 146, 152, 162, 165, 166, 168, 170, 171, 177, 202, 203, 207, 208, 209, 210, 213, 214

F

family assistance 27, 39, 40, 62, 63, 87, 88, 102, 205, 212
family reunification 7, 22, 24, 25, 26, 27, 28, 30, 49, 51, 102, 107, 112, 113, 115, 212, 213
Finland 18, 56, 57, 59, 62, 73, 76, 93, 97, 101, 109, 126, 127, 132, 135, 140, 142, 157, 158, 159, 161, 163, 175, 181, 196
Former Yugoslav Republic of Macedonia 2, 18, 38, 124, 157, 158, 160, 192, 195
foster care 13, 15, 21, 26, 28, 29, 34, 35, 36, 43, 47, 107, 120, 180, 211, 214
France 1, 3, 6, 36, 40, 41, 47, 58, 59, 64, 65, 71, 73, 93, 101, 106, 109, 124, 143, 150, 156, 160, 163, 167, 168, 170, 171, 175, 182, 197, 198, 199, 200, 201, 202, 203, 207, 209

G

Georgia 2, 6, 24, 31, 36, 46, 48, 73, 84, 97, 98, 107, 123, 133, 141, 156, 159, 164, 174, 178, 207
Germany 3, 6, 56, 58, 59, 60, 63, 69, 70, 71, 74, 97, 101, 107, 124, 136, 137, 141, 144, 159, 169, 175, 182, 196, 198, 204, 206, 212
Greece 3, 56, 59, 71, 73, 97, 101, 106, 128, 141, 142, 157, 158, 160, 161, 169, 175, 181, 193, 198
Guatemala 84, 90, 91, 93, 94, 100

H

Hague Convention 4, 7, 8, 11, 17, 18, 29, 30, 35, 51, 52, 53, 55, 82, 85, 89, 92, 94, 96, 97, 98, 99, 100, 101, 102, 103, 105, 120, 123, 150, 151, 153, 154, 155, 173, 177, 180, 189, 210, 212, 213, 215
article 1 4, 82
article 4 21, 52, 61, 82, 83, 89, 120, 133
article 8 96
article 16 100, 188
article 17 155
article 22 99
article 27 86
article 30 188
article 32 96

Hague Convention 1965 16
Hague Convention Special Commission 29, 88
Haiti 90
Hong Kong 32
Hungary 2, 18, 23, 38, 42, 48, 84, 112, 121, 126, 142, 148, 169, 193, 195, 198, 205

I
Iceland 3, 18, 23, 56, 68, 73, 76, 93, 127, 134, 141, 159, 167, 170, 191, 193
improper financial gain 8, 15, 98, 100, 215
independent adoption 8, 84, 103
India 90
institutional care 8, 13, 25, 26, 27, 28, 29, 31, 34, 40, 43, 44, 45, 47, 49, 58, 90, 91, 107, 111, 112, 115, 149, 151, 153, 176, 178, 180, 211
Ireland 3, 33, 59, 64, 65, 68, 73, 82, 107, 114, 129, 134, 149, 159, 165, 181
Italy 1, 3, 6, 23, 57, 97, 98, 105, 124, 135, 143, 148, 149, 152, 157, 158, 159, 167, 174, 177, 182, 191, 193, 198, 207, 209

K
kinship care 28, 66, 107, 120, 200, 205, 210, 212, 214

L
Latvia 2, 6, 23, 38, 46, 48, 56, 68, 73, 98, 106, 121, 123, 141, 148, 157, 159, 169, 174, 178, 195, 198
Liechtenstein 3, 106, 108, 130, 134, 157, 160, 162
Lithuania 2, 6, 24, 31, 36, 38, 42, 46, 56, 59, 62, 71, 73, 97, 106, 121, 123, 135, 141, 148, 157, 159, 161, 164, 169, 174, 177, 181, 193, 198
Luxembourg 3, 58, 71, 74, 106, 124, 156, 160, 164, 165, 166, 198, 202

M
Malta 3, 56, 67, 74, 106, 108, 109, 123, 133, 157, 158, 160, 164, 167, 169, 174, 181
Marshall Islands 61
Moldova 2, 24, 40, 59, 72, 74, 106, 112, 123, 133, 156, 160, 161
Monaco 3, 23, 58, 72, 74, 106, 124, 140, 156, 160, 168, 175
Montenegro 2, 18, 23, 36, 56, 74, 75, 97, 106, 141, 157, 158, 160, 161, 164, 167, 191

N
Netherlands 3, 6, 18, 23, 47, 68, 73, 93, 97, 106, 126, 127, 140, 143, 152, 157, 158, 160, 162, 165, 167, 169, 170, 174, 193, 194
Northern Ireland 168
Norway 3, 6, 18, 23, 56, 68, 74, 77, 93, 97, 98, 106, 124, 138, 141, 149, 160, 161, 170, 175, 181, 191, 193

O
older children 23, 42, 43, 47, 48, 91, 121, 164, 173, 216
Optional Protocol to UNCRC 8, 82, 89, 92

P
Paraguay 86
parallel planning 26
payments
    to children 81
    to institutions 29, 45, 46
    to parents 52, 82, 83, 95, 102, 103
Peru 165, 166
Poland 2, 6, 24, 46, 59, 72, 74, 98, 106, 109, 124, 134, 141, 157, 161, 168, 169, 175, 177, 187, 193, 198
Portugal 2, 3, 18, 46, 48, 56, 58, 60, 72, 97, 98, 124, 141, 158, 160, 161, 167, 168, 170, 174, 175, 178, 181, 195, 198, 207
private adoption 84, 103

R
revocation of consent 58, 59, 60
Roma 32, 54, 87
Romania 2, 18, 25, 26, 28, 29, 32, 35, 37, 38, 40, 43, 44, 46, 54, 56, 58, 61, 72, 87, 90, 95, 109, 112, 132, 140, 152, 157, 159, 169, 177

Russia 2, 6, 17, 24, 31, 36, 38, 40, 48, 59, 72, 74, 82, 93, 106, 107, 113, 121, 123, 135, 141, 149, 155, 156, 164, 180, 192, 195, 198

S
same-sex adoption 9, 172, 215
Samoa 61, 85
San Marino 3, 157, 158, 160
Serbia 2, 18, 24, 38, 42, 56, 58, 72, 74, 106, 133, 141, 157, 158, 159, 161, 164, 193
Slovakia 2, 24, 28, 32, 37, 38, 46, 48, 56, 74, 97, 101, 106, 121, 128, 133, 149, 157, 159, 161, 164, 169, 174, 178, 193, 198, 201
Slovenia 3, 23, 38, 56, 72, 74, 75, 97, 107, 123, 134, 142, 157, 159, 175, 181, 207, 212
Spain 3, 6, 18, 23, 56, 72, 74, 94, 97, 106, 124, 134, 140, 142, 149, 156, 160, 167, 169, 170, 174, 193, 195, 199, 200, 205
Sri Lanka 90
Sweden 3, 6, 23, 27, 47, 56, 68, 74, 77, 79, 94, 97, 127, 160, 169, 170, 174, 181
Switzerland 3, 6, 23, 56, 58, 68, 95, 101, 107, 111, 129, 135, 141, 143, 149, 157, 160, 161, 168, 175, 178, 179, 182, 193, 198, 199

T
Turkey 2, 56, 58, 129, 133, 157, 160, 168, 178, 179

U
Ukraine 2, 6, 17, 18, 24, 28, 36, 40, 48, 54, 56, 59, 63, 64, 72, 74, 92, 121, 129, 141, 155, 156, 159, 163, 169, 192, 193, 195, 214
UNCRC 4, 7, 11, 15, 18, 29, 35, 39, 52, 53, 55, 66, 75, 105, 118, 120, 124, 126, 127, 128, 129, 133, 141, 145, 149, 154, 168, 188, 189, 192, 196, 201, 202, 204, 206, 213, 215, 216
  article 2 202
  article 3 5, 13, 15, 117, 135, 202
  article 5 125
  article 6 13, 26, 201
  article 7 186, 187, 197, 199, 201, 202, 215
  article 8 187, 197, 201
  article 9 114, 119, 201, 205
  article 12 13, 118, 119, 126, 130, 134, 135, 137, 140, 144
  article 18 39
  article 19 39, 201, 204
  article 20 13, 30, 35
  article 21 4, 13, 14, 15, 21, 51, 60, 81, 96, 99, 110, 119, 140, 153, 170
  article 27 26, 153
  article 35 81
UN Guidelines for the Alternative Care of Children 39, 88
United Kingdom 3, 6, 18, 25, 32, 33, 71, 86, 94, 110, 114, 168, 186, 208, 212
United States 41, 47, 48, 55, 61, 78, 85, 91, 92, 97, 99, 180, 186, 208, 209, 215
unmarried fathers 72, 75, 200, 212, 214

V
Venezuela 96
Vietnam 44, 61, 90
views of the child 8, 49, 52, 146, 213, 214, 216

W
waiting period 30, 211

ABOUT THE AUTHOR

Claire Fenton-Glynn received her PhD in Law from the University of Cambridge in 2013, for which she received scholarships from the Cambridge Commonwealth Trust and the Modern Law Review. From October 2013 she worked as a College Teaching Officer and Director of Studies in Law at Lucy Cavendish College, University of Cambridge, before joining Kings College London in September 2014 as a Lecturer in Law. Since June 2013 she has acted as a consultant on child rights for the United Nations High Commissioner for Human Rights. She is an Associate Fellow of the Centre for International Sustainable Development Law.

European Family Law Series

1. *Legal Recognition of Same-Sex Couples in Europe*, K. Boele-Woelki and A. Fuchs (eds.)
2. *European Family Law in Action Volume I: Grounds for divorce*, K. Boele-Woelki, B. Braat and I. Sumner (eds.)
3. *European Family Law in Action Volume II : Maintenance Between Former Spouses*, K. Boele-Woelki, B. Braat and I. Sumner (eds.)
4. *Perspectives for the Unification and Harmonisation of Family Law in Europe*, K. Boele-Woelki (ed.)
5. *Family Law Legislation of the Netherlands*, I. Sumner and H. Warendorf
6. *Indépendance et interdépendance patrimoniales des époux dans le régime matrimonial légal des droits néerlandais, français et suisse*, B. Braat
7. *Principles of European Family Law Regarding Divorce and Maintenance Between Former Spouses*, K. Boele-Woelki, F. Ferrand, C. González Beilfuss, M. Jänterä-Jareborg, N. Lowe, D. Martiny and W. Pintens
8. *Inheritance Law Legislation of the Netherlands*, I. Sumner and H. Warendorf
9. *European Family Law in Action Volume III : Parental Responsibilities*, K. Boele-Woelki, B. Braat and I. Curry-Sumner (eds.)
10. *Common Core and Better Law in European Family Law*, K. Boele-Woelki (ed.)
11. *All's well that ends registered?*, I. Curry-Sumner
12. *Model Family Code – From a global perspective*, I. Schwenzer and M. Dimsey
13. *Harmonisation of Family Law in Europe. A Historical Perspective*, M. Antokolskaia
14. *Brussels II bis: Its Impact and Application in the Member States*, K. Boele-Woelki and C. González Beilfuss (eds.)
15. *Tensions between Legal, Biological and Social Conceptions of Parentage*, I. Schwenzer (ed.)
16. *Principles of European Family Law Regarding Parental Responsibilities*, K. Boele-Woelki, F. Ferrand, C. González Beilfuss, M. Jänterä-Jareborg, N. Lowe, D. Martiny and W. Pintens
17. *Juxtaposing Legal Systems and the Principles of European Family Law on Divorce and Maintenance*, E. Örücü and J. Mair (eds.)
18. *Convergence and Divergence of Family Law in Europe*, M. Antokolskaia (ed.)
19. *European Challenges in Contemporary Family Law*, K. Boele-Woelki and T. Sverdrup (eds.)
20. *Children and their parents*, M. Vonk
21. *La capacité de l'enfant dans les droits français, anglais et écossais*, L. Francoz-Terminal

22. *Joint Parental Authority*, C.G. Jeppesen de Boer
23. *Debates in Family Law around the Globe at the Dawn of the 21st Century*, K. Boele-Woelki (ed.)
24. *European Family Law in Action Volume IV: Property Relations between Spouses*, K. Boele-Woelki, B. Braat and I. Curry-Sumner (eds.)
25. *Foundational Facts, Relative Truths. A Comparative Law Study on Children's Right to Know Their Genetic Origins*, R. Blauwhoff
26. *Imperative Inheritance Law in a Late-Modern Society. Five Perspectives*, Christoph Castelein, René Foqué and Alain Verbeke (eds.)
27. *Juxtaposing Legal Systems and the Principles of European Family Law on Parental Responsibilities*, Esin Örücü and Jane Mair (eds.)
28. *La justice des mineurs en Europe*, Yann Favier and Frédérique Ferrand (eds.)
29. *The Future of Family Property in Europe*, Katharina Boele-Woelki, Jo Miles and Jens M. Scherpe (eds.)
30. *The Place of Religion in Family Law: A Comparative Search*, Jane Mair and Esin Örücü (eds.)
31. *Reconstructing Marriage. The Legal Status of Relationships in a Changing Society*, Caroline Sörgjerd
32. *Legal Recognition of Same-Sex Relationships in Europe*, Katharina Boele-Woelki and Angelika Fuchs (eds.)
33. *Principles of European Family Law Regarding Property Relations Between Spouses*, Katharina Boele-Woelki, Frédérique Ferrand, Cristina González Beilfuss, Maarit Jänterä-Jareborg, Nigel Lowe, Dieter Martiny and Walter Pintens
34. *Der nacheheliche Unterhalt: Grundlagen und Ausgestaltung im deutschen Unterhaltsrecht und in den Prinzipien der Commission on European Family Law*, Philipp Beuermann
35. *Family Law and Culture in Europe: Developments, Challenges and Opportunities*, Katharina Boele-Woelki, Nina Dethloff and Werner Gephart
36. *Children's Rights in Intercountry Adoption. A European Perspective*, Claire Fenton-Glynn

www.ingramcontent.com/pod-product-compliance
Ingram Content Group UK Ltd.
Pitfield, Milton Keynes, MK11 3LW, UK
UKHW051926100926
8556IPUK00022B/1403